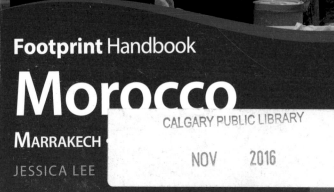

Footprint Handbook

Morocco

MARRAKECH •

JESSICA LEE

D0205426

This is
Morocco

Come to Morocco for its elusive magic and exotic mystery and you will probably leave with more intimate, human memories: watching kids play football in a dusty square, dodging donkey-carts while attempting to navigate narrow alleyways, enjoying mint tea and good-natured banter with a *babouche* seller in the local souk. The romantic image is real enough and is what draws most travellers here, but Morocco is a viscerally lived-in place, where modernity rubs shoulders with antiquity, and a melee of competing sounds, colours and pungent smells is waiting for you just outside the riad door.

So close to Europe, yet so very different, Morocco is hard to pin down. Around every bend in the road you'll spot a sweeping panoramic view or a half-crumbled kasbah. An alleyway turn in the medina can bring you face to face with either a scene from the medieval era or a street lined with chi-chi boutiques and cafés. Morocco is forever a surprise and an adventure, and the near impossibility of knowing it all just adds to the seduction of trying. This country is rewarding and remarkably good value as a destination for walking, surfing and yoga; for aimless exploring or for focused lazing. Whatever you do here, the nature of the place will soak into the very pores of your skin, and, once it does, don't expect any amount of exuberant hammam scrubbing to rub it off. Morocco's medley of medina mayhem, desert dunes, soaring mountains and verdant valleys has been beguiling travellers since they first set foot on this land. You're next in line to fall under its spell.

Jessica Lee

Best of
Morocco

❶ Marrakech

The Red City waves its magic wand over
all who visit, leaving them dazed by its
labyrinthine souks, dazzled by the dreamy
artistry of its palaces and heritage sites
and suffering sensory overload from a
night spent amid the riotous cacophony
of Jemaâ el Fna. Page 37.

❷ Essaouira

Taste the salt in the sea air from the ramparts while watching waves crash upon the fortified walls. Essaouira's seafront medina is a daydream of whitewashed walls and blue-shutter windows where surf fans, riad lovers and travellers hoping to catch some remnant of Essaouira's hippy past, all converge. Page 82.

❸ Toubkal National Park

When the mountains are calling you, make your way to Morocco's premier trekking destination, which is easily accessible from Marrakech. Trails between High Atlas villages provide mountain panoramas and an insight into rural life, while Jbel Toubkal is the peak that every trekker wants to bag. Page 108.

❹ Fès

Throw away the map; it's no use to you within the high-walled maze of Fès el Bali, where you'll fight donkeys for space along corkscrew alleys, breathe in the acrid stench of the tanneries, and weave your way through bustling souks to discover ancient *medersas*. Page 131.

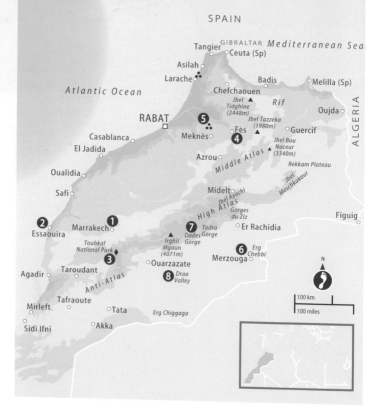

❺ Volubilis

Sit in the once-grand columned Capitol, cast your eyes up at the imposing Triumphal Arch and admire the startlingly well-preserved mosaics still in situ amid tumbled walls. These sprawling ruins are an evocative reminder of Rome's once-mighty rule over the region. Page 191.

❻ Erg Chebbi

For sublime desert scenes of giant rippling dunes head to Merzouga, where the vast orange crests of Erg Chebbi await. Sunset camel treks and a night surrounded by sand and stars are the stuff of Saharan fantasies. Page 218.

❼ Dadès Gorge

This is one of the prettiest corners of Morocco and a day-trekking paradise. Hike your way between red-earth kasbahs and tiny villages huddled beside lush green fields, all snugly sandwiched between the soaring orange cliffs of the gorge. Page 227.

❽ Drâa Valley

There are kasbahs and *ksour* galore along this ancient caravan route. Fortified villages and vast palm groves line the roadside all the way to Zagora. Stop off and explore the dark, mazy confines of these earthen-walled hamlets. Page 244.

Drawing water from a well near Merzouga

Route planner

There's a lot of ground to cover in Morocco, and trying to do too much in too short a time is a recipe for an unsatisfying trip. Bear in mind that journeys that appear relatively quick on a map can take far longer than you might imagine. This is especially true of routes that cross the Atlas mountains, where precariously perched switchbacks, wandering goats, fossil sellers and locals carrying absurd loads on decrepit bikes with no brakes or lights will inevitably slow you down. History and geography have created enormous variety in the country: it's possible to sample cities, mountains, coast, desert, Arabic and Berber cultures all on the same trip, just make sure you've also left enough time to sip mint tea and watch the sun set.

One week

a taster of city and countryside

Marrakech is the hub for routes across the High Atlas mountains to the south and towards the coast to the west. The sights are amazing, but there are also plenty of lower-key pleasures to discover in the maze of the city's streets; it's not a place to hurry. Three nights will give you enough time to acclimatize, to soak up the frenetic atmosphere of Jemaâ el Fna, explore the souks, and visit the tiled splendour of the heritage sites. If funds allow, try to spend at least one of those nights in a riad; the spectacular rooms and quiet courtyards of the city's beautifully adapted old houses are a highlight of any visit.

Then head east over the high mountain Tizi n'Tichka pass for a stop at the fairytale kasbah of **Aït Benhaddou** before driving on to the **Dadès Gorge**. The white-knuckle road that loops down into the gorge is an experience in itself, while a day or two spent on foot exploring the rural idyll of the valley floor with villages, verdantly green fields and crumbling kasbahs sitting snug between the red canyon walls, provides a snapshot of Morocco's gentler side after Marrakech's medina muddle.

Afterwards, turn west towards the coast and end up in the old fishing port of **Essaouira**, where thick ramparts, the oldest of which are Portuguese-built, protect the medina against the waves; a walk along them is a good way to appreciate the town. Seagulls wheel above the fishing boats in the port, from where the day's catch is taken to be sold in the central market, while the old town alleyways brim with souk stalls and a vibrant cafe-culture. It's a great place to wind down, take brisk walks along the sweep of beach and feast on seafood. Or, head out to sea for windsurfing and other watersports.

Two weeks

imperial cities and desert landscapes

After three nights in **Marrakech**, catch the train up to **Fès**, the spiritual capital of Morocco, spectacularly sited in a huge bowl of a valley. Fès can be difficult to get to know, with its attractions often hidden behind

> **Tip...**
> When you're exploring the medinas, don't fight the inevitability of getting lost; instead use the position of the sun roughly to orientate yourself.

high walls, but it's worth persevering. Once you find your feet, its streets reveal all sorts of treasures. Fès El Bali, the old medina, is the best place to stay. Spend two or three days exploring ancient *medersas*, grand and ornate arched gates, pungent tanneries and buzzing souks, and take time to climb to one of the vantage points above the old city. Spend a day wandering through Fès El Jedid too. The old Merinid capital is lined with dilapidated but still picturesque houses that were once home to the city's Jewish community; it is still home to a Jewish synagogue, cemetery and museum. If time permits, you could also take a day trip to nearby **Sefrou** whose rather tranquil medina is a stark contrast to the hustle of Fès.

Nearby, **Meknès** is Fès's smaller, more relaxed sibling. At one point the capital of Morocco, it has plenty of grand architecture as well as shopping opportunities in its souks. After a day's sightseeing, Meknès also makes a good base for excursions to the impressive, crumbling Roman ruins of **Volubilis** and holy pilgrimage site of **Moulay Idriss**.

Then head southeast towards **Merzouga**, exploring the **Gorges du Ziz** and the mud construction of **Rissani's** *ksour* en route. Almost on the Algerian border, Merzouga is little more than a string of hotels set up to take advantage of the cinematic splendours of the sand dunes of **Erg Chebbi**. Camel trek out to the desert and bed down for the night in the shadow of the dunes for a starry night and a Saharan sunrise.

After **Marrakech**, make a beeline for the **Vallée des Aït Bougmez**, south of Azilal, where hardy hill-walkers with time on their side could trek all the way to El Kelaâ des Mgouna. If you're not aiming for anything as ambitious, a couple of days spent exploring the valley floor here on day hikes allows you to soak up plenty of authentic High Atlas life as well as admire the rural scenery.

From here some serious backtracking is called for as the road peters out: head back towards Marrakech via a stop at **Cascades d'Ouzoud** to say hello to Morocco's largest waterfall, and then turn east again on the southerly route across the Tizi-n-Tichka. On the other side of the mountain pass is **Ouarzazate**, reigning queen of Morocco's film industry. The surrounding countryside has played various roles in a variety of Hollywood movies over the years. Nearby the stunning **Kasbah Aït Benhaddou** is the biggest film star of all.

From Ouarzazate follow the road south along the old caravan route of the **Drâa Valley**, through miles of lush oases and sleepy fortified villages until the ribbon of tarmac finally stutters to a halt at M'Hamid el Ghizlane and the Sahara beckons. From here it's still a substantial distance to the vast sands of **Erg Chiggaga** but the journey is worth it for the experience of isolation amid the towering dunes. Desert-fiends can pander to their Saharan daydreams by heading out on multi-day camel treks, while those who just want to dip their toes in the sand sea can 4WD there from M'Hamid.

If you take the road north from the Drâa through **Nekob**, you can make a loop of the Atlas via more desert dunes at **Merzouga**, the bucolic lush orchards and fields of the **Todra** and **Dadès gorges**, and **Skoura**'s peaceful *palmeraie*. From here it's back over the Tizi-n-Tichka and time to head due south from Marrakech, where tiny **Imlil** in **Toubkal National Park** is the hub of High Atlas hiking. Some travellers will be content to head out on day walks to nearby villages, but for others it's all about the multi-day treks, such as the nine-day Toubkal Circuit or the two-day Jbel Toubkal ascent.

ON THE ROAD
Improve your travel photography

Taking pictures is a highlight for many travellers, yet too often the results turn out to be disappointing. Steve Davey, author of Footprint's *Travel Photography*, sets out his top rules for coming home with pictures you can be proud of.

Before you go
Don't waste precious travelling time and do your research before you leave. Find out what festivals or events might be happening or which day the weekly market takes place, and search online image sites such as Flickr to see whether places are best shot at the beginning or end of the day, and what vantage points you should consider.

Get up early
The quality of the light will be better in the few hours after sunrise and again before sunset – especially in the tropics when the sun will be harsh and unforgiving in the middle of the day. Sometimes seeing the sunrise is a part of the whole travel experience: sleep in and you will miss more than just photographs.

Stop and think
Don't just click away without any thought. Pause for a few seconds before raising the camera and ask yourself what you are trying to show with your photograph. Think about what things you need to include in the frame to convey this meaning. Be prepared to move around your subject to get the best angle. Knowing the point of your picture is the first step to making sure that the person looking at the picture will know it too.

Compose your picture
Avoid simply dumping your subject in the centre of the frame every time you take a picture. If you compose with it to one side, then your picture can look more balanced. This will also allow you to show a significant background and make the picture more meaningful. A good rule of thumb is to place your subject or any significant detail a third of the way into the frame; facing into the frame not out of it.

This rule also works for landscapes. Compose with the horizon two-thirds of the way up the frame if the foreground is the most interesting part of the picture; one-third of the way up if the sky is more striking.

Don't get hung up with this so-called Rule of Thirds, though. Exaggerate it by pushing your subject out to the edge of the frame if it makes a more interesting picture; or if the sky is dull in a landscape, try cropping with the horizon near the very top of the frame.

Fill the frame
If you are going to focus on a detail or even a person's face in a close-up portrait, then be bold and make sure that you fill the frame. This is often a case of physically getting in close. You can use a telephoto setting on a zoom lens but this can lead to pictures looking quite flat; moving in close is a lot more fun!

Interact with people

If you want to shoot evocative portraits then it is vital to approach people and seek permission in some way, even if it is just by smiling at someone. Spend a little time with them and they are likely to relax and look less stiff and formal. Action portraits where people are doing something, or environmental portraits, where they are set against a significant background, are a good way to achieve relaxed portraits. Interacting is a good way to find out more about people and their lives, creating memories as well as photographs.

Focus carefully

Your camera can focus quicker than you, but it doesn't know which part of the picture you want to be in focus. If your camera is using the centre focus sensor then move the camera so it is over the subject and half press the button, then, holding it down, recompose the picture. This will lock the focus. Take the now correctly focused picture when you are ready.

Another technique for accurate focusing is to move the active sensor over your subject. Some cameras with touch-sensitive screens allow you to do this by simply clicking on the subject.

Leave light in the sky

Most good night photography is actually taken at dusk when there is some light and colour left in the sky; any lit portions of the picture will balance with the sky and any ambient lighting. There is only a very small window when this will happen, so get into position early, be prepared and keep shooting and reviewing the results. You can take pictures after this time, but avoid shots of tall towers in an inky black sky; crop in close on lit areas to fill the frame.

Bring it home safely

Digital images are inherently ephemeral: they can be deleted or corrupted in a heartbeat. The good news though is they can be copied just as easily. Wherever you travel, you should have a backup strategy. Cloud backups are popular, but make sure that you will have access to fast enough Wi-Fi. If you use RAW format, then you will need some sort of physical back-up. If you don't travel with a laptop or tablet, then you can buy a backup drive that will copy directly from memory cards.

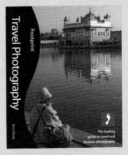

Recently updated and available in both digital and print formats, Footprint's Travel Photography by Steve Davey covers everything you need to know about travelling with a camera, including simple post-processing. More information is available at www.footprinttravelguides.com

When to go

… and when not to

Climate

Morocco is a good destination all year round, although it does get cold during January and February, particularly at night. This is especially true in the desert and pre-desert areas. Winter is also the season that sees the most precipitation, with occasional heavy showers turning dry riverbeds into dangerous flash floods and snow blocking the passes of the High Atlas. For most visitors, the best time to visit Morocco is during the spring (March through to May) when the days are bright and the heat is comfortable, meaning you won't suffer too much on long public transport journeys or while driving. After a wet winter, the countryside blooms into life; green fields are sprinkled with flowers, and the Dadès and Drâa valleys are filled with blossom. Spring can be good for hiking in the High Atlas, too, though lingering snow often makes higher routes difficult unless you have good equipment. In general, summer and autumn are best for walking and climbing in the mountains, and windsurfers will find the winds on the Atlantic coast are stronger in summer, although the swell for surfers is bigger in winter. Urban sightseeing is fine all year round, although in Marrakech and Fès the heat can be oppressive during the day from July to late September. Avoid desert trips to Merzouga and M'Hamid during the height of summer when most of the tourism infrastructure shuts down due to the heat.

> **Tip…**
> During winter visits, it pays to always keep an extra layer of clothing in your day bag to put on while walking through the shaded, cooler areas of the medinas in Marrakech and Fès. Budget travellers visiting in winter should be aware that most of the cheapest accommodation options in Morocco don't have heating, so it's a good idea to spend a little more on a bed for the night if travelling during this time.

Festivals

As well as a new generation of music and film festivals, Morocco has a number of local festivities, often focusing around a local saint or the harvest time of a particular product. These are fairly recent in origin. There are also religious festivals, whose timing relates to the lunar Islamic year. Ramadan is the most important festival in the Islamic calendar. Its starting date changes from year to year in the western calendar: it will be in May in 2017, 2018 and 2019. During Ramadan, Muslims must fast during daylight hours. The first day after Ramadan, Eid ul-Fitr, is spent celebrating and feasting. See also page 293.

March

Nomads Festival (M'Hamid, www. nomadsfestival.org) This celebration of the rich culture of Morocco's nomadic populations takes place over three days in March, offering a programme of concerts and cultural activities for visitors, as well as a range of debates, talks and workshops.

May/June

Rose Festival (El Kelaâ des Mgouna, Dadès Valley) Three days of celebration to welcome the new crop of rose petals, gathered from over 4000 km of hedges in the valley of the roses. A Rose Queen is elected and there are processions, music, dance and rose garlands.

Fès Festival of World Sacred Music (Fès, www.fesfestival.com) This hugely popular ten-day festival celebrates sacred music from across the globe. There are free open-air concerts as well as smaller ticketed events, most of which take place in various locations around the old town of Fès el Bali. Tickets are available online and can be bought individually for concerts or bundled together as a festival pass.

Festival Gnaoua et Musiques du Monde (www.festival-gnaoua. net) Tens of thousands of visitors flood the pretty streets of Essaouira and sway to the sounds of Gnaoua, the so-called Moroccan blues. A melding of sub-Saharan, Arabic and Berber styles, this was traditionally the music of black Moroccan slaves and is accompanied by acrobatic dance moves. The festival is often a place of exciting musical experimentation, as the age-old spiritual traditions of the music are combined with international jazz, reggae, blues and hip-hop influences.

Fête des Cerises (Sefrou) Sefrou's Cherry Festival is a four-day extravaganza culminating with a colourful parade and the crowning of the Cherry Queen. There are also free concerts during the evenings and a range of other events, including art and craft exhibitions. Dates change slightly annually but are usually around the beginning of June.

July

Festival National des Arts Populaires (Marrakech) A bringing together of music and dance troops from all over

Morocco to perform in the wide open space of the ruined Badi palace for a week. The festival kicks off with a parade of hundreds of artists from the Place la Liberté to Jemaâ El Fna. Some international acts also appear, and there are smaller performances around the city.

August/September

Moussem of Moulay Idriss (Moulay Idriss) Morocco's most important *moussem* centres round the Mausoleum of Moulay Idriss, founder of the Idrissid dynasty and great-great grandson of the prophet Mohammed. Pilgrims from far and wide flood into the village during the festival.

Moussem of Setti Fatma (Ourika Valley) The holy *koubba* (shrine) of Setti Fatma is the centrepiece of this four-day religious celebration. The *koubba* is closed to non-Muslims, but processions take place around the village and a carnival atmosphere pervades the valley.

Moussem des fiançailles (Allamghou) More than 2500 m up in the Atlas, isolated Imilchil's wedding festival in August/September is a chance, at the end of summer, for thousands of locals to dress up in their jewellery and finest clothes and find a partner. Music, dancing, sheep and cows accompany the party.

Oasis Festival (Marrakech, www.oasisfest.org) Morocco's first contemporary music festival is dedicated to underground electronica with three days of DJs and live music taking over the grounds of the Fellah Hotel in September. Advance booking is essential; tickets are available online.

October

Sufi Culture Festival (Fès) A celebration of Sufi music and culture held over eight days, bringing together Sufi musicians from across the globe for a series of concerts and other events at venues across the city.

December

Festival International du Film de Marrakech (www.festivalmarrakech.info) A celebration of the best of Moroccan and international film, Marrakech's film festival in December, chaired by Prince Moulay Rachid, awards the Golden Star to the best film of the past year and provides a chance to see the best of North African arthouse cinema.

What to do

Ballooning

Drifting over the Haouz plain near Marrakech, with the Atlas Mountains rising out of the red earth, is a great way to get a sense of the importance of the Red City to the surrounding area. Marrakech-based **Ciel d'Afrique** (www.cieldafrique.info) organizes hot-air balloon trips, leaving Marrakech around 0530 for a flight over the Jebilet hills north of Marrakech. A flight shared with other people will cost around €185.

Birdwatching

Home to 460 species, Morocco has the greatest diversity of birdlife north of the Sahara. One of Morocco's top destinations for birdwatchers is the reserve at **Tidzi**, south of Essaouira, which is home to Morocco's rarest resident bird, the bald ibis, which was once widespread in Central Europe. UK operators **Nature Trek** (T01962-733051, www.naturetrek.co.uk) and **Sunbird Tours** (T01767-262522, www.sunbirdtours.co.uk) offer several birding holidays to Morocco.

Camel trekking

The best places to arrange camel trekking excursions and longer trips are Mergouza, M'Hamid, and Zagora. All of the hotels in Mergouza can arrange sunset camel trips out to Erg Chebbi, while Zagora and M'Hamid are better locations for organizing longer multi-day trips. Travel agencies in Ouarzazate, such as **Désert et Montagne Maroc** (c/o Dar Daïf guesthouse, T0524-854949, www.desert-montagne.ma), also arrange camel trekking. Apart from a quick camel ride into the dunes, there are two options: the *méharée* and the *randonnée chamelière*. The *méharée* involves riding the camel, while the *randonnée chamelière* (camel hike) means you walk alongside the camels, which are essentially used as pack animals. In the former option, you can cover a lot more ground, riding for four to five hours a day. A good organizer will lay on everything apart from sleeping bags, although blankets are generally available. The best time of year for treks in the south is October to April (although sandstorms are a possibility between November and February). On a six-night camel hike out of Zagora you see a combination of dunes and plains, palm groves and villages en route to the dunes of Chigaga, with an average of five hours walking a day.

ON THE ROAD

Hammams

A ritual purification of the body is essential before Muslims can perform prayers. In the days before bathrooms, these 'major ablutions' were generally done at the hammam (bath). Segregation of the sexes was and still is the rule at the hammam. Some establishments are only open to women; others are only for men; most have a shift system (mornings and evenings for the men, all afternoon for women). In the old days, the hammam, along with the local *zaouïa* or saint's shrine, was an important place for women to gather and socialize, and even to pick out a potential wife for a son.

Very often separate hammams for men and women are next to each other on the ground floor of an apartment building. A passage leads into a large changing room/post-bath area, equipped with masonry benches for lounging on and (sometimes) small wooden lockers. Here you undress under a towel. Hammam gear today is usually shorts for men and knickers or swimsuits for women. If you're going to have a massage/scrub down, you take a token at the cash desk where shampoo can also be bought.

The next step is to proceed to the hot room: five to 10 minutes with your feet in a bucket of hot water will have you sweating nicely, and you can then move back to the raised area where the masseurs are at work. After the expert removal of large quantities of dead skin, you go into one of the small cabins or *mathara* to finish washing. (Before you do this, find the person with the dry towels so that they can bring yours to you when you're in the *mathara*.) In addition to a scrub and a wash, women may enjoy the pleasures of epilation with *sokar*, a mix of caramelized sugar and lemon. Men can undergo a *taksira*, which involves much pulling and stretching of the limbs. And remember, allow plenty of time to cool down, reclining in the changing area.

These days, a plethora of upmarket hammams – aimed squarely at foreign visitors – have opened up in Marrakech and Fès. These obviously don't have the local life appeal of the traditional Moroccan neighbourhood hammam but provide an easier experience for the uninitiated and higher standards of cleanliness. They also often have separate rooms where couples can hammam together. The most luxurious of these hammams are more like spas, with a range of add-on massage and beauty treatments on offer.

Horse riding

The horse is the object of a veritable cult in Morocco. A great opportunity to witness Moroccan riding skills is at a *Fantasia*, a spectacular ceremony where large numbers of traditionally dressed horsemen charge down a parade ground to discharge their muskets a few metres away from tents full of banqueting guests. The late King Hassan II assembled one of the world's finest collections of rare, black, thoroughbred Arab horses, and wealthy Moroccans are often keen for their offspring to learn to ride. Many towns have riding clubs, and national show-jumping events are shown on TV.

If you'd like time in the saddle, see www.ridingtours.com. Also try the following: **La Roseraie** at Ouirgane (on the Taroudant road, T0544-439128, www.laroseraiehotel.com); **Palmeraie Golf Palace** (Marrakech, www.pgp. co.ma); **Cavaliers d'Essaouira** (14 km inland from Essaouira on the Marrakech road, next to restaurant **Dar Lamine**, T0665-074889 mobile).

Mountain biking

Areas popular with mountain bikers include Ouarzazate and the region between the **Dadès Gorge** and **Toundoute**, north of Skoura. Clay washed onto the tracks by rain dries out to form a good surface for bikes. Most towns will have bike hire companies. **Unique Trails** (www.uniquetrails.com) and **Wildcat Adventures** (www.wildcat-bike-tours.co.uk) are UK-based operators running cycling trips to Morocco.

Skiing

Inconsistent snowfall dents Morocco's reputation as a ski destination: falls of snow rarely exceed 20 cm and often melt quickly in the bright sun, only to refreeze, leaving a brittle surface. On the occasions when there is good snow, Moroccans rush down from Casablanca or Rabat to **Oukaïmeden** (2600 m) in the High Atlas, an hour's drive south of Marrakech, which is Morocco's premier ski resort. The summit above the plateau is **Jbel Oukaïmeden** (3270 m). There is a ski-lift, and pistes range from black to green. Further east, in the High Atlas of Imilchil, the **Jbel Ayyachi** (3747 m) has some descents and good terrain for wilderness skiers.

The CAF Refuge of the **Club Alpin Français** in Oukaïmeden (T0524-319036, www.ffcam.fr) hires out ski gear and should be able to advise on skiing conditions. **Royal Moroccan Federation of Skiing and Mountaineering** (Parc de la Ligue Arabe, Casablanca, T0522-203798) is another useful source of information. Also contact **Ksar Timnay** (T0535-360188, www.ksar-timnay.com), at Aït Ayyachi near Midelt.

Surfing and windsurfing

Morocco is beginning to develop a watersports industry, mainly led by Europeans who have set up surf and windsurfing camps. There are also plenty of largely untapped surfing opportunities along the country's long Atlantic coastline. Essaouira has a surfing reputation but is actually better for windsurfing, thanks to the town's infamous wind. Conditions south of town are better, with the village of Sidi Kaouki a big destination for windsurfers in particular. **Explora Morocco** (www. exploramorocco.com) rents gear and arranges surfing, windsurfing, SUP and kitesurfing lessons in Essaouira.

Trekking

There are great opportunities for hiking in Morocco. The most popular area is the Toubkal National Park in the High Atlas (see page 108). However, as roads improve and inveterate trekkers return for further holidays, new areas are becoming popular. To organize your trip, you can either book through a specialist trekking operator from home or find a guide available when you arrive. Guides are plentiful in most settlements where trekking is an option, and in many towns your hotel can hook you up with one (see Independent trekking, below).

Where to go

Toubkal National Park offers various routes up into the mountains, including the extremely popular ascent of North Africa's highest peak, Jbel Toubkal (4167 m). South of Azilal, the beautiful Vallée des Aït Bougmez is also becoming popular. For weekend trekkers, there are gentle walks along the flat valley bottom, but the Aït Bougmez also makes a good departure point for tougher treks, including the north–south crossing of the west-central High Atlas to Bou Thraghar, near Boumalne and El Kelaâ des Mgouna. On this route, you have the chance to climb the region's second highest peak, Irhil Mgoun (4071 m). El Kelaâ des Mgouna is also one of the starting points for the Jbel Saghro trail, one of the few trails that can be walked in winter.

The area around the Ounila Valley has a good blend of village life and majestic scenery but is less well-known. Base yourself in the main settlement of Telouet, and hike out from there. Likewise, there are a lot of untapped walking opportunities in the Middle Atlas for those who really want to get off the beaten path. Certain parts are reminiscent of a Middle Earth landscape, especially between Azrou and the source of the Oum er Rabi river, where there is beautiful walking in the cedar forests. Despite its proximity to the rich farmlands of Meknès and the Saïs Plain, this is an extremely poor region that would benefit from increased eco-friendly tourism. For visitors with less time to spare, some of the prettiest day walks in Morocco can be found in the Dadès Gorge.

When to go

April to October is the best time for trekking. In the heat of summer, keep to the high valleys which are cooler and where water can be obtained. Note that the views are not generally as good in the High Atlas at the height of summer because of the heat haze.

Independent trekking

A good guide (minimum 300dh per day) is invaluable for any walk longer than a day-hike and highly recommended for treks that traverse the mountains. Check out their credentials by asking to see their guiding identity card; licensed mountain guides will be accredited as 'guides de montagne'. As well as a guide, the use of mules or donkeys to carry the heavy packs is common. If you are setting up a trek yourself, note that a good mule can carry up to 100kg (approximately three backpacks). A mule with a muleteer costs around 120dh per day. If you do a linear trek rather than a loop, you will generally have to pay for the days it takes for the muleteer and animals to travel back to their home village as well. A cook usually charges around 150dh per day. When buying food for the trek, remember to buy enough for the guide and muleteers, too.

What to expect

Vehicle pistes may look alluring but are, in fact, hard on the feet. Keep to the softer edges or go for footpaths when possible. Gorges are not the easiest places to walk in, so ask your local guide to recommend a higher route if there is one that is safe. Be particularly cautious if you have to walk on scree – you don't want to leave the mountains on a mule because of a sprained ankle. In order to fully appreciate the beauty of the Atlas, trekkers need to ensure that the walking is as comfortable as possible and this includes finding ways to deal with dehydration and fatigue. As on any hill trek, a regular pace should be maintained. If you are not used to walking at altitude, try to avoid high routes in the early stages of your trip. Slow and steady is the name of the game at altitude; ensure you pause if a dizzy feeling sets in. In villages that see a lot of trekkers passing through, local kids will be on the lookout, ever ready to see if they can get a dirham. They can, however, be useful in showing you the way through to the footpath on the other side of the settlement.

Where to stay

Camping or bivouacking is fine in summer but in spring and autumn indoor accommodation is necessary, in gîtes, refuges, shepherds' huts or local homes. Classified guest rooms in rural areas have the GTAM (Grande Traversée des Atlas Marocains) label of approval. Tents can be hired in some popular trekking destinations, such as Imlil.

Further information

Specialist maps and guidebooks are useful but can be difficult to find in Morocco. The few books on trek routes in English include Alan Palmer's *Moroccan Atlas: The Trekking Guide* (Trailblazer, 2014) has 66 trail maps; Des Clark's *Mountaineering in the Moroccan High Atlas* (Cicerone, 2011) concentrates on winter walking for the experienced mountaineer, covering 40 peaks over 3000 m. Experienced Atlas walker Hamish M Brown's *The High Atlas* (Cicerone, 2012) covers 48 routes, details the area's culture and offers practical guidance. For further information, you can also contact the **Royal Moroccan Federation of Skiing and Mountaineering** (Parc de la Ligue Arabe, Casablanca, T0522-203798).

Shopping tips

Morocco is a shopper's paradise. The famous souks in Marrakech and Fès, in particular, are great places to hunt down traditional artisan work as well as experience the cut and thrust of haggling with the experts. To buy in the souks you will have to engage in the theatre and the mind games of the haggle. In order to come out of the process happy, there are some things to bear in mind.

- Don't get too hung up on the idea of 'a good price'; the best price is the one you are happy to pay.
- Have a figure in mind before you start and don't go above it.
- Be prepared to walk away if the price is too high – whatever you're buying, there will almost certainly be another stall around the corner selling the same thing.
- Keep a sense of humour and be friendly and polite but firm.
- Don't suggest a price unless you're sure you want to buy a particular item: once you start talking numbers, you are in negotiation and you may find it hard to extricate yourself.

The price you are first quoted might be twice as much as the seller is prepared to accept, or three times as much, or ten times as much – there is absolutely no firm rule about this. A decent starting point from the buyer's point of view is to take about a half to a third off the amount you'd be prepared to pay and start by offering that. In the souks, you'll usually get a better price if you buy from the smaller specialist stalls rather than big emporiums that line the more popular thoroughfares.

As a very rough guide, and depending on quality, size, etc, expect to pay these sort of prices: *babouches* 50-150dh; leather bag 200-400dh; teapot 50-200dh (more for silver); spices 30-60dh per kg; pouffe 150-450; blanket 300-600dh.

Good items to buy include argan oil, metalwork (particularly beautiful copper tangines and contemporary takes on traditional lamps), leatherware, Berber blankets, *babouches* (shoes/slippers), ceramics (especially the blue-and-white painted rustic pottery once typical of Fès and zellige tilework) and, of course, carpets, although carpet-buying can be especially complex and has many potential pitfalls – don't be too swayed by offers of mint tea/declarations of antiquity/tales of the years of hard toil the seller's elderly aunt spent making it…

Where to stay

romantic riads and shepherds' shelters

Morocco has a good range of accommodation to suit all budgets. There are several well-appointed business hotels in the main cities, luxurious places for the discerning visitor and clean basic hotels to suit those with limited funds. Independent travellers appreciate the growing number of *maisons d'hôte* or guesthouses (generally referred to as riads, see box, page 63), some of which are very swish indeed, while, in the mountain areas, walkers and climbers will find rooms available in local people's homes. Modern self-catering accommodation is also becoming more popular, particularly in Marrakech.

There is an official star rating system, although few hotels will boast about their membership of the one-, two- or even three-star categories, and there does not appear to be very tight central control on how the prices reflect the facilities on offer so standards vary considerably. It's probably best to ignore the star rating completely. Note, too, that breakfast is often not included in the room price of hotels at the budget end of the spectrum.

Price codes

Where to stay

€€€€ over €140
€€€ €71-140
€€ €35-70
€ under €35

Prices are for double rooms.
Singles are marginally cheaper.
See page 290 for exchange rates.

Restaurants

€€€ over €30
€€ €15-30
€ under €15

Prices are for a two-course meal
for one person, excluding drinks
or service charge.

Cheap

At the budget end of the market are simple hotels, often close to bus or train stations. At the cheapest end of the spectrum, toilets and showers are usually shared (although the room will often have a washbasin) and you may have to pay for a hot shower. The worst of this sort of accommodation is little better than a concrete cell, stifling in summer and cold during winter. The best, though, is often quite pleasant (except in high summer and mid-winter), with helpful staff, lots of clean, bright tiling and rooms opening on to a central courtyard. Outside the big tourist cities, such hotels have almost exclusively male Moroccan customers and some solo female travellers will feel uncomfortable in them. Although such hotels are generally clean, it may be best to bring a sheet with you if you're planning to use them a lot. Water, especially in the southern desert towns, can be a problem, but generally, there will be a public bath (hammam) close by for you to take a shower after a long bus journey.

Mid-range

More expensive one-star hotels are generally in the new part of town (*ville nouvelle* neighbourhoods). Showers may be en suite, and breakfast (coffee, bread and jam, a croissant, orange juice) should be available, possibly at the café on the ground floor, for around 20dh. Next up are the two- and three-star places. Most will also be in the *ville nouvelle* areas of towns. Rooms will have high ceilings and en suite shower and toilet. Light sleepers need to watch out for noisy, street-facing rooms. Some of these hotels are being revamped, not always very effectively. In this price bracket are a number of establishments with a personal, family-run feel.

Expensive

Top hotels are generally run by international groups, such as **Accor** and **Le Méridien**. Upmarket hotels in Morocco can either be vast and brash, revamped and nouveau riche, or solid but tasteful and even discreet with a touch of old-fashioned elegance. The main cities also have large business hotels.

Riads and guesthouses

The big phenomenon of the late 1990s and 2000s in the Moroccan tourist industry was the development of the riad. Wealthy Europeans bought old properties in the medinas of Marrakech, Fès and Essaouira and converted them into boutique-style guesthouses, while locals converted their old family homes into hotels as well. By far the nicest and most atmospheric places

to stay, riads range from the super-
luxurious to more modest offerings,
but the vast majority are at the higher-
end of the accommodation spectrum.
See box, page 63.

Tip...
Riads will usually send someone to
meet you at the airport – a good
reason to spend your first night in one.

Youth hostels (Auberges de jeunesse)

There are 11 hostels in Morocco all affiliated to HI, including ones in Essaouira,
Fès, Meknès Marrakech, Azrou (Middle Atlas) and Asni (High Atlas). Priority
is given to the under-30s but you don't need a HI card to stay the night.
A maximum stay of three nights is the rule at some hostels. Overnight charges
are 20-40dh, with use of the kitchen 2dh. For information try the **Moroccan
Youth Hostel Federation** ⓘ *Parc de la Ligue Arabe, Casablanca, T0522-220551*.
The Fès hostel has had good reviews but is in the *ville nouvelle*, as is the
Marrakech hostel. Both are convenient for the train station, but a long way
from sights and old-town atmosphere. It may be better to go for a cheap
hotel, more conveniently located and with better toilets and showers.

Mountain accommodation

In the mountains, you can easily bivouac out in summer or, in the high
mountains, sleep in a stone *azib* (shepherd's shelter). There are three main
options for paid accommodation: floor space in someone's home, a gîte of
some kind, or a refuge run by the **CAF (Club Alpin Français)**. The refuges
have basic dormitory and restaurant facilities. Rates depend on category
and season. The CAF can also be contacted via BP 6178 (Casablanca, T0522-
270090), and BP 4437 (Rabat, T0537-734442).

In remote villages, there are *gîtes d'étape*, simple dormitory
accommodation marked with the colourful **GTAM (Grande traversée de
l'Atlas marocain)** logo. The warden generally lives in the house next door.
Prices here are set by the **ONMT** (tourist board), and the gîte will be clean if
spartan. The board also publishes an annual guide listing people authorized
to provide gîte-type accommodation.

In mountain villages where there is no gîte, you will usually find space in
people's homes, provided you have a sleeping bag. Many houses have large
living rooms with room for people to bed down on thin foam mattresses. It
is the custom to leave a small sum in payment for this sort of service. On the
whole, you will be made very welcome.

Camping

There are campsites all over Morocco – the **ONMT** quotes 87 sites in well-chosen locations. Few sites, however, respect basic international standards. Security is a problem close to large towns, even if the site is surrounded by a wall with broken glass on top. Never leave anything valuable in your tent. Many campsites also lack shade, can be noisy and the ground tends to be hard and stony, requiring tough tent pegs. As campsites are really not much cheaper than basic hotels and, as even simple things like clean toilets and running water can be problematic, hotel accommodation is usually preferable. There are some notable exceptions, however, which are listed throughout the book.

Food
& drink

tagines, tea and pastry treats

Moroccan cuisine

The finest of the Moroccan arts is possibly its cuisine. There are the basics: harira and bissara soups, kebabs, couscous, tagine and the famous *pastilla*: pigeon, egg and almonds in layers of filo pastry. And there are other dishes, less well known: gazelle's horns, coiling *m'hencha* and other fabulous pastries. The Moroccans consider their traditional cooking to be on a par with Indian, Chinese and French cuisine; although the finest dishes are probably to be found in private homes, upmarket restaurants, notably in Marrakech, will give you an idea of how good Moroccan food can be. On the international stage, Moroccan cuisine is also beginning to get the respect it deserves, with new restaurants opening in European capitals. However, the spices and vegetables, meat and fish, fresh from the markets of Morocco, give the edge to cooks in old medina houses.

The climate and soils of Morocco mean that magnificent vegetables can be produced all year round, thanks to assiduous irrigation. Although there is industrial chicken production, in many smaller restaurants, the chicken you eat is as likely to have been reared by a small-holder. Beef and lamb come straight from the local farms.

In addition to the basic products, Moroccan cooking gets its characteristic flavours from a range of spices and minor ingredients. Saffron (*zaâfrane*), though expensive, is widely used; turmeric (*kurkum*) is also much in evidence. Other widely used condiments include a mixed all spice referred to as *ra's el hanout* ('head of the shop'), cumin (*kamoun*), black pepper, oregano and rosemary (*yazir*). Prominent greens in use include broad-leaved parsley (*ma'dnous*), coriander (*kuzbur*) and, in some variations of couscous, a sort of celery called *klefs*. Preserved lemons (modestly called *bouserra*, 'navels', despite their breast-like shape) can be found in fish and chicken tagines. Bay leaves (*warqa Sidna Moussa*, 'the leaf of our lord Moses') are also commonly employed. Almonds, much used in patisserie, are used in tagines too, while powdered cinnamon (Arabic *karfa*, or French *cannelle*) provides the finishing touch for *pastilla*. In patisserie, orange-flower water and rose water (*ma ouarda*) are essential to achieve a refined taste.

Eating times vary widely in Morocco. Marrakech gets up early and goes to bed early, too, so people tend to sit down to dine around 2000. Across the country, the big meal of the week is Friday lunch, a time for people to gather in their families. The main meal of the day tends to be lunch, although this varies according to work and lifestyle. As anywhere, eating out in plush eateries is a popular upper-income occupation. Locals will tend to favour restaurants with French or southern European cuisine, while Moroccan 'palace' restaurants are patronized almost exclusively by tourists.

Starters

Harira is a basic Moroccan soup; ingredients vary but include chickpeas, lentils, vegetables and a little meat. It is often accompanied by hard-boiled eggs. *Bissara* is a pea soup and makes a cheap and filling winter breakfast. *Briouat* are tiny envelopes of filo pastry, akin to the Indian samosa, with a variety of savoury fillings. They also come with an almond filling for dessert.

Snacks

Cheaper restaurants serve kebabs (aka *brochettes*), with tiny pieces of beef, lamb and fat. Also popular is *kefta*, mince-meat brochettes, served in sandwiches with chips, mustard and *harissa* (red-pepper spicy sauce). Tiny bowls of finely chopped tomato and onion are another popular accompaniment. On Jemaâ el Fna in Marrakech, strong stomachs may want to snack on the local *babouche* (snails).

Main dishes

Seksou (couscous) is the great North African speciality. Granules of semolina are steamed over a pot filled with a rich meat and vegetable stew. Unlike Tunisian couscous, which tends to be flavoured with a tomato sauce, Moroccan couscous is pale yellow. For most families, couscous is the big Friday lunch.

A tagine is a stew and is the basic Moroccan dish. It is actually the term for the two-part terracotta dish (base and conical lid) in which meat or fish are cooked with a variety of vegetables, essentially carrots, potato, onion and turnip. Tagine is everywhere in Morocco. Simmered in front of you on a *brasero* at a roadside café, it is always good and safe to eat. Out trekking and in the South, it is the staple of life. For tagines, there are four main sauce preparations: *m'qalli*, a yellow sauce created using olive oil, ginger and saffron;

ON THE ROAD
Dishes for Ramadan

During the holy month of Ramadan the daily fast is broken at sunset with a rich and savoury *harira* (see above), *beghrira* (little honeycombed pancakes served with melted butter and honey) and *shebbakia* (lace-work pastry basted in oil and covered in honey). Distinctive too are the sticky pastry whorls with sesame seeds on top.

m'hammer, a red sauce which includes butter, paprika (*felfla hlwa*) and cumin; *qudra*, another yellow sauce, slightly lighter than *m'qalli*, made using butter, onions, pepper and saffron, and finally *m'chermel*, made using ingredients from the other sauces. Variations on these base sauces are obtained using a range of ingredients, including parsley and coriander, garlic and lemon juice, *boussera*, eggs, sugar, honey and cinnamon (*karfa*).

In the better restaurants, look out for *djaj bil-hamid* (chicken with preserved lemons and olives), sweet and sour *tajine barkouk* (lamb with plums), *djaj qudra* (chicken with almonds and caramelized onion) and *tajine maqfoul*. Another tasty dish is *tajine kefta*, basically fried minced meat balls cooked with eggs and chopped parsley. In eateries next to food markets, delicacies such as *ra's embekhar* (steamed sheep's head) and *kourayn* (animal feet) are popular.

A dish rarely prepared in restaurants is *djaj souiri*, aka *djaj mqeddem*, the only *plat gratiné* in Moroccan cuisine. Here, at the very last minute, a sauce of beaten eggs and chopped parsley is added to the chicken, already slow-cooked in olives, diced preserved lemon, olive oil and various spices.

All over Morocco, lamb is much appreciated, and connoisseurs reckon they can tell what the sheep has been eating (rosemary, mountain pasture, straw, or mixed rubbish at the vast Mediouna tip near Casablanca). Lamb is cheaper in drought years, when farmers have to reduce their flocks, expensive when the grazing is good, and is often best eaten at roadside restaurants where the lorry drivers pull in for a feed.

Desserts

A limited selection of desserts is served in Moroccan restaurants. In the palace restaurants, there will be a choice between *orange à la cannelle* (slices of orange with cinnamon) or some sort of marzipan patisserie like *cornes de gazelle* or *ghrayeb*, rather like round short-cake. *El jaouhar*, also onomatopoeically known as *tchak-tchouka*, is served as a pile of crunchy, fried filo pastry discs topped with a sweet custardy sauce with almonds. Also on offer you may find *m'hencha*, coils of almond paste wrapped in filo pastry, served crisp from the oven and sprinkled with icing sugar and cinnamon, and *bechkito*, little crackly biscuits.

Most large towns will have a couple of large patisseries, providing French pastries and the petits fours essential for proper entertaining. Here you will find *slilou* (aka *masfouf*), a richly flavoured nutty powder served in tiny saucers to accompany tea, but don't expect to find *maâjoun*, the Moroccan equivalent of hash brownies, made to liven up dull guests at wedding parties.

In local *laiteries*, try a glass of yoghurt. Oranges (*limoun*) and mandarins (*tchina*) are cheap, as are prickly pears, sold off barrows. In winter, in the mountains, look out for kids selling tiny red arbutus berries (*sasnou*) carefully packaged in little wicker cones. Fresh hazelnuts are charmingly known as *tigerguist*.

Eating out

Cafés offer croissants, petit-pains and cake (Madeleine), plus occasionally soup and basic snacks. Snack eateries in the medina and *ville nouvelle* are generally cheap and basic; some are modelled on international themed fast-food restaurants. *Laiteries* sell yoghurt, fruit juices and will make up sandwiches with processed cheese, salad and *kacher* (processed meat). Full-blown restaurants are generally found only in larger towns, and some are very good indeed. And, finally, in cities like Fès, Meknès and Marrakech, you have the great palaces of Moroccan cuisine, restaurants set in old, often beautifully restored private homes. These can set you back 500dh or even more. Some of these restaurants allow you to eat à la carte (**El Fassia** in Marrakech), rather than giving you the full banquet menu (and late-night indigestion).

Eating out cheaply

If you're on a very tight budget, try the ubiquitous food stalls and open-air restaurants serving various types of soup, normally the standard broth (*harira*), snacks and grilled meat. The best place for the adventurous open-air eater is the Jemaâ el Fna square in Marrakech. Another good place is the fish market in the centre of Essaouira. There is a greater risk of food poisoning at street eateries, so go for food that is cooked as you wait, or that is on the boil. Avoid fried fish that is already cooked and is reheated when you order it. Each city also has a colourful central market, generally dating back to the early years of the 20th century, stuffed with high-quality fresh produce. Try the Guéliz market in Marrakech, on Avenue Mohammed V, on your left after the intersection with Rue de la Liberté as you head for the town centre.

ON THE ROAD
Eating in people's homes

Moroccan families may eat from a communal dish, often with spoons, sometimes with their hands. If invited to a home, you may well be something of a guest of honour. Depending on your hosts, it's a good idea to take some fruit or pâtisseries along. If spoons or cutlery are not provided, eat using bread with your right hand only – do not use your left hand since it is ritually unclean. If the dishes are placed at floor level, keep your feet tucked under your body away from the food. In a poorer home, there will only be a small amount of meat, so wait until a share is offered. Basically, good manners are the same anywhere. Let common sense guide you.

Vegetarian food

Moroccan food is not terribly interesting for vegetarians, and meals can turn into endless repetition of the same couple of choices. Vegetable tagines and seven-vegetable 'Casablanca' couscous are easy to come by in larger towns. Pizza, omelettes and excellent salads are also readily available and can be good options. In Marrakech, Essaouira and Fès, vegetarians will find plenty more dishes to choose from. Outside the main centres, though, vegetarianism is really quite alien to most Moroccans, as receiving someone well for dinner means serving them a tagine with good chunk of meat. If you're heading into seriously rural areas that don't see a lot of foreign visitors, be prepared to eat lots of processed cheese and omelettes.

Drink

Tea

All over Morocco the main drink apart from water is mint tea (*thé à la menthe/ attay*), a cheap, refreshing drink which is made with green tea, fresh mint and masses of white sugar. The latter two ingredients predominate in the taste. If you want a reduced sugar tea, ask for *attay msous* or *bila sukar/sans sucre*). In cafés, tea is served in mini-metal tea pots, poured from high above the glass to generate a froth (*attay bi-rizatou*, 'tea with a turban') to use the local expression. Generally, tradition has it that you drink three glasses. To avoid burning your fingers, hold the glass with thumb under the base and index finger on rim. In some homes, various other herbs are added to make a more interesting brew, including *flayou* (peppermint), *louiza* (verbena) and even *sheeba* (absinthe). If you want a herb tea, ask for a *verveine* or *louiza*, which may be with either hot water or hot milk (*bil-halib*).

Coffee

Coffee is commonly drunk black and strong (*kahwa kahla/un exprès*). For a weak milky coffee, ask for a *café au lait/kahwa halib*. A stronger milky coffee is called a *café cassé/nuss-nuss* (literally half-half).

Other soft drinks

All the usual soft drinks are available in Morocco. If you want still mineral water (*eau plate*) ask for Sidi Harazem, Sidi Ali or Ciel. The main brands of fizzy mineral water (*eau pétillante*) are Oulmès and Bonacqua, a water produced by Coca Cola.

The better cafés and local *laiteries* (milk-product shops) do milkshakes, combinations of avocado, banana, apple and orange, made to measure. Ask for a *jus d'avocat* or a *jus de banane*, for example, or for a usually excellent mixed juice known as panache.

Wines and spirits

For a Muslim country, Morocco is fairly relaxed about alcohol, although be aware that most mid-range and budget restaurants don't have alcohol licences, and standalone bars are few and far between. In the top hotels, imported spirits are available, although at a price. If you want to buy alcohol outside a restaurant, every major town will have a few licensed sales points. Often they are very well stocked with local and imported wines. Foreign supermarket chains, in all the major cities, also have an off-licence section. In Ramadan, alcohol is on sale to non-Muslim foreigners only and many of the off-licences shut down for the month.

The main locally made lager **beers** are Casa, Flag and Flag Spécial. In the spring, look out for the extremely good Bière de Mars, made only in March with Fès spring water. Morocco produces **wine**, the main growing areas being Guerrouane and Meknès. Reds tend to prevail. **Celliers de Meknès** (CdM) and **Sincomar** are the main producers. At the top of the scale (off-licence prices in brackets) are Médaillon (90dh) and Beau Vallon (CdM, 90dh, anything up to 185dh in a restaurant). A CdM Merlot will set you back 45dh. Another reliable red is Domaine de Sahari, Aït Yazem, a pleasant claret, best drunk chilled in summer (30dh). The whites include Coquillages and Sémillant, probably the best (40dh). At the very bottom of the scale is rough and ready Rabbi Jacob, or, cheaper and still cheerful, Chaud Soleil. The local fig firewater is Mahia la Gazelle.

Menu reader

Amlou Runny 'butter' from argan kernels

Arganier Tree producing an almond-like nut. The kernel of the nut produces the highly valued argan oil

Beghir Thick pancakes often served for breakfast

Bestila Elaborate sweet and sour pie made of alternating layers of filo-pastry and egg, pigeon, and crushed almonds. Speciality of Fès

Bissara Bean and pea soup, workingman's breakfast

Briouet Filo pastry envelopes, filled with crushed nuts and basted in olive oil, then dipped in honey

Brochettes Kebabs made with tiny pieces of liver, meat and fat

Chermoula Marinade sauce

Couscous Steamed semolina made from durum wheat, heaped with meat and vegetables. Couscous may also be served with nuts, dates, raisins, sugar and milk for dessert. In the countryside, couscous is made from barley

Fliou Peppermint, also used in tea preparations

Harcha Thick round unleavened 'bread', popular for breakfast

Harira Chickpea and mutton soup, especially popular when breaking the fast in Ramadhan

Kaâb el-ghizal Gazelles' horns. Traditional marzipan-filled pastry

Kahoua Coffee

Kefta Minced meat

Khliaâ Preserved meat (dried, boiled). Fr 'viande boucanée')

Líkama Mint

Luiza Verbena herbal tea

Mahchi (or **mo'ammar**) Stuffed (chicken, vegetables, etc)

Mechoui Barbecued meat

Mqali Meat dishes simmered with sauce reduced rapidly on high flame at end

Mouhallabiya Milk pudding

Na'na Mint, essential for preparing tea, also called 'likama' The best mint is produced in Meknès

Orz bil-bahiya Paella

Qa'ida Tradition – vital to any meal prepared for guests in a Moroccan home

Ra's el Hanout (lit. 'master of the shop') Special spice mix

Roumi (lit. 'from Rome). Adjective designating things foreign or modern, especially with regard to food and recipes. Used in opposition to things 'bildi' (qv), indigenous and traditional

Seksou (Amz) Couscous, qv

Tajine Moroccan stew traditionally cooked slowly in a clay pot on a brasero

Tajine barkouk Sweet and sour prune and mutton stew

Zitoun Olives

Zit el oud Olive oil

Marrakech
& Essaouira

a tale of two cities

The starting point for most visitors to Morocco, Marrakech is one of the great cities of North Africa. Nicknamed the Red City due to the uniform terracotta wash used on its buildings, this ancient town has been on tourist tick-lists since at least the 1920s.

Lying within easy reach of both the High Atlas valleys and the Atlantic coast, Marrakech makes a good base from which to plot further journeys into the countryside. For many, though, the city itself is the main attraction. Famed for the chaotic open-air revelry and street theatre of its main square, Jemaâ el Fna, and for the mazy narrow alleys and souks of the medina, where you can find handicrafts of every shape and size, Marrakech continues to dazzle all who arrive here.

When the buzz of the medina gets too much, many travellers head west to the coast and the photogenic fishing port of Essaouira. Its ramparts have been battered by naval conquests and Atlantic waves over the centuries, but today it is a rather sleepy and relaxing place to visit. Its fishing industry survives, but tourism is increasingly taking over as the main business of the coast, which is popular with windsurfers. Wandering through the compact old town and strolling along the beach provide the perfect antidote to Marrakech's more frenetic energy.

Best for
Riads ▪ Shopping ▪ Sightseeing ▪ Windsurfing

Marrakech 37
Essaouira. 82

Footprint
picks

★ Jemaâ el Fna, page 43

Spend an evening amid the colourful, chaotic entertainment of
the Jemaâ.

★ Marrakech souks, page 50

Chuck away the map and shop till you drop in the labyrinthine
souks of the Marrakech medina.

★ Medersa Ben Youssef, page 51

Gaze in wonder at the intricate artistry of one of North Africa's
best-preserved Islamic buildings.

★ Bed down in a riad, page 63

Sleep amid *zellige* tiles and oodles of old world ambience at a
riad – there's something to suit all budgets.

★ Lunch at Essaouira port, page 84

Munch on fresh fish and breathe in the sea air at Essaouira's port.

★ Sunset on the Skala, page 86

Watch the sun dip below the horizon atop the ramparts of
Essaouira's skala.

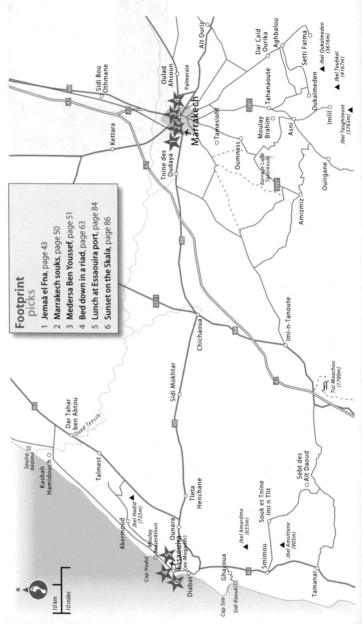

Footprint picks

1 Jemaâ el Fna, page 43
2 Marrakech souks, page 50
3 Medersa Ben Youssef, page 51
4 Bed down in a riad, page 63
5 Lunch at Essaouira port, page 84
6 Sunset on the Skala, page 86

Marrakech

Marrakech's labyrinthine medina of skinny alleys, overlooked by a dramatic backdrop of snow-capped High Atlas mountains, is Morocco's big drawcard and many visitors never venture far beyond its old red earth walls. This city is where sophisticated modernity and traditional North African culture collide and merge. Glamorous riad-living and chi-chi boutiques are now as much part of the experience as the metal-workers banging their hammers in the back corners of the souks and the snake charmers and soothsayers entertaining the seething crowds of Jemaâ el Fna square. Marrakech may be a favoured city-break for Europeans seeking out the North African sunshine, but this ancient city hasn't lost its soul to tourism. Lose yourself in the backstreets of the medina, and you'll discover the residential heartbeat of the old city. Admire the dazzling displays of artistry at the Saâdian Tombs and the Medersa Ben Youssef, then spend an evening Marrakchi-style amid the bedlam of musicians, dancers and roaming acrobats at Jemaâ el Fna. For many, Marrakech is their first taste of Morocco and North Africa as a whole, and what an impression it leaves. This is a city that doesn't do things by halves. Pulsating with energy and crowded with people, Marrakech is overwhelming to the senses and occasionally nerve-jangling, but never, ever boring.

Essential Marrakech

Finding your feet

Accessible by air and situated at the meeting point of routes to Essaouira (on the Atlantic coast), Ouarzazate to the south and the northern imperial cities, Marrakech makes an excellent central point of arrival in Morocco. Marrakech **Menara Airport**, T0524-447910, www.marrakech.airport-authority.com, is 6 km west of the city, by the Menara Gardens. From the airport, the medina and the Guéliz district are both easily accessible by *petit taxi*, *grand taxi* (beware overcharging), hotel transfers, or by the airport shuttle bus. The **railway station** is to the west of the central area, a 10-minute walk from the *ville nouvelle* or 30 minutes from Jemaâ el Fna; taxis and buses are available. Inter-city public **buses** arrive at the *gare routière*, next to the Bab Doukkala gate into the medina, a 15-minute walk from Jemaâ el Fna. Bus companies **CTM** and **Supratours** also stop at Bab Doukkala but have their main terminals in Guéliz near the train station.

Tip...

If you're staying in a riad, pre-arrange a meeting point at the edge of the medina (usually Jemaâ el Fna) upon arrival, from where someone will escort you to the riad.

Getting around

Marrakech is a great city for walking. Much of the medina is made up of skinny alleyways, impossible to navigate by car, which means that walking is the best way to explore the old city. It's an easy 20-minute amble between the medina and the *ville nouvelle*. Renting a bicycle

Best accommodation

Riad Tizwa, page 62
Riad Zolah, page 62
Tchaikana, page 62
Equity Point Hostel, page 64
Le Gallia Hotel, page 64

or scooter is also an option for confident riders. Short taxi rides in Marrakech should not cost more than 10 or 15dh, longer journeys, 20dh. Unfortunately Marrakchi taxi drivers are renowned for overcharging and for not using their meters; try to have change and insist on using the meter. A scenic alternative is a *calèche* (a horse-drawn carriage), particularly popular for trips between the Jemaâ and the Kasbah or the Jardin Marjorelle.

Orientation

Marrakech is a spread-out city hemmed by sprawling suburbs but its central area is relatively compact. At the centre of the *ville nouvelle* is Place du 16 Novembre. Directly to the north of this is bustling Guéliz, the modern shopping district with plenty of café-culture and restaurants and Jardin Majorelle at its northeast end. Directly to the south is leafy, mostly residential Hivernage, with a scattering of hotels and restaurants. The *ville nouvelle* and the medina (Marrakech's old city) are connected by Avenue Mohammed V which runs eastwards to the Koutoubia Mosque and the main medina entry at Jemaâ el Fna from where you can dive into the labyrinthine souks. Head south from the Jemaâ to reach the Kasbah district with the Bahia Palace, the Saadian Tombs, El Badi Palace and the *mellah* (the old Jewish quarter).

Hassle

Most of Marrakech's once notorious fake guides and scammers have now disappeared thanks to the work of the city's Brigade Touristique. That's not to say you won't get hassled – you will – but even in the centre of Jemaâ el Fna, vortex for roaming vendors and touts, the atmosphere is mostly relaxed. Do watch out for the henna-ladies on the square, who have a habit of making a sales pitch by grabbing your hand. And, don't pay any attention to young men in the souks who hang about on street corners shouting out that you're going the wrong way or that the sight you're heading towards is closed. If you do get lost, always ask directions from a vendor at a stall, shop or café rather than from any nearby loiterer.

Best cheap eats

Jemaâ el Fna stalls, page 69
Marrakech Henna Art Café, page 70
Amal Women's Training Centre, page 71

Best restaurants for a treat

Dar Zellij, page 67
Al-Fassia, page 71

When to go

December to February can get cold (particularly during the evenings), so pack a jumper and jacket if you're travelling at this time. Around Christmas and Easter is peak holiday time, when prices rise for accommodation throughout the city. July and August are hot; though the high walls of the medina provide lots of shady areas, this time is best avoided unless you thrive on sweating it out. May, June and October are by far the nicest times to visit with pleasant sunny days galore.

Time required

Allow at least three days to explore the city, or more if you want to really soak up the atmosphere.

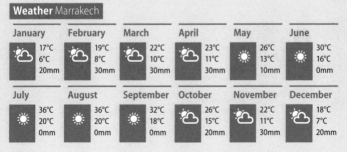

Weather Marrakech

January	February	March	April	May	June
17°C	19°C	22°C	23°C	26°C	30°C
6°C	8°C	10°C	11°C	13°C	16°C
20mm	30mm	30mm	30mm	10mm	0mm

July	August	September	October	November	December
36°C	36°C	32°C	26°C	22°C	18°C
20°C	20°C	18°C	15°C	11°C	7°C
0mm	0mm	0mm	20mm	30mm	20mm

1 Marrakech

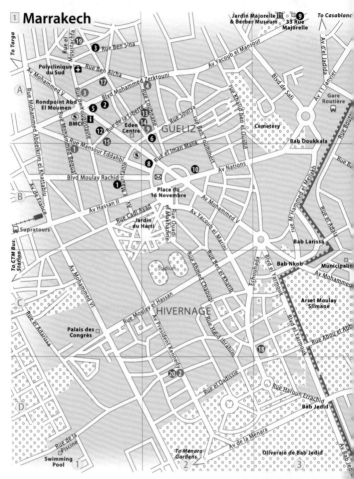

Where to stay
Bab 1 *B1*
Dar Rhizlane 2 *D2*
Diwane 3 *A1*
Moroccan
 House 4 *A2*
Riad El Fenn 5 *C4*
Riad Tizwa 6 *B4*
Riad Viva 7 *D4*
Tchaikana 8 *B6*
Toulousain 9 *A2*

Restaurants
Al Bahriya 1 *B1*
Al Fassia 2 *A1*
Amal Women's
 Training Centre 3 *A1*
Café Clock 4 *E5*
Café Les Négociants 5 *A1*
Catanzaro 6 *A2*
Dar Zellij 7 *A4*
Grand Café de la Poste 8 *B2*
Kaowa 9 *A3*
Le 16 10 *B2*
Le Tobsil 11 *C4*
Loft 12 *A1*

Bars & clubs
68 Bar Au Vin 13 *A2*
Café de Livre 14 *A2*
Kechmara 15 *A1*
Kosybar 16 *D5*
L'Auberge Espagnole 17 *A1*
Le Comptoir Darna 18 *C3*
Le Point Bar 19 *A1*
Sky Bab Bar 20 *D2*

ON THE ROAD

The desert and the mountains

Marrakech is surrounded by extensive palm groves into which suburbs are gradually spreading. Yet there are also sandy, arid areas around the city, which give it a semi-Saharan character. And then, there are the mountains. Arriving from Fès or Meknès you run alongside the bald, arid Jebilet ('the little mountains'), or cross them at Sidi Bou Othmane as you come from Casablanca or Rabat. Perhaps the most beautiful approach to Marrakech is on the N7 from Casablanca and Sidi Bennour, which crosses the Plateau des Gantours and the end of the Jebilet. However, from most points in Marrakech, cloud and heat haze allowing, it is the High Atlas, the Adrar (literally 'the mountains'), which dominate. At times the optical illusion is such that the snow-covered mountain wall appears to rise from just behind the city.

Sightseeing in Marrakech

exploring Marrakech by neighbourhood

Central Marrakech is clearly divided into two parts: the large historic city of the medina, and the *ville nouvelle*, Guéliz. The focal point of the medina, and indeed of the whole city, is the Jemaâ el Fna, an open space full of street entertainers and food sellers. Handily for the tourist, it is located in the middle of the main sightseeing area, opposite the Koutoubia Mosque. North of Jemaâ el Fna are the souks, the Sidi Ben Youssef Mosque, the Medersa Ben Youssef, the Maison de la Photographie, and the Musée de Marrakech. South of Jemaâ el Fna, down Riad Zitoun el Jedid, are the Dar Si Said, Bahia Palace, Badi Palace and the Saâdian Tombs.

The western side of the medina is taken up by the **Bab Doukkala** and **Leksour/ Mouassine** neighbourhoods. The latter is the old city's most chic enclave, home to boutiques and bijou gallery places as well as more traditional souk stalls. Travellers with more time, could explore the lesser visited neighbourhoods of the north and east sections of the medina: the Thursday flea market at **Bab el Khemis** is ideal for those seeking gems amongst junk and second-hand treasures, while the **tanneries** at Bab Debbagh provide a pungent behind-the-scenes look at the city's leather manufacturing process.

Most visitors will spend some time in **Guéliz**, the suburb laid out by the French in the 1920s. Despite all the new apartment buildings and traffic, it is worth a wander for its cafés, upmarket boutiques and art galleries, and its many eating options and bars. The main thoroughfare is Avenue Mohammed V and the evening promenade here is popular.

Ramparts

Except for those around the Agdal Gardens, the extensive ramparts of Marrakech (20 gates and 200 towers stretching for 16 km) are predominantly Almoravid,

ON THE ROAD

Marrakech for kids

Snake charmers, acrobats, jugglers and monkey-tamers: Jemaâ el Fna is a wide-eyed world of wacky entertainment for kids. Exploring the maze of the souks and watching craftspeople at work is always fascinating, and entering Bab Debbagh's tannery area is sure to result in exclamations about the smell. However, when the heat and noise begin to frazzle both parents and young ones, try out these:

A family-friendly bike tour run by AXS, page 78.
A ride through the palm groves of the Palmerai, page 79.

A day at a pool outside the city, page 80.
A horse-drawn *calèche* tour of the city walls, below and page 81.

although they have been extensively restored since that period. Repairs and reconstruction are a continual process as the *pisé*-cement walls, made of the distinctive earth of the Haouz plains, crumble over time. The ramparts and gates are one of the distinctive sights of Morocco and can be viewed on a ride in a horse-drawn *calèche*. In places, there has been much beautification, with fancy wrought-iron railings and rose gardens taking the place of the dust on the Hivernage side of town. (Details of individual gates are given in the sights text, below.)

★ Jemaâ el Fna

the beating heart and soul of the city

The Jemaâ el Fna, unique in Morocco, is both the greatest pull for tourists and still a genuine social area for Marrakchis and those flooding in from the surrounding regions. 'La Place' is full of people hawking their goods or talents and others watching, walking, talking and arguing. From sunset until late into the night, a weird and wonderful mix of musicians, acrobats, snake charmers and showmen keep the crowds entertained. It is particularly memorable during Ramadan when the day's fast ends. Whatever the time of day or year, Jemaâ el Fna is somewhere that visitors return to again and again, responding to the magnetic pull that affects locals as much as tourists, to mingle with the crowd or watch the chaos from above on one of the café terraces that line the square (see box, page 69).

Jemaâ el Fna means 'assembly of the dead' and may refer to the traditional display of the heads of criminals executed here until the 19th century. In 1956, the government attempted to close down the square by converting it into a corn market and car park, but it soon reverted to its traditional role. In the late 1980s, the bus station was moved from here out to Bab Doukkala and in 1994, the square was fully tarmacked for the GATT meeting. In 2001, thanks to campaigning by a team

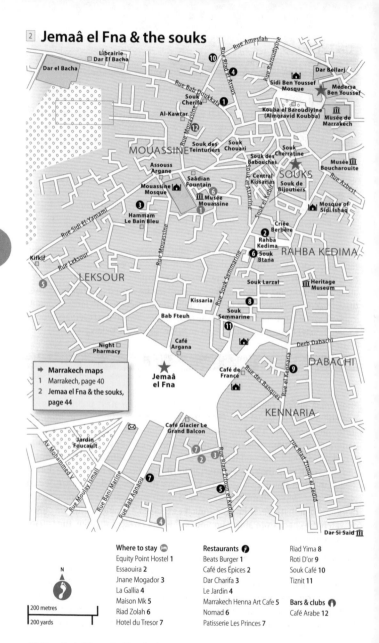

Jemaâ el Fna & the souks

Librairie Dar El Bacha

Dar el Bacha

Rue Amesfah

Rue Riad Zitoun

10

4

Rue Bab Doukkala

Dar Bellarj

Sidi Ben Youssef Mosque

Medersa Ben Youssef

Souk Cherifa

1

Al-Kawtar

12

Kouba el Baroudiyine (Almoravid Koubba)

Musée de Marrakech

MOUASSINE

Souk des Teinturiers

Souk Chouari

Souk des Babouches

Souk Cherratine

Assouss Argane

Saâdian Fountain

6

Musée Mouassine

Central Kissarias

SOUKS

Musée Boucharouite

Mouassine Mosque

1

Souk de Bijoutiers

Rue Azbest

3

Hammam Le Bain Bleu

Criée Berbère

Mosque of Sidi Ishaq

Rue Sidi El Yamami

2

Rahba Kedima

RAHBA KEDIMA

Kifkif

Rue Leksour

6

Souk Btana

5

LEKSOUR

Souk Larzal

Heritage Museum

Kissaria

8

Bab Fteuh

Souk Semmarine

11

Night Pharmacy

Café Argana

Derb Dabachi

DABACHI

➡ Marrakech maps
1 Marrakech, page 40
2 Jemaa el Fna & the souks, page 44

Café de France

9

Jemaâ el Fna

KENNARIA

Café Glacier Le Grand Balcon

Jardin Foucault

7

2

3

Marrakech Henna Art Cafe

5

Dar Si Said

Where to stay 🏠
Equity Point Hostel 1
Essaouira 2
Jnane Mogador 3
La Gallia 4
Maison Mk 5
Riad Zolah 6
Hotel du Tresor 7

Restaurants 🍴
Beats Burger 1
Café des Épices 2
Dar Charifa 3
Le Jardin 4
Marrakech Henna Art Cafe 5
Nomad 6
Patisserie Les Princes 7

Riad Yima 8
Roti D'or 9
Souk Café 10
Tiznit 11

Bars & clubs 🍷
Café Arabe 12

N

200 metres
200 yards

ON THE ROAD

Jemaâ el Juice

Ask people about their impressions of Jemaâ el Fna and they'll mention the snake charmers, the food, the acrobats, the swarming mass of humanity, but also the orange juice. From dawn until late at night, the west and east sides of the square are home to stalls piled high with immaculately stacked oranges, touting cheap and delicious freshly squeezed juice that makes for a refreshing pit-stop while exploring the medina. Orange is 4dh per glass; grapefruit, pomegranate, or mixed is 10dh. Make sure the vendor squeezes it freshly in front of you as some water down their 'ready made' containers with squash.

led by Spanish writer and Marrakech resident Juan Goytisolo, UNESCO labelled the Jemaâ as a 'Masterpiece of the oral and intangible heritage of humanity' for its role in preserving street theatre.

During the day you can explore the stalls and collections of goods: fruit, herbs and spices, clothes, shoes, alarm clocks and radios, as well as handicrafts. There are snake charmers and monkey tamers, water-sellers and, sheltering from the sun under their umbrellas, henna tattoo artists, fortune tellers and public scribes awaiting their clients. You may find an astrologist-soothsayer tracing out his diagram of the future on the tarmac with a stubby piece of chalk. And should you need an aphrodisiac, there are stalls with tea urns selling cinnamon and ginseng tea and little dishes of black, powdery *slilou*, a spicy sweet paste.

Just before sunset the crowds begin to flood in, a mix of students and people pausing on the way home from work, smart tourists strolling to restaurants in the medina and backpackers ready for hot tagine or harira soup at one of the food stalls. As dusk sets in the entertainment begins: wildly grinning Gnaoua musicians with giant metal castanets, Berber folk musicians, slapstick boxers and Ouled el Moussa tumblers. After coaxing a few dirhams from the crowd, an acoustic band will get some Berbers dancing, while around a hissing gas lamp a group will perform a song by Jil Jilala, an activist group popular in the 1970s. Sometimes (though the tradition has mainly died out on the square), if you're lucky, you'll see a storyteller enthralling the crowd. A modern variation on the traditional *halka* or storyteller's circle touches harsh social reality: local people listen to a true tale told with dignity by the relatives of a victim of poverty or injustice. More recent additions to entertainment in the square include a variety of games which you can join in for a dirham or two, including 'hook the ring over the coke bottle' and bowling a football between two impossibly narrow goal posts.

Tip...

Entertainers will expect a tip if you stop to watch or take photos of them, so keep plenty of small change handy. Pickpockets are occasionally a problem and visitors should be extra vigilant while strolling the square or while standing amid the crowds that huddle around the buskers; keep wallets or handbags out of view.

Koutoubia Mosque

The 65-m high minaret of the Koutoubia Mosque dominates the whole of Marrakech because, unlike the Qarawiyin Mosque in Fès, it is set apart from the dense building of the old town. Visible from afar, it provided the focal point for urban planner Henri Prost when he laid out the modern neighbourhood of Guéliz.

Tip...

Non-Muslims cannot enter the mosque but are permitted to walk through the surrounding plaza. As this is a place of prayer, and in every way the most important mosque in the city, dress decently if you are going to approach the site to view it at length.

Unusually, the Koutoubia is a double mosque, both parts dating from the reign of the second Almohad ruler, Abd el Mumin (1130-1163). Standing on the esplanade facing the minaret, the ruins of the first Koutoubia are behind railings to your right (first excavated in the late 1940s). The bases of the prayer hall's columns and the cisterns under the courtyard are clearly visible. The ground plan of the second Koutoubia, still standing, is the same as that of the ruined one (17 naves). The Almohad mosque at Tin Mal (see page 104), open for visits by non-Muslims, has a similar plan.

The name 'Koutoubia' derives from the Arabic *kutub* (books) and means the 'Booksellers' Mosque', reflecting the fact that manuscripts were bought and sold in a souk close by. The site of the mosque was originally occupied by a late 11th-century Almoravid kasbah, the Dar al Hajar. The successful Almohads destroyed much of the Almoravid city and, in 1147, built a large mosque, close to the fortress. In all likelihood they had to do this because, puritan as they were and considering the Almoravids to be heretics, they could not pray in a tainted building. Unfortunately, the orientation of the new Almohad mosque was not quite right – the focus point in a mosque is the direction of Mecca and should be indicated by the mihrab, or prayer niche. The solution was to build a second mosque – the present Koutoubia – even though the faithful at prayer can correct this directional problem themselves, under the direction of the imam, once the right direction has been worked out.

Thus two mosques existed for some time side by side, the first probably functioning as a sort of annexe. Today, the bricked-up spaces on the northwest wall of the Koutoubia Mosque indicate the doors which connected the two buildings. However, the older structure fell into disrepair and eventual ruin. Excavations in 1948 revealed a *maqsura*, or screen, in front of the mihrab, which could be wound up through the floor to protect the Sultan, and a *minbar*, or

Fact...

An unlikely local legend tells that the Koutoubia minaret once overlooked the harem and so only a blind muezzin was allowed to climb it to call the faithful to prayer.

ON THE ROAD

Inside the mosque

In all Muslim countries, mosques are built orientated towards Mecca, as the believers must pray in the direction of their holy city. In Morocco's case, this means that the orientation is east-southeast. A large mosque has four main areas: prayer halls, courtyard and colonnade, minaret and, in all likelihood, attached ablutions facility and hammam. Most mosques will have: the **qibla wall**, facing east-southeast, with a decorated niche or **mihrab** in the middle, towards which the believers pray; a colonnaded **prayer hall** and a large **courtyard**, often with a fountain; a **minaret** or *midhana* from which the call to prayer is made five times a day; an **entrance**, through which the non-Muslim visitor may glimpse the courtyard if there is no wooden lattice-work screen.

On Fridays, there will often be so many people for the weekly midday prayers and accompanying sermon that latecomers, equipped with their rugs, will have to pray outside in the street.

---

pulpit, which was moved into position on wooden rollers. The two cisterns in the centre may have been from a previous Almoravid structure. On the eastern flank of this mosque was an arcade of which a niche and the remains of one arch remain.

The existing Koutoubia Mosque, built by Abd el Mumin in 1162, was a vast structure for 12th-century North Africa. Held to be the high point of Almohad building, it is here that the innovations of Hispano-Moorish art reach perfection. The minaret is 12.5 m wide and 67.5 m to the tip of the cupola on the lantern and is the mosque's principal feature, rightly ranked alongside later Almohad structures, the Hassan Tower in Rabat and the Giralda in Seville. The minaret, composed of six rooms, one on top of the other, was a great feat of engineering in its day and influenced several subsequent buildings in Morocco. The cupola on top is a symmetrical square structure topped by a ribbed dome and three golden orbs, which are alleged to have been made from the melted-down jewellery of successive Almohad leader, Yaqoub al Mansour's wife, in penance for her having eaten three grapes during the Ramadan fast. The cupola has two windows on each side, above which is a stone panel in the *darj w ktaf*, 'step-and-shoulder', motif, and a band of coloured tiles at the top. Ultimately, the Koutoubia is striking because it is the work of one ruler, Abd el Mumin. Comparable buildings in western Islam – the Great Mosque of Córdoba and the Alhambra – were built over a couple of centuries.

> **Tip...**
> For a good view of the minaret, head to the gardens behind the mosque (great for photographs). A close-up of the top of the minaret and its *darj w ktaf* design also features on the 100dh banknote.

BACKGROUND
Marrakech

In some early European maps Marrakech appears as 'Morocco city', although 'Maraksh' is the Arabic name. The origins of the name are obscure: some see it as a corruption of 'aghmat-urika', the name of an early town. Marrakech was first founded in 1062 by Youssef Ibn Tachfine, the Almoravid leader, as a base from which to control the High Atlas mountains. A kasbah, Dar al Hajar, was built close to the site of the Koutoubia Mosque. Under Youssef Ben Tachfine, Marrakech became the region's first major urban settlement. Within the walls were mosques, palaces and extensive orchards and market gardens, made possible by an elaborate water transfer and irrigation system. The population was probably a mixture of people of black-African descent from the Oued Drâa, Imazighen from the Souss Valley and the nearby Atlas, and Amazigh Jews. The city attracted leading medieval thinkers from outside Marrakech.

Marrakech was taken by the Almohads in 1147, who almost totally destroyed and then rebuilt the city, making it the capital of their extensive empire. Under the Almohad Sultan Abd el Moumen, the Koutoubia Mosque was built on the site of Almoravid buildings, with the minaret added by Ya'qub al Mansour. Under the latter, Marrakech gained palaces, gardens and irrigation works, and again became a centre for musicians, writers and academics, but on his death it declined and fell into disarray.

While the Merinids added several *medersas* to Marrakech, Fès received much more of their attention and was preferred as the capital, although from 1374 to 1386 Marrakech was the centre of a separate principality. Marrakech was revitalized by the Saâdians from 1524, with the rebuilding of the Ben Youssef Mosque and the construction by Ahmed al Mansour Ad Dahbi of the El Badi Palace and the Saâdian Tombs. Marrakech also became an important trading post, due to its location between the Sahara and the Atlantic.

The Alaouites took control of Marrakech in 1668. In the early 18th century the city suffered from Moulay Ismaïl's love of Meknès, with many of the major buildings, notably the El Badi Palace, stripped to glorify the new capital. The destructive effects of this period were compounded by the civil strife following his death. However, from 1873, under Alaouite Sultan Moulay Hassan I and his son, the city's prestige was re-established. A number of the city's fine palaces date from this time and are still open to visitors.

From 1898 until independence, Marrakech was the nerve-centre of southern Morocco, ruled practically as a personal fiefdom by the Glaoui family from the central High Atlas. The French took control of Marrakech and its region in 1912, crushing an insurrection by a claimant to the Sultanate. Their policy in the vast and rugged southern territories was to govern through local rulers, rather as the British worked with the Rajahs of India.

With French support, Pacha T'hami el Glaoui extended his control over all areas of the south. His autonomy from central authority was considerable; his cruelty notorious. And, of course, there were great advantages in this system, in the form of profits from the new French-developed mines. In the 1930s, Marrakech saw the development of a fine *ville nouvelle*, Guéliz, consisting of wide avenues of jacarandas and simple, elegant bungalow houses. On acquiring a railway line terminus, Marrakech reaffirmed its status as capital of the south. It was at this time, when travel for pleasure was still the preserve of the privileged of Europe, that Marrakech began to acquire its reputation as a retreat for the wealthy.

Marrakech today

Marrakech is Morocco's fourth largest city. In recent decades the population has grown enormously to around 1.5 million (or nearer two million including the suburbs), swelled by civil servants and armed forces personnel. Its people are a mix of Arab and Amazigh; many are recent migrants from surrounding rural regions and further south attracted by the city's reputation as 'city of the poor', where even the least qualified can find work of some kind. However, for many rural people, the urban struggle is hard and, as the Tachelhit pun puts it, Marrakech is *ma-ra-kish*: 'the place where they'll eat you if they can'. For centuries an important regional market place, Marrakech now has a booming service economy and there is still a wide range of handicraft production and small-scale industry, particularly in the medina. Out in the western suburbs are new factories. Increasingly, tourism is seen as the mainstay of the city's economy. Marrakech is one of the major tourist attractions of Morocco and many of the city's large number of unemployed or under-employed supplement their incomes by casual work with tourists.

The Brigade Touristique, set up to reduce the hassling of tourists, has been reasonably successful. Tourist activity, property development and riad businesses were booming during the first decade of the new millennium, but, with the global economic recession post-2008, this progress has reached a plateau. In April 2011 an explosion rocked the famed Café Argana in the main square of Jemaâ el Fna (see page 270). After a short hiatus where travellers avoided the city, Marrakech has now fully recovered and in 2015, the Café Argana reopened to customers once more. Today, the city continues to maintain its hold on the Western imagination. Despite the creeping gentrification, the Red City retains a sense of rawness, and with budget airlines making travel here a great-value escape from the grey northern European winter, Marrakech looks set to maintain its popularity. The ongoing problem for the city is how to deal with this tourist influx to ensure that the magic of the place is not diluted by the massive numbers of visitors.

Many of the souks of Marrakech retain their original function and a morning's souking is one of the great pleasures of the city. Before leaping into impulse purchases, get an idea of prices in shops in Guéliz, or in the Ensemble Artisanal on Avenue Mohammed V. Once you have threaded your way up Souk Semmarine, onto Souk el Kebir and past Souk Cherratine, you are in the neighbourhood of some of the city's most important heritage monuments and sites, including the magnificent Medersa Ben Youssef, the Musée de Marrakech and the Maison de la Photographie. West of the main souk area, the Leksour and Mouassine neighbourhoods are among the most upmarket and fashionable in the city, with plenty of shops and galleries.

★Souks

The main souks lie to the north of Jemaâ el Fna. The entrance to them is to the left of the mosque. Follow this round to the left and then turn right into the main thoroughfare, **Souk Semmarine**. Alternatively, enter through the small tourist market, further round to the left on Jemaâ el Fna. Souk Semmarine is a busy place, originally the textiles market, and, although there are a number of

> **Tip...**
> To explore the souk area north of the Jemaâ without the crush of the crowds, head out early in the morning. The souks start to get busy after 1100. Note that many souk vendors take Friday off, so this is a great chance to discover usually bustling alleys at their most silent.

large, expensive tourist shops, there are still some cloth sellers. To the left is a *kissaria* (small covered alley) selling clothes. The first turning on the right leads past **Souk Larzal**, a wool market, and **Souk Btana**, a sheepskin market, to **Rahba Kedima**, the old corn market, now the square is rimmed by spice shops touting traditional cures and cosmetics, as well as cooking spices. The main carpet souk **Criée Berbère,** where slaves, mainly from across the Sahara, were auctioned until 1912, has its entranceway off Rahba Kedima. Walk back onto the main souk via a short alley with wood-carved goods. Here the souk forks into **Souk el Attarine** (perfumers' souk) on the left and **Souk el Kebir** on the right.

To the right of Souk el Kebir is the **Souk des Bijoutiers**, with jewellery. To the left (west) of Souk el Kebir is a network of *kissarias*, selling *babouches* and clothing. From here, if you head north along Souk Smata, you'll get to Souk Haddadine where the blacksmiths and coppersmiths ply their trade, and then to the **Souk Cherratine**, with leather goods; somewhere to bargain for camel or cowhide bags, purses and belts. This souk leads on to Place Ben Youssef.

From here, you could take Souk Smata west to Souk Lebbadine, where you can see carpenters at work, then wander into Souk des Teinturiers, or the dyers' market, where wool recently dyed is festooned over the doorways. Just south of here is the Saâdian fountain and the 16th-century **Mouassine Mosque**.

Koubba el Baroudiyine
Pl Ben Youssef. Not open to the public.

This 11th-century shrine is the only complete Almoravid building surviving in the city. It dates from the reign of Ali bin Youssef (1107-1143) and, perhaps, formed part of the toilet and ablutions facilities of the mosque that at the time existed nearby. The *koubba* is walled off and can't be entered but you can get a decent look at its exterior design by peering between the wrought-iron railings that surround it on Place Ben Youssef. At first glance it is a simple building, with a dome surmounting a square stone and brick structure. However, the dome has a design of interlocking arches, plus a star and chevron motif on top. The arches leading into the *koubba* are different on each side.

Standing with the Almoravid Koubba behind you, the minaret of the large 12th-century Ben Youssef Mosque, rebuilt in the 19th century, is clearly visible.

Musée de Marrakech
Pl Ben Youssef, T0524-441893, www.museedemarrakech.ma. Daily 0900-1800. 50dh adult, 30dh child. After the entrance courtyard, there's a good café on the left and a bookshop on the right.

The entrance to the museum is just off Place Ben Youssef, nearly opposite the Almoravid Koubba. It is housed in Dar M'nebhi, the early 20th-century palace of a former Moroccan minister of war. The simple whitewashed walls of the domestic wing shelter temporary exhibitions of contemporary art by local artists while off the main courtyard, protected by a plexi-glass roof and a brass chandelier the size of a small UFO, are displays of Koranic manuscripts, coins, ceramics and textiles. The actual exhibits though, are not the primary reason to visit. The Dar M'nebhi's palatial interior – in particular, its central courtyard's dazzling zellige tilework – are what most visitors are here to see. Note the Portuguese influence in the elaborate wooden façades to the rooms on the left of the courtyard. A small passageway to the left of the main reception room takes you through to the restored hammam, now home to a small collection of early engravings on Morocco.

★Medersa Ben Youssef
Daily 0900-1800. 20dh.

Turning right out of the Museé de Marrakech, follow the street round to the entrance to the city's most important Islamic monument, the 16th-century Medersa Ben Youssef. One of the few Islamic buildings in Morocco open to the general public, it was restored by the Fondation Ben Jelloun and is Marrakech's architectural highlight. Cool, calm corridors, beautiful arches, *zellige* tiles and the light reflecting in the central pool make it a breathtaking place to visit. Founded in 1564-1565 by the Saâdian Sultan Moulay Abdellah, on the site of a previous Merinid *medersa*, it functioned as a boarding school for students of the religious sciences and law. The Medersa is centred around a square courtyard containing a rectangular pool and with arcades on two sides. Each student had a separate cell with a sleeping loft and a window looking onto the courtyard. Note the much worn but still fine cedar wood of the upper façades around the courtyard. You will see fine *zellige* tiling on the arcade floor, walls and pillars. Inscriptions are in Kufic and cursive lettering, interwoven with floral patterns.

At the far end is the prayer hall covered with an eight-sided wooden dome. Beneath the dome-plaster open-work windows illuminate the tilework. In the *qibla* wall is a five-sided mihrab. Note the stalactite ceiling of the mihrab, and the carved stucco walls with pine cone motif. The inscription here, dedicated to the Sultan, translates as: "I was constructed as a place of learning and prayer by the Prince of the Faithful, the descendant of the seal of the prophets, Abdellah, the most glorious of all Caliphs. Pray for him, all who enter here, so that his greatest hopes may be realized." Note also the massive Carrara marble columns.

On the way out of the Medersa, the toilets on the right of the vestibule have an elaborate stalactite design on the ceiling.

Dar Bellarj
9 Toulalat Zaouïat Lahdar, T0524-444555. Daily 0900-1800. Free.

Turning right out of the Medersa, then left under a covered street, you will come to the entrance of Dar Bellarj, 'the House of Storks', on your left. The building, restored recently by a couple of Swiss artists, dates from the 1930s. Prior to this there was a fondouk (caravanserai, or inn) on the site which housed the only hospital for birds in North Africa, run by a wise man with a gift for curing wounded storks. Today, the building, austerely but simply refurbished, is used as gallery space for contemporary arts and has a programme of exhibitions.

Maison de la Photographie
46 Rue Ahal Fès, T0524-385721, www.maisondelaphotographie.com. Daily 0930-1900. 40dh, children free,

This gallery of vintage Moroccan photographs is the work of collectors Hamid Mergani and Patrick Menac'h and provides a fascinating glimpse into Morocco's past. Sepia-tinted photos and glass negatives dating from the 1870s up to the 1950s are displayed over the three floors of this restored riad, showcasing Moroccan traditional lifestyles and culture as well as the raw landscapes of the High Atlas and a look at cities such as Marrakech and Tangier before modern suburban sprawl. On the top floor you can watch an interesting 1956 documentary about the High Atlas filmed by photographer Daniel Chicault, and the roof terrace has a café.

Musée de Mouassine
4-5 Derb el Hammam, Mouassine, T0524-377792, www.museedemouassine.com. Sat-Thu 1000-1800. 30dh,

Tucked away, down an alley behind the Mouassine Mosque, this little gem of a heritage site is a Saâdian-era *douiria* (guest annex) which has been able to retain its original decorative features due to them being covered up for years under layers of white plaster. A painstaking five-year restoration job has revealed an amazingly intact example of a residential Saâdian building (dating to circa 1560). The salon interiors are a sumptuous frenzy of intricate woodwork and plasterwork decoration in a jewel-box of vivid colours, which showcase the craftsmanship of the 16th century. The museum also hosts a program of art exhibitions and occasional music recitals and concerts.

Musée Boucharouite
107 Derb el Cadi, off Rue Azbest, T0524-383887, Mon-Sat 0930-1800. 40dh, children free.

Boucharouites are Berber rag-rugs made using recycled cloth and because of their humble origins have long been sniffed at by the carpet world, but this small restored riad, south of Musée de Marrakech, puts this craft firmly in the spotlight. On display here is Patrick Maillard's boucharouite collection as well as an eclectic array of Moroccan popular art, which showcases the natural artistry of Morocco, beyond the typical palatial views associated with it. The boucharouites, with their colourful, geometric designs, resemble pieces of modern art while vibrantly painted woodwork, interesting household and agricultural objects are scattered throughout the rooms.

Heritage Museum
25 Rue Rahba Kedima, T0524-390280, www.heritagemuseummarrakech.com. Daily 0900-1700. 30dh,

This private museum displays the Alouani Bibi family's eclectic collection of Moroccan art and artefacts ranging from granary doors and Roman amphorae to tribal costumes and Jewish artefacts. It's all been beautifully collated across two floors of this small riad with explanations in French and English provided. Upstairs, the displays of various Berber clothing outfits and tribal weavings is particularly interesting for textile fans. There's a small café on the rooftop too.

North of Medersa Ben Youssef
North of the Medersa Ben Youssef, you can wander through more recent residential neighbourhoods, built on the site of former orchards and market gardens. Whereas Fès has steep and narrow streets, accessible only by pedestrians and mules, flat Marrakech is teeming with bicycles and mopeds, mini-taxis and handcarts. Eventually, your wandering might take you to the open square of Bab Taghzaoute and on to **Zaouïa of Sidi Bel Abbes**. Usually considered the most important of the seven saints of Marrakech, Bel Abbes was born in Ceuta in 1130. He championed the cause of the blind in Marrakech and was patronized by Sultan Yaqoub al Mansour. You are free to wander through the religious complex, though non-Muslims are barred from the mausoleum. It's a striking place, with bright squares and shady alleyways. A series of arches is filled with potted plants and blind people chatting and waiting to receive alms. Nearby is the **Zaouïa of Sidi Ben Slimane el Jazouli**, a 14th-century sufi.

On the northeast side of the medina ramparts, **Bab el Khemis** opens into the Souk el Khemis (Thursday market) and an important area of mechanics and craftsmen. Check out the junk-market here on a Sunday morning. There is a small saint's tomb inside the gate building. Bab Doukkala, on the northwest side by the bus station, is a large gate with two towers. The medina side has a horseshoe arch and a cusped, blind arch, with a variation on the *darj w ktaf* (step and shoulder) motif along the top. There are occasional exhibitions in the guardroom inside the gate. The esplanade here has been badly neglected and many of the orange trees have died off.

Kasbah quarter

grand palace ruins and a mausoleum to die for

The kasbah quarter dates from the late 12th century and the reign of the Almohad Sultan Ya'qub al Mansour. To get to it, follow Avenue Prince Moulay Rachid (also known as Rue Bab Agnaou) south from Jemaâ el Fna, or enter the medina at Bab Rob, near the buses and *grands taxis* on the southwest side. Bab Rob is Almohad and is named after the grape juice which could only be brought through this gate.

Bab Agnaou and the Kasbah Mosque

Bab Agnaou, meaning the 'gate of the black people', marks the entrance to the kasbah quarter. Bab Agnaou itself is an Almohad gateway surrounded by a series of arches within a rectangle of floral designs, with a shell or palmette in each corner and an outer band of Kufic inscription. The road from the gate leads to Rue de la Kasbah; turn right along here and then take the first left. On this road is the much restored **Kasbah Mosque**, dating from 1190. The minaret has Almohad *darj w ktaf* and *shabka* (net) motifs on alternate sides, with a background of green tiles, above which is a band of coloured tiles. Though not as impressive as the tower of the Koutoubia Mosque, the minaret is a notable landmark en route to the Saâdian Tombs. The entrance to these lies directly to the right of the mosque.

Saâdian Tombs

Rue de la Kasbah. Daily 0900-1700. 10dh, children 3dh. Try to visit early in the day as the place gets very crowded with tour groups.

The late 16th-century Saâdian Tombs were discovered thanks to aerial photography in 1917, having been sealed off by Moulay Ismaïl in the 17th century in a vain attempt to condemn the Saâdian rulers to oblivion. A series of chambers around a small garden, decorated with carved cedar and plaster, is the final and, ultimately rather moving, resting place of the Saâdian family. The mihrab of the first main burial chamber is particularly impressive. Here lies the prince Moulay Yazid. The second room contains the tomb of Ahmed al Mansour. The second and older mausoleum was built for the tombs of Ahmed al Mansour's mother, Lalla Messaouda, and Mohammed esh Sheikh, founder of the Saâdians. In the rather dilapidated garden and courtyard are the tombs of numerous other princelings and followers.

El Badi Palace
Daily 0900-1700. 10dh plus another 10dh to see the Koutoubia minbar, children 3dh.

From the Bab Agnaou, head right inside the ramparts, and then take the second right to reach Place des Ferblantiers, a square which is normally home to a number of metalwork workshops and cheap and cheerful restaurants, though at the time of research the square was undergoing redevelopment. If you pass through Bab Berima, the gate on the southern side of the square, the entrance to the El Badi Palace is on the right, between high *pisé* walls. The huge barren spaces of the ruined 16th-century palace come as a bit of a shock after the cramped streets of the Marrakech medina. Orange trees grow in what were once enormous pools in the central courtyard, and storks nest noisily on the ruined walls which protect the vast courtyard from the hubbub of the surrounding streets.

The palace was built by the Saâdian Sultan Ahmed al Mansour ed-Dahbi (the Golden) between 1578 and 1593, following his accession after his victory over the Portuguese at the Battle of the Three Kings, at Ksar el Kebir in northern Morocco. It marks the height of Saâdian power, the centrepiece of an imperial capital. It was a lavish display of the best craftsmanship of the period, using the most expensive materials, including gold, marble and onyx. The colonnades were of marble, apparently exchanged with Italian merchants for their equivalent weight in sugar.

The palace was largely destroyed in the 17th century by Moulay Ismaïl, who stripped it of its decorations and fittings and carried them off to Meknès. No austere royal fortress, the Badi was probably a palace for audiences – and it was at one of these great court ceremonies that the building's fate was predicted: 'What do you think of this palace?' asked the Sultan El Mansour. 'When it is demolished, it will make a big pile of earth,' replied a visionary. El Mansour is said to have felt a sinister omen.

On the palace's southern side, just after the entrance, stairs lead down to a subterranean passageway which showcase some old photos of the palace on the walls. In the southwest corner of the walls you can climb up to the top of the ramparts for great views over the courtyard and the city rooftops beyond. At the southeast corner, steps lead down to a forecourt with preserved tile flooring.

The ruins on either side of the courtyard were probably summer houses, the one at the east end being called the **Koubba el Khamsiniya** (The Fifty Pavillion) after either the 50 cubits of its area, or the fact that it once had 50 columns. Other scattered ruins, with odd fragments of decoration amidst the debris, include stables and dungeons.

> ### Fact...
> To the south of the El Badi Palace is the Dar el Makhzen, the Royal Palace of the late King Hassan II. The present king has had a new palace constructed, close to the Mamounia.

ON THE ROAD

Tanning secrets

The tanneries are one of the most interesting (if smelly) sites in Marrakech. The tanners are said to have been the first to settle in Marrakech, close to the seasonal Oued Issil on the edge of the city, with access to plenty of water and space to expand away from residential areas. The tanneries were accessed via Bab Debbagh ('Tanners' Gate'), the only gate to be named after a craft corporation. 'Bab Debbagh, bab deheb' (Tanners' Gate, gold gate), the old adage goes, in reference to the tanners' prosperity. Located on the east side of the ramparts, this is an intricate defensive gate with a twisted entrance route and wooden gates, which could shut off the various parts of the building for security. One legend runs that seven virgins are buried in the foundations of the gate (sisters of the seven protector saints of Marrakech) and that women who desire a child should offer them candles and henna. Another legend says that Bab Debbagh is inhabited by Malik Gharub, a genie who dared to lead a revolt against Sidna Suleyman, the Black King, only to be condemned to tan a cowhide and cut out *belgha* soles for eternity as punishment.

The tannery was considered both a dangerous place – as it was the entrance to the domain of the Other Ones – and a beneficial one, since skins were a symbol of preservation and fertility. Because the tanners spent their days in pits working the skins, they were said to be in contact with the unseen world of the dead and to be masters of fertility, being strong men, capable of giving a second life to dry, dead skin. The process of tanning skins is strongly symbolic – the tanners say that the skin eats, drinks, sleeps and 'is born of the water'. When the skin is treated with lime, it is said to be thirsty; when it is treated with pigeon dung, it is said to receive *nafs*, a spirit. The *merkel* (treading) stage prepares the skin to live again, while the *takkut* of the tanning mixture is also used by women to dye their hair. At this point, the skin receives *ruh* (breath). Leather is thus born from the world of the dead and the *ighariyin*, the people of the grotto, and is fertilized in the swampy pool, the domain of the dead – who are also said to have the power to bring rain.

Marrakech Museum for Photography and Visual Arts (MMPVA) ⓘ *www. mmpva.org, Wed-Mon 0900-1645, free*. On the palace's north side is the Khaysuran Pavilion which is now the temporary home of the MMPVA, which utilizes it as a gallery space for Moroccan and North African artists. The MMPVA is scheduled to move into a purpose-built museum near the Menara Gardens (which will form the largest museum space dedicated to photography and visual arts in the world), but various project setbacks mean that it is likely to remain at the El Badi Palace site for the near future.

Tanning in Marrakech is still a pre-industrial process, alive and functioning not far from the heart of the medina – even though the traditional dyes have largely been replaced with chemical products. Wandering towards the tanners' area, you are likely to be approached by some lad who will offer to show you around (20dh is a reasonable tip). You will be given a sprig of mint to hold to your nostrils and, through a small metal door, you will be shown an area of foul-smelling pits, where men tread and rinse skins in nauseous liquids and dyes, while other artisans scrape and stretch the skins in small, lean-to buildings. You will probably be told that there are two tanneries: one Arab, the other Berber. In fact there are several, and workforces are ethnically mixed. Specialists remain, however, with one set of tanners working mainly on the more difficult cow and camel skins, and the other on goat and sheep skins.

The complex process of tanning starts with soaking the skins in an *iferd* in the middle of the tannery, filled with a fermenting mixture of pigeon guano and tannery waste. Fermenting traditionally lasted three days in summer, six in winter. Then the skins are squeezed out and put to dry. Hair is scraped off, then the skins are put into a pit of lime and argan-kernel ash. This removes any remaining flesh or hair, and prepares the skin to receive the tanning products. The lime bath lasts 15-20 days in summer, up to 30 in winter. Then the skins are washed energetically, trodden to remove any lime, and any extra bits are cut off. Next the skins spend 24 hours in a *qasriya*, a round pit of more pigeon dung and fresh water. At this stage the skin becomes thinner and stretches. There follows soaking in wheat fibre and salt for 24 hours to remove any traces of lime and guano.

Then begins the actual tanning process. (The word *debbagh* actually means tannin.) Traditional tanneries used only plants – roots, barks and certain seeds and fruits. In Marrakech, acacia and oak bark are used, along with takkut, the ground-up fruit of the tamarisk. A water and tannin mix is prepared in a pit, and the skins get three soakings. After this, the skins are prepared to receive the dye. They are scraped with pottery shards, beaten and coated with oil, alum and water. Then they are dyed by hand and left to dry in the sun (traditionally on the banks of the nearby Oued Issil). Finally, the skins are worked to make them smoother and more supple, stretched between two ropes and worked on smooth pottery surfaces.

To the west of the pavilion is a small **museum** exhibiting the restored *minbar* from the Koutoubia Mosque. Mark Minor, one of the conservators from the Metropolitan Museum of Art in New York who carried out the restoration, called it "one of the finest works of art in wood created by mankind." Constructed in Córdoba in Spain in 1139, it is covered in around 100 carvings. The *minbar* remained in use until 1962.

Two museums devoted to Moroccan artistry sit close together at the south end of Riad Zitoun el Jedid. From Jemaâ el Fna, follow Rue des Banques from just past Café de France. At the first junction, continue through to the right onto Riad Zitoun el Jedid and head straight down this road until you come to a car park on your left. The signposted alleyway on the right leads first to Maison Tiskiwin and then to the Dar Si Said. Afterwards, make your way back to Riad Zitoun el Jedid and keep heading south until you hit Bahia Palace.

Maison Tiskiwin

8 Rue de la Bahia, T0524-389192, www.tiskiwin.com. Daily 0930-1230 and 1430-1800. 20dh, children 10dh.

The fantastic Maison Tiskiwin ('the House of the Horns') is home to a fine collection of items related to Northern African and Saharan culture and society. This small museum was lovingly put together by the Dutch art historian Bert Flint, who still lives here, though he has given the museum to Marrakech University. Flint still spends some of the year travelling and collecting to add to the collection, and there is a strong sense of enthusiasm for the artefacts here (in contrast to some of the state-run museums). There are crafts from the Rif and the High Atlas, though the collection focuses primarily on the Sahara, and includes jewellery and costumes, musical instruments, carpets and furniture. The building itself, around a courtyard, is an authentic and well-maintained example of a traditional riad. There are excellent and copious notes in English. Groups tend to visit in the morning – if you go along in the afternoon you may get the museum all to yourself.

Dar Si Said

Derb el Bahia, Riad Zitoun el Jedid, T0524-389564. Wed-Mon 0900-1630. 10dh, children 3dh.

Built by Si Said, Visir under Moulay el Hassan and half-brother of Ba Ahmed Ben Moussa, the Dar Si Said is a late 19th-century palace housing the **Museum of Moroccan Arts and Crafts**. The collection includes pottery, jewellery, leatherwork, carved wooden doors and Chichaoua carpets and is particularly strong on Amazigh artefacts. On the first floor is a salon with Hispano-Moorish decoration and a colourful, carved cedarwood ceiling that alone is worth the visit. The tranquil garden courtyard boasts some gloriously preserved tilework.

Bahia Palace

Corner Rue Riad Zitoun el Jedid and Rue Bab Mellah. Daily 0900-1630. 10dh, children 3dh.

At the southern end of Rue Riad Zitoun el Jedid is the Bahia Palace (Bahia means 'brilliant', and it is). It was built in the last years of the 19th century by the Vizir Ba Ahmed Ben Moussa, or Bou Ahmed, a former slave who exercised power under sultans Moulay Hassan and Abd el Aziz. Sunlight shines through wrought-iron bars creating beautiful patterns on the *zellige* tiles and, in the courtyard, water ripples over green tiles around a beautiful fountain, surrounded by trees. There are nearly always tour groups wandering through, but there are also plenty of quiet corners in which lingering until they've passed is a pleasure. The palace is a maze of patios planted with fruit trees, passageways and empty chambers with painted ceilings. Guides will tell you that each wife and concubine had a room looking onto the patio. The story goes that Bou Ahmed was so hated that, on his death in 1900, his palace was looted and his possessions stolen by slaves, servants and members of his harem. Subsequently, the building was occupied by the French authorities. Bareness is still a feature of the palace, but it is one that accentuates the beauty of the architecture.

Mellah (Jewish quarter)

South of Bahia Palace and east of the El Badi Palace, the *mellah* (Jewish neighbourhood) was created in 1558. The Jewish community has all but vanished, and the claustrophobically narrow alleyways here only hold a few remnants of this district's former role in the life of Marrakech. Wind your way to **Lazama Synagogue** ⓘ *Rue Talmud Torah, Sun-Thu 0900-1700, 10dh*, one of the few synagogues still functioning today. The synagogue can be tricky to find as it's not signposted but most locals are happy to point out the way for you. From Bahia Palace, head east down Rue Bab Mellah and take the second alley entry on your right (the first entry after passing through Rue Bab Mellah's archway). The synagogue is in the second block of this alley, entered through a nondescript doorway. Hemming the eastern side of the *mellah* is the *miaâra* (the Jewish cemetery). Now somewhat scruffy and overgrown, this huge walled cemetery filled with white tombs demonstrates how large Marrakech's Jewish community once was. The cemetery caretaker will expect a tip when you leave.

Gardens

green lungs of the city

Central Marrakech is framed by gardens. Close to the medina, those between Koutoubia and Mamounia have been totally replanted with roses, and even once scruffy Arset Moulay Slimane, opposite the Municipality on your way to Jemaâ el Fna, has been spruced up.

Jardin Majorelle and the Musée Berbère

Av Yacoub el Mansour, T0524-313047, www.jardinmajorelle.com. May-Sep daily 0800-1800, Oct-Apr daily 0800-1730. 70dh, plus 30dh for the museum.

The Jardin Majorelle, also called the Bou Saf-Saf Garden, is off Avenue Yacoub el Mansour in Guéliz and is well worth the walk from Bab Doukkala. This is a small tropical garden laid out in the inter-war period by a French artist, Jacques Majorelle, son of a family of cabinet-makers from Nancy who made their money with innovative art nouveau furniture. Majorelle portrayed the landscapes and people of the Atlas in large, strongly coloured paintings, some of which were used for early tourism posters. The carefully restored garden belonged to Yves St Laurent until his death in 2008 and his ashes were scattered here. Strong colours and forms are much in evidence: the buildings are vivid cobalt blue, the cactuses sculptural. Bulbuls sing in the bamboo thickets and flit between the Washingtonia palms. Even if gardens aren't your thing, a trip here is thoroughly worthwhile to visit the Musée Berbère. Inside the garden, the bright blue pavilion, once used as Majorelle's studio, now houses this excellent museum devoted to highlighting the artistry of Morocco's Imazighen culture. By far the most beautiful museum in Morocco, it contains a carefully curated collection from household objects and religious artefacts to a stunning display of traditional costumes worn by different tribal communities. The jewellery room, with the walls dramatically draped in black with star-like spotlights so that the cases containing the huge array of decorative pieces really stand out, is a particular highlight. There are also plenty of information boards (in French, English, German and Spanish) to help you understand the context of the displays.

Agdal Gardens
Open only when the King is not in residence: Fri-Sun 0900-1800.

The Agdal Gardens, stretching south of the medina, were established in the 12th century under Abd el Moumen, and were expanded and reorganized by the Saâdians. The vast expanse, over 400 ha, includes several pools, and extensive areas of olive, orange and pomegranate trees. Of the pavilions, the Dar al Baida was used by Sultan Moulay Hassan to house his harem. The largest pool, Sahraj el Hana, receives coachloads of tourists, but at other times is a pleasant place to relax, although not to swim.

Menara Gardens
From the medina and the Agdal Gardens, Avenue de la Menara leads to the Menara Gardens, essentially an olive grove centring on a rectangular pool. A short moped hop from central Marrakech, the area is much appreciated by locals for picnics. The presence of such a large expanse of water generates a pleasant microclimate. The green-tiled pavilion alongside the pool was built in 1866; with the Atlas Mountains as a backdrop, it features heavily on postcards.

Palmeraie
Marrakech is surrounded by extensive palm groves. In the original Prost development plan of the 1920s, no building was to be higher than a palm tree. It is also illegal to cut down a palm tree – hence palms have been left growing in the middle of pavements. In recent years the Palmeraie has suffered as the urbanized area round Marrakech has expanded, and certain areas have been divided up for upmarket holiday development. Nevertheless, it is a good place for a drive or a *calèche* tour. Take the Route de la Palmeraie, off the N8 to Fès, to explore it.

Tourist information

Office du Tourisme
*Pl Abd el Moumen Ben Ali, Gueliz
(on Av Mohammed V opposite
Café Les Négociants), T0524-436131.
Mon-Fri 0830-1830.*
Has a range of leaflets but not much
actual information.

Where to stay

It is a good idea to reserve rooms in
advance during the peak visiting times
of European holidays (particularly
Christmas and Easter) when demand
for accommodation can outstrip supply.
Riads aside, the larger upmarket hotels
are located in 3 areas: in the Hivernage
garden city area and along the
neighbouring Av Mohammed VI; in a
development on the Casablanca road
in the Semlalia neighbourhood; and in
the Palmeraie east of the city. Hivernage
is close to Guéliz, and a short taxi ride
into Jemaâ el Fna in the old town. Riads
in the medina fall into both the luxury
and mid-range price brackets. There's
also a cluster of budget options in the
alleys off Rue Bab Agnaou (Av Prince
Moulay Rachid), Riad Zitoun el Kedim
and the Kennaria neighbourhood
behind the Café de France; all are within
a 5- to 10-min walk from Jemaâ el Fna
(see also box, page 63).

Medina

€€€€ Maison MK
*14 Derb Sebaai, Quartier Ksar, T0524-
376173, www.maisonmk.com.*
A fairyland for adults, Maison MK is
the medina's hipster address with its
6 warm, spice-toned rooms resplendent
with quirky, clever lighting and plush
contemporary linens that bring a
funky-edge to riad design. All come with
bags of extras, including in-room iPods,
mobile phones for guest use, an honour
bar and hot water bottles to snuggle
during colder months. The cinema room
has a 2.5-m screen as well as an Xbox,
and the riad's hammam offers plenty of
spa-style pampering treats. Maison MK
is also known for its restaurant, Gastro
MK, with a 5-course tasting menu that's
something of a foodie favourite in
Marrakech. Breakfast, Wi-Fi and airport
transfers included.

€€€€ Riad El Fenn
*Derb Moullay Abdullah Ben Hezzian, Bab
el Ksar, T0524-441210, www.el-fenn.com.*
The epitome of laid-back glamour,
El Fenn is strikingly sumptuous yet
completely unstuffy. Owned by Vanessa
Branson (sister of Richard), this 28-room
mansion whips riad-living into the
21st century without ever losing sight of
the building's rich history. Jewel-toned
rooms, graced with large contemporary
artworks and colourful seating areas,
lead on to curvy *tadelakt* bathrooms with
generous-sized tubs for soaking away a
hard day's haggling in the souks. Many
have open fires for the colder months,
and all effortlessly merge traditional
Marrakchi artisan features and modern
style. There's a fine restaurant and bar,
a hammam offering spa-style treats,
3 swimming pools, a family of tortoises
that freely roam around the palm-draped
courtyard and, of course, oodles of
cosy cushioned seating nooks for when
chill-out time comes a-calling. Wi-Fi and
breakfast included.

€€€€ Riad Zolah
114-116 Derb el Hammam, Mouassine,
T0524-387535, www.riadzolah.com.
Step inside and receive a masterclass
in traditional Moroccan artistry. The
painstaking restoration of these
2 adjoining 17th-century houses has
allowed many original features to be left
in place, while the newer additions sit in
perfect harmony with the old. Intricate
zouak doors, mashrabiyya windows,
antique carpets and kilims and original
tadelakt plasterwork all summon up a
true sense of this building's history while
the courtyard plunge pool, in-room
iPod docks and chic rooftop terrace
bring you pleasantly back into the 21st
century. With only 6 rooms and oodles
of space, the Zolah is intimate yet not
claustrophobic as some smaller riads
can be. Take in the 360° views across the
tumble of medina's rooftops from the
terrace; pamper yourself in the riad's own
hammam, or chill out with your better
half in one of the many cosy alcoves
downstairs; once you've slapped on your
pair of complementary *babouches*, Zolah
is the kind of place that is hard to leave. If
you do manage to drag yourself out the
door, mobile phones are lent to guests in
case you get lost. Airport transfers, Wi-Fi
and breakfast included.

€€€-€€ Tchaikana
25 Derb el Ferrane, off Rue Azbest,
T0524-385150, www.tchaikana.com.
Leave the medina madness behind as
soon as the door closes, to cross the
threshold into this chicly minimalist
haven that is a tribute to African art. The
central courtyard is decked out in plenty
of soothing white and comes complete
with orange trees and chirping birds.
The 3 room and 2 suites (from €90 in
high season) are generously sized with

gorgeous taupe linens on the beds and
beautiful African objets d'art, artefacts
and masks scattered throughout. Bag the
Nomad suite if you can for the 4-poster
bed made using stunning Tuareg tent-
posts. The rooftop, with plenty of pot
plants, vines and shady seating, has good
views out to the mighty Atlas Mountains.
Tchaikana also gets top marks for
service, with friendly manager Khadijah
providing an orientation walk for guests
at the start of their stay and always ready
to help with queries. Breakfast and Wi-Fi
included. Recommended.

€€ Riad Tizwa
26 Derb Gueraba, Dar el Bacha, T0668-
190872 (Morocco) or T+44 (0)7973-115471
(UK), www.riadtizwa.com.
There's plenty of bright and breezy
casual style at the Bee brothers'
Marrakech riad, squiggled down an
alleyway, just off bustling Dar el Bacha.
The 6 rooms (doubles start from €80 in
high season) come in different shapes
and sizes, some with enormous 4-poster
beds and colourful kilims. All have a
fresh, modern feel. The big taupe-
coloured *tadelakt* bathrooms have
innumerable thick towels, plenty of local
Moroccan pampering products and soft
hooded dressing gowns you may never
want to take off. Rooms open onto a
central courtyard with a small fountain
and are shaded from the sun by blousy
white curtains which wrap around
the upper corridor. Climb the staircase
(clinging on to its original tiles) to the
rooftop for breakfast in the sunshine
or to flop out on one of the sunbeds.
Breakfast and Wi-Fi included.

€€ Riad Viva
107 Derb Mbarek, Sidi Mimoun,
T0524-382006, www.charming-
riads-in-marrakech.com.

★The riad experience

The riad (*maison d'hôte* or guesthouse) gives you the experience of staying in a small but fine private medina house that has often been painstakingly restored by an expat or local owner. There are hundreds in Marrakech, probably around 1000, and rates (usually quoted in euros) vary enormously; some riads are extremely luxurious while others are geared to the budget-conscious traveller. In general, prices tend to be high for Morocco, but you're paying for service and style in bucketloads. Riads are managed either directly by their owners or via an agency which deals with everything from reservations to maintenance. The riads have created a lot of work for locals (and pushed property prices up), so many Marrakchis feel they have a stake in the guesthouse system. (With regard to tipping, err on the generous side.)

Guests are usually met either at the airport, or on the edge of the medina to be escorted to their accommodation, since an individual riad can be impossible for first-timers to find in the maze-like streets. All riads should provide breakfast, included as part of the price, and most will also cook an evening meal on request, though advance warning is usually required. Cooler, darker ground floor rooms are preferable in summer; lighter, warmer first floor rooms in winter. When booking a stay in winter, check for details of heating. Most riads are available to rent in their entirety, making a great base for a group or family holiday. Staff are usually included, and meals and entertainment (acrobats, musicians, dancers) can often be arranged. What riads consider to be high season varies but always includes Christmas and Easter holidays. Rates often fall substantially outside these times.

Riad rental agencies

It may pay to shop around and see what is offered by riad rental agencies – they usually add a commission to the price, but they can also have special offers available.

Hôtels & Ryads, UK T+44 (0)207 570 0336, www.riads.co.uk. Have 64 riads in Marrakech and one of the easiest-to-use websites, a good place to get an idea of what's available. **Marrakech Riads**, 8 Derb Charfa Lekbir, Mouassine, T0524-391609, www.marrakech-riads.net. Friendly and highly recommended agency with 8 excellent riads, including the simple **Dar Sara** and the beautiful **Al Jazira**. The headquarters, the beautiful **Dar Cherifa**, a 17th-century house converted with gallery space on the ground floor, is worth a visit in its own right (see page 70). **Villas of Morocco**, Immeuble Berdai, 1st floor, Guéliz, T0522-942525, www.villasofmorocco.com. For the ultimate in luxury beyond the confines of the medina, this agency has a portfolio of magnificent private villas in the Palmeraie and elsewhere. All are fully staffed to cater for weddings, events and deluxe holidays. On average from around €3600 per night for exclusivity.

One step removed from the central medina's hustle, Riad Viva sits in the peaceful, high-walled back alleys of the Sidi Mamoun district. The 7 rooms (€75-110; great discounts in low season), wrapped around a palm frond-shaded courtyard, use lashings of white against splashes of bold colour for an elegant yet casual feel. The riad's major drawcard is the rooftop terrace with its plunge pool, sunbeds lined up for duty and comfy shaded seating with the added perk of a view over the gardens of the 5-star Mamounia Hotel (so you can sneak a peek at the rich and famous guests).

€€-€ Hotel du Tresor
77 Derb Sidi Boulokat, off Rue Riad Zitoun el Kedim, T0524-375113, www.hotel-du-tresor.com.
For bags of eclectic style, look no further. This riad's rooms (doubles €40-90/ singles €37-40) may be small but they're crammed with character. Crystal chandeliers, antique mirrors, 4-poster beds draped in rainbow colours and 19th-century armchairs sit alongside original painted wood ceilings and doors, creating a cleverly mismatched style that adds to the cheerful, quirky whimsy of the place. The petite central courtyard is home to a huge orange tree, strung with lanterns, and a slim plunge pool for cooling off on a hot medina day. Service is personable and friendly, and the location, down a twist of alleys a short stroll from the Jemaâ, can't be beaten.

€ Equity Point Hostel
80 Derb el Hammam, Mouassine, T0524-440793, www.equity-point.com.
Riad styling on a pauper's budget. Yes, for the princely sum of €13 you too can sample life within one of Marrakech's grand old mansions. The Equity hostel group have spared no effort in turning

these 2 adjoining houses into one of the most stylish hostels around, replete with lashings of Marrakchi flavour. Big comfy lounging areas strewn with cushions are the perfect place to swap travel tales with new friends, while the surprisingly large pool is a welcome treat after a long day trudging the souks. Dorms come in 4-bed (€18), 6-bed (€16) and 8-bed (€13) options – cheaper in low season – all with en suite bathrooms, a/c and lockers. There's a computer room, a restaurant and a bar. The 4-bed dorms can also be sold as private twin rooms if you really don't want to share with others. Wi-Fi and breakfast included.

€ Hotel Essaouira
3 Derb Sidi Bouloukat, off Rue Riad Zitoun el Kedim, T0524-443805.
The medina has plenty of cheap-as-chips digs, but the Essaouira is one of the best of the bunch for no-frills accommodation. The small rooms (single/ double 70/100dh), sporting some scuffed but pretty floor tiles and coloured glass details, don't come with much more than a bed and washbasin but are kept tidy, while rooms with shared bathroom are small but also spick-and-span. Management are friendly, and the central location is a definite plus-point.

€ Le Gallia Hotel
30 Rue de la Recette, T0524-445913, www.hotellegallia.com.
It's no surprise that Le Gallia has a lot of repeat guests; this 1930s building, festooned with corridors of vibrantly coloured tiles, offers plenty of home-from-home appeal which ensures plenty of repeat custom. Snug rooms (single/double 300/450dh) are kept in apple pie order and come with recently renovated bathrooms with plenty of hot water, a/c and heating. Most have

windows that look out onto the central courtyard, complete with palm trees, vines, blooming flowers, caged birds and 2 friendly resident cats. Only a hop-skip-jump from the Jemaâ, yet a soothingly quiet place to stay, Le Gallia is one of Marrakech's budget traveller gems. Room are often cheaper than the rack rates; breakfast is an extra 45dh. Wi-Fi. Recommended.

€ Riad Jnane Mogador
116 Riad Zitoun el Kedim, T0524-426324, www.jnanemogador.com.
So popular that management advises booking 6 months in advance, this place was one of Marrakech's original lower-end riads, filling a gap in the market between the bare-bones budget hotels and the luxury boutique riads. It's a blueprint that many have copied, but still nobody else does it quite this well. The 18 rooms (single/double/triple 360/480/580dh; good discounts in low season) aren't large, but they're kitted out with plenty of traditional character and have blue *tadelakt* bathrooms, a/c and TV. There's a pretty courtyard with a petal-filled fountain, roof terrace with spectacular views to the Koutoubia and a hammam offering massages. Wi-Fi included. Breakfast is 40dh.

Ville nouvelle

€€€€ Dar Rhizlane
Av Jnane el Harti, Hivernage, T0524-421303, www.dar-rhizlane.com.
One of the grandest addresses in the *ville nouvelle*, Dar Rhizlane's 19 rooms and suites are decorated with swags of European old-world elegance, including richly hued kilims on the floor, regally-sized beds and black-and-white etching of old Marrakech on the walls. The setting, on an olive tree-lined boulevard

in Hivernage, allows a sense a space that is lacking at medina properties and some rooms even come with their own private garden. There's an air of tranquillity here that is normally reserved for the luxury pads in the Palmeraie but Dar Rhizlane has the bonus of being within walking distance of the city centre. There's a rose garden a pool, spa, and a restaurant open to non-guests. Wi-Fi, breakfast and afternoon tea included.

€€€-€€ Bab Hotel
Crnr Rue Mohammed el-Beqal and Blvd Mansour Eddahbi, Guéliz, T0524-435250, www.babhotelmarrakech.ma.
A sleek boutique hotel in the heart of Guéliz. Rooms (from €76) follow the crisp white-on-white minimalist trend with black-and-white photos on the walls and pops of colour provided by cushions. Many come with terraces, while all have TV and minibar. The roof terrace is home to the **Sky Bab Bar** (see page 74), which attracts Marrakech's arty-types in the evening and there's a bright, modern restaurant fitted out with plenty of retro style, and a pool. Wi-Fi and breakfast included.

€€ Diwane
24 Rue Yougoslavie (just off Av Mohammed V), Guéliz, T0524-432216, www.diwane-hotel.ma.
If you're looking for a hotel with all the trimmings, Diwane is one of the most human of the city's super-hotels. It has a great pool with grassy surrounds, café, restaurant, gym, hammam and a boutique which actually sells some useful maps and books. The 115 rooms offer generous desks, balconies, fridges and bathrooms that have a touch of local style with tiles and *tadelakt* details. A good choice for disabled travellers as it offers adapted rooms. Wi-Fi and breakfast included.

€ Hotel Toulousain
44 Rue Tarik Ibn Ziad, Guéliz, T0524-430033, www.hoteltoulousain.ma.
This long-running backpacker favourite is a friendly, laid-back kind of place with a handy central location. Rooms are simple and come in a variety of prices from basic options with shared bathroom (single/double 150/220dh), and vintage rooms with small en suites and a flurry of wall tiles (single/double 250/300dh), to modern renovated rooms which lack the cute character of the vintage rooms but gain a TV (single/double 300/400dh). Mobile fans and heaters can be provided if needed. During mid-summer it's best to steer clear of the ground floor rooms as they can get too hot. The large central courtyard is full of greenery and is a good place to kick back at the end of the day. Wi-Fi and breakfast included.

€ Moroccan House Hotel
3 Rue Loubnane, T0524-420305, www.moroccanhousehotels.ma.
The 50 rooms in this modern hotel are decorated in a rather over-the-top recreation of riad style, but, if you can put up with the frilly decor, they provide excellent value for money. Rooms (doubles from 425dh) come with 4-poster beds and exuberant use of pastel pinks, blues and purples – sort of like entering a sparkly dolls' house for grownups – while all have TV, a/c and minibar as standard. There's a good pool (not heated) and a big roof terrace for breakfast, plus a traditional hammam in the basement. Family suites are well-priced, and there are also have facilities for guests with mobility issues. Wi-Fi included.

Outskirts of the city
In the Palmeraie, to the north of the centre, the old palm groves are increasingly being taken over by large, smart hotels and villa-style boutique hotels. These can feel a bit far from the action, though there is usually the advantage of large pools and luscious gardens. Many provide transport into the city centre.

€€€€ Jnane Tamsna
Rte Douar Abiad, Palmeraie, T0524-328484, www.jnanetamsna.com.
Spread over 5 villas within a 9-acre property scattered with fruit trees, date palms, herb and flower beds, a tennis court and 5 pools, Jnane Tamsna is an exclusive retreat from the worries of the world. There are just 24 rooms in this intimate resort, all decorated with owner, Meryanne Loum-Martin's, keen eye for mixing traditional Moroccan artistry with cool contemporary lines. The roll-call of celebrity visitors bears testimony to the highly personalized service here. Cooking courses are one of the resort's specialities, and the restaurant sources much of its produce from the property's organic gardens, expertly created by Meryanne's ethnobotanist husband, Gary Martin, who also set up the Global Diversity Foundation. Breakfast, all soft drinks and Wi-Fi included.

€€€€-€€€ Dar Ayniwen
Off Rte Dour Abiad, Tafrata, Palmeraie, T0524-329684, www.dar-ayniwen.com.
Luxury of the ornate, antique sort is on offer at this palm grove guesthouse, converted from the owner's family home. Very different to the minimalist-chic style favoured by many Palmeraie places, Dar Ayniwen's merging of Victorian and Edwardian furniture, Oriental artwork, and art nouveau creates an elegant but wonderfully lived-in atmosphere that makes it stand out amid some of it's more over-the-top modern neighbours. A great choice if you still want easily to

explore Marrakech: Dar Ayniwen provides a complementary shuttle service into the central city hourly. For those simply interested in a tranquil getaway, there's really no reason to leave the grounds, with a pool, sprawling gardens with fruit trees, cacti and English lawn, complimentary cooking classes offered, and an on-site spa. Dar Ayniwen's restaurant is also highly regarded among Marrakchi foodie circles and is open to non-guests (reservations essential, tasting menu 500dh, including return transfer from central Marrakesh). Minimum stay 2 nights. Breakfast, airport transfers and Wi-Fi included. Recommended.

€€€€-€€€ Fellah Hotel
KM 13, Route de L'Ourika, Tassoultante, T0525-065000, www.fellah-hotel.com.
This is luxury done with oodles of eclectic-cool plus a big spoonful of sustainable vision. Just to Marrakech's south, the village of Tassoultante is home to this unique boutique hotel where the rooms are kitted out in a medley of vintage finds, contemporary Moroccan designer furniture and local textiles, and guests are encouraged to dig a bit deeper into their surroundings. Of course there's a hammam, spa, pool and restaurant (serving slap-up organic fare pulled fresh out of the garden) but the Fellah has much more to it than boutique credentials. It's also one of the main sponsors of the Dar al-Ma'mun Foundation; a UNESCO-recognized cultural centre that is on the hotel grounds. The centre's activities include educational programs for Tassoultante village, supporting Moroccan artists and writers, and promoting cultural awareness, and the centre regularly hosts events ranging from literature readings to art exhibitions. Recommended.

Restaurants

Upmarket Moroccan restaurants in restored riads with garden courtyards are part of the Marrakech experience. Generally, they can be tricky to find but if you reserve your table in advance, many offer a service where a staff member will guide you to the restaurant door. Cheap eats are plentiful and are found throughout the medina. For contemporary eating, the *ville nouvelle* has plenty of good options and, whatever your budget, you shouldn't miss the experience of dining with the locals in Jemaâ el Fna.

Medina

€€€ Dar Zellij
1 Derb Kaa Essour, off Rue Bab Tagzaoute, Sidi Ben Slimane, T0524-382627, www.darzellij.com. Wed-Mon from 1900, also Fri-Sun 1200-1600.
This 17th-century riad offers one of the most spectacular settings in the city in which to enjoy an evening meal. It's not easy to find but is well worth the effort. Waiters seem to float around the tree-filled courtyard in long white gowns, and the live music is subtle rather than intrusive. Tables come sprinkled with petals, there's an open fire, dark red walls, candles, enormous high ceilings, curtains and calligraphic art. The menu is traditional Moroccan with a choice of set menus for dinner (300-550dh) which offer a range of typical tajine and couscous options that allow you to sample Moroccan favourites cooked with care and full-bodied flavour. For slap-up dining, you really can't beat the extravagance of the setting here or the service. Lunch menus are cheaper.

€€€ Le Tobsil
22 Derb Abdallah Ben Houssein, Bab Ksour,
T0524-444052. Wed-Mon 1500-0100.
One of the longest established
addresses for fine dining in the medina.
Elegant Moroccan cuisine is cooked and
served with more subtlety than usual in
this ochre-walled little riad. The 5-course
banquet menu is fixed price and, though
it's expensive at 625dh, it does include
wine and aperitif plus there is live Gnawa
music during the evening. Put on your
glad-rags as this isn't the place for casual
dress. Reservations are essential, as there
are not many tables, and it can get a
little cramped.

€€ Le Jardin
32 Souk Sidi Abdelaziz, T0524-378295,
www.lejardin.ma. Daily 1000-2300.
This large courtyard restaurant, with
tables surrounded by trees for shady
dining, is enclosed in a 17th-century
mansion. It's a lovely place to sit and enjoy
a mint tea, one step removed from the
frenetic energy of the medina's alleys. The
menu offers something for everyone, from
traditional Moroccan dishes of couscous
and tagines (100-120dh) to spinach ravioli
and steaks. There are decent options
available for vegetarians here and also
a children's menu. In summer there are
outdoor screenings of arthouse movies in
the garden, while in winter you can enjoy
a meal in front of the crackling fire.

€€ Nomad
1 Derb Aarjan, T0524-381609, www.
nomadmarrakech.com. Daily 1100-2300.
The hippest place to eat in the central
medina area, Nomad's sleek rooftop
terrace is always packed with diners
lapping up the sunshine while they
munch on North African dishes that
have been given a modern makeover.
For starters opt for their contemporary

version of a Tunisian briq (pastry parcel)
packed with spiced lamb and green
harissa paste, and fill up on Agadir
calamari or a tagine with a fusion-twist
for your main. Alcohol is served.

€€ Souk Café
11 Derb Souk Jdid, T0662-610229.
Daily 1100-2300.
It is well worth stopping by to sample the
authentic Marrakchi cuisine served up
inside this stylishly converted house with
its cinnamon-coloured *tadelakt* walls and
colourful textiles. The rooftop terrace is
a pleasant place to dally away an hour or
two over a smoothie, while this is also a
good place to tuck into the Marrakech
speciality tangia, along with all the usual
tagines. Vegetarians will find enough
options on the menu here too.

€ Beats Burger
35 Souk Jeld Zimakine, www.
beatsburger.com. Daily 1100-2100.
A completely unexpected find while
you're searching the souks, Beats
Burger is all about gourmet burgers,
bagels and salads (55-115dh). There are
cheeseburger sliders, a vegan bagel and
great fillings such as hash browns and
harissa mayonnaise. Eat either inside, in
the small dining room decorated with
LPs and an ornate *tadelakt* ceiling, or
upstairs on the dinky roof terrace. Thirst-
quenching smoothies are on offer and
there's an excellent music soundtrack.

€ Café Clock
224 Derb Chtouka, Kasbah, T0524-378367,
www.caféclock.com. Daily 0900-2300.
Sister to the original Café Clock in Fes
(see page 157), Clock Marrakech offers
up a menu of salads, snacks (including
some great vegetarian options such
as chargrilled vegetable and cheese
toasted sandwiches), and larger meals

ON THE ROAD
Café culture

Around Jemaâ el Fna there are lots of cafés which exist primarily because of their terraces overlooking the square. None are licensed, and none would be great cafés in other locations, but they are all rightfully popular, especially late in the afternoon, for the opportunity they offer to survey the frenzy below from the relative calm of a terrace. As a response to the hordes of tourists coming up to these cafés just to take photos, many will only let you onto their terraces after you've bought a drink.

Café Argana is the most famous of the Jemaâ cafés. Having being targeted in 2011s suicide bombing and closed for several years, the café has been fully rebuilt and reopened with its large terraces a prime spot to overlook the square below.
Café de France has several levels and an excellent panorama over the square and the medina beyond.

Café Glacier Le Grand Balcon, on the southeast edge of the square, has perhaps the best views of sunset through the rising smoke from the food stalls below.
Les Terrasses de l'Alhambra, just opposite the Café de la France, is a strategic meeting place near the entrance to the souks and just beyond the mayhem of the foodstalls with good views from the top terrace.

such as Clock's famed camel burger, that merge Moroccan culinary traditions with modern café-style cooking. This place is much more than just another dining option, though, with a regular programme of evening concerts and events that showcase local musicians and Marrakchi culture. If you're in town on a Thu, don't miss the Hikayet (oral storytelling) performance that is helping to keep this Moroccan tradition alive. The café is also a venue for a range of cultural activities such as cooking classes and quick survival courses in basic Moroccan Arabic (see page 78).

€ Jemaâ el Fna food stalls
Daily 1700-late.
One of Marrakech's great experiences, eating in Jemaâ el Fna is not to be missed. Piles of salads and steaming

tagines are set up under hissing gas lamps from early evening onwards. Each stall has a different variety of cooked food, from sheep heads to snails to less adventurous fried fish, tagines and brochettes. Walking along between the stalls is an experience in itself – you will be cajoled onto benches from all sides by young Moroccans who have somehow picked up a surreal line in mock cockney patter. Although some travellers are wary about hygiene at the Jemaâ stalls, eating here is no less safe than in most Moroccan restaurants. Just choose a stall that is popular as obviously it will have a faster turnover of food.

Stall 22 is a winner for typical brochettes and the servers are more laid-back with their sales pitch than most of their neighbours, while stall 14 specializes in fresh fried fish. If you fancy dessert there's a roving sweets cart that does the rounds between the stalls.

€ Marrakech Henna Art Café
35 Derb Sqaya, www.marrakechhenna artcafé.com. Daily 1000-2100.
Look for the distinctive blue door decorated with henna art to find this welcoming place, just off Rue Riad Zitoun el Kedim. Once inside, you'll find a healthy menu of Middle Eastern and Moroccan-inspired dishes (20-40dh) including good salads, hummus, falafel sandwiches and more substantial mains like turkey brochette with caramelized pumpkin. Vegans get a good look-in on the menu too. The blue walls inside are often home to art exhibitions, and you can get your hands decorated with henna after you dine. Cutlery is served in *babouches* which adds to the cuteness appeal. Wi-Fi available.

€ Roti D'or
17 Rue el Kennaria. Daily 1000-2100.
Just a couple of tables and a few seats at the counter are available at this cheap and cheerful diner which dishes up an eclectic menu of comfort food favourites for when you tire of tagines. Whether you're hankering for enchiladas (40dh), macaroni cheese (35dh), or a falafel or shwarma sandwich (25dh), they've got you covered. Portions are generous and the service is quick and super-friendly. Order their home-made mint iced tea for a seriously refreshing accompaniment to your meal.

€ Tiznit
28 Souk el Kassasabine, just off Jemaâ el Fna, T0524-427204. Daily 0800-2300. Closed during Ramadan.
Climb up the steep tiled steps to enter this little restaurant jammed with a few plastic tables and locals tucking into the best rabbit tagine in town. It's clean and tidy, though there are definitely no frills, and the welcome is genuine. Tagines here start from 40dh.

Cafés and patisseries

Café des Épices
75 Rahba Kedima, T0524-391770, www. cafédesepices.net. Daily 0800-2000.
The open space of Rahba Kedim, thronged with hat and basket vendors, and lined with spice and soothsayer stalls, makes a great setting for the medina's best café. Its street-side seating and rooftop terrace are nearly always overflowing with people. This is pole position in the souks for sitting down and supping some mint tea, a juice, or coffee, while contemplating your next shopping mission. It offers good sandwiches and salads as well and there's Wi-Fi.

Dar Cherifa
8 Derb Charfa Lakbir, off Rue Mouassine, T0524-426463. Daily 1200-1900.
Tricky to find and when you do you'll probably need to ring the bell to be let in, but that just adds to the rarefied air of this gallery café in a tall, spacious riad, snaffled down a narrow alley in the Mouassine area of the medina. Downstairs is a contemporary art space which also hosts occasional cultural evenings while the quiet café is on the roof terrace upstairs and serves mint tea and saffron coffee. There are 2 lunch menus (90dh/120dh).

Patisserie Les Princes
32 Rue de Bab Agnaou (also known as Av Prince Moulay Rachid), T0524-443033. Daily 0600-2230.
One of the medina's most famous patisseries, Les Princes is something of a Marrakech institution. There's an excellent selection of pastries and

petits fours; croissants are 3dh while scrumptious mille-feuille go for 10dh. Out the back is a *salon du thé* if you want to eat in. It's on the pedestrian street south of Jemaâ el Fna.

Riad Yima
52 Derb Aarjane, Rahba Lakdima, T0524-391987, www.riadyima.com. Daily 1000-1800.
This café, gallery and boutique in one brims with quirky pop-art charm. Created by artist, photographer and designer Hassan Hajjaj, the space is filled with his humorous recycled objets d'art and is tucked down a side-alley off Rahba Kedima. It's a tranquil place to stop amid the bustle and serves herbal teas, a variety of coffees and organic fruit juices.

Ville nouvelle
While Marrakech's medina restaurants serve mostly Moroccan food, the *ville nouvelle* is more about international cuisine and offers contemporary dining, with more options that serve alcohol.

€€ Al Fassia
55 Blvd Zerktouni, Guéliz, T0524-434060, www.alfassia.com. Wed-Mon 1200-2230.
Run by 3 sisters and employing a staff of nearly all women, this excellent Moroccan restaurant is the place in town to try pigeon pastilla. Unlike many of the more upscale restaurants which serve traditional Morrocan cuisine in Marrakech, Al Fassia is not about set menus (great if you just can't handle the major food coma that sets in after the marathon of dishes). The menu has an excellent choice of tagine and couscous mains (110-150dh), including a fish kefta tagine spiced with ginger, and a vegetarian couscous, and there's a good wine list too. The interior is all European-style white tablecloths and

soft lighting rather than palatial pizazz, so there's little to detract from the food, which works just fine because you're guaranteed excellent eating here. There's a 2nd branch of Al Fassia in Aguedal (KM2, Route de L'Ourika, T0524-381138), though locals still say Guéliz is the best of the pair. Highly recommended.

€€ Catanzaro
11 Rue Tarak Ibn Ziad, Guéliz, T0524-433737. Mon-Sat 1200-1430 and 1915-2300.
Seriously vying for the title of Morocco's best pizzeria, Catanzaro has rustic, chequered-tablecloth charm in spades, friendly service and great wood-fired pizza (along with pasta and some meat grills). It's also good value, with pizzas starting at 60dh and good Moroccan wines priced from 160dh per bottle. Usually packed with both locals, foreign residents and tourists, it's a good idea to reserve a table though you can usually also simply turn up and wait around for a table to become free.

€€ Loft
18 Rue de la Liberte, Guéliz, T0524-434216. Daily 1200-2400.
Neutral tones offset by splashes of turquoise blue and exposed brick walls hung with statement art give Loft a modern vibe that would be as at home in New York as it is in Marrakech's *ville nouvelle*. The menu veers distinctly to French traditions with the odd hat-tip to Morocco, with dishes such as lamb shank with mashed potato and salmon steak on the menu. Alcohol served.

€ Amal Women's Training Centre
Rue Ibn Sina, Guéliz, www.amalrestaurant. wordpress.com. Daily 1200-1600.
The Amal Centre trains disadvantaged local women to be chefs, and the centre's restaurant provides vital funds as well

as providing on-the-job practice for the trainees. The menu changes daily but there's always a couple of both Moroccan and international main dishes available, and with tagines priced from 35dh it is a winner for value too. A great place for a casual lunch, plus it's all for a good cause.

€ Restaurant Al Bahriya
75 Av Moulay Rachid, Guéliz, T0524-846186. Daily 1000-midnight.
Just round the corner behind **Café de la Poste** you'll find this street-restaurant usually chock-a-block with Moroccan families munching on fresh fish, prawns, and calamari, all fried in batter and served up with wedges of lemon and spicy olives. Seafood lovers shouldn't miss a meal here, and it definitely won't break the bank either with meals starting from 40dh.

Cafés and patisseries

Café Les Négociants
On the corner of Av Mohammed V and Blvd Mohammed Zerktouni, Guéliz, T0524-435762. Daily 0700-2300.
In Guéliz, this busy intersection has popular cafés on each side, but this is the granddaddy, an old-timer still at the heart of *ville nouvelle* life and the place to come for important conversations, for long, lingering mint teas and to watch the world go by.

Grand Café de la Poste
Corner of Blvd El Mansour Eddahbi and Av Imam Malik, Guéliz, T0524-433038, www.grandcafédelaposte.com. Daily 0800-0100.
Built in 1925, the extravagant Grand Café has immaculately restored 1920s colonial styling and a very pleasant outdoor terrace under umbrellas. It's a place people come to see and be seen, and, despite the inflated prices and lacklustre service, sitting out on the terrace on a sunny afternoon watching Marrakech's la-di-dah set quaff mint tea can't be beaten. Alcohol served.

Kaowa
34 Rue Yves Saint Laurent (opposite the entrance to Jardins Majorelle), Guéliz, T0524-330072. Daily 0900-1900.
This funky place serves up an array of tasty fruit smoothies as well as coffees and teas, with healthy organic salads and wrap-sandwiches (and much less healthy huge slices of cheesecake) to munch on. The bright, modern interior could have jumped straight out of a hipster neighbourhood in London or New York, while the wooden deck terrace, strewn with potted bamboo plants, is a good place to people watch as the throngs enter the gardens across the road.

Le 16
Pl du 16 Novembre, Guéliz, T0524-339670. Daily 0700-midnight.
With its lime-green umbrellas spilling into the central Pl du 16 Novembre, Le 16 is one of the *ville nouvelle*'s most popular pit-stops for a coffee break or café lunch. On a hot summer's day, don't miss the ice cream here, which comes in a huge range of imaginative flavours. There are decent salads and light meals, though most people are here for the sweets, the fruit juices, or just a simple pot of mint tea.

Bars and clubs

Marrakech has never been much of a drinking city but the times they are a'changing with a handful of modern café-bars and tapas bars sprinkled throughout Guéliz. In the medina drinking venues remain thin on the ground. Clubbers should note that the club scene in the city is expensive and can be sleazy.

68 Bar Au Vin
Rue de la Liberte, Guéliz, T0524-449742.
Daily 1800-0100.
A small, friendly wine bar, slap in the
centre of Guéliz, which only opened
in 2015 and is rightfully popular for its
slick yet friendly service and low-key
ambience. The decor has plenty of
modern style, with dark painted walls,
exposed brickwork and funky low-
lighting. It's a favourite with Marrakech's
foreign resident crowd who come to
munch on a menu of antipasto and
mezze and enjoy a bottle of wine, or
two. The space (over 2 floors) is tiny
though, and it can get crowded and
extremely smoky as the night wears on.

Café Arabe
184 Rue Mouassine, Medina, T0524-429728,
www.cáféarabe.com. Daily 1200-2300.
Conveniently located on one of the
main routes through the medina,
this café-bar offers good, if slightly
unimaginative, Moroccan and Italian
fare on the ground floor in a lush riad
setting while upstairs is a rare medina
bar and a relaxing rooftop terrace.

Café du Livre
44 Rue Tarik Ben Ziad, Guéliz, T0524-
432149, www.cáfédulivre.com.
Mon-Sat 0930-2100.
This great café/bar has second-hand
novels in English and French for sale,
a decent soundtrack of music, lots of
information about what's going on in
the city, and Wi-Fi. It's a friendly, casual
kind of place that attracts a good mix of
locals, foreign residents and travellers.
There are good cocktails, decent coffee,
beer on tap and a menu of international
bar-style food. Cigarette smoke can be
a problem. It's off a courtyard next to
Hotel Toulousaine.

Kechmara
3 Rue de la Liberté, Guéliz, T0524-422532,
www.kechmara.com. Mon-Sat 1130-0100.
One of Marrakech's most happening
joints, Kechmara is a very cool
contemporary bar-café with a killer
wine list, beer on tap and a menu of
gourmet-style burgers (110dh) in case
you get hungry. It attracts an arty hipster
crowd and plenty of Marrakech's foreign
residents, who flock here after the sun
sets to sit on the designer plastic chairs
and gossip. Live music at the weekends
and frequent host art exhibitions. If the
cigarette smoke downstairs gets too
much, head to the shaded roof terrace.

Kosybar
47 Pl des Ferblantiers, Kasbah, Medina
T0524-380324. Daily 1200-0100.
Pl des Ferblantiers was traditionally the
location of Marrakech's metalworkers but
was undergoing major reconstruction
during the update of this book.
Occupying several floors, Kosybar
functions as a restaurant and café, but the
food is nothing special. Instead, its roof
terrace is a great place to hang out with a
drink at sunset; cocktails are expensive at
around 100dh, but bottles of Moroccan
wine are reasonably priced from 150dh.

L'Auberge Espagnole
Corner Rue Tarik Ibnou Ziad and
Rue Moulay Ali, Guéliz, T0524-458913.
Daily 1700-0100.
Cheerfully decked out in lots of white,
yellow and red, this narrow tapas bar with
an eclectic mix of sporting photos taking
over the walls, is a pleasant place for drinks
and an especially good spot to come and
watch football games on the two big
screens. Despite the sporty theme, this is
a relaxed venue with a fun vibe that often
has live music in the evenings.

Le Comptoir Darna
Av Echouhada, Hivernage, T0524-437702, www.comptoirmarrakech.com. Daily restaurant 2000-0100, club 1900-0300.
Muted lighting, kaftan-clad waiting staff and seriously over-the-top decor set the tone for this oriental-fantasy venue where high-rollers come to drink late into the night. There's a restaurant downstairs, but Le Comptoir Darna is better known for its club on the 1st floor where a cabaret fusion of live music, belly dancers and weekend DJs entertain a cocktail-sipping crowd.

Le Point Bar
3 Rue Abu Hayane Taouhidi, Guéliz, T0614-554254. Daily 1800-0200.
This tapas bar is a fine place to while away an evening, tucking into small plate dishes, having a few beers or wines and checking out the interesting mix of people who come here for the friendly ambience and decently priced drinks. Make a beeline for the garden, complete with pot-plants and palm trees, for the best seats in the house.

Sky Bab Bar
Bab Hotel, corner Rue Mohammed el-Beqal and Blvd Mansour Eddahbi, Guéliz, T0524-435250, www.babhotel marrakech.ma. Daily 1130-2400.
A chilled-out, loungey bar, doused in white, with plenty of comfy seating, perfect for kicking back with a glass of wine. Definitely one of the more laid-back venues for a drink in the city. During the evening there's often a DJ or live music.

Entertainment

Cinemas
The major cinemas showing films in French (and Hollywood films sometimes in their original English with French subtitles) are the **Colisée** (Blvd Mohammed Zerktouni, Guéliz, T0524-448893) and the 9-screen multiplex **Megarama** (Av Mohammed VI, Agdal, T0890-102020, www.megarama. ma/marrakech), south of the centre.

Cultural centres
Instituto Cervantes, *14 Av Mohammed V, Guéliz, T0524-422055, www.marrakech. cervantes.es. Mon-Fri 1100-1300 and 1600-1830, Sat 1100-1230 and 1530-1800.* Spanish cultural and language school, with occasional concerts, films, exhibitions and special events.
Institut Français, *Route de la Targa, Guéliz, www.if-maroc.org/marrakech. Tue-Sat 1000-1230 and 1500-1900 (library).* With a recommended café, open-air theatre and pleasant garden, the French Institute shows films and holds exhibitions and other cultural events. The library has a small stock of books and films in French on Morocco-related subjects. **Café** Tue-Sat 0900-1900.

Festivals

Jan Marrakech Marathon (www. marathon-marrakech.com). A completely flat route marks out Marrakech's annual race as a good choice for 1st-time marathon runners as well as the more experienced.
Feb-May Marrakech Biennale (www.marrakechbiennale.org). Held every 2nd year (2016, 2018, etc), this celebration of art brings exhibitions and art installations to heritage sites throughout the city such as Badi Palace and Bahia Palace.
Jul Festival National des Arts Populaires. Brings together traditional regional music and dance troops from all over Morocco to perform at Jemaâ el Fna.

Sep Oasis Festival (www.oasisfest.org). Marrakech's 1st music festival dedicated to underground electronica. Held in the grounds of the Fellah Hotel (13 km south of the central city).

Dec Festival International du Film de Marrakech (www.festivalmarrakech. info). The city's glitziest event with free open-air screenings of films at Jemaâ el Fna, along with a jury-judged selection of world cinema.

Shopping

Crafts, fabrics and clothes

Marrakech is a shopper's paradise. Craft production has taken off in a big way, with a range of new products, notably in metal and ceramic, being added to classic leather and wood items. The influence of the international decorator set can clearly be felt. Close to the Dar el Bacha, in the Bab Doukkala neighbourhood, are plenty of antique dealers and, in Guéliz, the keen shopper will find chic boutiques with clothing, fine leather and other items. Prices in Guéliz are fixed and more expensive than the medina. A feel for prices can also be gained by visiting the workshops in the large **L'Ensemble Artisanale**. In the medina, prices are, of course, negotiable. If you are buying non-essential decorative items and are prepared to walk away, haggling is likely to be a less awkward experience, and you'll probably get a better deal (see box, page 76).

Medina

Al-Kawtar, *Rue Mouassine, Mouassine, www.alkawtar.org. Daily 0930-1400 and 1500-1800.* This non-profit organizations sells beautiful bed linens and other embroidered homewares, all produced by disabled women.

Al-Nour, *57 Rue Laksour, www.alnour-textiles.com. Sat-Wed 0900-1400 and 1500-1830.* Embroidered homewares and clothing made by a worthy female cooperative that supports local disabled women.

Assouss Argane, *94 Rue Mouassine, Mouassine, T0524-380125, www. assoussargane.com. Daily 0900-1800.* Authentic and undiluted Moroccan argan oil and beauty products, direct from a women's co-operative near Essaouira. The friendly all-female staff are happy to provide explanations and help.

Khartit Mustapha, *3 Fhal Chidmi, Rue Mouassine, Mouassine, T0524-442578. Daily 0800-2100.* Specializing in baubles, bangles and beads, Mustapha is the friendly owner of this Berber jewellery shop. He can make necklaces and bracelets to order using the semi-precious stones and colourful beads (once used as currency) that he also sells by weight. Credit cards accepted.

KifKif, *8 Rue Laksour, T0661-082041 (mob), www.kifkifbystef.com.* Colourful textiles, jewellery, toys and funky leather bags, selected by expat designer and manufactured by local craftworkers.

Le Trésor des Nomades, *142-144 Rue Bab Doukkala, T0524-385240. Daily 0900-1930.* Run by Mustapha Blaoui, this is a warehouse chock-full of treasures: lanterns, carved wooden doors, goatskin-covered chests in fantastic colours, Tuareg woven mats, kilims, antique *babouches* and much more. There's no sign outside, but look for the large double wooden doors. Shipping available.

Souk Cherifa, *Souk el Attarine, Mouassine. Daily 1000-1930.* This old fondouk has been transformed into the medina's most chi-chi shopping area, with the rooms on the ground and 1st floor home to young local designers selling

ON THE ROAD
Where to buy what in the souks

The souks can be confusing for shopping but they're also great fun. Originally each souk specialized in one type of product but this system has largely broken down on the main tourist drag (Souk Semmarine and its continuation, Souk el Kebir) up to the area around the Medersa Ben Youssef where stalls sell a wide range of souvenirs and crafts, trying to attract more custom.

If you enter the souks from opposite the **Café de France** in Jemaâ el Fna you will pass olive stalls and mint sellers on your right, then bend round to the right and you'll find yourself in the eastern corner of a small square called Bab Fteuh. Straight in front of you, through an arch, is the wide **Souk Semmarine** with some big antique shops and carpet emporia. Remember, prices tend to be higher along this section of the souk. **Rahba Kedima**, a rare open space off to the right (about 200 m up Souk Semmarine), is lined with spice stalls selling harissa, ras el-hanout, and saffron as well as a huge range of more regular spices. The middle of the square is home to open-air stalls selling woolly hats and raffia baskets. Further on, Souk Semmarine successively becomes **Souk el Kebir**, **Souk el Najjarine** and, under a wooden lintel, **Souk Chkaïria** where there are plenty of leather goods shops.

The other reasonably major route through the souks is via **Rue Mouassine**, which also runs north-south from the western end of Bab Fteuh, past the Mosque Mouassine. After the mosque and Saâdian fountain, veer right to head onto Souk el Attarine for lantern stalls and then spiral your way up to Souk el Haddidine for copper work. To the west of Rue Mouassine is **Rue Dar el Bacha**, the street running out towards Bab Doukkala. It has many interesting antiques, artwork, and jewellery shops.

homeware and fashion, featuring distinctly contemporary twists on traditional Marrakchi artistry.

Ville nouvelle

There are a number of little boutique-type places on **Rue de la Liberté**, **Rue Mauritanie** and **Rue Sourya**, all of which cut across Av Mohammed V between Pl du 16 Novembre (Marrakech Plaza) and Pl Abdelmoumen Ben Ali. Also have a quick trawl along the streets around **Rue Mohammed Bequal** (turn left just after the restaurant La Taverne, which itself is almost opposite the **Cinéma Colisée**). At the **Marrakech Plaza** on

Pl du 16 Novembre are branches of major European chains where young Marrakchis pay high prices for western labels.
33 Rue Majorelle, *33 Rue Yves Saint Laurent, T0524-314195*. Opposite the Jardin Majorelle, this smart new shop has a selection of quality clothing, jewellery and gifts from the new wave of Moroccan designers. Art gallery also attached.
Alrazal, *55 Rue Sourya, T0524-437884, www.alrazal.com. Mon-Sat 0930-1300 and 1530-1930*. Exquisite handmade clothing for children that's somewhere between fancy dress box and party outfit. Silk-embroidered miniature kaftans and Ali Baba pants in a rainbow of colours.

Galerie le Caftan, *Immeuble 100, No 2, Rue Mohammed Bequal, T0661-765260.* As the name suggests, a good choice of upmarket traditional women's gear made to order on the premises. Beautiful *babouches* with a modern touch.

L'Ensemble Artisanale, *Av Mohammed V (on the right past the Koutoubia as you head to Guéliz). Mon-Sat 1000-1230 and 1500-1900.* At this showcase craft centre prices are non-negotiable and slightly more expensive than in the old city. You can see people at work at practically all the main crafts, including embroidery, ceramic mosaic and basketry, felt hats, wood painting and slipper making. However, it's a tame experience compared to the sights and sounds of the souks.

Sidi Ghanem Industrial Zone, *a few kilometres on Rte de Safi, best reached by taxi or bus No 15, www.sidighanem.net. Open Mon-Fri.* If you're in the market for serious home decoration, you may want to take a trip out of town to Sidi Ghanem, where lots of Moroccan contemporary designers have outlets, focusing on home interiors, candles, designer furniture, crafts and fashion. Their main income is from exports but most are also open to visitors.

Books

Marrakech is not the most bookish of towns. Nevertheless, there are a few shops where you can stock up on large coffee table books, maps and recent Moroccan fiction in French. It's also worth trying the **Café du Livre** in Guéliz (page 73). Foreign newspapers, a day or 2 old, can be bought from the stands along Av Mohammed V.

Darart Librairie, *79 Rue Yves Saint Laurent.* A decent selection of Morocco guidebooks in English as well as French, city maps, coffee books and a few novels (mostly in French).

Librairie Chatr, *19/21 Av Mohammed V, T0524-447997.* Under the arcades at the top end of Av Mohammed V, near the Shell station and the intersection with Rue Abd el Krim el Khattabi. The best choice of books in the city, from coffee table books to novels and Atlas Mountain guidebooks (in French).

Librairie Dar El Bacha, *2 Rue Dar el Bacha, T0524-391973.* A small but well-stocked shop in the medina, with maps and guidebooks on its shelves (mostly in French).

Supermarkets

Aswak Assalam, *opposite the bus station at Bab Doukkala.* The nearest supermarket to the medina.

Carrefour, *Eden Centre, Av Mohammed V.* Smack in the centre of Guéliz, this handy large supermarket is your best bet for stocking up on essentials. Has a large alcohol section.

Hypermarché Marjane, *on the Casablanca road.* Stocks just about everything including electrical goods, clothes, household items, food and alcohol.

What to do

Ballooning

Ciel d'Afrique, *Imm Ali, Apt 4, 2nd floor, Av Youssef Ben Tachfine, Route de Targa, Guéliz, T0524-432843, www.cieldafrique. info.* An early morning hot-air balloon flight over the palm groves and villages to the north of Marrakech is a great way to start the day. Starts from 2050dh per person. They also organize balloon trips further afield in the south of the country.

Climbing and outdoor activities

Terres d'Amanar, *35 km Rte de Asni (30 mins from Marrakech), T0524-438103, www.terresdamanar.com.* In the foothills of Mt Toubkal National Park is a new eco-adventure forest park offering professionally supervised outdoor pursuits. Day courses include climbing, abseiling, zip wire, trekking, horse riding and archery. There's also accommodation in eco-lodge or tents for longer stays.

City tours

AXS Cycling Tours, *Rue Fatima el Fihria (east from Agdal Gardens), T0524-400227, www.argansports.com*. See Marrakech from the saddle of a bike on these recommended cycling tours using high-quality bikes (with cycling helmets). There are 2-day tour options for the city: the Magical Marrakech Tour (350dh per person) which weaves through the medina, and the Marrakech Tasting Tour (600dh) which threads a trail between local culinary stops, such as the souk's hidden bread ovens and the medina's tangia stalls. Both tours are family friendly. Longer tours and bike rental are also available.

Marrakech Private Tours, *T0641-903550, www.marrakechtours.wix.com/kamal*. Marrakchi BenMoussa Kamal runs customizable walking tours of the medina that take in both its historical highlights and lesser-seen corners. A good choice if you're interested in discovering more about Marrakech's local culture as well as seeing the sights.

Cooking classes

Café Clock, *224 Derb Chtouka, Kasbah, T0524-378367, www.caféclock.com*. 1-day cooking classes (600dh) include shopping in the souk before learning how to prepare a 3-course Moroccan menu with a choice of salads, mains and desserts to learn how to master. They can also arrange 2-hr bread-baking workshops and specialist patisserie classes.

Souk Cuisine, *5 Derb Tahtah, T0673-804955, www.soukcuisine.com*. A recommended cooking class (520dh) that involves shopping in the souk for fresh produce with Marrakech resident Gemma van de Burght and then learning to cook a selection of Moroccan tagines and salads under the watchful eyes of 2 Moroccan female chefs. Lunch afterwards includes wine.

Golf

PalmGolf, *Circuit de la Palmeraie (7 km north of the central city, in the Palmeraie), T0524-368766, www.palmeriemarrakech. com/en/golf/*. 27-hole course, designed by Robert Trent and opened in 2009.
Royal Golf Club, *7 km south, off the Ouarzazate road (N9), T0524-409828, www. royalgolfmarrakech.com*. Three 9-hole interconnected courses set in orchards.

Hammams

Public hammams The Islamic requirement for ablutions combined with the lack of bathrooms in many Moroccan homes mean that the city's public hammams are well used. They cost around 10dh per person and are either single sex or have set hours or days for men and women. Massage and black soap scrubs cost extra. Remember to keep your knickers or shorts on in the hammam and take a spare dry pair with you.
Hammam Dar el Bacha, *Rue Fatima Zohra. Daily men 0700-1300, women 1300-2100*. This is a large hammam dating from the early 1930s. The vestibule has a huge dome, and inside are 3 parallel marble-floored rooms, the last with underfloor heating.

Private hammams For a calmer, less confusing, hammam experience many riads have private hammams and a

flurry of deluxe hammams have opened
up in the medina offering a spa-style
environment. These are very obviously
a long way away from the real thing and
are aimed squarely at travellers simply
looking to relax and rejuvenate. Expect a
full scrub, soak and massage to cost from
300dh upwards.

Hammam Ziani, *14 Rue Riad Zitoun Jdid,
T0662-715571, www.hammamziani.ma.
Daily 0800-2200.* A favourite with budget
travellers, this private hammam offers
good-value scrub, soak and massage
packages with female masseurs.

Le Bain Bleu, *32 Derb Chorfa Lakbar,
T0524-383804, www.lebainbleu.com.*
The top address for a luxury hammam
experience in Marrakech medina, Le
Bain Bleu does bathing in style. Advance
booking is essential.

Horse riding

Cavaliers de l'Atlas, *Rte de Casablanca
(opposite Afriquia Station), Palmeraie,
T0672-845579, www.lescavaliersdelatlas.
com.* Riding in the palm groves outside
Marrakech or longer treks for several
days. Novices and experienced riders
catered for.

Trekking and tour operators

Atlas Sahara Trek, *6 bis Rue Houdhoud,
Quartier Majorelle, T0524-313901, www.atlas-*
sahara-trek.com. One of the best trekking
agencies in Marrakech, with 20 years'
experience. Moroccan-born founder
Bernard Fabry knows his deserts well.

Mountain Safari Tours, *64 Lot Laksour,
Route de Casa, Guéliz, T0524-308777,
www.mountainsafaritours.com.* Specialist
travel agency with 20 years' experience
in guiding travellers through Morocco.
Puts together itineraries focused on
photography, gastronomy and fishing
as well as more regular tours.

Mountain Voyage, *Immeuble El Batoul,
2nd Floor, 5 Av Mohammed V, Guéliz,
T0524-421996, www.mountain-voyage.
com.* High-end tailor-made tours in the
Toubkal area and beyond (5-14 days).
Owners of the luxurious **Kasbah du
Toubkal** mountain hotel (see page 111).

SheherazadVentures, *55 Residence
Ali, Av Mohammed VI, Guéliz, T0615-
647918, www.sheherazadventures.com.*
English-Moroccan travel company
offering a range of special interest trips,
including pottery making, photography,
volunteering and date picking as well as
more classic itineraries.

Transport

Air

Airport Marrakech Menara (www.
marrakech.airport-authority.com) is
clearly signposted, 6 km from the centre.
A *petit taxi* (3 passengers) or *grand taxi*
(6 passengers) from the airport takes
15 mins and should cost 100-150dh (more
after 2000) to the medina or Guéliz.
Although fares are supposedly fixed and
published on an airport noticeboard,
taxi drivers at the airport are notorious
for overcharging, so agree the price first.
To save hassle, most hotels and riads can
arrange airport transfers for about 200dh.
Alternatively, there's a handy airport

ON THE ROAD

A day by the pool

Many of Marrakech's riads have plunge pools but these are rarely bigger than a few metres. The coast is a bit too far away for a day trip, so out-of-town pools, usually with attached bars and restaurants, or hotels that open their pools to non-residents, can make an attractive day out, especially as the temperature rises in summer.

Beldi Country Club, Km 6, Rte du Barrage, T0524-383950, www.beldicountryclub.com. With four swimming pools, and one dedicated for children, Beldi is a prime escape from the city. Spend a tranquil afternoon lounging poolside after a delicious three-course lunch on the terrace. 370dh including lunch, 250dh children. Ring to reserve.

Les Jardins de la Medina, 21 Derb Chtouka, Kasbah, T0524-381851, www.lesjardinsdelamedina.com. Leave the medina behind without actually leaving the medina. This hotel on the edge of the Kasbah quarter, with its pool amid lush foliage offers lunch and pool combo passes for 350dh. The spa here offers luxurious hammam rituals and beauty treatments as well.

Oasiria, Km 4, Rt d'Amizamiz, T0524-380438, www.oasiria.com. This huge waterpark offers two pools, huge water-slides and a pirate ship to keep little ones happy plus there are restaurants, cafés and acres of gardens. Free shuttle from the city centre. 210dh, 130dh children.

---

shuttle bus, No 19, which runs every 30 mins to Jemaâ el Fna via Guéliz and Hivernage (20dh single, 30dh return).

EasyJet (www.easyjet.com), **Ryanair** (www.ryanair.com) and **Royal Air Maroc** (197 Av Mohammed V, T0890-00080, www.royalairmaroc.com, daily 0830-1215 and 1430-1900) all fly daily to/ from **London**. There are also flights to/ from **Manchester**, **Bristol**, **Nottingham** and **Edinburgh**. Other international destinations include **Paris** and **Madrid** (daily), plus **Brussels**, **Copenhagen**, **Geneva** and **Milan**.

Bus

Local City buses, run by **AlsaCity**, can be caught at the Pl de Foucauld, just off Jemaâ el Fna next to the calèches. There are also stops along Av Mohammed V and Av Hassan II. No 1 and No 7 are the most useful services, running from Jemaâ el Fna along Av Mohammed V, through Guéliz. No 3 and No 8 run from the railway station to the bus station, via Jemaâ el Fna; No 10 from Jemaâ el Fna to the bus station; No 11 from Jemaâ el Fna to the Menara Gardens and airport. No 4 goes to the Jardin Majorelle.

Long distance Supratours (T0524-435525, www.oncf.ma) buses leave from alongside the train station on Av Hassan II. CTM buses (T0524-448328, www.ctm.ma) have their terminal on Rue Abou Bakr Seddiq, near the Theatre Royal in Guéliz. For all other private long-distance bus companies, the *gare routière* is just outside Bab Doukkala, T0524-433933.

There is often a choice between different companies with varying prices and times. When leaving Marrakech, make sure the number of the booth where the tickets are bought matches the bus stop number where you intend to catch the bus. Always be there in advance. It is wise to call at the station the previous day as some services, notably across the High Atlas to Taroudant and Ouarzazate, leave early in the morning. Note that buses to the **Ourika Valley**, **Asni** and **Moulay Brahim** run from outside Bab Rob rather than Bab Doukkala.

Destinations served by bus from Marrakech include **Agadir**, **Casablanca**, **El Jadida**, **Er Rachidia**, **Essaouira**, **Laâyoune**, **M'hamid** (CTM only), **Oualidia**, **Ouarzazate**, **Rabat**, **Safi**, **Skoura** and **Taroudant**.

Calèche
Green-painted horse-drawn carriages can be hired from the stands at Jemaâ el Fna. There is a fixed price of 120dh per hr (displayed inside the carriage). The most common routes are a tour around the ramparts and trips to Jardin Marjorelle.

Car hire
You should be able to get something like a small Dacia or Renault Clio for 350dh per day, unlimited km, but avoid the lesser-known firms, if possible, and make sure there's cover, or at the very least a plan B, in case you break down in the middle of nowhere. A driver will cost you around 250dh a day extra. 4WD hire with driver is around 1200dh per day. If driving, once out of Marrakech, the roads are rarely crowded. However, the Marrakech–Casablanca road has a notoriously high number of accidents. International agencies in Marrakech include **Avis**

(137 Av Mohammed V, T0524-433727); **Europcar** (63 Blvd Mohammed Zerktouni, T0524-431228, and at the airport); **Hertz** (154 Av Mohammed V, T0524-431394, airport T0524-447230).

Taxi
Petits taxis The city's khaki-coloured *petits taxis* can take up to 3 passengers. Marrakchi taxi drivers are renowned for overcharging. Most taxis have meters but most drivers will refuse to use them. From the medina to Guéliz should cost around 10dh during the day, 20dh after 2000. Be aware that taxis at the railway station are particularly notorious at quoting ridiculous fares (see below).

Grands taxis These run on fixed routes, with prices depending on route. 6 passengers are normally squeezed in, but you can make a private trip if you pay for the empty spaces. Major *grands taxis* stands are found at Bab Doukkala (for **Essaouira** and **Ouarzazate**) and Bab Rob (to **Asni**, **Ourika Valley** and **Ouirgane).**

Train
The railway station is in Guéliz, on Av Hassan II at the corner with Av Mohammed V (T0890-203040 call centre, www.oncf.ma). A taxi into the city from the station is around 15dh but expect to be quoted up to 50dh by taxi drivers who hang about at the station entrance; walking away from the station entrance to hail off the street should get you a more reasonable fare. Alternatively, take bus No 3 or 8 from outside the station, along Av Hassan II and Av Mohammed V, to the medina. There are regular express trains for **Casablanca** (3½ hrs), **Rabat** (4 hrs) and **Fès** (7 hrs).

Essaouira

Essaouira, 'little picture', is one of those stage set places: you half expect to see plumed cavalry coming round the corner, or a camera crew filming some diva up on the ramparts. It is a beautifully designed 18th-century military port and, somehow, hasn't changed too much since. The walls are white, the windows and shutters are often cracked and faded blue, while arches and columns are sandy camel-brown. Three crescent moons on a city gate provide a touch of the heraldic; tall feathery araucaria trees and palms along the ramparts add a Mediterranean air, while surfers and fanciful Jimi Hendrix myths hint at Essaouira's hippy days, a few decades ago. Above it all seagulls glide and dive in squawking flocks keeping beady eyes on the fishing boats hauling their catch in at the port.

Essential Essaouira

Finding your feet

The best way to arrive in Essaouira is by the **Supratours** bus as its office is right outside Bab Marrakech (one of the main entrances into the medina). Both **CTM** (www.ctm.ma) and other private line buses arrive at the bus station about 300 m northeast of the medina's Bab Doukkala entrance – a five-minute walk with luggage or a 10dh *petit taxi* ride (15dh at night). The *grands taxis* stand is next to the bus station, although arrivals will be dropped off at Bab Doukkala. Drivers can use the car park (24-hour warden) close to the harbour next to Place Prince Moulay el Hassan. See Transport, page 96, for further details.

Getting around

One of the most appealing aspects of Essaouira is that all the principal tourist sites can be comfortably reached on foot; this is a city for strolling and the medina is compact so you can't really get lost.

Best stays

Villa Maroc, page 89
Villa Garance, page 90
Riad Nakhla, page 91

For longer walks, head south along the windswept beach to Borj el Beroud. You can also walk further along the sand to Cap Sim (an all-day excursion).

Best restaurants

Elizir, page 92
Les Alizés Mogador, page 92
Des Arcades, page 93

When to go

May brings the Gnaoua Festival to Essaouira and, with it, lots of visitors; book your hotel as far in advance as possible if you're planning to be here during the festival period. July and August is peak local holiday season and can also be busy. By far the best months for Essaouira travels are April to June and September to October, but remember that the famed *alizée* wind howls over the city throughout the year so always pack something to throw over your shoulders for when the wind whips up.

Time required

Unless you're a keen windsurfer, three days is time enough to explore the medina and relax on the beach.

scale the ramparts then meander through a medina that's too compact to get lost in

Medina

Essaouira does not have a lot in the way of formal sights but has plenty of gently atmospheric streets to compensate. Enclosed by walls with five main gates, the medina is the major attraction. Entering from **Bab Doukkala** the main thoroughfare is Rue Mohammed Zerktouni, which leads into Avenue de l'Istiqlal, where there is the **Grand Mosque**, and just off, on Rue Laalouj, the **Museum of Sidi Mohammed Ibn Abdallah** ① *T0524-475300, Wed-Mon 0830-1200 and 1430-1800, 10dh*. This house, once the home of a pasha, has a collection of weapons and handicrafts, such as woodwork and carpets, and also has an interesting ethnographic collection, including examples of stringed instruments beautifully decorated with marquetry and documents on Berber music.

Avenue de l'Istiqlal leads into Avenue Okba Ibn Nafi. At the end of the street a gate on the right leads into **Place Moulay Hassan**, the heart of the town's social life. The town's souks are mainly around the junction between Rue Mohammed Zerktouni and Rue Mohammed el Gorry, although there is an area of woodworkers and craft stalls inside the Skala walls to the north of Place Moulay Hassan. At the northeast end of Rue Zerktouni, close to Bab Doukkala, is the much-decayed **mellah** (the old Jewish quarter). Although the Jewish community no longer remains, some of the synagogues have been renovated and opened to the public. The **Rabbi Haïm Pinto Synagogue** ① *Rue Mellah, Sun-Fri 0900-1200 and 1400-1800, donation appreciated*, on the second floor of a residential building, is one of the best examples.

Outside Bab Doukkala is the Consul's **cemetery** for the British officials who died here while converting Mogador into a trading post with strong UK links. Behind the high wall on the road to the bus station is the **Jewish cemetery**. If you find the man with the key, you may discover the resting place of Leslie Hore-Belisha, inventor of the first pedestrian crossing light.

★Harbour and Skala du Port

Off Place Moulay Hassan is the small harbour, busy with its fishing fleet. The open-air foodstalls serving grilled fish are prime lunching territory – a meal here is a quintessential Essaouira experience. The sea gate (**Porte de la Marine**), which serves to link the harbour with the medina, was built in 1769, it is said, by an Englishman who converted to Islam during the reign of Sidi Mohammed Ibn Abdallah. The gateway is built of stone in the classical style, and the year of its construction (1184 of the Hegira) is inscribed on the pediment. From the sea gate a bridge spans small primitive dry docks to the ramparts on the **Skala du Port** ① *entry 10dh payable at a kiosk close to the Porte de la Marine*, an old Portuguese sea defence and battery. From the top of the bastion there are extensive panoramic views of the harbour and the offshore islands, the **Îles Purpuraires**. The Skala du Port is also famed for being featured in Orson Welles' *Othello*.

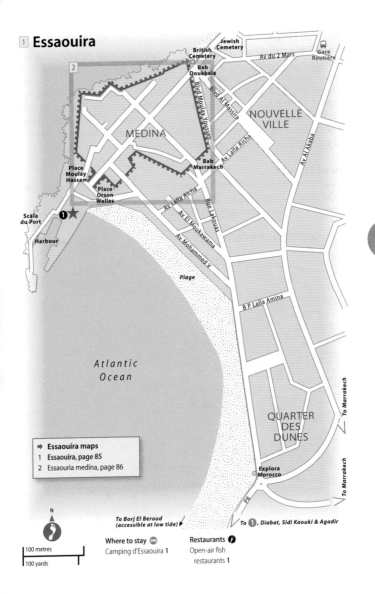

1 Essaouira

Jewish Cemetery

Av du 2 Mars

Gare Routière

British Cemetery

Bab Doukkala

Blvd Moulay Youssen

Blvd Al Massira

NOUVELLE VILLE

MEDINA

Av Lalla Aïcha

Av Al Akaba

Place Moulay Hassan

Bab Marrakech

Place Orson Welles

Scala du Port

Harbour

Av Lalla Aïcha

Av El Moukawama

Rue La Kouas

Av Mohammed V

Plage

B P Lalla Amina

Atlantic Ocean

→ **Essaouira maps**
1 Essaouira, page 85
2 Essaouria medina, page 86

QUARTER DES DUNES

To Marrakech

To Marrakech

Explora Morocco

P8

To Marrakech

N

100 metres

100 yards

To Borj El Beroud
(accessible at low tide) ▶

To ➊, Diabat, Sidi Kaouki & Agadir

Where to stay 🛏
Camping d'Essaouira 1

Restaurants 🍴
Open-air fish
restaurants 1

★Skala de la Ville

Further to the north of Place Moulay Hassan, it is possible to get onto the ramparts of the Skala de la Ville from Rue de la Skala close to its junction with Rue Darb Laalouj. Entry here is free. Crenellated walls protect a 200-m-long raised artillery platform and an impressive array of decorated Spanish and other European cannon. From the tower of the **north bastion** there are fine views of the old *mellah*, the medina, with its white buildings and blue shutters, and the coastline to the north; this is a good spot from which to watch the sunset. The **woodworkers' souks** are situated here in arched chambers underneath the ramparts.

Around Essaouira

Essaouira has fine beaches, but the prevailing wind, known as the *alizée*, stirs up a lot of sand, keeping all but the hardiest sunbathers away, and makes it cold for swimming. Conditions are ideal for windsurfing, though not necessarily

2 Essaouira medina

➡ Essaouira maps
1 Essaouira, page 85
2 Essaouira medina, page 86

Where to stay 🛏
Dar Liouba 21
Dar Loulema 5
Essaouira Hostel 3
Jack's Apartments 1
La Maison des Artistes 4
Riad Chakir Mogador 6
Riad Lalla Mira 23
Riad Lalla Zina 2
Riad Nakhla 24
Ryad Watier 19
Villa Garance 10
Villa Maroc 17

Restaurants 🍴
Café des Arts 10
Chez Mermoz 3
Des Arcades 5
Elizir 4
Ferdaouss 9
La Cantina 6
La Triskalla 8
Les Alizés Mogador 15
Mega Loft 1
Patisserie Chez Driss 11
Umia 2
Yoo 7

Bars 🍸
Café Taros 12

100 metres
100 yards

BACKGROUND
Essaouira

Essaouira is a quiet sort of place with a long history. There was a small Phoenician settlement here, previously called Magdoura or Mogador, a corruption of the Berber word Amegdul, meaning 'well-protected'. The Romans were interested in the purple dye produced from the abundant shellfish on the rocky coast, which they used to colour the robes of the rich. Mogador was occupied in the 15th century by the Portuguese, who built the fortifications around the harbour. The town was one of their three most important bases but was abandoned in 1541, from which time it went into decline. Mogador was also visited by Sir Francis Drake in Christmas 1577. In 1765, the Alaouite Sultan Sidi Mohammed Ibn Abdallah transformed Mogador into an open city, enticing overseas businessmen in with trade concessions, and it soon became a major commercial port, with a large foreign and Jewish population establishing the town as a major trading centre.

The Sultan employed the French architect Théodore Cornut to design the city and its fortifications. In his design, Cornut chose a rectangular layout for the main streets, resulting in a uniform style, and constructed ramparts in the Vauban style. The fortifications were not always that effective, however. From time to time, the tribesmen of the region would raid the town, carrying off booty and the merchants' wives – who it is said, were not always that happy to return: perhaps life in rural Morocco was more pleasant than listening to the wind in the damp counting houses of Mogador.

At Independence the town's official name became Essaouira, the local Arabic name meaning 'little picture'. In the 1960s Essaouira had a brief reputation as a happening place, attracting hippies and rockstars, including Jimi Hendrix. In recent years, the town has emerged from several decades of decline, attracting greater numbers of tourists, notably surfers. The burgeoning number of riads and their accompanying upmarket tourism has also brought some wealth to the inhabitants of this most relaxed town, without spoiling its gentle atmosphere, though an increase in the number of oversized hotels outside the city walls may have a more detrimental effect.

surfing. The northern **Plage de Safi** is fine in the summer, but can be dangerous during windy weather.

South of the town, the wide beach is great for football, and there are usually games going on here. The mouth of **Oued Ksob** (reached along the beach at low tide, or from a track off the N1 south of the town) is noted for a variety of migrating seabirds, including black, little, sandwich, whiskered and white-

Fact...
Stories linking the ruins of Borj el Baroud with Hendrix's 'Castles Made of Sand' are spurious – the song was released 18 months before the singer visited Essaouira.

winged terns. Eleonora's falcons can also be seen here. Past the Oued Ksob, you will see the waves breaking against the remnants of **Borj el Baroud**, an old fortress and watchtower dating from the 18th century. Local legend states that the people of Souss put a curse on the building because their trade was being ruined.

From here, it's just a short stroll inland to the village of **Diabat**, about 5 km from Essaouira (or 40 dh in a taxi). Diabat was once a favourite hippy destination, but its bohemian flavour has mostly now vanished as the surrounding area is now part of a luxury resort development that includes a golf course.

> **Tip...**
> If you're planning on walking far along the beach south of town, note that the Oued Ksob below the village of Diabat becomes an impassable river at high tide.

Îles Purpuraires

These islands to the southwest are a bird sanctuary, particularly for rare Eleonora's falcons, which can be seen with a good telescope from the end of the jetty. Although it's now a nature reserve, it is possible to visit the main island, **Île de Mogador**, outside the April to October breeding season. You can negotiate a private trip with a local fishing vessel to ferry you there and back, but first you must obtain a permit (free) from the Port office.

Listings Essaouira *maps p85 and p86*

Tourist information

Délégation Provincial de Tourisme
10 Av du Caire, T0524-783532.
Mon-Fri 0900-1630.
Rather basic office with helpful staff, maps, leaflets and bus timetables.

Where to stay

The best place to stay is the medina, with its upmarket guesthouses, riads and occasionally damp cheap hotels. It's also possible to stay to the south of the medina, where a few large hotels and guesthouses stretch along the beachfront as far as the main Marrakech road. Alternatively, head for a country guesthouse a few miles south around Diabat, Ghazoua or Cap Sim. When searching for cheap hotels make

sure you get a well-ventilated room with windows and, preferably, a view of the ocean.

Medina

Essaouira is 2nd only to Marrakech in the quantity and quality of restored properties in the old town operating as guesthouses. Though many of these are not riads in the strictest sense, they are usually referred to as such, and the style will be familiar to those who have stayed in riads in Marrakech. If you can afford it, these are the best option. The typical Essaouira house has 2 storeys around a courtyard with rooms opening onto balconies. Most guesthouses can do evening meals for around 150-200dh, if given advance warning. In many cases, the whole establishment can be rented for a few days for a house party. It is important to book well ahead, especially during the annual **Gnaoua Festival**. Many guesthouses do not accept credit cards; check in advance.

For a selection of apartments and studios in the medina, try agency **Jack's Apartments** (1 Pl Moulay Hassan, T0524-475538, www.jackapartments.com), which offers a range of accommodation options, all with Wi-Fi and daily cleaning service, and most with sea views and private or shared terrace.

€€€€-€€€ Villa Maroc
10 Rue Abdallah Ben Yassin, T0524-476147, www.villa-maroc.com.
Sublime service and an exceptional eye for aesthetics make Villa Maroc one of Essaouira's best stays. The rooms, in a clutch of 18th-century merchant houses, have retained their air of history yet have been given a thoroughly contemporary makeover, with white, cream and shades of blue used in abundance, day beds and spacious *tadelakt* bathrooms. Some have rustic wood-beam ceilings, while oversized lamps and local embroidery on bed linen offer a thoroughly Essaouira twist. There's a hammam and spa, restaurant, bar and a rooftop with views that stretch across to the long swathe of beach. Breakfast and Wi-Fi included. Recommended.

€€€-€€ Casa Lila
94 Rue Mohammed el Qorry, T0524-475545, www.casalila-riad.com.
Exceptionally photogenic, even by riad standards, Casa Lila goes big on dusty pastel shades, with lots of purples, lemons, lilacs and pinks. Rooms come in different colour schemes but all are fit for a princess fantasy with luscious fabrics and beds sprinkled with rose petals, while open fires and checkered floors add to the chic quotient. There is

a stunning roof terrace where you can soak up the sun and a hammam offering essential oil massages. Minimum 2-night stay. Breakfast and Wi-Fi included.

€€€-€€ La Maison des Artistes
19 Rue Laâlouj, T0524-475799, www.lamaisondesartistes.com.
There's an entertaining air of artistic eccentricity at this 8-room guesthouse overlooking the sea, with lots of conversation point pieces of furniture and striking art among the colourful decoration. Rooms (from €65) are decorated with a fine eye for bohemian-chic, with plenty of quirky decoration touches offset by lashings of white. To really treat yourself opt for the loft-style suite, 'Le Pavilion de Cesar', and wake up to stunning wrap-around sea views. An enticing menu of home-made meals can be prepared upon request; staff go out of their way to help, and the roof terrace is just the ticket for basking in the sun while listening to the waves. Breakfast, Wi-Fi and soft drinks included. Recommended.

€€€-€€ Ryad Watier
16 Rue Ceuta, T0524-476204, www.ryad-watier-maroc.com.
The French owner of this large and spacious riad has filled it with a quirky mix of old and new that gives the entire place an ambience of relaxed charm – there's even a resident tortoise. There are stunning artworks by local painters and the owner's father, stained-glass window details and a cosy library full of interesting books, while the huge, airy rooms (doubles from €85) blend bright modern colour palettes with tiles, rugs and terracotta *tadelakt*. Some have mezzanine sleeping platforms and all feature big showers in the bathroom; there are roomy family suites for those with kids in tow. There's also a hammam

and massage room for relaxing after long strolls on the beach. Minimum 2-night stay. Breakfast and Wi-Fi included.

€€ Dar Loulema
2 Rue Souss, T0524-475346, www.darloulema.com.

Centrally situated, just a stone-throw from café-crammed Pl Moulay Hassan, this boutique hideaway has just 8 beautifully styled rooms (doubles from €68) each decked out with a mix of antique furnishings, colourful fabrics and traditional tiled floors. Choose the Todra room for plenty of Berber appeal or the Mogador room to bring Essaouira's blue and white aesthetic into your bedroom. There are great views over the fishing port and across the beach from the rooftop. Breakfast and Wi-Fi included.

€€ Riad Lalla Mira
14 Rue d'Algerie, T0524-475046, www.lallamira.net.

A solid bet, German-run Lalla Mira emphasizes its eco-credentials and also houses a beautiful mosaic-tiled hammam (the oldest in Essaouira), free for guests. Some of the rooms (single/double 439/692dh) are on the small size and can be a tad dark (the singles in particular) but all come with TV and have solar-powered underfloor heating and use a water-recycling system. The restaurant here serves good vegetarian food. Breakfast included.

€€ Villa Garance
10 Rue Eddakhil, T0524-473995, www.essaouira-garance.com.

Well looked after by its French owners, Villa Garance is a charming place to stay with a homely lounge, complete with open fireplace, downstairs, a pretty rooftop for long and lazy breakfasts, and 10 ample-sized and high-ceilinged

rooms (€63-89) complete with original art deco tiled floors and lots of original features. Some have 4-poster beds and 6 of the rooms have large shutter-windows that look down onto the street below. The large suites are a winner for travelling families with two connecting rooms. Breakfast and Wi-Fi included. Recommended.

€€-€ Dar Liouba
28 Impasse Moulay Ismaïl, T0524-476297, www.darliouba.eu.

This guesthouse, with rooms surrounding an octagonal courtyard, has lots of intimate appeal with a very warm welcome from staff and French owner Patricia. The decoration is bright and simple, with lots of white offset with splashes of textile colour. Rooms aren't particularly big but are bright and airy, some with open fireplaces and all with nice homely touches such as stacks of paperbacks to read. Breakfast and Wi-Fi included.

€ Essaouira Hostel
17 Rue Laghrissi, T0524-476481, www. hihostels.com/hostels/essaouira-hostel.

Tricky to find (ring ahead and somebody will come to meet you), this 'boutique' hostel in an 18th-century riad has superb friendly management and a fun, youthful vibe. Mixed dorms start from €7, while private double rooms with en suite begin at €23. There's a communal kitchen if you want to cook and a lounge, terrace and bar for hanging out with new friends. Laundry can be done for free and Wi-Fi is included.

€ Riad Chakir Mogador
13 Rue Malek Ben Morhal (off Av Istiqlal), T0524-473309, www.riadchakir.com.

This good-value riad amps up the charm with friendly staff and loads of traditional Moroccan character spread over 3 adjoining houses featuring chunky wooden beams and colourful painted ceilings. Some of the 26 rooms (single/double €35/45, good discounts in low season) can be rather cramped but if you don't need to swing a cat, they more than make up for it with 4-poster beds draped with billowy fabrics and *tadelakt* bathrooms. The central location, just off Av Istiqlal, is handy as well. Wi-Fi and breakfast included.

€ Riad Lalla Zina
17 Rue d'Agadir, T0610-026998.
Long-term Essaouira resident, Anne, has turned this rather quirky guesthouse into a jewel-box of charms. A bohemian style flows through the 9 bijoux rooms (single/double/triple 200/300/400dh) which feature vibranty painted wood ceiling centrepieces and original floor tiles; some have large shutter-windows that look straight down onto the courtyard below. Up on the rooftop, there are great medina vistas, while downstairs in the courtyard, they occasionally organize musical performances. Breakfast included.

€ Riad Nakhla
12 Rue d'Agadir, T0524-474940, www.riadnakhla.com.
Stunning affordability here. Ably run by manager Rachid, Riad Nakhla has 16 cosy and colourful rooms all with super-comfortable beds and satellite TV. To be fair, the rooms don't have the wow-factor features of Essaouira's riad offerings, but at 250dh for a single and 360dh for a double room, this is one of Essaouira's best bargains, particularly due to the excellent standard of cleanliness kept up here. It's all topped off by a roof terrace with knock-out views across the medina

rooftops. Wi-Fi and breakfast included. Recommended.

Around Essaouira

€€€ Jardins des Douars
Douar Sidi Yassine (15 km south of Essaouira, 3 km inland off the road to Agadir), T0524-474003, www.jardindesdouars.com.
Walls of warm, spice-toned *tadelakt*, huge wooden doors, fireplaces and antique furniture make this an elegant stay with plenty of luxury trimmings. For those just here to relax and rejuvenate, there is little reason to walk out the door, since the hotel's tranquil surroundings are replete with botanical gardens, a pampering spa and hammam, 2 pools for lazy sunbathing days and a restaurant and bar. Breakfast and Wi-Fi included.

€€€-€€ Baoussala
El Ghazoua, T0524-792345, www.baoussala.com.
This small, pretty eco-guesthouse is set in a peaceful location 10 km from Essaouira and 10 km from Sidi Kaouki. Purpose-built by owners Dominique and Bruno Maté, it has gardens full of cacti and hammocks strung between eucalyptus trees and a solar-heated pool. The 6 bright, large rooms (€100-130) are the perfect blend of contemporary chic and Moroccan artistry, with wood-beam ceiling features, open fires, big comfortable beds on raised platforms, plenty of traditional decoration touches and plentiful scattered cushion seating areas. It all adds up to a wonderful tranquil and relaxing place to stay. The whole house can be rented together. Lunch and evening meals are available and breakfast and Wi-Fi are included.

€ Auberge de la Plage
Sidi Kaouki, T0524-476600,
www.kaouki.com.
A colourful, chilled-out place just 100 m
from the beach – the perfect pit-stop
for watersports fans who want to be
near the waves. The 10 bright rooms
(350-500dh), are simple but homely
with showers heated by solar-power
(2 with shared bathroom), and the lovely
shaded garden is a fine place to rest up
after the rigours of the road. As well as
watersports, horse riding and camel
excursions can be easily organized here.

€ Dar Kenavo
13 km out of Essaouira on Agadir
road, after 8 km take the left turn for
Casablanca/Marrakech and it's 4 km
along on the left, T0661-207069 (mob),
www.darkenavo.com.
Out in argan country, this rural
guesthouse is a nature-lover's hideaway
with 8 rooms and 3 bungalows (from
€50) plus a shared Berber tent dormitory
(€11). All open out into the quiet garden
with its heated pool, where resting up
and enjoying the peace and quiet is the
main activity to savour. A good choice if
you want to see something of Moroccan
rural life. Disabled access in private
rooms. Breakfast and Wi-Fi included.

Camping

Camping d'Essaouira
2 km out of Essaouira near the
lighthouse, on the Agadir road.
Well protected, clean loos.

€€ Elizir
1 Rue d'Agadir, T0524-472103.
Daily for lunch and dinner.
Creative food using top-notch
ingredients, Elizir is run by a Moroccan
returned from Italy, who cooks up
a storm of Mediterranean-inspired
flavours. Try the ravioli with ricotta,
basil and pistachio, or organic chicken
with figs and gorgonzola. The eclectic
decoration touches – vintage finds
mixing with black-and-white portraits
on the walls and original Moroccan
tiles – adds plenty of charm to the dining
experience. Its reputation as one of the
best restaurants in town is well deserved
so advance booking is advisable. Alcohol
served. Recommended.

€€ Les Alizés Mogador
26 Rue de la Skala, T0524-476819.
Daily for lunch and dinner.
One of the most popular places in town,
and rightfully so. You can't reserve, but
waiting at the small tables just inside the
entrance with some olives and a bottle
of wine is one of the great pleasures of
the place. Once you get a table, you'll be
plied with seriously flavourful Moroccan
food – there's not an enormous choice
on the menu, but what they do offer
is all good, and the place is run with a
rare combination of efficiency and good
humour. Alcohol served. Recommended.

€€ Mega Loft
49 Rue el Yeman, T0613-981987.
Daily for lunch and dinner.
Is it a homeware store? Is it a café? Is it a
live music venue? Is it an art gallery? Mega
Loft is a little slice of hipster-style cool
near the ramparts with a boutique selling
funky pan-African style homewares

and a restaurant with a menu that veers between European café-bites and more traditional Moroccan with dishes such as aubergine millefeuille, seafood pastilla, and crabmeat and mushroom gratin. Service is swift and friendly, and, during the evening, musicians usually play on the small stage.

€€ Umia
22 Rue de la Skala, T0524-783395.
Daily for lunch and dinner.
This chic, contemporary restaurant on the alley that faces the skala walls is one of Essaouira's top tickets for modern European cuisine. The small menu concentrates on doing just a few dishes right, with crowd-pleaser choices such as beef wellington and duck confit, all served with top-notch presentation. A great choice if you're looking for a stylish yet casual place to eat. Alcohol served.

€ Chez Mermoz
Pl Chrib Atay, off Rue Laalouj.
Daily for lunch and dinner.
This ramshackle little place, with its covered patio decorated in Essaouira's blue-and-white aesthetic, serves up typical tagines for seriously good-value prices. 3-course set menus are a budget dining bonanza, starting from 65dh with no scrimping on portion size. There are no frills here, and the seemingly never-ending soundtrack of Bryan Adams hit songs can be wearying, but the family who run the show are lovely, and you can't beat the value.

€ Des Arcades
3 Av Istiklil.
This intimate place is a friendly choice with a small but exceptionally well-executed menu (mains 60-90dh) of tagines, couscous and a couple of daily

Tip…
For cheap eating Essaouira style head to the open-air fish stalls between Place Moulay Hassan and the port. Here you'll find freshly caught fish, straight from the harbour. Grilled up and served with a tomato salad, it is the town's best budget eating option. Prices are fixed by weight and displayed on boards, but make sure you are clear on what you have and haven't ordered. Another cheap fish option is the little fish barbecue place in Souk el Hout, the fish market on the left as you come from the port area down Avenue Istikal.

dishes that lean towards fish. This is a great place to come and try fish couscous or sardine kefta tagine, while the home-made pickled sardines, served as a complementary starter, are delicious. The upstairs mezzanine has a very low ceiling, so taller diners will definitely want to dine downstairs. Recommended.

€ Ferdaouss
27 Rue Abdesslam Lebadi, T0524-473655.
Mon-Sat lunch and dinner.
For a taste of Moroccan home cooking with a few twists head to this family-run place in an upstairs apartment. Tagines are the star menu item here, but there are lots of little innovations instead of the usual chicken-preserved lemon and lamb-prune options. Here you can have a goat tagine with the slow-cooked meat falling off the bone or tuck into a chicken tagine flavoured with fennel. There's also a decent selection of pastillas and couscous. Alcohol isn't served but you can bring your own wine.

€ La Triskalla
58 Rue Touahen, T0524-476371.
Daily 1100-1900.

A very laid-back café replete with low lighting, candles, a cat, plenty of low seating and a fine soundtrack of blast-from-the-past favourites. The menu is strong on fresh seafood and vegetarian options and usually there is a daily set menu (50-60dh) which provides a good-value, filling and tasty meal. It's a friendly and fun place, with welcoming staff, and you can easily lose an hour or so here just sitting down and drinking one of their extensive and imaginative selection of juices.

€ Yoo
204 Place Marché aux Grains.
Daily 0900-2000.

A café devoted completely to vegan and vegetarian options and slow-pressed juices. This little place, with seating on a bustling square, is the No 1 place to come to get your lunchtime healthy salad fix. As well as salads, there are chickpea burgers and some tasty sandwich options, all vegetarian friendly. For sweet treats on hot days they offer a large selection of frozen yoghurts and an imaginative menu of juices.

Cafés and patisseries

Pâtisserie Chez Driss
Pl Moulay Hassan.

Those with a sweet-tooth should make a beeline for Chez Driss as soon as they get into town. This is Essaouira's most famous patisserie, in business since 1928 and still churning out a dazzling selection of petits fours, cakes, tarts, millefeuille and all sorts of other sugary treats daily. Eat inside where the walls are covered from top to bottom with old photos and vintage posters, or outside on the little terrace, or takeaway some delicacies to munch on the beach. Highly recommended.

Café des Arts
56 Av Istikal, T0612-134742.

Upstairs on the main street, this place has a young vibe, with occasional live music, lots of local art adorning the walls and a menu of Moroccan food. Right in the thick of things, a stop in here for coffee makes a good break between shopping forays.

La Cantina
66 Rue Boutouil, T0524-474515.

Feeling the need for a proper scone or a slice of cake? This English-run bistro-café will sort you out. Tucked in a small square near the beginning of the *mellah*, La Cantina has a rather eclectic menu that veers between home-made scones, breads and cakes to burgers and chilli con carne. It's a good place to sit down and have lunch or a pot of tea while exploring the back streets of the medina.

Bars

Essaouira is not really the place for wild nightlife, although it livens up nicely during the annual Gnaoua Music Festival. The main alcohol off-licence is near Bab Doukkala: turn right out of the gate and the off-licence is on your left after about 100 m, identifiable by small black-and-white tiles and beer posters.

Café Taros
2 Rue de la Skala, T0524-476407,
www.taroscafé.com. Mon-Sat till late.

Up the street on your left as you face Pl Moulay Hassan with the port behind you, this café-bar's rooftop terrace is the top destination in town for sundowners. There's a large selection of cocktails as well as beer and wine and decent food as well.

Festivals

May Essaouira Festival of Gnaoua and World Music (www.festival-gnaoua.net). This 4-day feast of music is Essaouira's big annual event and one of Morocco's most important festivals. A huge program of outdoor concerts at Pl Moulay Hassan and other more intimate venues throughout the city are held in a celebration both of traditional Gnaoua music and other musicians from throughout Africa and beyond.

Shopping

The main thoroughfares of the southern and central medina are all packed with little boutiques, from traditional jewellery stores and carpet merchants to funky modern designer shops and scrap-metal sculpture studios. More expensively, you can pick up paintings by the local school of naïve and pointillist artists.

What to buy Traditionally, the town's women wore all-enveloping cotton/wool mix wraps, in cream or brown, just the thing to keep out the ocean mists. Islamic fashions change and, happily, the weavers have found a new market providing fabrics for *maisons d'hôtes* and their denizens. New colours and stripes have been added, and you can get a nice bedspread for 300dh. Raffia-work sandals and handbags are also a major local industry. Essaouira is also the place to pick up the much-prized argan oil used for cosmetic and food products. Objects made in fragrant, honey-brown thuya wood, native to the area, are for sale everywhere in Essaouira's shopping streets, from small boxes inlaid with lemon-wood to chunky, rounded sculptures. However, the demand for thuya products has resulted in mass deforestation, so buying thuya should be avoided.

Argan d'Or, *5 Rue Ibn Rochd*. Sells a range of argan beauty products and soaps from pure oils to moisturisers and hand creams.

Co-operative Tiguemine Argan, *15 km Rte de Marrakech, T0524-784970*. Get to understand the argan oil production process by visiting this women's co-operative 15 km out of town on the road to Marrakech. There are several other co-ops along this stretch of highway.

KifKif, *Place Marché aux Grains*. Locally made accessories, jewellery and knick-knacks with a contemporary edge.

Raffia Craft, *82 Rue d'Agadir*. This is a tiny outlet shop for the raffia products of local designer, Miro. His shoes are in demand in Europe and much copied by other local artisans.

What to do

Art and crafts

Yellow Workshop, *Derb Mohammed Diouri (next to the Institut Français), T0660-313605, www.yellowworkshop.com*. Run by a Moroccan/Dutch husband and wife team who are artists, musicians and avid birdwatchers, the Yellow Workshop is where you can learn collage and folk-style pattern art (100dh per hour) as well as lessons on traditional Gnaoua music guembri instruments. Also some walking activities (see below).

Cycling

Bikes, including mountain bikes, can be hired from various places in the medina from about €15 for the day.

Hammams

There are several public hammams in the medina, with prices from around 10dh for entry (extra for glove, soap and scrub-down). Try the oldest called **Hammam Pabst** on Rue Annasr in the *mellah*. Orson Welles once used it as a location in the filming of *Othello*. The following are private hammams:

Hammam Lalla Mira, *14 Rue d'Algerie, T0524-475046, www.lallamira.net. Daily women 1030-1900, men 1930-2300.* Super-friendly service from the female staff here makes this a great option for newbies to the hammam experience. A hammam and black soap scrub costs 130dh, and massage add-ons, with argan oil, start from 140dh for 30 mins.

Mounia Hammam, *17 Rue Oum Errabia.* Prices from 50dh for a basic hammam and up to 250dh for the full works.

Horse riding

Ranch de Diabat, *Diabat, Quartier des Dunes, T0670-576841, www.ranch dediabat.com.* This ranch just 3 km south of Essaouira organizes everything from 1-hr horse rides along the beach (150dh) to multi-day treks along the Atlantic coast. The 3-hr horse ride (350dh) and 1 day ride (600dh) are great ways to see some of the surrounding countryside. Also organizes camel treks.

Surfing and windsurfing

As a whole, Essaouira is a more popular destination for windsurfing rather than surfing. Winter is the better surfing season, while Apr-Oct the wind is up and the windsurfers are out in force. If you don't have your own gear, you can rent it, but do check it carefully before taking it out. For both sports, the southern end of Essaouira beach (at Cap Sim) and the beach at Sidi Kaouki (to the south of Essaouira) are the best spots.

Explora Morocco, *T0611-475188, www. exploramorocco.com.* Right on the main

beach this place has English-speaking staff and good value surf, windsurfing, kitesurfing and SUP lessons (in English, French, Spanish and Arabic) from €30 for 2 hrs. They also do gear rental for all the aforementioned watersports and have a shop in the medina on Av Istiklal.

Walking

Ecotourism and Randonnées, *T0615-762131, www.essaouira-randonnees.com.* Half-day and full-day walks through argan forests, out to local waterfalls, beside the ocean and to local villages. English guide available.

Yellow Workshop, *Derb Mohammed Diouri (next to the Institut Français), T0660-313605, www.yellowworkshop. com.* Arranges day walks along the beach to Sidi Kaouki and birdwatching in the Essaouira area.

Transport

Air

Small and quiet **Aéroport de Mogador**, T0524-476709, is 13 km south of town. **RAM** has daily flights to/from **Casablanca** and regular flights to/from **Paris**.

Bus

Buses from Essaouira can get very full in summer and during the **Gnaoua Festival**. Check your departure times the day before you travel and try to reserve. The best onward option is the service run by **Supratours** (office on the square just outside Bab Marrakech, T0524-475317, www.oncf.ma) to **Marrakech** at 0645, 0900, 1145, 1515, 1700 and 1800 (70dh), which connects with onward trains to **Casablanca–Rabat**. Buy your ticket at the kiosk on the square at least a day before, as this is a popular bus. **CTM** (T0524-784764, www.ctm.ma) and private line bus services operate from the terminal near Bab Doukkala, with connections to **Casablanca** (6 or 9 hrs, depending on route), **Safi**, **Marrakech** (3 hrs) and **Agadir** (3½ hrs). You can also buy CTM bus tickets from the office on Rue de Caire near Bab Sabaa. Lots of touts compete for custom – go inside the terminus and look at ticket windows where departure times are clearly posted. **CTM** has departures daily to Casablanca (145dh) via Safi and El Jadida at 1015, 1145, 1345, and 1715. Buses south to **Agadir** depart at 1430, 1830 and 2000 (70dh), and there are daily buses to **Marrakech** at 1230 and 1700 (75dh).

Taxi

Grands taxis operate from a parking lot beside the bus terminal. (You may have to wait a while for the vehicle to fill up if you are going to Marrakech.) There are frequent departures for **Diabat**, **Ghazoua**, **Smimou** and other places in the region. *Grands taxis* heading to Marrakech also hang around the square opposite the Supratours ticket office. *Petits taxis* are numerous and charge 5dh for a short ride in town. There are numerous calèches to be caught from the cab rank outside Bab Doukkala.

High Atlas

Morocco's magnificent spine

Snow-topped for half the year, the High Atlas rise out of the plains south of Marrakech. They stretch across Morocco west to east, from the Atlantic coast just north of Agadir until they fade into the desert on the Algerian border.

In winter, there is scope for skiing; in spring, apple and cherry blossom fills the valleys with colour, and, in summer, the cooler air is a draw for escapees from the oppressive cities. All year round there are good walking opportunities, from short strolls to waterfalls, to serious treks to mountain summits.

Within easy day-trip distance south of Marrakech, the Toubkal National Park, named after Jbel Toubkal, the highest peak in North Africa, has long been a draw for tourists. The region also has other popular destinations, including pretty Setti Fatma in the Ourika Valley and the ski resort of Oukaïmeden. The striking, restored mosque of Tin Mal is high on the spectacular road to the Tizi-n-Test pass. Southeast of Marrakech is another dramatic pass, the Tizi-n-Tichka, and the village of Telouet, with its brooding Glaoui fortress.

Less visited is the Eastern High Atlas, where you can discover the Cascades d'Ouzoud, Morocco's highest waterfalls, and the beautiful high valley of the Aït Bougmez.

Best for
Landscapes ▪ Rural life ▪ Trekking ▪ Views

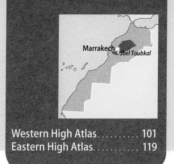

Western High Atlas......... 101
Eastern High Atlas.......... 119

Footprint
picks

★ **Tizi-n-Test**, page 106

This hair-raising high mountain pass is one of Morocco's best drives.

★ **Toubkal National Park**, page 108

Morocco's premier trekking destination gives intrepid visitors the chance to bag North Africa's highest peak.

★ **Oukaïmeden**, page 114

During winter, snow-bunnies grab their skis and head for Oukaïmeden's slopes.

★ **Telouet**, page 117

Base yourself in Telouet to explore the hiking and biking potential of the sleepy Ounila Valley.

★ **Cascades d'Ouzoud**, page 120

Thundering waterfalls provide a cooling respite when summer turns the heat-dial up.

★ **Aït Bougmez Valley**, page 121

Enjoy gorgeous day walks between traditional mudbrick villages.

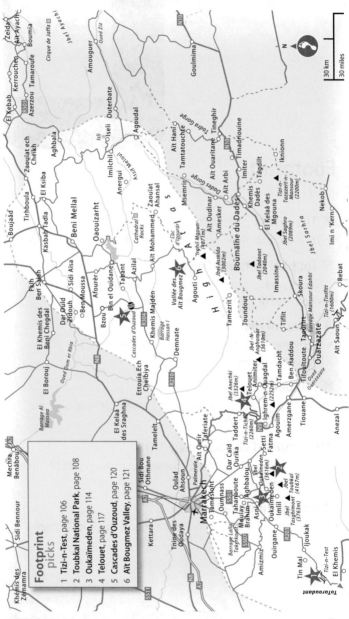

Footprint picks

1 Tizi-n-Test, page 106
2 Toubkal National Park, page 108
3 Oukaïmeden, page 114
4 Telouet, page 117
5 Cascades d'Ouzoud, page 120
6 Aït Bougmez Valley, page 121

Western
High Atlas

Three main roads lead south out of Marrakech into the Western High Atlas. The westernmost heads over the Tizi-n-Test pass towards Taroudant; the next runs up the Ourika Valley to Setti Fatma, Oukaïmeden and the Toubkal National Park, while the easternmost road heads over the Tizi-n-Tichka pass towards Ouarzazate.

On the R203 to the Tizi-n-Test, Asni is an important market town and Ouirgane is a strung-out holiday destination in the hills. Further south, the road curves and rises through the spectacular mountain valley to the awe-inspiring 12th-century mosque of Tin Mal, one of Morocco's most significant buildings, now partially restored. Back at Asni, a road branches south to Imlil and the Toubkal National Park, centring on North Africa's highest mountain. The landscapes are spectacular, and there are some great walking routes.

The route up the Ourika Valley from Marrakech is, initially at least, a gentler one, splitting to terminate at either the village of Setti Fatma, with its waterfalls and riverside restaurants, or the ski resort of Oukaïmeden.

Most dizzying of all, the N9 climbs to cross through the Tizi-n-Tichka pass at 2260 m. Just east of here is the precipitous kasbah of Telouet.

The main S501 road south out of Marrakech (straight over at the junction near the Hivernage) forks a few kilometres after the Club Royal Equestre, left on the S501 to Asni and right on the S507 to Amizmiz in the foothills of the Atlas. Both routes are worth exploring. Beyond Asni, the R203 from Marrakech to Taroudant is one of the most spectacular routes in Morocco, winding its way up and then down through the High Atlas mountains, above beautiful valleys and past isolated villages, eventually reaching the Tizi-n-Test pass.

Lalla Takerkoust

The S507 passes through a number of small settlements, including Tamesloht and Lalla Takerkoust. Often referred to as 'the lake', Lalla Takerkoust, 40 km southwest of Marrakech, is actually a reservoir, formed by a hydroelectric dam (the Barrage Lalla Takerkoust) that provides Marrakech with a good portion of its

> **Tip...**
> Note that in a wet year, clay from the hillside may crumble onto the upper sections of the Amizmiz to Ouirgane road.

Essential High Atlas

Getting around

Trips out from Marrakech to Imlil and a few other popular destinations in the Western High Atlas are fairly easy using buses or *grands taxis*. In order to travel between villages, however, your own transport is invaluable. Once in the mountains, many of the roads are narrow and winding, with vertiginous drops.

Best mountain rooms

Kasbah Africa, for making families welcome, page 108
Kasbah du Toubkal, for supporting the local community, page 111
Riad Dar Ouassaggou, for great value, page 112
Kasbah Bab Ourika, for luxury with a conscience, page 114
Dar Itrane, for star-gazing, page 123

Time required

A day trip into the mountains from Marrakech will give you small taste of the scenery. A week will give you a good overview of the region, but if you want to do some multi-day trekking as well, then 10 days to two weeks is a better option.

When to go

The Atlas are best explored in summer or autumn, as the winter weather can make getting around difficult. At altitude, snow lingers through the spring, though blossom in the high valleys can also make this a rewarding time to visit. The peaks of the Atlas mountains remain snow-capped until at least early summer, and temperatures at night can often drop below zero. Make sure to pack a fleece and thermals.

ON THE ROAD
Un stylo, un bonbon, un dirham

All over the country the sight of children begging is not uncommon. But in the mountains it seems particularly prevalent, encouraged perhaps by generations of well-meaning trekkers who have happily handed out coins, pens or sweets. The mechanical chorus of "Un stylo, un bonbon, un dirham" will follow you, echoing through many remote mountain valleys.

In the past, the advice has been to bring a supply of pens or, in some worrying cases, medicine to hand out. Today, however, community leaders will almost certainly advise against giving the local children anything at all. Even giving out pens encourages systematic begging, damaging the education system and family structures. It also detrimentally affects the way foreign visitors are seen: as resources to be mined, rather than human beings to interact with.

Talk to the local children, teach them something, but save your pen money and donate it instead to organizations like the Global Diversity Foundation (www.globaldiversity.org.uk) or the High Atlas Foundation (www.highatlasfoundation.org).

electricity. It is a popular swimming and picnicking place for Marrakchis wanting to escape the oppressive heat of the city. Lapping at the red-earth foothills of the High Atlas, and with the high peaks as a backdrop, it's a strikingly beautiful place, and there are a couple of places to stay and eat too. If you have a car, the route across the Kik plateau from here to Asni has extraordinary panoramic views across the high pastures to the Atlas peaks beyond.

Amizmiz and around
Amizmiz, 55 km southwest of Marrakech at the end of the S507, is a growing rural centre interesting as the starting point for some pleasant hikes and for its Tuesday souk. Turning off right just after the 'administrative zone', you can wind up into the foothills to the *maison forestière*. Parking in the shade, there is some gentle walking along a track above the Assif Anougal, with views down over the villages. From Amizmiz, there is also a road eastwards to **Ouirgane**, via the Tizi-n-Ouzla (1090 m), where you can get a view of the Assif Amassine valley, with the Toubkal Massif as backdrop. There then follows a winding descent to the junction with the S501, where you can go right for Ouirgane or left for Asni and Marrakech.

Moulay Brahim
With small hotels and eateries, Moulay Brahim is a popular weekend stop for Marrakchis, off the S501. The village gets particularly busy from June to September, with people coming to visit the shrine of Moulay Brahim, visible with its green-tiled pyramid roof in the middle of the village. Stalls sell various scraggy pelts, chameleons and incense as offerings to Moulay Brahim, who is said

to be particularly good at solving women's fertility problems. There is a festive atmosphere, with whole families coming to rent small semi-furnished apartments.

Asni

After the rather nerve-racking drive through the gorges of Moulay Brahim, the approach to Asni, with its poplar and willow trees, comes as something of a relief. If you arrive on Saturday, you will be able to see the souk in a big dusty enclosure on your left as you come from Marrakech, with its accompanying chaos of *grands taxis*, mules and minibuses. The village is scattered in clusters in the valley and makes a good place for a quick break en route to Ouirgane, Tin Mal or Taroudant, if you can deal with the attentions of the trinket sellers. There are good walking routes along the Plateau du Kik to the west of Asni, north to Moulay Brahim and southwest to Ouirgane.

> **Tip...**
> A popular driving route goes from Asni up onto the Plateau du Kik and then through the villages around Tiferouine, before heading some 8 km northwest cross-country to the settlement of Lalla Takerkoust and its reservoir.

Ouirgane

Ouirgane is another pleasant place to pause on the R203, about one hour's drive (61 km) from Marrakech. The settlement's houses are scattered on the valley sides, and there are pleasant, easy rambles through the countryside. It's a favoured summer weekend destination for Marrakchis seeking cooler climates during summer. Ouirgane can be reached by bus from Marrakech (the Taroudant service) or by *grand taxi* from Asni. Hotels in Ouirgane (see page 107) have good food and offer the opportunity to explore the valley.

Tin Mal

Tin Mal is about 2 hrs' steady drive from Marrakech, 8 km past the village of Ijoukak. You can also take a Taroudant bus or a grand taxi *as far as Ijoujak, where there are several basic cafés with rooms. Tizi-n-Test is another 37 km further southwest.*

A small settlement high in the Atlas mountains, Tin Mal was once the holy city of the Almohad Dynasty (see box, opposite). It offers a rare opportunity for non-Muslims to see the interior of a major Moroccan mosque, with examples of 12th-century Almohad decor intact amidst the ruins. The Koutoubia at Marrakech (the Almohad capital from 1147) was modelled on Tin Mal. Completed in 1154, under Abd el Mu'min, the **Tin Mal Mosque** has a simple exterior. The *mihrab* (prayer niche) is built into the minaret. To the left, as one stands before the mihrab with the imam's entrance to the right, is a space for the *minbar*, the preacher's chair, which would have been pulled out for sermons. The decoration is simple: there are several cupolas with restored areas of stalactite plasterwork and there are examples of the *darj w ktaf* and palmette motifs but little inscription. The technique of applying plaster to brick is a forerunner of later and larger Almohad decorative

BACKGROUND
Tin Mal

In 1122, Ibn Toumert, after much roaming in search of wisdom, returned to Morocco. He created too much trouble in Marrakech, with his criticisms of the effete Almoravids, but the mountain tribes swore to support him and fight the Almoravids in the name of the doctrines he had taught them. He was proclaimed Mahdi, the 'rightly guided one', and in 1125 he established his capital at Tin Mal, a fairly anonymous hamlet strategically situated in the heartland of his tribal supporters. The rough-and-ready village was replaced with a walled town that was soon to become the spiritual centre of an empire. The first mosque was a simple affair; the building you see today, a low square structure, was the work of Ibn Toumert's successor, Abd el Mu'min – a student whom the future Mahdi had met in Bejaïa.

Tin Mal was the first *ribat*, as the austere Almohad fortresses were called, and was subject to a puritan discipline. The Mahdi himself was a sober, chaste person and an enemy of luxurious living. All his efforts went into persuading his followers of the truths of Islam as he conceived them. Prayers were led by the Mahdi himself and all had to attend. Public whippings and the threat of execution kept those lacking in religious fervour in line. As well as prayer leader, the Mahdi was judge and jury, hearing and trying cases himself according to Muslim law, which had barely begun to penetrate the mountain regions.

After Ibn Toumert's death, his simple tomb became the focal point for a mausoleum for the Almohad sovereigns. Standing in the quiet mosque, today mostly open to the sky, looking down the carefully restored perspectives of the arcades, it is difficult to imagine what a hive of religious enthusiasm this place must have been.

When the Almohad empire acquired Marrakech, a fine capital well located on the plain, Tin Mal remained its spiritual heart and a sort of reliable rear base. It was to Tin Mal that Abd el Mu'min sent the treasures of Ibn Tachfin the Almoravid. Even after the Merinid destruction of 1275-1276, the tombs of of Ibn Toumert and his successors inspired deep respect.

Eventually, the Almohads were to collapse in internecine struggles. The final act came in the 1270s, when the last Almohads took refuge in Tin Mal. However, the governor of Marrakech, El Mohallim, pursued them into their mountain fastness, then besieged and took the seemingly impenetrable town. The Almohad caliph and his followers were taken prisoner and executed, and the great Almohad sovereigns Abu Yaqoub and Abu Youssef were pulled from their tombs and decapitated. The Almohads, one time conquerors of the whole of the Maghreb and much of Spain, were destroyed in their very capital, barely 150 years after they had swept away the Almoravids.

schemes. In the 1990s, around US$750,000 was put forward for restoration of the ruins. Work now seems to have ground to a halt, though the building is doubly impressive in its semi-ruined, semi-open-to-the-sky way. The mosque guardian will let you in and enthusiastically point out features such as the original doors piled up in a corner. He'll also ask for a donation when you leave.

★ Tizi-n-Test

The R203 road leaves Marrakech heading south through various small villages on its way to Tin Mal and the Tizi-n-Test pass before dropping down again to Taroudant, gateway to the south, beyond. The pass offers breathtaking views across the Souss valley to the Anti-Atlas mountains. Driving has been possible since the road, a traditional trading route, was formally opened in 1928, following the work of French engineers. Some of its sections are downright scary, but it is a recommended experience, particularly when tied in with visits to Asni, Ouirgane and Tin Mal. Signs on the exit to Marrakech will indicate if the pass is open. The R203 joins the N10 from Taroudant to Ouarzazate (see page 232).

Tip...
There are buses between Marrakech and Taroudant, but check that they are going via Tizi-n-Test.

Where to stay

Lalla Takerkoust

€€ Le Flouka
Barrage Lalla Takerkoust, T0664-492660, www.leflouka.com.

Right on the water's edge of Lalla Takerkoust, this tranquil resort is a great place to come up for air after the medina madness of Marrakech. Rooms (double €60, €80 for a lake view) are simply decorated with lamps, local art, rugs and bare beams, and some have open fires for colder months. There are 2 pools (1 heated) but you can just as easily head out into the lake. Swimming in the lake with the Atlas Mountains in front of you is hard to beat. The restaurant serves a decent selection of international and Moroccan mains and there's a bar here too for when you want to put your feet up with a beer. It's a friendly, laid-back spot with helpful staff who can organize day-hikes and other excursions in the surrounding countryside.

Asni

€€€€ Kasbah Tamadot
T0208-600 0430 (UK), T877-577 8777 (USA) or T0524-368200 (Morocco), www.kasbahtamadot.com.

Expect all the bells and whistles on display here at one of Morocco's best-known hotels. Purchased by Sir Richard Branson and run by Virgin (despite calling itself 'Sir Richard Branson's Moroccan Retreat', don't expect to bump into him here), Kasbah Tamadot comes complete with all the creature comforts you can imagine. Rooms (the cheapest of the 27 rooms and suites is more than €700 per night) are an indulgent and colourful mix of antiques, art and swish contemporary styling while there are indoor and outdoor pools, gardens, spa and a hammam, as well as some spectacular views. The restaurant uses ingredients from the hotel's own gardens and the library comes equipped with a telescope. Despite all its good points, however, it has a little less character than its major rival for Morocco's ultimate luxury treat (see page 114); **Kasbah Bab Ourika**.

€€€ Kasbah Angour
T0524-484121, www.kasbahangour.com.

If you're feeling a bit frazzled after Marrakech medina exploits, head here for a spot of decompression. This charming countryside retreat, run by English owner Paul Foulsham, sits high on a hill just off the main road, a few kilometres before Asni. Spacious, light-filled rooms (from €145) have exposed wood-beam ceilings and stone-cladding features and are decorated with an eye for calming simplicity, and all have dinky patios for admiring the mountain scenery. There's a pool and sprawling gardens for when you simply want to sit back and do nothing, plus excursions and hikes are very easily arranged here.

Ouirgane

€€€-€€ Chez Momo II
Coming from Marrakech, 800 m past La Roseraie, up a road on the left, T0524-485704, www.aubergemomo.com.

After the original Chez Momo was engulfed in the water of Ouirgane's new reservoir in 2008, Chez Momo II was born, further up the hill, using local craftsmen and materials. Rooms (doubles from 560dh) are homely and elegant, with wrought-iron beds, bare wooden beams and lamps in alcoves. There's a beautiful horseshoe arch pool at the front of the house, with trees, roses and sun loungers around, and trekking, on foot or on mule, is easily organized.

€€ Kasbah Africa

T0524-484312, www.kasbahafrica.com.
Well-run and good value, Kasbah Africa is a particularly good spot for travelling families with generously sized family suites (€112) which could fit up to 5, and a policy that kids under 15 stay free of charge if they're sharing the parents' room. Stone-clad rooms (single/double €74/80) are big, light and airy, and lead out to private patios. Their interiors are just the ticket for chic countryside-retreat living with Berber rugs on stone floors, soft-toned textiles on beds and cushions and lovely extras such as a telescope for star gazing and binoculars for wildlife spotting enthusiasts. There's a large pool, restaurant and sweeping views over the hills plus plenty of excursions and hiking trips are able to be organized. Wi-Fi and breakfast included.

Restaurants

Hardly anywhere in the Atlas operates just as a restaurant, though there are standalone cafés. There are a number of stalls and cafés in the centre of Asni cooking harira soup and tagines. This is the last major place to stock up on basic supplies for a visit to the Toubkal region. The hotels in Ourigane all have restaurants attached.

For a lunch stop close to the Tizi-n-Test, the cheap **Restaurant La Belle Vue** (boumzough.free.fr) is about 1 km after the pass on the Taroudant side. Cheap rooms are also available, but have a sleeping bag ready – it gets cold at 2100 m altitude.

Transport

Asni

There are regular buses, and much quicker *grands taxis* between Asni and Bab Rob in **Marrakech** (2½ hrs). Regular minibuses trundle between **Imlil** and Asni throughout the day. To get off the beaten track, though, you'll need your own wheels.

★ Imlil and the Toubkal National Park See also map, page 110.

Morocco's top trekking destination

Northern Africa's highest peak is one that many mountaineers like to tick off their list, but the national park that surrounds it has plenty of other good walks, from afternoon strolls to serious treks.

Imlil and around

Imlil, 17 km south-southeast from Asni, is the most important village of the Aït Mizane Valley. At 1790 m, it is the start of the walks in this area. As well as the ascent of Jbel Toubkal, walking options include the **Aremd circuit**, a refreshing hike through remote villages with breathtaking views; the walk to the **Lac d'Ifni**, or the walk to **Setti Fatma** in the Ourika Valley.

Imlil is also a good place to hang out for a while. In the centre of the village is the car park/taxi area, with the stone-built **Club Alpin Français (CAF)** hut at the corner of the road and a guides hut. There are small cafés and shops, a good baker, a highly recommended spice shop and tour operators who can help you get biking and hiking in the local area. Mules are 'parked' to the south of the village. There is a utilitarian concrete route indicator on the right, should you be unsure of your direction. When you arrive, you may be besieged by lots of underemployed blokes, keen to help you in some way or other. The town's **hammam** has been built with money from the kasbah (see Where to stay) and is recommended.

Jbel Toubkal ascent

The ascent of Jbel Toubkal, the highest mountain in North Africa at 4167 m, takes two days. Most trekkers spend the night at the **Club Alpin Français Toubkal Refuge** ⓘ *www.refedu toubkal.com*, a simple dormitory place with a basic restaurant providing meals at 3106 m. In winter this is a difficult trek and full equipment is essential. A specialist hiking book, such as Richard Knight's *Trekking in the Moroccan Atlas* (Hindhead: Trailblazer, 2008), is also recommended. If you're organizing the trek independently, mules and guides can be easily hired in Imlil upon arrival.

Day 1 Imlil is the end of the surfaced road, but it is possible to reach Aremd (also spelt Aroumd) by car up the rough track. Alternatively, it takes about 45 minutes to walk. **Café Lac d'Ifni** makes a good stop here. Sidi Chamharouchouch is reached in another 2½ hours, going steadily uphill. It is important to bear right after the *marabout* to find the initially very steep, but later steady, slope up to the **Toubkal Refuge** (3207 m). Allow 4½ hours from Imlil. The **Toubkal Refuge**, with dormitory space for 90 people (€11 per night May-October/€13 per night November-April)

Essential Toubkal National Park

When to go

The best time for walking is during blossom time in spring, after the main snows. Mules cannot negotiate passes until March/April. Summers are likely to be too hot for many walkers, and visibility in the heat haze is poor. November to February is too cold, and there is too much snow for walking, although frozen ground is often more comfortable than walking on the ever-moving scree. Deep snow and ice present few problems to those with ropes, ice axes, crampons and experience. Without these, stay away in winter.

Information and advice

It's wise to purchase specialist hiking books (such as Alan Palmer's *Moroccan Atlas*) and maps. Mules and guides can be hired in Imlil. Having a local Tachelhit-speaking guide is essential on treks as conditions can be dangerous. The number of people who have to drop out of treks in the area due to stomach problems is high, so try to check on hygiene when deciding who to use. If you're planning a trek in advance, **Mountain Voyage** (www.mountain-voyage.com, see page 79), based in Marrakech and **Mountain Travel Morocco** (www.mountain-travel-morocco.com, see page 113), based in Imlil, are both recommended.

is often crowded. On the plus side, the warden sells bottled water and soft drinks, and the food whipped up in the restaurant is good value (breakfast €3/dinner €7). Campers using the level site below the hut can also use the facilities.

Day 2 The usual approach for walkers is via the South Cwm, a long day's walking and scrambling if you want to go up and back. The route is clearer on the map than

Jbel Toubkal region

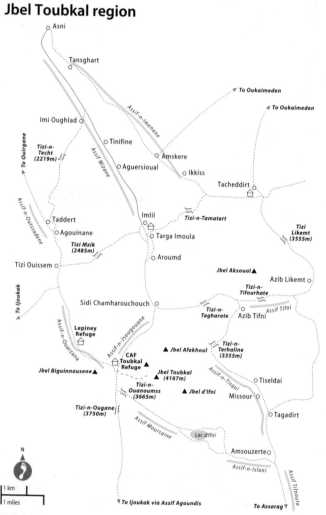

it is on the ground. First observe the route from the rear of the Toubkal Refuge: the large boulders on the skyline are a point to aim for. Leave the refuge and go down to the river. Cross over and go up the other side to the main path to the foot of the first of the many screes. Take the scree path up to the boulders, which can be reached in just over an hour. From here, there is a choice: the long scree slope to the north of the summit, or the shorter, steeper slope to the south of the summit ridge. Either way, allow 3½ hours.

The summit is not in itself attractive but the stone shelters make fairly comfortable overnight camping for a good view of sunrise. Views to the Jbels Saghro and Siroua are excellent – if there is no haze –but, as the summit here (4167 m) is a plateau, other views are limited. Be prepared for low temperatures at this altitude and for the bitter winds that blow three out of four days in the spring and autumn. The descent is quicker; allow 2-2½ hours.

Toubkal Circuit

In nine days, a good walking circuit can give you a feel for life in the High Atlas and take in Jbel Toubkal too. The map (see opposite) shows the main places to overnight. Day one would take you from Imi Oughlad or Aguersioual to Amskere. Day two is the first full day and involves a five-hour trek to Tacheddirt. A long day three runs via the Tizi Likemt (3555 m) to Azib Likemt. From here, you have another long day four over to Amsouzerte, where there is a difficult-to-find gîte or Landrover taxis back down to Marrakech. From Amsouzerte, on day five you head for Lac Ifni (2290 m). Day six takes you to the Toubkal Refuge (3106 m), via the Tizi-n-Ouanoumss (3665 m), and a long day severn is the climb up Jbel Toubkal and back down to the refuge. Day eight takes you down to Aroumd/Aremd (1920 m), via the shrine of Sidi Chamharouch (2340 m) and its tiny collection of stalls. At the time of the pilgrimage, this shrine is very busy. From Aremd, on day nine, you head back to Imi Oughlad (1300 m). This last long stretching of the legs takes you via the Tizi Oussem (1850 m) and the small settlements of Agouinane and Taddert before the last pass, Tizi-n-Techt (2219 m), taking you down to Imi Oughlad.

Listings Imlil and the Toubkal National Park

Where to stay

The Bureau des Guides, in the centre of Imlil, can provide information on accommodation in homes: locals, who are used to walkers, are generally keen to provide a floor or mattresses to sleep on.

€€€€-€€€ Kasbah du Toubkal
Imlil, T0524-485611, www. kasbahdutoubkal.com.

Imlil's restored kasbah, once HQ of the local caïd, is perched spectacularly above the village and played the role of a Tibetan fortress in director Martin Scorsese's film Kundun. It is run by the UK-based travel agent **Discover Ltd** in conjunction with locals and helps fund the Imlil village association (which, among many worthy community projects has provided ambulance service to the district, a community hammam, and school-building in remote villages) by adding a 5% levy onto the final bill. It's a great example of how sustainability and community involvement can work in tourism. Rooms (doubles from €160) are minimalist in style with *tataoui* ceilings, warm wood furnishings, coffee and tea facilities, and million-dollar views from the windows. The restaurant cooks up hearty Moroccan fare and the welcome and friendliness of staff provides a home-from-home atmosphere. They can organize a variety of treks in the local area including Jbel Toubkal ascents. Breakfast and use of onsite hammam included.

€€€ Riad Dar Imlil
Imlil, T0524-484917, www.darimlil.com.
Run by Kasbah du Toubkal, this is a relaxing place for a mountain escape. Riad Dar Imlil (rooms from €130) has comfortable standard rooms and more deluxe options with plenty of swish-factor and private balconies, all with local textiles providing colourful accents. The restaurant with its roaring open-fire in cold months, and the large communal terraces provide plenty of places to sit back and admire the views. Wi-Fi and breakfast included.

€ Chez Les Berberes
T0667-910760, www.chezlesberberes.com.
Rustic, homely bliss awaits hikers here; friendly Khadija and Hassan go out of their way to make sure guests feel at home. Simple, snug rooms (doubles €15) come with *tataoui* ceilings, small bathrooms and plenty of authentic Berber flavour. Some have little balconies overlooking the countryside. Khadija rustles up tasty Moroccan dishes for dinner and hiking is easily arranged. Wi-Fi and breakfast included.

€ Dar Atlas
T0676-738329, www.daratlasimlil.com.
Cosy Dar Atlas is a solid budget traveller bet with small, simple rooms (doubles €10) with plenty of blankets on beds, all sharing clean bathrooms with hot showers. The owners here are trekking guides and can offer plenty of advice to independent hikers, as well as arranging full trekking trips. Meals here get top marks for being great value home-cooking. Breakfast and Wi-Fi included.

€ Riad Dar Ouassaggou
T0667-491352, www.guesthouse ouassaggou.com.
A warm welcome, on-the-ball management and a whole swag-load of peace and quiet: Riad Ouassaggou is a great deal. 6 good-sized rooms (doubles €35-45, family suite €60) come with colourful carpets, stained-glass accents and homely touches, such as a kettle and free fruit, while the terrace has sweeping views across the mountains beyond. Staff can sort out all your trekking needs, and the kitchen rustles up crowd-pleasing wholesome and tasty Moroccan meals guaranteed to fill you up after a day's walking. Wi-Fi and breakfast included. Recommended.

Restaurants

Most places offer half board, so the standalone eating options are limited, but Café Soleil and Atlas Tichka offer good lunches. Les Amis does good chicken brochettes and genuine coffee; Café Grand Atlas is more of a local place, where you can eat tagine on the roof terrace. Café Imlil was the first café in town and hasn't changed much since. For something smarter, and for the best views, go to the Kasbah de Toubkal.

What to do

Trekking and tours

Brahim Ait Zin, *T0667-690903, trekadventurer@yahoo.fr*. Brahim knows the mountains very well and speaks good English.

Bureau des Guides, *in the centre of Imlil, T0524-485626, bureau.guides@yahoo.fr. Daily 0700-1900 summer, 0800-1700 winter.* You can find a guide here.

Mountain Travel Morocco, *T0524-485784, www.mountain-travel-morocco. com.* Highly regarded local company with a whole host of treks to choose from: easy walks to winter ascents of Jbel Toubkal, as well as day trips and other activities. Guides here are all multi-lingual and the standard of service is excellent.

Trek Morocco, *T0667-491352, www. trekmorocco.com.* Multi-lingual Ahssine (a co-founder of Mountain Travel Morocco) can sort out all your hiking needs, whether it's a 2-day Jbel Toubkal ascent or longer circuits traversing the countryside between Berber villages. All activities can be fully customized. Also can arrange horse riding and 4WD tours.

Transport

Regular minibuses trundle between Imlil and **Asni** throughout the day.

Setti Fatma and the Ourika Valley

a taste of the Atlas within easy reach of Marrakech

The Ourika Valley is a beautiful area of steep-sided gorges and green terraced fields along the winding Oued Ourika, about 45 minutes' drive south of Marrakech. The accessibility of the valley makes it a very popular excursion for Marrakchis and tourists, so, in summer, sections of the valley get crowded with campers and day trippers happy to be away from the hot, dusty air of the plain. Just before Aghbalou, the P2017 splits, with a right-hand road taking you up to the ski resort of Oukaïmeden. The trail-head village of Setti Fatma is reached by going straight ahead. The valley has occasional problems with flash floods, the worst of which, in 1995, destroyed most of Setti Fatma and killed many people.

Setti Fatma

The road ends at Setti Fatma, famous for its waterfalls and 100-year-old walnut trees. There is a small weekly market, a Bureau des Guides de Montagne and a good choice of basic accommodation and riverside tagine outlets. Setti Fatma must once have been idyllic. There is breeze-block housing among the older stone homes now, but the pretty setting and the sound of the river make it picturesque nonetheless. For walkers, Setti Fatma makes a good base for exploring the **Jbel Yagour**, a plateau region famed for its numerous prehistoric rock carvings. Most visitors, though, are on an day trip from Marrakech and stop only to walk up to the waterfalls and then have lunch. Be aware that due to the popularity of these trips, the waterfalls trail can be extremely crowded so don't expect a peaceful ramble.

The cascades are a 30-minute hike up from Setti Fatma, following a well-defined path up behind the first café. There is some minor scrambling over rocks on the way to the first waterfall where there is a good café; plenty of local guides along the route are available to assist the less able. From here the crowds thin out slightly as some groups descend back the way they came, while others continue on the more difficult trail up to the second waterfall. Another alternative is to take an indirect trail along a ridge path with great views over the surrounding hills, back to Setti Fatma.

★ Oukaïmeden

Oukaïmeden, 'the meeting place of the four winds', is Morocco's premier ski resort and Africa's highest. It's some 2600 m up in the Atlas and a 1½-hour drive from Marrakech, making it a good day trip. The highest lift goes up to 3250 m, and there are various runs down, though these are not always very well marked. There are also four drag lifts and a tobogganing area. The resort is open for skiing from December to March but in summer it's less busy and many places are closed.

The quality of skiing is variable, and good skiable snow cannot be counted on, though there's new investment and talk of snow cannons. The hot African sun means that the snow melts easily, only to freeze again at night, leaving slopes icy. Instructors work in the resort, and there are ski shops that rent equipment and donkeys to carry your gear between lifts.

In summer, visitors can walk, climb and even paraglide here. Look out for the prehistoric carvings on the rocky outcrop below the dam wall. There are further carvings on the flat rocks among the new chalets.

> **Tip...**
> In a 4WD, you can take winding roads and tracks from Oukaïmeden to Tahanaoute and Asni on the R203 Tizi-n-Test road. Although the villages and landscapes are beautiful, the villages are very poor, and children are eager for pens, notebooks and dirhams (see box, page 103). When you pull away from a village, watch out that no children are clinging onto the back of your vehicle for a thrilling (if dangerous) dare.

Listings Setti Fatma and the Ourika Valley

Where to stay

Setti Fatma and around

€€€€-€€€ **Kasbah Bab Ourika**
45 mins from Marrakech off the Setti Fatma road near Dar-Caid-Ouriki, T0524-389797, T0661-252328 (mob), www.kasbahbabourika.com.
Unfussily elegant, this kasbah is in an extraordinary location, perched on its own personal hill overlooking the mouth of the Ourika valley, with craggy red mountain rock to one side and Marrakech in the distance behind. Decorated with insouciant style, rooms (from €160) are huge and have an antique, rustic atmosphere that makes guests feel immediately at home, but they are also luxurious, with thick rugs, generous bathrooms, open fires and wonderfully comfortable beds. The pool is spectacular, with views to the

mountains, and the food is exquisite, with dishes such as chilled carrot soup and lemongrass beef brochette with stir-fried spinach and turmeric expertly mixing flavours. The environmental and social policies of the place are ground-breaking with solar-powered heating, grey water recycled for the gardens, and plenty of involvement in the local community. Guests here are truly in for a treat whether they're here mainly to chill out or to head out on guided hikes through the extraordinarily fertile valley and Berber villages below. The track that needs to be navigated to reach the front door is an eroded adventure, but one that increases the dramatic sense of arrival, and of being in a very special place indeed. Wi-Fi and breakfast included.

€ Hotel Asgaour
Setti Fatma, T0524-485294, T0666-416419 (mob).
A friendly place with basic, clean rooms and small but comfy beds, most with shared bathroom. Some rooms have views over the valley, and the hotel has a pretty terrace across the other side of the river, as well as some chairs and tables outside. Rooms with private shower and toilet are more expensive.

€ La Perle d'Ourika
T0661 56 72 39, www.laperledourika.com.
A couple of mins downstream from Setti Fatma, the Perle has a degree of decoration rare in Setti Fatma, with furry sequined bed covers, painted floors and plenty of vibrant colour. Its eccentric style is all part of its laid-back charm. Rooms (€20-45) all share sparkling-clean bathrooms with plenty of piping hot water and the roof terrace has great views up and down the lush valley. The restaurant here is great too and serves alcohol.

Oukaïmeden
Oukaïmeden has a small but adequate supply of accommodation. In practice, the resort only gets crowded on snowy weekends, and many visitors from Marrakech prefer to return home to sleep. Out of season, rooms in mountain chalets can be found.

€€ Chez Juju
T0524 319005, www.hotelchezjuju.com. Open all year (except Ramadan).
8 clean and well looked-after wood-clad rooms (from 550dh in summer/900dh during ski season), with a decent restaurant serving French as well as Moroccan cuisine, and a bar with cold beer. It's rather pricey for the amenities but it still represents one of the resort's better sleeps. Half-board is obligatory. Wi-Fi (in communal areas only) included.

€ CAF Refuge of the Club Alpin Français
T0524-319036. Open all year.
Dorm bunks cost 210dh during winter and 120dh in summer (with kids at half-price) and the refuge rents out skiing equipment and mountain bikes plus there's a bar and games room. Breakfast is 30dh extra. Wi-Fi included.

Restaurants

Setti Fatma and Ourika Valley
There are a huge number of places in Setti Fatma that set up to catch the lunchtime trade from Marrakech, offering excellent tagines freshly cooked at stalls near the river. There's little to choose between them; wander around and pick one that smells good, or go for a table with a view.

What to do

Rafting
Splash Rafting Morocco,
*Albakech House, Av Mohammed VI,
Agdal, Marrakech, T0618-964252,
moroccoadventuretours.com.* The best
rafting conditions are in the winter and
spring. Class III and IV whitewater rafting
takes place in the Ourika Valley Dec-May.
Splash also run 3-day rafting trips to the
Ahansal river Mar-Jun. 650dh per person
for a half-day rafting trip.

Trekking
About 10 km from Setti Fatma is
Tachedirt, where there is a Refuge
du CAF. To set up a trek, contact the
Bureau des Guides de Montagne,
on your right before the hotels. The
place is run by the very capable and
English-speaking Abderrahim ('Abdou')
Mandili, T0524-291308, T0668-562340
(mob), abdoumandili@yahoo.fr.

Transport

Setti Fatma and Ourika Valley
Buses and *grands taxis* go to Bab Rob in
Marrakech. If driving from Marrakech,
head straight for the mountains on
the P2017, starting from the fountain
roundabout just outside the city walls at
Bab Jedid, next to the Hotel Mamounia.
Once in Ourika, a possible means of
transport is a lift in the open-top vans
and lorries which speed along the valley.

Oukaïmeden
From Marrakech, Oukaïmeden is reached
via the P2017 Ourika Valley road, but
forking right 43 km out of Marrakech,
instead of left for Setti Fatma. Another
option is to walk the piste which leaves
the road south of Oukaïmeden, and
cross the hills to the R203 to south of
Asni. There are daily buses to/from
Marrakech in winter.

Towards Ouarzazate via Tizi-n-Tichka
gateway to the hiking and 4WD potential of the Ounila Valley

Completed in 1936 by the Foreign Legion, the N9 road from Marrakech to
Ouarzazate gives stunning views. It runs through the full range of Atlas
environments, from the Haouz plains, through the verdant foothills of the Oued
Zat, to the barren peaks of the Atlas and the arid regions to the south.

Drivers need maximum concentration on this route, especially in the twilight,
when you will meet donkeys and flocks of sheep wandering across the road,
guided by small children. Clapped-out local buses break down, and there are
some especially narrow and vertiginous stretches leading up to the pass after
Taddert. A further hazard is the group of eager fossil sellers who hang out at
viewpoints and café stops. Note that in winter there can be heavy cloud, snow
storms and icy rain, reducing visibility and making the road extremely slippery.
In such conditions, the road is not much fun at night. If snow blocks the pass,
the snow barriers will be down. The total distance from Marrakech to Ouarzazate
is nearly 200 km. Good places to stop include upper Taddert (busy, 86 km from
Marrakech), the Tizi-n-Tichka pass (2260 m) itself, which is almost exactly halfway,
or Ighrem-n-Ouagdal, about 118 km from Marrakech, where there is an old *agadir*

(granary) to visit. Driving in good conditions, Marrakech to Taddert will take you two hours, while Taddert to Ouarzazate is about another two.

★ Telouet

A narrow road, in need of resurfacing and with nasty tyre-splitting edges, takes you from the Tizi-n-Tichka road to Telouet (turn left 106 km from Marrakech). An eagle's nest of a place, high in the mountains, Telouet's spectacular kasbah is legendary. Today, it is on the tourist circuit – as the hordes of 4WD vehicles testify. Within living memory, however, its name was synonymous with the repressive rule of the Glaoui brothers, sons of an Ethiopian slave woman, who, by force of arms and character, managed to achieve absolute dominance over much of southern Morocco in the early 20th century. Gavin Maxwell's *Lords of the Atlas* describes this turbulent, bloodthirsty period, as first the Moroccan monarchy and then the French skirmished with the southern tribal leaders to achieve dominance. The denouement, which came shortly after Moroccan Independence in 1956, was fatal to Glaoui power.

Abandoned before completion, the Kasbah of Telouet as it survives today is mainly the result of 20th-century building schemes by the last great Glaoui lord, T'hami. Generally, as you arrive, someone will emerge to show you around. The great reception rooms, with their cedar ceilings and crumbling stucco, a transposition of 19th-century Moroccan urban taste to the mountains, are worth a visit.

Telouet to Ouarzazate via Aït Ben Haddou

Telouet is also the starting point for an 80-km route down to Ouarzazate. The route was resurfaced in 2015 and should be manageable for most vehicles, but it's wise to check before you set off. Leaving Telouet, ask for the road to Animiter, the first main village. After a few kilometres, a turn-off to the left, near the foot of Jbel Amassine, takes you up to the source of the Glaoui family's wealth, a salt mine. **Animiter**, some 9 km east from Telouet, was famous in the early days of Moroccan tourism because its kasbah, painted by Jacques Majorelle, was featured on an early poster. It should be possible to camp near the Oued Mellah. The next village, **Timsal**, lies a few kilometres to the south. After Timsal, follow the road along the Adrar Taqqat, used when they put in electricity lines. You reach **Tioughassine**, and the road follows the Ounila Valley. At **Assaka**, look out for abandoned granaries under the cliffs. The track then continues up onto a sort of plateau above the canyon, before dropping down to the valley bottom; **Tizgui-n-Barda** is the next main village, about 29 km from Telouet. Continue along the Assif Ounila to reach **Tamdacht**, meeting point of the *oueds* Marghene and Ounila. The next stop, **Aït Ben Haddou** (see page 241), is 50 km from Telouet.

This route was used in earlier times by caravans coming up from the south to pick up salt from the Telouet mine. Today, it is increasingly popular as an excursion and for hikes in the area. The first 10 km of piste from Animiter is very potholed, but the remainder of the road is in very good shape.

Where to stay

Telouet

€ Dar Aissa
T0670-222247, www.daraissa
telouet.onlc.eu.
As humble as they come, this family-run guesthouse has super-clean basic rooms (130dh) with colourful walls and painted shutters, all with shared bath. The genuine welcome and home cooking are what makes this place really shine; Aissa and his wife will go out of their way to make you feel at home as well as helping you organize walks and activities around Telouet. A place for those who prefer atmosphere over amenities. Breakfast included.

€ Kasbah Tigmi N' Oufella
T0661-235953, www.nuances
morocaines.com.
To get off the beaten track, this restored kasbah, overlooking the sleepy Ounilla Valley village of Angeulz, may be just the ticket. There are just 3 rooms (from €38), decorated in an artful and clever style that fuses minimalism with hanging lamps, Berber motifs and a scattering of antiques. Home-cooked meals can be rustled up for lunch and dinner, and there are plenty of walking opportunities in the local area. No English is spoken. Wi-Fi and breakfast included.

Transport

Telouet

For those without their own vehicle, the trip to Telouet is problematic; the easiest option is to hire a *grand taxi* privately.

390651472
33637
Transited:
April 30,
2019 11:30
AM

Eastern
High Atlas

A mountainous hinterland, the Atlas to the east of Marrakech are wild and little-visited. Towns are strung out along the N8 from Marrakech to Fès, on the northern edge of the mountains. South of this main route, the town of Azilal gives access both to the beautiful, remote high valley of the Aït Bougmez, an area increasingly popular with walkers, and to the Cascades d'Ouzoud, Morocco's highest waterfall. The High Atlas region south of Azilal has a very traditional character. The people here are Tamazight-speaking; their limited contact with mainstream Morocco and their lack of formal education make the culture more conservative. The architecture of the villages is largely unspoiled by concrete, and semi-nomadic lifestyles continue in the high pastures.

There is more vegetation here than further west, with conifer forests surviving at high altitude. The Eastern High Atlas have wide flat valleys, deep ravines and small rivers that can easily turn to flood after a rainstorm. The highest mountain in the region is the long, rounded ridge of the Ighil Mgoun, which reaches 4071 m.

Further east is an area of shoulder mountains, snow-capped into early summer, bare plateaux and occasional deep canyons. Imilchil is the most obvious 'capital' of this area, and trekking expeditions set off from here.

Demnate and Imi-n-Ifri

On the R210 about 1½ hours from Marrakech, Demnate was once a picturesque, whitewashed place. These days the crumbling kasbah, once set in the middle of olive groves, is surrounded by unsightly new buildings, but the old *mellah*, where Demnate's long-gone Jewish population lived, still survives in the centre of town. Sunday is market day. Nearby, **Imi-n-Ifri** ('the door to the cave') is a natural rock bridge formed by the partial collapse of a huge cavern. If you don't have transport, there are transit vans that do the short run up from Demnate. Opposite the closed auberge of the same name, a path winds down to the stream bed and a small reservoir where it's possible to swim and camp. Concrete steps, partly gone, take you up to the **grotto**. Above your head, there are great sheets of calcareous rock and, above that, cawing choughs circle overhead. You may also see the odd Barbary squirrel.

★ Cascades d'Ouzoud

These waterfalls, about 2½ hours' drive from Marrakech, make a long day trip but are, nevertheless, hugely popular with Marrakchis, so prepare to share them with plenty of others. The left turn off the R304, about 20 km before Azilal, is signposted. From here, the road heads north through beautiful landscapes where the dominant colours are red earth, dark green thuya and the paler grey green of the olive trees. Arriving in the village of Ouzoud, various local men will emerge waving sticks to help you park. For the cascades, head past the riad and through a few market gardens crossed by rivulets of fast-flowing water to reach the edge of the precipice (watch out for slippery clay). Look out for the traditional water-driven barley mills. Tumbling 110 m down cliffs, the Cascades d'Ouzoud are an impressive sight from above as well as below, especially when they turn red with clay after heavy rains. The word *ouzoud* comes from the Amazigh *izide*, meaning delicious. There are various paths that will take you down to cafés on the rocks below the falls. Unfortunately, the area around the waterfalls and pools can be litter-strewn, which spoils the experience somewhat. It's possible to swim at the base of the falls, but be careful diving in, as the pool is shallow.

Azilal

Sprawling west from a small core of kasbah and French military buildings, terracotta-red Azilal is less of a one-mule place than it used to be. In fact, it is turning into a major town with stilt-legged buildings, a big *gare routière*, a Thursday souk and a **tourist office** ① *Av Hassan II, T0523-488334.* There is little here of sightseeing interest, but it makes for a great coffee or lunch break on the road to Aït Bougmez, a slow 2¾-hour drive southeast over the mountains from here.

★ Vallée des Aït Bougmez

The Aït Bougmez is one of the most beautiful valleys of the High Atlas. Since the main access roads into the valley were tarmacked a few years ago, the area has really opened up to tourism, but the valley's stone- and *pisé*-built villages above the fields still retain their sleepy charm. The Aït Bougmez is an excellent walking destination; **Tabant**, 1850 m up, is the main centre. Good day walks include heading up to the dinosaur footsteps near Rbat and an easy 8-km walk along the road from Tabant to Agouti with a side trip up to the granary of Sidi Moussa on a mound-like hill along the way. There is another, slightly longer route from Tabant to Ifrane along the old main piste to Aït M'hamed. Longer, more serious treks, head to the **Massif du Mgoun**, Morocco's second-highest mountain massif.

Massif du Mgoun

Although not the most aesthetically pleasing of mountains (it has no soaring peaks), Mgoun has the largest area of land above 3000 m in the whole country. The best time to climb the mountain is probably summer or early autumn, for snow remains late into the year in these highlands. The easiest route to the summit is from the south side of the mountain, which means starting from El Kelaâ des Mgouna in the Dadès Valley (see page 230). The alternative is to head south from the Aït Bougmez to approach the massif from the east. Taking this option, head

> **Tip...**
> A popular multi-day trekking option is to trek from the Aït Bougmez south to Bou Thrarar and Kelaât Mgouna. This is a six-day trip, with possible camps at Tarzout, Aguerzka and Bou Thrarar. It will be up to your guide to break up the route as they see fit. Apart from the high pass on the first day, there are no huge climbs, and you will be walking for between six and seven hours a day.

south from **Tabant** over the Tizi-n-Aït Imi (2905 m) to **Tighremt-n-Aït Ahmed**, and then west to the foot of the mountain along the course of the Assif Oulliliymt on a second day's trek. The ascent to the highest point (4071 m) is not actually difficult. Note that the summit is sacred: in a survival of pre-Islamic tradition, the mountain's help (protection) may be asked, even today.

Listings Azilal and the Aït Bougmez Valley

Where to stay

Demnate and Imi-n-Ifri

€€€ Kasbah Timdaf
T0523-507178, www.kasbah-timdaf.com.
A beautiful eco-lodge surrounded by flower-filled gardens and, beyond, its own farm. Traditionally designed Berber

rooms (single/double €65/80) are spacious and airy; some have open fires for the chillier months. There's a good restaurant here with food cooked by the French owners, and cooking lessons are available on request. Breakfast and Wi-Fi included.

€€ Tiziout Maison d'Hôtes
Just north of Demnate, T0658-346148,
www.tizouit.ma.
This rather charming eco-lodge,
constructed from stone by the owners,
is an elegant but low-key kind of place
with 8 large, bright rooms (from €60),
all with their own private terraces for
relaxing after a day out walking. There's
a pool for splashing about in, great
views and a tranquil garden filled with
fruit trees. It's all thoroughly relaxing
and a good de-stress stop for a few
days. Good day-hikes exploring the local
countryside can be easily arranged.
Breakfast and Wi-Fi included.

Cascades d'Ouzoud

€€ Riad Cascades d'Ouzoud
T0523-459658, www.ouzoud.com.
The best accommodation option
near the waterfalls, this riad has a
combination of whitewashed and
rough *pisé*-style walls, 9 tastefully
decorated rooms (single/double
570/710dh in high season) and a
spacious roof terrace with panoramic
views over the surrounding countryside.
There are wooden beamed ceilings
and some rooms have open fireplaces.
The riad also does decent food, both
Moroccan and French, using good
local ingredients, served either on the
terrace or in a traditional Moroccan
lounge downstairs. Breakfast and
Wi-Fi included.

€ Hotel Chellal d'Ouzoud
T0523-429180, hotelchellal.weebly.com.
A cheerful, colourful place with simple,
clean en suite rooms (single/double
250/400dh in high season) and a nice
communal terrace. It's got a great central
location, just a super-quick amble from
both the waterfall trail and the main
square. Management are friendly and
the food here is tasty. Breakfast included.

Camping

Camping Zebra
T0666-328576, www.campingzebra.com.
This friendly, well-organized campsite
is run by Dutch couple Paul and
Renata with aplomb. There are both
good pitches for tents (camping plus
1/2 people 65/85dh) and a range of
rooms available from 200-400dh. It's
well placed about 1 km from town and
the waterfall trail.

Aït Bougmez
Most of the accommodation options
(mainly simple auberges and gîtes)
are strung out in the villages that
surround Tabant.

€€ **Dar Aya Atlas Moroccan Guesthouse**
Plateau de Tamezrit, Agouti,
T0524-308777, T0661-242034 (mob),
www.morrocan-guesthouse.com.
Traditional earth-built guesthouse in a beautiful setting. 7 en suite rooms decorated in colourful Berber style. Activities available.

€€ **Dar Itrane**
Imelghas, T0523-459312,
www.origins-lodge.com.
One of the best options in the area is this fine, French-managed eco-lodge in a traditional red adobe building 1800 m up near the village of Imeghas. There are 17 en suite rooms (double €80 in high season with half-board), a roof terrace, a hammam and a chef who prepares local Berber dishes. The name means 'House of the Stars', because the remoteness of the place make it perfect for viewing the night sky. Excellent hiking and other excursions can be arranged here. Full-board options also available.

€€ **Touda Ecolodge**
Zawyat Oulmzi.
You wouldn't necessarily know it from the simple, traditional exterior, but this is a cut above most of most of the accommodation in Aït Bougmez. The 7 good-sized, simple rooms (doubles €70 with half-board in high season) have *tadelakt* bathrooms with solar-powered hot water, and the communal spaces are accented by traditional Berber textiles and art. More importantly, the eco-lodge is an excellent base for organizing hikes in the valley, with plenty of information available for both independent walks and guided trips.

€ **La Casbah M-Goun**
Douar Agerd-n-ozro, T0662-778148,
www.hotel-ait-bouguemez.com.
There's a spectacular setting for this traditional place, surrounded by great views of the green fields and stark mountains. Simple rooms (single/ double €40/50) are generously kitted out with rugs and blankets, and there's a dorm (€13 per person) as well. There's a relaxed, unhurried air to the entire place which adds to the appeal if you're looking for some down-time after a few weeks of hard travelling. Breakfast included.

Transport

Azil al
Azilal is the transport hub for the regions of the High Atlas to the south, with a *gare routière* next to the main mosque. There are buses for **Marrakech**, **Casablanca**, **Denmate** and **Beni Mellal**. *Grands taxis* also run to Marrakech and Denmate as well as to Tabant. **Tabant** is also served by local minivans.

Beni Mellal and around
Morocco's little-visited provincial heartland

One of the major centres of central Morocco, Beni Mellal, on the northern edge of the Atlas, has an important souk on Tuesday. Like a number of other towns in the region, it has grown thanks largely to money sent back by migrant workers in Italy. The main monuments include the Kasbah Bel Kush; built in the 17th century by Moulay Ismaïl, it was heavily restored in the 19th century. It's also worth a walk up to the small, quiet gardens below the ruined Kasbah de Ras el Aïn, perched precariously on the cliffside. There is a nice café in the gardens.

Kasbah Tadla

Kasbah Tadla, to the northeast of Beni Mellal, was founded in 1687 by the Alaouite Sultan Moulay Ismaïl, no doubt because it is ideally located more or less halfway between Marrakech and Meknès and Fès, the imperial cities of the Saïss Plain. The crumbling terracotta ramparts sit above the shrivelled course of the river and, except for a new social-housing project on the flood plain, the view has changed little since the town's foundation. On the platea behind the kasbah is a rather derelict public garden, splendid in a quiet sort of way when the purple jacarandas are in flower. Within the kasbah there is a lot of self-built housing, put up by soldiers and their families, and two mosques, one with the distinctive Almohad lozenge design on the minaret. The other has poles protruding from the minaret. Someone might offer to show you into the courtyard building behind the mosque, which was the sultan's residence. Today, it is inhabited by poor residents. The 10-arched bridge over the Oum er Rbia is a fine example of 17th-century engineering. Kasbah Tadla's souk day is Monday.

The best view of the kasbah is from the austere **monument** to four resistance heroes on a low rise on the south side of the town. Four parallel concrete blades rise skywards, but there is no inscription to recall who the heroes were.

Boujaâd

Just a 25-minute drive from Kasbah Tadla, Boujaâd is something of a surprise. In recent memory, it was an important town – essentially a pilgrimage centre for the semi-nomadic inhabitants of the Tadla plain. The historic medina has an almost Mediterranean character, with its arcaded square, whitewashed walls, shrines, paved streets and white houses. Much of the town was destroyed in 1785. The key buildings are the **Zaouïa of Sidi Othman** and the **Mosque of Sidi Mohammed Bu'abid ech Cherki**, the town's founder.

Listings Beni Mellal and around

Tourist information

Beni Mellal

The **tourist office** is on the 1st floor of Immeuble Chichaoui (Av Hassan II, T0523-483981).

Where to stay and eat

Beni Mellal

There's a selection of tired budget hotels dotted around the centre; they're nothing fancy but adequate for a night. There are *laiteries* and cafés along the main street.

€€-€ Les Belles Terrasses
26 Rue Essaouira, T0523-481010, www.lesbelleserrasses.com.
By far the nicest place to stay in town, this guesthouse opened in 2011 and has small but elegantly decorated rooms (from 550dh) with lots of crisp white bed

linen, satellite TV and a/c, and extensive gardens with a pool for cooling dips after a hot drive. It's all very comfortable and rather lovely. Service here is on-the-ball, tasty meals are dished up in the restaurant (the best place in town), and management can help with information on arranging activities in the local area. Breakfast and Wi-Fi included. Recommended.

Transport

Beni Mellal
CTM buses leave from the terminal in the town centre, with services for Casablanca (80dh, 4 hrs) at 0900, 1330, 1500 and 1800; 2 services to **Marrakech** (55dh, 3½ hrs) at 1030 and 1250; and 2 to **Fès**

(90dh, 5 hrs) at 0500 and 1045. From the bus station it is a 10-min walk up Av des FAR to the centre. *Grands taxis* head to Azilal from where you can pick up transport to the **Aït Bougmez**.

Kasbah Tadla
CTM buses for **Fès**, **Marrakech** and **Beni Mellal** run via Kasbah Tadla. There are private line buses from **Agence SLAC** for **Beni Mellal**, **Boujaâd** and **Oued Zem** and **Rabat**. These can all be caught from the bus station on the Boujaâd side of town (the far side from the old kasbah).

Boujaâd
Regular buses and *grands taxis* leave for **Kasbah Tadla** and **Oued Zem** from the main square.

Imilchil to Zaouïat Ahansal

traverse Morocco's rural heart

One of the best treks in the Atlas takes you from the plateaux of the Imilchil region, via the Assif Melloul and the beautiful village of Anergui, to the former pilgrimage centre of Zaouïat Ahansal. This route, part of the Grande traversée de l'Atlas marocain, takes you through remote regions where knowledge of French (and even Arabic) will be rudimentary to say the least.

Take a local, preferably Tabant-trained, guide, who will be aware of potentially snowy conditions (if travelling outside summer) and water levels in the Assif Melloul. At Zaouïat Ahansal, you link in with further routes southwest to the Aït Bougmez and north to the Cathedral rocks of Tilouguite and Ouaouizaght. A number of European-based travel companies organize treks in this region. Accommodation is in mountain gîtes, camping out or in locals' homes.

Imilchil and around
Southeast of Kasbah Tadla, though marginally more easily approached from Rich to the east, Imilchil centres on a beautiful crumbling kasbah topped with storks' nests. The town has a dusty, sloping main street, where you will find a couple of small cafés, the local dispensary and the entrance to the souk. Behind the kasbah, the **Hotel Izlane** can provide a little information on possible treks and may be able to put you in contact with suitable guides. Quiet for most of the year, the town comes alive for the annual marriage fair in September

ON THE ROAD

Moussem des fiançailles

Imilchil is famous for its annual summer wedding festival, **Moussem des fiançailles**, which was traditionally an occasion for people from all over the region to get together. The *moussem* site is in fact at Allamghou, signed left off the route from Rish, some 20 km before Imilchil and near the junction with the mountain piste up from Tinghir.

The *moussem* is based on a local legend in which two young people fell in love and wanted to marry. Their parents said no, and the couple cried so much that two lakes formed: Tislit for the girl and Isli for the bridegroom. After such a display of grief, the parents could hardly continue to refuse and so allowed each of their offspring to marry their heart's desire.

The *moussem* was traditionally a great occasion for locals to turn out in all their finery and celebrate marriages with plenty of dancing and singing. In recent years, the occasion has suffered from the incursion of tourists – and from drought. Weddings are expensive, once-in-a-lifetime occasions, and, in Morocco's rural communities, the capital available for such an event is severely limited in drought years. Nevertheless, in villages along the route to Imilchil, there is evidence of some new prosperity, with lots of new building, for the most part using traditional packed-earth construction methods.

(see box, above), when young people descend from the mountains to find themselves a partner.

Lac Tislit, 5 km to the north, is an exquisite if austere oval of blue ringed by reeds, set in an arid hollow of the mountains. The natural splendour is a little marred by a bogus kasbah, complete with plastic ceremonial tents. Beyond Lac Tislit, the larger **Lac Isli** can be reached on an easy day's 4WD trip.

Imilchil to Anergui

With the green of its fruit and walnut trees, **Anergui** is one of the most beautiful sites in the Eastern High Atlas. There are various trek routes from Imilchil to Anergui, a distance of roughly 57 km. The route you take will depend

> **Tip...**
> Note that some routes require better-than-average fitness.

on weather and river conditions. If the **Assif Melloul** is not in flood, your guide will take you along the riverside route, which involves some wading and goes via the small settlements of Oudeddi and Oulghazi. After Oulghazi, you may head up out of the river valley to Anergui via the **Tizi-n-Echfart** pass. The other option is a more perilous route high above the river and is used when the river is in full flood in spring. Bear in mind that at this time of year, ice in shady areas can make high paths perilous for both people and mules.

Anergui to Zaouïat Ahansal

The Assif Melloul continues west from Anergui to meet the **Assif ou Ahansal** near the so-called **Cathedral Rocks** near Tamga. The basic track from Anergui to Zaouïat Ahansal can just about be traversed with 4WD, a distance of around 92 km. For walkers, this route is especially fine, taking you through the beautiful gorges of the Assif Melloul. Zaouïat Ahansal (altitude 1600 m) became important due to its location at a meeting of the ways between the Eastern and Central High Atlas. There are a couple of gîtes here.

Azilal to Zaouïat Ahansal

Coming from the west, the easiest way to reach Zaouïat Ahansal is from Azilal, a distance of 83 km. There are fairly frequent 4WD taxis doing this run. About 17 km out of Azilal there is a junction where you either go right for the Aït Bougmez or left for Aït M'hamed (Saturday souk), 3 km further on. From here, it's another 63 km to Zaouïat Ahansal. The tarmac runs out a few kilometres out of Aït M'hamed, but the track continues east-southeast towards the **Tizi-n-Tsalli-n-Imenain** (2763 m, 50 km from Azilal), in the shelter of the great Jbel Azourki (3677 m). A further col, the **Tizi-n-Ilissi** (2600 m), is 16 km further on, below Jbel Arroudane (3359 m). Then comes the drop down to Zaouïat Ahansal.

Listings Imilchil to Zaouïat Ahansal

Where to stay

Imilchil

Options are few but adequate. Apart from the places listed below, there is some simple dorm accommodation in the village.

€ Complexe Collier d'Ambre
T0672-992679, www.imilchil-collier-dambre.com.
This little place is the best place in town to overnight. Rooms (single/double 170/280dh) are en suite, and communal areas are bedecked with plenty of rustic, Berber flavour. The food rustled up in the kitchen here is seriously good Moroccan home cooking, and the staff go out of their way to make it a welcoming place to stay. Breakfast included.

€ Hotel Izlane
Clearly visible behind the kasbah, T0523-442806, www.hotelizlane.com.
Run by mountain guide Khalla Boudrik, the hotel has a large restaurant and 15 basic rooms which all share bathrooms. There is good information here on local trekking options.

Transport

A long way from anywhere else, Imilchil is hard to reach unless you have your own transport, though you might find a *grand taxi* heading that way from the north on the market days of Fri and Sun. There are fairly frequent 4WD taxis between Azilal and Zaouïat Ahansal.

Fès, Meknès & Middle Atlas

monriments, medinas and mountains

The area of central Morocco around the Jbel Zerhoun and the Saïss Plain was important even in ancient times: a strategic, fertile region on the trade routes leading from eastern North Africa to the Atlantic coast.

The imperial cities of Fès and Meknès may be only one hour apart and both home to medinas filled with spooling alleyways but they're as different as chalk and cheese in ambience. Combining both in one trip allows you to get a sense of the power which was once concentrated in this region. Both also make good bases for day trips into the surrounding countryside. Volubilis is the main highlight. One of the finest Roman sites in North Africa, its ruins still manage to evoke life in a prosperous frontier town in the second and third centuries AD. Nearby, Moulay Idriss, the father of the Moroccan state, is honoured in the pilgrimage town of the same name, where houses cascade down the twin hills in a rainbow of pastel hues.

Further out, the rolling countryside of the Middle Atlas is great road-tripping terrain. Here you'll find cedar woodland, lakes, cork-oak forests, magnificent mountains and one of North Africa's most startlingly huge cave systems.

Best for
Architecture ▪ History ▪ Landscapes ▪ Road trips

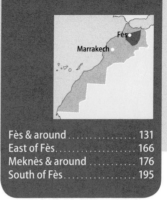

Fès & around 131
East of Fès. 166
Meknès & around 176
South of Fès. 195

Footprint
picks

★ Fès el Bali, page 134

Test your navigation skills while *medersa*-viewing and souk-strolling amid the medieval maze of Fès's old city.

★ Sefrou medina, page 163

Escape the full-on bustle of Fès and experience a medina without the crowds.

★ Gouffre du Friouato, page 171

Spelunking hats at the ready to head underground into one of North Africa's deepest caverns.

★ Meknès, page 178

Discover Morocco's most laid-back imperial city and cast your eyes upwards at the imposing Bab Mansour.

★ Moulay Idriss, page 190

Time seems to have stood still within the narrow, pastel-washed alleys of Morocco's pilgrimage centre.

★ Volubilis, page 191

Mosaic mastery amid the villa ruins at Morocco's most important Roman site.

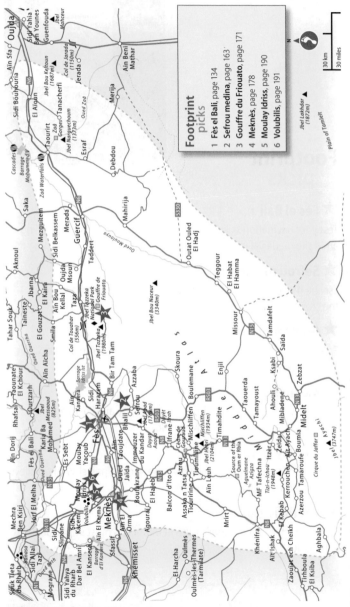

Footprint picks

1 Fès el Bali, page 134
2 Sefrou medina, page 163
3 Gouffre du Friouato, page 171
4 Meknès, page 178
5 Moulay Idriss, page 190
6 Volubilis, page 191

Fès
& around

Fès (also spelt Fez in English) is spectacular, but not as immediately attractive as Marrakech. Unlike the capital of the south, a crossroads for caravans and peoples, Fès is more secretive, its traditional ways tucked behind cliff-like walls in the old city. Fès is fascinating – perhaps as close to the Middle Ages as you can get in a couple of hours by air from Europe – but it is not an easy city to get to know. Hidden within the jigsaw puzzle streets of its medina are magnificent *medersas*, craftsmen at work in the souks, half-crumbling monuments and fountains at every turn. At first glance, many visitors find it baffling, and the crush of the crowds on the narrow medina streets can make sightseeing hard work. Let's get one thing straight: you're going to get lost. The squiggling alleyways will defeat even the best navigator at least once. However, Fès repays the time and effort spent on it. Slow down your travel itinerary a little, spend a couple of days here, and you'll gradually ease into the city's rhythms. When the medina muddle gets too much, you can always strike out into the countryside. Both Sefrou and Bhalil make easy side trips, while sites further afield, such as Meknès, Volubilis and Moulay Idriss, are close enough to visit on day trips.

Essential Fès and around

Finding your feet

Fès lies at a crossroads in Morocco and is an excellent base from which to plan and carry out the next stage of your travels. **Royal Air Maroc (RAM)** has a daily flight from Casablanca to **Aéroport de Fès-Saïss**, 15 km south of the centre and accessible by bus or grand taxi. The main bus station is outside the Fès el Bali walls near Bab Mahrouk, while the **CTM** station is at Place de l'Atlas on Avenue Mohammed V in the southern section of the ville nouvelle, about 4 km from Fès el Bali. If you've arrived from the east using the **Supratours** bus service, you'll be dropped at their office beside the railway station, at the end of Boulevard Chenguit in the ville nouvelle. To get to the centre of the ville nouvelle from here, head down this road and slightly to the left into Avenue de la Liberté; this joins Avenue Hassan II at Place de Florence. A petit taxi from the train station to Bab Boujeloud (for the medina) should cost 10dh (20dh after 2000). Be aware that taxi drivers at the train station are known to try and overcharge. See also Transport, page 161.

Getting around

Fès is a spread out sort of place, and distances are greater than they may at first seem, so be prepared for some considerable hikes from one place to another or pay for a few petit taxi rides. If you are based in a ville nouvelle hotel, it's roughly a 3 km trot to Bab Boujeloud on the edge of Fès el Bali. There are petit taxi stands on Place Mohammed V, and at the main **PTT** on the Avenue Hassan II, or you can simply flag one down on the street. In the medina, petit taxi stands are at Place de l'Iskiqlal (near the Musée Dar Batha) and at Bab Mahrouk. Much of the medina area is pedestrianized so you'll need to get your walking shoes on to explore. The complex network of lanes and alleys here will be a test of your internal

Tip...

If you do hire a guide, expect to be taken into a shop at some stage along the tour. Always try to agree the balance between sights and shops in advance with your guide.

Weather Fès

January	February	March	April	May	June
16°C	18°C	19°C	21°C	25°C	29°C
6°C	7°C	8°C	9°C	12°C	15°C
73mm	59mm	90mm	51mm	36mm	9mm

July	August	September	October	November	December
34°C	34°C	31°C	25°C	20°C	17°C
18°C	19°C	17°C	13°C	9°C	6°C
1mm	5mm	25mm	60mm	68mm	76mm

Best hotels

Riad Laaroussa, page 151
Dar Finn, page 152
Riad Tizwa, page 154

compass, so, if time is limited, it may be better to engage an official guide, rather than get lost and have (possibly unpleasant) dealings with an unofficial guide. While Fès el Jedid is fairly flat, Fès el Bali has long sloping streets.

Fact...

The word Fès in Arabic means axe – a possible reference to tools used in the city's construction.

Orientation

Essentially, there are three main areas to visit: **Fès el Bali**, the oldest part of the city, is a medina divided by the river into Adwa al Andalusiyin (the Andalucían quarter on the east bank) and Adwa al Qaraouiyine (the Qaraouiyine quarter on the west bank); **Fès el Jedid**, containing the royal palace and the *mellah* was founded under the Merinids and requires half a day's exploration; the **ville nouvelle**, built by the French, lies to the south of the historic core and is not so rich in sights but has taken over many of the political, administrative and commercial functions of old Fès.

Best restaurants

Dar Roumana, page 152
The Ruined Garden, page 157
Café Clock, page 157

When to go

Spring (April, May and even June) are by far the best time to visit, with late September and early October good choices too. This region gets very cold in winter and heating in many hotels (not just budget accommodation) can be inadequate due to poor insulation and high-ceilinged rooms. Bring warm clothing and don't forget to pack your umbrella and a pair of sturdy footwear; when it rains in Fès, the hilly streets of Fès el Bali can become a slosh-fest.

Time required

Ideally allow at least three days for Fès (including a side trip to Sefrou).

Tip...

Save some energy to get up to the Borj Nord/Merinid tombs for views across Fès el Bali at sundown.

Fès el Bali is the main attraction. Although it has few well-structured heritage sites, sightseeing here is more about winding your way through the narrow alleys and souks, soaking up the atmosphere. If time is very short, then the minimum half-day circuit will allow you to cover the main street, Talaâ Kebira, the Medersa Bou Inania, the central souks area (with the Nejjarine Museum of Wooden Arts and Crafts) and the alleys surrounding the Quaraouiyine Mosque where there's a scattering of religious monuments. From there you can then head to the Chouwara tanneries. With more time up your sleeve you can visit the Musée Dar Batha, fully explore the souks and head over the Oued Boukhrareb to the right bank to get lost amid the narrow lanes of this lesser-seen section of the old city.

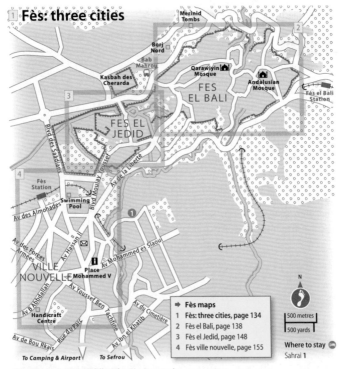

1 • Fès: three cities

Merinid Tombs

Borj Nord

Bab Mahrou

Kasbah des Cherarda

Qarawiyin Mosque

FES EL BALI

Andalusian Mosque

Fès el Bali Station

FES EL JEDID

Fès Station

Swimming Pool

Av des Almohades

Av des forces Armees

Av B Abdallah

VILLE NOUVELLE

Place Mohammed V

Av Hassan II

Av Mohammed es Slaoui

Av Youssef Ben Tachfine

Av du Cimetière

Av Ibn el Khatib

Av de Bou Rkais

Rue du Parc

Handicraft Centre

To Camping & Airport   To Sefrou

N

➡ Fès maps
1 Fès: three cities, page 134
2 Fès el Bali, page 138
3 Fès el Jedid, page 148
4 Fès ville nouvelle, page 155

500 metres
500 yards

Where to stay
Sahrai 1

ON THE ROAD
The Fès effect

Fès does not have the immediate friendliness of the villages, the mountains or the desert, but it's worth spending time getting to know the city. Like it or not, Fès will not leave you indifferent. Driss Chraïbi in his 1954 breakthrough novel *Le Passé Simple* did not mince his words: "I do not like this city. It is my past and I don't like my past. I have grown up, I have pruned myself back. Fès has quite simply shrivelled up. However, I know that as I go deeper into the city it seizes me and makes me entity, quantum, brick among bricks, lizard, dust – without me needing to be aware of it. Is it not the city of the Lords?"

Bab Boujeloud and around

If you're staying in a cheap hotel, it's likely that you'll be somewhere near Bab Boujeloud. The neighbourhood takes its name from the striking gate, which marks the main western entrance to Fès el Bali. With blue *zellige* tiles on the outside and green on the inside, Bab Boujeloud makes a fittingly stylish access point to the city and was revamped under the French in 1913.

Just to the right of the gate, as you arrive from the Place Boujeloud, there is a small gate in the wall, generally kept closed, which leads into the restored **brick water collector**. Though this may not sound very exciting, it is a good piece of late medieval hydraulic engineering, channeling the waters of the Oued Fès into underground pipes, which supplied the distributors of each neighbourhood. The whole system was still in operation in the late 19th century.

The two minarets visible from the gate are those of the 14th-century **Medersa Bou Inania** and the simpler ninth-century **Sidi Lazzaz Mosque**. On your left as you arrive at Bab Boujeloud, the impressive gate flanked by twin octagonal towers is **Bab Chorfa**, leading into Kasbah En Nouar, or Kasbah Filala, so named because it was once occupied by people from the Tafilalet who arrived with the early Alaouite rulers.

There are two main thoroughfares in Fès el Bali. From Bab Boujeloud, **Talaâ Seghira** leads to the right, while **Talaâ Kebira** leads to the left, directly past the Sidi Lazzaz Mosque and the Bou Inania Medersa, one of the most important sites in Fès; from here Talaâ Kebira continues straight on down through the medina to the Qaraouiyine Mosque.

Medersa Bou Inania
Rue Talaâ Kebira. Daily 0830-1730. 20dh, children 10dh.

Fès's most spectacular sight, and one of Morocco's most beautiful buildings, the 14th-century Medersa Bou Inania is located handily close to Bab Boujeloud, with its entrance near the top of Talaâ Kebira. Built by the Merinid Sultan Abu

> **Tip...**
> For the best view of the *medersa*'s minaret, go for a coffee and a cake on the roof terrace of **Café Clock**, opposite (see page 157).

BACKGROUND

Fès

Fès has a highly strategic location in the Oued Sebou basin, astride the traditional trade route from the Sahara to the Mediterranean, as well as on the path from Algeria and the Islamic heartland into Morocco. For centuries, the dominant axis within Morocco was between Fès and Marrakech, two cities linked by their immense power as well as by their rivalry. Even today, while Rabat and Casablanca dominate the country in political and economic terms, Fès continues to make its presence felt as the country's spiritual capital. The people of Fès have long been noted for their religious devotion. Dr Edmond Secret, writing in the 1930s, said that "the majority do their five daily prayers. Draped in modesty in the enveloping folds of their cloaks, the bourgeois, prayer carpets under their arms, recall monks in their dignity." This air of religiosity still clings to the city, especially during Ramadan.

The first settlement here was the village of Medinat Fès founded in 789/790 by Moulay Idriss. However, the town proper was founded by his son Idriss II 'El Azhar' (the Splendid) as Al Aliya in 808/809. Soon after, Muslim refugees from Córdoba and surrounding areas of Andalucía took up residence in the Adwa al Andalusiyin quarter. Later, 300 families from Kairouan (in contemporary Tunisia) settled on the opposite bank, forming Adwa al Qaraouiyine. The life of the city gravitated around the Qaraouiyine Mosque, still perhaps the foremost religious centre in Morocco. On the right bank of the Oued Boukhrareb, the Jamaâ Madlous or Andalucían Mosque was founded in the ninth century and remains the main mosque of Adwa al Andalus.

The city's religious life was closely tied to education: "If learning was born in Medina, maintained in Mecca and milled in Egypt, then it was sieved in Fès," went the adage. The university of the Qaraouiyine Mosque was founded in 859 and remains one of the most prestigious in the Arab World. Its influence grew under the Merinids, with the construction of colleges or *medersas*, so that, during the early Middle Ages, the city was a centre of cultural exchange. One Gerbert d'Aurillac, later to become Pope Sylvester II from 999 to 1003, studied in Fès in his youth and brought Arabic numerals back to Europe. Famous names to have studied or taught in Fès include the Jewish philosopher and doctor Maimonides; the mystic Ibn' Arabi (died 1240); Ibn Khaldoun (died 1282), and the mathematician Ibn el Banna (died 1321).

The two parts of Fès el Bali were united by the Almoravids in the 11th century, and Fès became one of the major cities of Islam. In the 12th century the Qaraouiyine mosque was enlarged to its present form, making it one of the largest in North Africa. The Almohads strengthened the fortifications of the great city. Under both dynasties Fès was in competition with the southern capital of Marrakech.

Fès reached its peak in the Merinid period, when the dynasty built the new capital of Fès el Jedid containing the green-roofed Dar al Makhzen still occupied by the monarch, the Grand Mosque with its distinctive polychrome minaret dating from 1279, and the *mellah*, to which the Jews of Fès el Bali were moved in 1438. The Merinid sultans Abu Said Uthman and Abu Inan (see box, page 142) left a particularly notable legacy of public buildings, including the Medersa Bou Inania, several mosques and the Merinid Tombs. The *zaouïa* of Moulay Idriss II was rebuilt in 1437 and became a major centre of pilgrimage. In the 15th century Fès consolidated its position as a major centre for craft industries and trade.

Under the Saâdians (15th to 16th centuries) Fès declined, with a degree of antagonism between the authorities and the people. The Saâdians did, however, refortify the city, adding the Borj Sud and Borj Nord fortresses on the hills. Under the Alaouites, Fès lost ground to the expanding coastal towns, which were far better located to benefit from trade with Europe. The occupation of Algeria also meant Fès was out of touch with the huge changes taking place to the east. In 1889 the French writer Pierre Loti described it as a dead city. However, the dynasty had added a number of new *medersas* and mosques, and reconstructed other important buildings.

The French entered Fès in 1911 but proved unable to gain full control of the city and its hinterland. Plans to make it the Protectorate's capital were thus abandoned. Although many Fassi notables did well out of the Protectorate – witness the palaces and splendid houses of the Ziat, Douh and Batha areas of the medina – Fès was largely overshadowed by the growth of Rabat and Casablanca. The *ville nouvelle*, also often referred to as Dar Dbibagh, was founded in 1916, but it dates principally from the late 1920s.

The city declined further in the post-Independence period as the elite moved to the cities of the Atlantic coast, leaving their fine courtyard homes to poorer members of the family or to rural immigrants. By the late 20th century the medina faced critical problems: residents and tenants were unable to afford the upkeep of large, ageing buildings (and were often living in unsanitary conditions); the Oued Fès and the Oued Sebou were dangerously polluted, and the historic but much decayed drinking water network was disintegrating.

In 1981, the city was added to the UNESCO World Heritage List. In the 1990s, the ADER (Agence pour la dédensification et la réhabilitation de Fès) was set up to improve living conditions within the medina, and, in 1995, the World Bank came up with US$14 million for infrastructure improvement. Since the early 1990s, the city has exploded beyond its former limits, with huge new areas of low-rise housing on the hills behind the Borj Sud at Sahrij Gnaoua and to the north at Dhar Khemis and Bab Siffer. More than 20 years after conservation schemes first began, you'll still see many alleyways held up by scaffolding as you wander through the medina. Nevertheless, improvements have been made to the city walls and a number of historic *medersas* have been fully restored. Tourism is also playing a role, as increasing numbers of old buildings are being renovated as upmarket riad accommodation.

Inan between 1350 and 1355 (see box, page 136), it was used to accommodate students until the 1960s and is now open to the public after a lengthy restoration. You enter through a highly decorated vestibule roofed by a stalactite dome. The building centres on a large, stone-flagged courtyard separated from the prayer hall at the far end by a sort of dry moat, where water taken from the Oued Fès once flowed. The courtyard is decorated with ceramic mosaic, Koranic inscriptions

2 Fès El Bali

and some fine carved woodwork. On the ground and first floors are the students' cell-like rooms, some with decorated ceilings.

The mosque area has a highly decorated minaret, indicating that it was far more important than most *medersas*, which normally do not have minarets or even pulpits for the Friday prayer. Indeed, the *medersa* has the status of a Friday mosque and, for a time, rivalled the Qaraouiyine Mosque. On exiting the

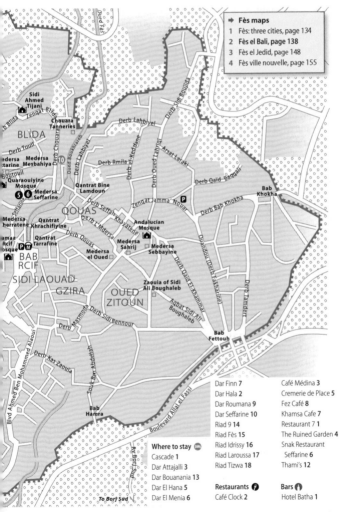

➡ **Fès maps**
1 Fès: three cities, page 134
2 Fès el Bali, page 138
3 Fès el Jedid, page 148
4 Fès ville nouvelle, page 155

Where to stay 📷
Cascade 1
Dar Attajalli 3
Dar Bouanania 13
Dar El Hana 5
Dar El Menia 6
Dar Finn 7
Dar Hala 2
Dar Roumana 9
Dar Seffarine 10
Riad 9 14
Riad Fès 15
Riad Idrissy 16
Riad Laroussa 17
Riad Tizwa 18

Restaurants 🍴
Café Clock 2
Café Médina 3
Cremerie de Place 5
Fez Café 8
Khamsa Cafe 7
Restaurant 7 1
The Ruined Garden 4
Snak Restaurant
  Seffarine 6
Thami's 12

Bars 🍸
Hotel Batha 1

ON THE ROAD

A child's survival guide to Fès

When your parents say to you "son, we're going to Fès," your first reaction might be: "Where's Fès?" The next is: "Will they have pizza?" In reality Fès is one of the most brilliant cities I've ever been to. Wandering around the medina, you see groups of street children, vibrant coloured washing hanging over into the streets and, best of all, the amazing market. In the markets nothing is fixed-price and there's always some clever deal or haggling going on.

Me and my brother and sister decided to test our haggling skills to the limit by playing a Moroccan version of *The Apprentice* and seeing who could buy the same standard items – a coloured glass, a slipper keyring and a pencil case – for the least money. Sadly, I lost by quite a bit!

At least I was helped in my bargaining by having done the Café Clock download course. This is a short session (about 1½ hours, 150dh) that Café Clock runs to teach you some simple Arabic phrases and a bit about the culture and what hand signals mean. My favourite was 'smehily' meaning "sorry", which you pronounce "smelly", and I used a lot bumping into people.

Café Clock is a great place to be, in the heart of the medina, and it does great milkshakes and burgers – and when I say burger I don't mean beef, pork or even lamb – but camelburger! (Which is actually delicious.)

And about the pizza – no, you won't find much in the medina, but they do have Malawi bread, like a thin wide sugary crêpe which is good for breakfast with soft cheese.

Do
- Have a chocolate and banana milkshake at Café Clock.
- Go for a swim in one of the hotels.
- Learn a few phrases of Arabic.

Don't
- Go into a carpet shop unless you've got half an hour to spare and don't mind being patted on the head by the owner.
- Visit the Roman ruins at Volubilis. Because 1) they are ruins 2) they are Roman 3) you have to drive three hours to get there and back. And no, they're not educational.

by Leo Thomson (age 11)

Bou Inania Medersa, look up at the wall on the opposite side of the street to see a bizarre and intricate wooden contraption built into the wall. This is a complex 14th-century *clepsydra* (**water clock**), which used brass bowls, dripping water and chimes to signal the correct time for prayer to both the Qaraouiyine Mosque and the Mosque of Fès el Jedid. The wooden structure has been finely restored, although, alas, it doesn't actually work.

ON THE ROAD

Pottery and belief

Until perhaps the 1960s, old-fashioned heavy pottery plates and dishes were in general use in Fassi homes. A study on Fassi ceramics quotes an elderly housewife recounting how her father, back in the 1930s, insisted on eating from Fassi pottery: "I want to eat from *fakhar* (traditionally made) dishes, made from the *trab* (clay) of Morocco, because such plates and vessels have been made with a prayer, in accordance with religion. Any foreign vessel is *haram* (sinful)."

For great family occasions, the poorer families would rent large dishes called *tabaq* or *mtirda*. The great families did not use *mokhfia* dishes, but other shapes and forms. Today, these traditional forms are often recycled in less hard-wearing pottery for the tourist market, often decorated with metal or bone insets.

Pottery also accompanied the Muslim in the cemetery. A *ghorraf* or *zlafa* of water was left on top of tombs, the idea being that birds would come to drink and sing to the dead. Maybe some believed the birds to be God's messengers – and it was seen as a very worthy charitable action to leave them water to drink. Pigeons and doves were particularly appreciated, nicknamed *deker Allah*, as their cooing was said to sound like the words for 'remember Allah'.

But old-style pottery was also delicate. Oil and butter penetrated the surface, rendering the glaze fragile. Large plates were expensive, and would be repaired, sometimes with metal patches or occasionally staples. Sometimes a small piece of pot was cemented in to replace a missing piece.

This attachment to pottery shows the material value of tableware in times gone by. But it also indicates a sentimental, maybe even religious value. After all, the members of a family would have sat round a large communal dish to eat together hundreds of times, saying the words *bismillah*, 'in the name of God', at the start of each meal. The *hadith*, or saying of the Prophet, runs that anything you do starting with the *bismillah* will go well.

Musée Dar Batha

Off Pl de l'Istiqlal, T0535-634116. Wed-Mon 0830-1630, 10dh. Photography of exhibits not allowed, although you may take photographs of the gardens and courtyard.

This 19th-century Hispano-Moorish palace is home to a display of Moroccan arts and handicrafts. Like many museums in Morocco, it's worth visiting more for the artistry of its exterior and interior decoration than for the dusty exhibits themselves. The covered walkways that surround the Andalucían garden in the centre of the palace are definitely worth walking through for their beautifully preserved painted-wood ceilings. The most important exhibit here is the beautiful collection of Moroccan ceramics, including distinctive Fès pottery. (A 10th-century technique used cobalt to produce the famous 'Fès blue'.) The *minbar*, or preacher's chair, from the Medersa Bou Inania is also on display.

BACKGROUND
Saintly Sultan Abou Inane

A number of ancient colleges in the medinas of Morocco – among them *medersas* in Meknès, Salé and Fès – bear the name Bou Inania, after their royal founder. Sultan Abou Inane's most important building works were in Fès: he constructed the Jamaâ Zhar, a fine mosque close to his palace, and the Koubba of the Qaraouiyine Library. Today's non-Muslim visitor can see the Medersa Bou Inania, considered to be one of the finest in existence. Tradition has it that when the sultan was presented with the final accounts, he tore up the paperwork, declaring that "Beauty is not expensive, whatever the sum may be. A thing which pleases man cannot be paid too dear."

Born in Fès in 1329, Abou Inane Faris de-throned his father at the tender age of 20, and had himself proclaimed sultan at Tlemcen in June 1348. By all accounts he was an imposing figure. Wrote Ibn el Ahmar, chronicler of the Merinids: "He was taller than everybody else. His body was slim, his nose long and well-made. He had hairy arms. His voice was deep, but he spoke quickly in a staccato manner, so that it was sometimes difficult to understand him. He had beautiful, finely shaped eyes, full eyebrows, and an agreeable face of great beauty … My eyes have never seen in his army a soldier with a fuller beard, a finer and more pleasing figure." Abou Inane was also, apparently, a skilled horseman, and had a good knowledge of law, arithmetic and Arabic. Ibn el Ahmar also mentions that he left behind 325 children.

On being proclaimed sultan, Abou Inane took the throne name of El Moutawakkil, 'he who places trust in God'. Although a strong ruler, he was also a pious man (he knew the Koran by heart). He instituted a tradition of having a blue flag hoisted to the top of the minarets on Friday to indicate prayer time, and had oil-lamps placed on the minarets to show prayer times at night.

Like many a medieval ruler, however, Abou Inane had an unfortunate end. In 1358, returning to Fès from Tunis, he fell sick. Arriving in his capital on the eve of Aïd el Kebir, he had sufficient strength to lead the great prayers on the *musalla* outside the city. He was too ill, however, to receive homage from the notables of the realm. The vizier, Hassan el Foudoudi, who had been plotting in the wings, had the sick sultan smothered in his bedclothes.

The burial place of Abou Inane remains something of a mystery. Perhaps it was too risky for the sultans that followed to allow such a good ruler to have a mausoleum, which might then become a focus for public gatherings and discontent.

Talaâ Kebira

The narrow Talaâ Kebira, the principal street in Fès el Bali, descends steeply towards the spiritual and commercial heart of the city, a tangle of streets and alleys around the shrine (*zaouïa*) of Moulay Idriss and the Qaraouiyine Mosque (both off limits to non-Muslims). The 20-minute walk from Bab Boujeloud is many people's most memorable experience of Fès, an extraordinary wander through noises, smells, and sights of the souk, from camels' heads on display at the butchers' to aged mint sellers to heavily laden mules carrying goods across the city, guided by muleteers crying out 'Balak!' to warn pedestrians.

As Talaâ Kebira descends, it goes through frequent identity changes, taking on the name of the different crafts which are (or were) practised along different sections of the street. First it becomes **Rue Cherabliyine** (slippermakers), where each afternoon except Friday people hawk second-hand shoes and slippers. The **Cherabliyine Mosque** dates from 1342, the reign of Sultan Abul Hassan, and has a small and attractive minaret tiled in green and white with the *darj w ktaf* motif. Further on, Rue Cherabliyin is called **Aïn Allou**, where leather articles are auctioned every day except Friday. After Aïn Allou, the street is named for the basket weavers (Msamriyine) and bag makers (Chakakyrine), before becoming the **Souk el Attarine**, the former perfumers' souk, the most prestigious in the medina.

Between Attarine and the Zaouïa of Moulay Idriss is the lively main **kissaria**, the place to buy traditional clothing.

At the bottom of Talaâ Kebira, in the immediate vicinity of the mosque, are four *medersas*: going clockwise, **Medersa Attarine** (the most important), **Medersa Mesbahiya** (partly ruined), **Medersa Seffarine** (the Coppersmiths' Medersa, recently restored) and **Medersa Cherratène** (more modern, three storeys). All were in use well within living memory.

> **Fact...**
> Traditionally, the end of each summer saw great celebrations for the *moussem* of Moulay Idriss, when the craftsmen's corporations would take part in processions to the shrine of the city's founder; a sacrificial bull, its horns and head decorated with henna, was at the heart of every procession.

Nejjarine Museum of Wooden Arts
38 Rue Abdelazuz Boutaleb, T0535-621706. Daily 1000-1700. 20dh, children 10dh.

Before getting tangled up in Souk el Attarine, take a right and then a left down some steps off Cherabliyine to get to the square in front of the 18th-century **Fondouk Nejjarine**, an impressive building now home to an interesting museum of wooden crafts and tools. The beautiful space is filled with some interesting pieces that showcase Fassi carpentry to great effect, such as carved doors and windows, handsome coffers and musical instruments. There's also an impressive doorknocker carved from one piece of wood. Just outside, on the square, the **Nejjarine Fountain**, also carefully restored, is reputed to have fever-curing properties. On the far side of the square from the fondouk is **Hammam Laraïs**, the wedding baths, once much used by grooms and brides before a pre-marriage trip to the *zaouïa* of Moulay Idriss.

Shrine of Moulay Idriss II
Inaccessible to non-Muslims.

Surrounded by narrow streets, this 18th-century *zaouïa* (shrine) is the last resting place of the ninth-century ruler Idriss II. It is off-limits to non-Muslim visitors, although parts of the interior can be seen by tactful glances through the large, unscreened doorways. Shops around the *zaouïa* sell candles and other artefacts for pilgrims, the distinctive nougat sweets which are taken home as souvenirs of a pilgrimage, and silverware. Each entrance to the precinct is crossed by a wooden bar, ensuring no pack animals go wandering into the sacred area. On your way round, note a circular porthole through which offerings can be discreetly passed.

Medersa el Attarine
Daily 0830-1730. 20dh, children 10dh.

Dating from 1323, the **Medersa Attarine** (currently undergoing restoration) was built by Merinid Sultan Abu Said. It used to accommodate students studying at the nearby Qaraouiyine University. The courtyard is one of the most elaborately decorated in Morocco, with the usual carved stucco, cedar wood and *zellige* tiling. The courtyard has a solid, white marble fountain bowl. In the dark prayer hall, a chandelier bears the name of the *medersa's* founder and the date. As with most *medersas*, the second floor has a succession of students' cells.

Qaraouiyine Mosque
Inaccessible to non-Muslims. From the narrow streets, you may be able to take diplomatic glances through unscreened entrances.

At the end of Souk el Attarine, the Quaraouiyine Mosque, the focal point of Fès el Bali, is probably the most important religious building in Morocco and was once a major centre of medieval learning, with professors in law, theology, algebra, mathematics, philosophy and astronomy. With space for up to 22,000 worshippers, it is one of the biggest mosques in North Africa. Original funding to build this mosque was provided in 857 by a wealthy immigrant family from Kairouan (in present day Tunisia), hence the name. The building was enlarged in 956 and again – most importantly – under the Almoravids between 1135 and 1144. The Almohads added a large ablution hall, while the Merinids rebuilt the courtyard and minaret. The twin pavilions in the courtyard are 17th-century Saâdian additions. The minaret dates back to 956, but the 'Trumpeters' Tower' or Borj an-Naffara is later and is used during Ramadan to signal the time to begin fasting again. Built under Sultan Abou Inan in the second half of the 14th century, the tower originally functioned as an observatory. The Qaraouiyine has 14 doors, 275 pillars and three areas for ablutions. Features include elaborate Almohad carving and a venerable wooden pulpit. Some of the chandeliers were made from church bells. Women have a separate worship area, on a mezzanine floor, behind the men.

A minor sight on the Derb Bou Touil, the street running along the eastern side of the mosque, is the 14th-century three-storey **Fondouk Titouani**, originally built to

BACKGROUND

Bathtime stories

Early in the 19th century, Fès was visited by the Spaniard Domingo Badia y Leblich, travelling under the pseudonym Ali Bey el Abbassi. He noted the importance of the public baths or hammams of Fès: "The baths are open to the public all day. The men go in the morning, the women in the afternoon. I generally used to go in the evening, taking the whole bathhouse for myself so that there would be no outsiders ... The first time I went there, I noted that there were buckets of water placed symmetrically in the corner of each room and each cubicle. I asked what they were for.

'Do not touch them, sir,' the personnel of the hammam replied in haste.
'Why?'
'These are buckets for the people down below.'
'Who are they?'
'The demons who come to wash during the night'."

A few centuries earlier, Leo Africanus described the traditions of the hammams of Fès:
"The companions and the owners of the steam-baths hold festivities once a year, celebrating in the following way. First of all they invite all their friends, and go through the city to fife, tambourine and trumpets, then they take a hyacinth bulb, placing it in a fine copper container which they cover with a white cloth. Then they go back through the city, accompanied by music, to the door of the hammam. There they put the bulb in a basket which they hang over the door, saying, 'This will bring seed to the hammam, because of it there will be many visitors'."

Traditions related to the hammam seem to have died away today. But, even in the 1920s and 1930s, superstitions were very much alive. Dr Edmond Secret, a French doctor working in Fès, noted how those who went to the hammam very early, washing alone, were considered courageous, and genies were held to live in damp corners and the water pipes.

accommodate merchants from Tetouan and, today, used by artisans and a carpet shop. Both this and the nearby **Palais de Fès** restaurant have good views of the Qaraouiyine's courtyard.

Place Seffarine

On the southeast side of the Qaraouiyine, the triangular Place Seffarine (Brassworkers' Square) is surrounded by metalworker shops and marked by a tree visible from the north or south Borj. On the right is the **Qaraouiyine Library**, founded in 1349 and still operational. You can usually enter the courtyard and entrance hall; non-Muslims are not allowed in the library itself.

If you head left of the tree on Seffarine, you can reach one of the bridges over the Oued Boukhrareb, either Qantrat Kharchifiyine or, after Sebbaghine, Qantrat

Tarrafine. Here you come out onto **Rcif**, home to the best fresh produce market in the medina.

Chouara tanneries

The most colourful sight in Fès, the Chouara tanneries have not really changed since medieval times. At the bottom of the valley, they use the water of the Oued Boukhrareb, as well as a smelly mix of urine and guano, to turn animal hides into dyed, usable leather. To get there from Place Seffarine, follow Derb Mechattine (the narrow right-hand street of the two at the top of the square) around to the left onto Zanka Chouara. The best views of the tanneries are from the terraces of the surrounding leather shops, from where you can view the work going on below. Afterwards, you'll be expected to have a look at the handiwork for sale; there's no obligation to buy anything, although the quality is high, and you could do much worse for a souvenir of the city. See box, page 56, for a full account of the traditional tanning process.

Adwa al Andalus

Probably the poorest area of the medina, the Andalus quarter on the right bank of Fès el Bali has fewer obvious sights than the left bank. However, the **Medersa Sahrij**, next to the Mosque al Andalus, is worth a visit. You can approach the neighbourhood from the southeast, taking a *petit taxi* to Bab Fettouh, or by climbing up out of Bab Rcif, losing yourself in the maze of streets of the Qouas neighbourhood.

> **Fact...**
> On every night of the year, in the hours which precede the dawn, a company of muezzins maintains a vigil in the minaret of the Andalucían Mosque, praying for those asleep and those awake.

With its green and white minaret, the **Mosque al Andalus** is a distinctive building dating from the same period as the great Qaraouiyine Mosque. The minaret dates from the 10th century, and the mosque was enlarged in the 13th century, with an architect from Toledo designing the grand main doorway, which is particularly impressive if you approach the mosque coming up the steps from below. If interested in a relic of the city's commercial life, take a look at the **Fondouk el Madlous**, a few steps down from the mosque entrance on the left. Restored under Moulay Hassan I in the 19th century, this fondouk is still used for accommodation and storage.

As you face the main door of the mosque, go right along Derb Yasmina to reach the entrance of the nearby **Medersa Sahrij** ('School of the Reflecting Pool'), built 1321-1323 to house students studying at the mosque. There has been no major restoration campaign here yet, and cats snooze on the weathered wood screens topped with scallop designs. The white marble basin, after which the *medersa* was named, has been removed from the courtyard. The large prayer hall contained the library against the *qibla* wall at either side of the mihrab. Try to get up onto the roof for the view. In between the mosque and the *medersa* is the **Medersa Sebbayine**, now closed. After visiting the Medersa Sahrij, you could carry along the same street, past the unmarked Medersa el Oued on your right. A few metres further on, a sharp right will take you onto Derb Gzira. Just after the turn is a house which bears the strange name of **Dar Gdam Nbi**, the 'house of the Prophet's foot', so called because a sandal which supposedly once belonged to the Prophet Mohammed was conserved there. Once a year, just before the Prophet's birthday or Mouloud, the Tahiri family would open their home to allow the faithful to approach the semi-sacred item of footwear. Unfortunately, the owners have sold up, and the property has been divided. Continue therefore on Derb Gzira, which winds back down to Rcif, where you could find a bus (No 18) to take you back up to Place de la Résistance in the *ville nouvelle*. There are plenty of red *petits taxis* here as well.

Views of Fès el Bali

The **Borj nord**, built by the Saâdian Sultan Ahmad al Mansour in 1582, is a small but interesting example of 16th-century fortress architecture. There are good views of parts of Fès el Bali from the road running up to it. Inside is an **Arms Museum** ① *T0535-645241, Wed-Mon 0900-1300, 1500-1730, 10dh*, with displays of weapons and military paraphernalia from all periods, including European cannon. The collections have been built up mainly as a result of royal donations and include a number of rare pieces. Many of these killing tools have a certain splendour as crafted items. Look out for the largest weapon of all, a 5-m-long cannon weighing 12 tonnes used during the Battle of the Three Kings.

For the best panoramic views over the city, head up the hillside from the Borj nord to the 14th-century **Merinid Tombs**. The tombs are ruins, and much of the ornamentation described by earlier visitors has not survived. In the late afternoon, the garden promenade behind the Borj nord and tombs is busy with locals out for a stroll, but note that this is not a safe place to go alone at night. The views over Fès el Bali, and the surrounding rolling hills are excellent.

From the 13th-century **Borj sud**, south of the centre, occupied by the military, you can also look north over Fès.

Also known as the *madina al bayda* (the white city), this area was founded by the Merinids as their capital in 1276. It contains the Royal Palace and the old Jewish quarter (the *mellah*), and is now a pleasant haven between the hustle and bustle of Fès el Bali and the *ville nouvelle*. Allow half a day here, perhaps in the late afternoon, before heading for the Merinid Tombs at sunset.

Mellah

The best place to start is probably at the **Place des Alaouites**, close to the Royal Palace and instantly recognizable by its spectacular doors giving onto a vast esplanade used on ceremonial occasions – or, in the early 1990s, during urban riots. Over on the right, at the edge of a small garden terrace, is the elegant **Bab Lamar**. Between this

> **Fact...**
> The term *mellah*, used for Jewish neighbourhoods throughout Morocco, probably derives from the Oued Melah, literally 'salty river', which once ran close to this part of Fès, but which, like so many of the watercourses in the region, has disappeared.

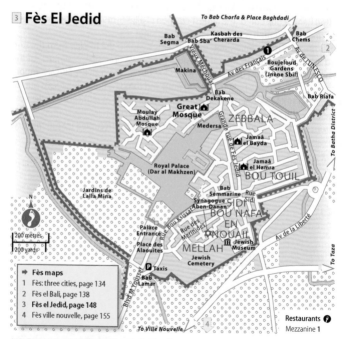

3 Fès El Jedid

To Bab Chorfa & Place Baghdadi
Bab Segma
Bab Sba
Kasbah des Cherarda
Bab Chems
Vieux Méchouar
Av des Français
Rd de TUNIS
Makina
Boujeloud Gardens (Jnène Sbil)
Bab Dekakene
Bab Riafa
Moulay Abdullah Mosque
Great Mosque
Grand Rue de Fès Jedid
ZEBBALA
Medersa
Jamaâ el Bayda
To Batha District
Royal Palace (Dar al Makhzen)
Jamaâ el Hamra
BOU TOUIL
Jardins de Lalla Mina
Bab Semmarine
Synagogue Aben-Danan
Rue Sidi
SIDI BOU NAFA EN NOUAIL
Rue des Mérinides
Palace Entrance
Jewish Museum
Place des Alaouites
MELLAH
Jewish Cemetery
Av de la Liberté
To Taza
200 mètres
200 yards
N
Taxis
Bab Lamar
Bhd M. el Ouazzani
To Ville Nouvelle

Fès maps
1 Fès: three cities, page 134
2 Fès el Bali, page 138
3 Fès el Jedid, page 148
4 Fès ville nouvelle, page 155

Restaurants
Mezzanine 1

The palaces of Fès

Hidden in the narrow streets of the Douh, Zerbatana and Ziat neighbourhoods, just east of the Batha, are some truly huge 19th- and early 20th-century palaces. The heirs have long since migrated to more promising elsewheres, and the high-ceilinged rooms are semi-squatted by poor relatives or rural migrants. If your time is limited, try to see Dar el Glaoui and Dar el Mokri. You will need to hire a guide to gain access and expect to tip the building owners (a tip of around 20dh per visitor is probably reasonable for the disturbance). A good guide is multilingual Abdellatif Riffi Mbarki, T0668-220112 (mob).

Most often visited, as it is right on Talaâ Seghira, is the **Palais Mnebhi**, which now functions rather efficiently as a restaurant. Its former owner was a minister of war under Sultan Moulay Abd el Aziz, and Maréchal Lyautey, first résident-général, once resided here.

Try to also get a peek at the garden patio of **Dar Ba Mohamed Chergui**, on Derb Horra, linking Talaâ Kebira to Talaâ Seghira. The overgrown raised flowerbeds are laid out according to the *mtemmen*, figure-of-eight motif traditional in *zellige* (ceramic-mosaic). On Rue Sidi Mohammed el Haj, a right off Talaâ Seghira as you descend, is **Dar Ababou**, which has a garden courtyard overlooked by balconies.

Dar el Glaoui is the most easily visited of the big palaces. Three tennis courts, if not four, would have easily fitted into the main courtyard. From the roof terraces there are views across the city. When the Glaoui family fell from favour after Independence, the palace was abandoned.

No less splendid is **Dar el Mokri**, named for the grand vizir El Mokri who held office for the whole of the French period. There are some 1930s additions and a sadly run-down garden. Off the big courtyard, the rooms are partly converted to workshops, partly squatted. There is an off-chance that, if you are passing down Derb Chaq Bedenjala on your way to Bab Jedid, a lad will spot you and ask if you want to take a look at the palace.

Close to the Batha (*batha* is Arabic for open area) are a number of easily located patrician residences. Right on the square, **Dar Mekouar**, once a cradle of the nationalist movement, is a few metres to the left of the Maison Bleue guesthouse (see plaque on wall). Next to the café to the right of the Maison Bleue, a narrow street, Derb Salaj, runs directly into Fès el Bali. Follow along and you will find, down a blind alley, the house used by the local **Institut Français** for occasional concerts. Further along, the very chic **Riad Fès** guesthouse is signposted, and you will find **Dar Cheikh Tazi**, now headquarters of the Association Fès-Saïss, an organization working to promote the region.

---

and the Rue Bou Ksissat is a small gate which takes you into Rue des Mérinides in the *mellah*. All along this street are the elegant façades of houses, with distinctive exterior balconies, built by prosperous Jewish families in the early 20th century.

Take the fourth street on the right, Rue de Temara, to arrive at the **Synagogue Aben-Danan**. In the main hall of the synagogue, there is a collection of objects giving some idea of the material context of Fassi Jewish life. After the synagogue, pass a small square and head across to the **Nouaïl** area. Next to the Jewish cemetery, the **Jewish Museum** has an intriguing collection of photos, newspaper clippings and artefacts of the community that lived here. (If you go right here, the street leads down to a door which will take you down to the American animal hospital or **Fondouk el Amerikan**.) From the Nouaïl area try to cut through to the continuation of Rue des Mérinides, Rue Sekkakine and the imposing **Bab Semmarine**, which leads you to Fès el Jedid proper. (If you double back on Rue des Mérinides, you'll find **Bab Magana**, the 'clock gate', whose scruffy timepiece stopped a while ago.)

Bab Semmarine to Bab Sba'

Bab Semmarine, a chunky structure characterized by a double horseshoe arch and lozenge motifs, takes you through into the wide main street of Fès el Jedid, often referred to as Avenue Moulay Slimane. This cuts through Fès el Jedid and takes you through to **Bab Dekakene**. On the right, **Jamaâ el Hamra** 'the red mosque' is the first of the two mosques, so called because it was founded by a red woman from the Tafilalelt. The second mosque on your right is the **Jamaâ el Bayda**. Continue straight ahead and, at the end of the avenue, you can cut through an arched gate in the walls to your right, taking you past the dry course of the Oued Chrachar to a decrepit waterwheel and a small café-restaurant. Double back, cut through left, and you are at **Bab Dekakene**. Here you want to go through to the right to the walled square referred to as the **Vieux Mechouar**. On the left are the Italianate entrance gates to the **Makina**. Originally built in the 19th century to house an arms factory, it now has various functions, including a rug factory and youth club. Going straight ahead, you come to **Bab Sba'**, which takes you through onto the main road running along the north side of the city, linking the *ville nouvelle* to Fès el Bali. You might take a look at the unusual twin octagonal towers of **Bab Segma**, flanking the ring road. The fortified structure to the north is the **Kasbah des Cherarda**, built in 1670 by Sultan Moulay Rachid and today housing a branch of the university and a hospital.

> **Tip...**
> For those with plenty of time, a trail through Fès el Jedid should include a dawdle through the Moulay Abdullah neighbourhood, north of the palace. There are a couple of mosques for non-Muslims to look at from the exterior here. If you have the energy, head through the Boujeloud gardens and along Avenue des Français to Bab Boujeloud at the western end of Fès el Bali.

Where to stay

There are hotels and riads in Fès to suit all budgets, including some very luxurious ones in and around the tangled lanes of the medina. This is certainly the best place to stay if you want to get a real feel of old Fès. Reservations are essential at most of the higher-end riads. If you reserve in advance, most places will send someone to meet you at Bab Boujeloud when you arrive. **Fez Riads** (T0672-513357, www.fez-riads. com), is an excellent agency offering luxury accommodation in the medina. Budget accommodation in the medina is mostly in the Bab Boujeloud area and can fill up very quickly in spring and summer. If you're struggling to find somewhere to stay, it can be worthwhile checking out the budget hotels in the *ville nouvelle*.

Fès El Bali

€€€€ Riad Fès
5 Derb Ben Sliman Zerbtana, T0535-741206, www.riadfes.com.
This vast house, originally built in 1900, was one of the first in Fès to be transformed into upscale accommodation, and it remains one of the city's most luxurious places to stay. Particularly at night, its poolside bar is spectacular. The 30 rooms are split into 3 different design themes depending on your tastes – Baraco Andalous, traditional Moroccan or Oriental – and although they don't quite live up to the wow-factor of the communal areas, they still feel exceedingly special. Service here is top-notch, and the rooftop Sky Bar (open

to non-guests) has one of the best views over the medina rooftops in the city. Wi-Fi and breakfast included.

€€€€-€€€ Riad Laaroussa
3 Derb Bechara, T0674-187639, www.riad-laaroussa.com.
One of the first wave of contemporary riads in Fès, this 17th-century riad opens out around a grass and pebble courtyard with fountains and orange trees. As well as 4-poster beds, fireplaces in some of the rooms (a huge bonus during the rather damp and cold winters) and a striking *tadelakt* roof terrace, there are plenty of quirky touches like kettles for taps, adding an air of the unexpected. The dining room has black-and-white photos and jazz playing, while the 8 bedrooms (from €120) are all themed around a colour. There's an elegant hammam and spa and copious amounts of intricately carved plaster. Wi-Fi and breakfast included.

€€€€-€€ Dar Bensouda
14 Zkak El Bghel, Quettanine, T0535-638949, www.riaddarbensouda.com.
This chic hotel is in one of the more obscure parts of the medina and is well worth the effort of finding. Owned by Moroccan hotelier Abdellatif Aït Ben Abdellah, who made his mark with several respected riads and restaurants in Marrakech, he's brought his own sense of style to Fès. A large courtyard is minimally furnished with butterfly chairs, linen drapes and saffron-coloured rugs. Rooms are individually decorated with pared-down elegance, and 1 luxury suite has a private courtyard at an accessible price. Another courtyard is home to an inviting plunge pool, the

restaurant (warmed by a log fire in the winter) serves a wide range of Moroccan cuisine, while the roof terrace provides a full 360-degree view of the medina and surrounds.

€€€€-€€ Riad 9
9 Derb Lamsside, Souiket Ben Safi, Zkak el Ma, T0535-634045, www.riad9.com.
Sophisticated and elegant, Riad 9 has everything necessary to make a stay in Fès unusually stylish, from books, jazz, Chinese lanterns and panoramic views to a hyperactive cat. Run by a French designer, there are just 3 suites here (€100-200) brimming with traditional architectural features and an artful mix of old and modern textiles, as well as vintage finds, and quirky features such as dentists' chairs in bathrooms. Highly chic yet playful at the same time, Riad 9 is the epitome of inventive contemporary design. Their restaurant next door (Riad 7, see page 157) is one of the hippest spots to eat in the medina. Wi-Fi, breakfast and pick-up from the airport or train station included.

€€€-€€ Dar Attajali
2 Derb Qettana, Zqaq Rommane, T0535-637728, T0677-081192 (mob), www.attajalli.com.
Attajali is one of the most exquisite renovations in the medina, highly traditional with lots of soft, silky textiles, soothing Arabic music and an air of quiet serenity. 4 individually decorated rooms (€85-115) have wooden ceilings, pretty *zellige* tiles, antiques, comfortable extra-long mattresses, imported German duvets and traditional Moroccan beauty products in the bathrooms. The 'purple suite' has a spectacular draped 4-poster bed, if you're after a romantic weekend away. The food here is excellent, making good use of locally sourced fruit and

vegetables. Breakfast and dinner are served in a rooftop dining room, with wonderful views across the medina. Those looking for a soothing respite after a day amid the souks can join in one of the hatha yoga or meditation sessions. Wi-Fi and breakfast included.

€€€-€€ Dar Finn
27 Zqaq Rowah, Cherabliyine, T0655-018975, www.darfinn.com.
Dar Finn (rooms from €85-130) is ideal for style-savvy travellers who want to get off the beaten path. Owners Rebecca Eve and Paul O'Sullivan, who named it after their son, have brought an upbeat boutique concept to the medina. Half the house has retained its traditional architecture – such as in the courtyard and tearoom – but there is a modern façade, garden and plunge pool, and an intimate dining room to create a groovy hangout for guests. Large balconies off the suites have the clean lines of nouveau art deco, while the upper floors and 3 roof terraces offer softer, chill-out zones with jaw-dropping views. The vibe is laid-back and relaxed, and there's an honesty bar. Wi-Fi and breakfast included.

€€€-€€ Dar Roumana
30 Derb el Amer, Zkak Roumane, T0535-741637, www.darroumana.com.
One of the first foreign-owned guesthouses to open in the medina (and still one of the best). The American owner Jennifer Smith has created one of the friendliest places you could hope to stay. Big on traditional Moroccan decor, such as *zellige*, intricate plaster work and painted ceilings, it has a wonderful feeling of space and light, with a large central courtyard, library, TV room and sprawling roof terrace with excellent views of the Merinid tombs. All 5 suites

(€85-145) are large, well proportioned and feature the works of local craftsmen, as well as unique characteristics, such as the claw-footed bath in the Roumana suite, or the private balcony off the Yasmina suite. Jennifer has always been known for her excellent cuisine, and with French chef Vincent Bonnin heading Dar Roumana's restaurant (see page 156), you're guaranteed some of the best eating in the city here. Wi-Fi and breakfast included.

€€€-€€ Dar Seffarine
14 Sbaa Louyate, T0535-635205, www.darseffarine.com.
Widely recognized as being the most spectacular renovation in Fès, the 750-year-old Dar Seffarine is an architectural gem built around a spectacular tiled courtyard with high arches. Thanks to Kate (a Norwegian graphic designer and photographer) and Alla (an Iraqi architect), the attention to detail, from the restoration of the house's intricate features to the choosing of antique carpets, furniture and linens, is impeccable. Decor is minimal to allow the house to speak for itself, but a museum it's not. The couple are gregarious hosts: every evening guests are invited for drinks in their small, homely courtyard just off the kitchen, or to dine together in the rooftop dining room (the food is excellent). Located just around the corner from the Qaraouiyine Mosque, it's also well positioned for some of the medina's key sights, and with easy access to the parking and taxis at Rcif. Wi-Fi and breakfast included.

€€€-€€ Riad Idrissy
Derb Siaj, T0649-191410 (Robert), T0535-633066 (the riad), www.riadidrissy.com.
A great example of the laid-back new vibe of the Fès medina, this 4-suite riad feels more like a private home than a hotel, with a big personality, thanks to lots of irreverent personalized touches and quirky finds by the owners, John Twomey and interior designer and gardener Robert Johnstone. Check out the beaded animal tables from Cameroon and the raffia wedding cake covers refashioned as lampshades, or the 4-poster bed that needs box steps to climb onto it. And when you want to chill out, head to the tree-shaded rambling oasis of their restaurant next door, The **Ruined Garden** (see page 157). Wi-Fi and breakfast included.

€€ Dar el Hana
22 Rue Ferrane Couicha, Cherabliyine, T0535-635854, T0676-286584 (mob), www.darelhana.com.
A homely little riad, you'll be fantastically well looked after here whether you rent the whole place or just a room (doubles €65-85). Carefully restored, Dar el Hana has wooden beamed ceilings and shuttered windows, and the Jacaranda suite and Hibiscus room have a 'secret' window just above the pillows. All rooms have private bathrooms but in the smaller rooms they are not en suite. Guests breakfast together in the courtyard or on the terrace. The whole place can be rented out for €240. Wi-Fi and breakfast included.

€€-€ Dar El Menia
7 Derb el Menia el Kebira, T0535-633164, T0655-206961, www.medinafes.com.
This small but immaculately renovated little guesthouse, just off the Talaâ Kebira, has just 4 rooms (doubles €45-65, family suite €75) each with their own character. Around 250 years old, you'll find plenty of traditional Moroccan decoration here, from painted wood and intricate plasterwork, to pristine *zellige*

tiles and carved cedar wood doors. It's a great place to get a taste of traditional Moroccan living while being perfectly placed at the heart of the medina for exploring. There's a roof terrace for chilling out, and the sumptuous traditional dinners of couscous and tagine (by prior arrangement) are a bargain. Wi-Fi and breakfast included.

€€-€ Riad Tizwa
Derb Guebbas 15, Douh Batha, T07973-238444 (UK mob) or T0668-190872 (Morocco mob), www.riadtizwa.com.
Sibling to the more established Tizwa in Marrakech, Tizwa Fès has 7 chic bedrooms (doubles €40-105) and a sprawling, lushly planted roof terrace, where excellent breakfasts are served. All rooms are generously appointed with some useful modern details, such as iPod docking stations, which is indicative of the Bee brothers' laid-back approach to hospitality that makes the place so pleasurable. Bathrooms are all done out in *tadelakt*, with organic rose petal soap and luxuriously thick bathrobes, and tea and coffee is secretly delivered to your door in the mornings, a nice touch. Communal spaces are warm and welcoming, with an open fireplace in the living room and a richly furnished courtyard for chilling out over mint tea in the afternoons. A truly comfortable home-away-from-home. Wi-Fi and breakfast included.

€ Dar Hala
156 Derb Lakram, off Talaâ Kebira, T0535-638687, www.riadfeshala.com.
The traditional rooms (single/double 400/500dh) decked out with local embroidered textiles, a/c and satellite TV, are a great budget choice to bed down in, with friendly owner Mohammed on hand to help with any queries. Rooms are generously sized and have an abundance

of scuffed floor tiles, worn down by years of wear, which gives a sense of the history of this old family home. Budget-conscious families can sleep in the good-value suite (850dh), which can fit up to 6. The pick of the rooms is the double at the top of the house leading onto the communal roof terrace, from where there are good views over the medina. Wi-Fi and breakfast included.

€ Dar Bouanania
21 Derb Ben Salem, off Talaâ Kebira, T0535-637282.
Packed with painted wood, plaster and wonky traditional tiled floors, Dar Bouanania is one of a rare breed of budget riad-style hotels. At these prices you aren't getting fancy services, but the good-sized rooms (from 250dh) brim with higgledy-piggledy character and the staff are very friendly. Wi-Fi and breakfast included.

€ Hotel Cascade
26 Rue Serrajine, T0535-638442.
A backpackers' institution, the busy **Cascade** is in the very heart of the action, just inside the main gate of Bab Boujeloud. Rooms with shared bathroom (150dh) are very basic but clean, and you can sleep on the roof for 40dh if you're really watching your pennies. They also have a few slightly more upscale rooms with en suite. The rooftop terrace here, overlooking the comings and goings of the main thoroughfare into the medina, is a major plus-point. Wi-Fi included.

Fès ville nouvelle

€€€ Hotel Sahrai
Bab Lghoul, Dhar el Mehraz, T0535-940332, www.hotelsahrai.com.
One of the city's most sumptuous new openings, Hotel Sahrai lords it up on the hill above the *ville nouvelle* with

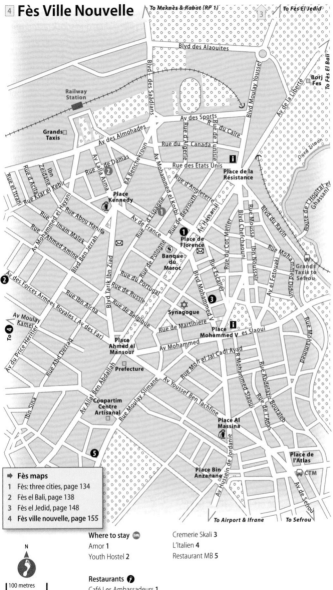

4 Fès Ville Nouvelle

To Meknès & Rabat (RP 1)

To Fès El Jedid

Blvd des Alaouites

Railway Station

Grands Taxis

Av des Almohades

Av des Sports

Rue du Caire

Rue du Tunisie

Rue du Dr Canada

Rue des Etats Unis

Blvd des Saâdians

Blvd Moulay Youssef

Av de la Liberté

Bori Fes

To Fès El Bali

Oued Zitoun

Place de la Résistance

Rue Ibn Zeidoun

Rue el Achir

Rue Ksar el Kebir

Rue el Irfani

Rue de Damas

Rue el Hayani

EA Benchekroun

Rue Laila Asma

Rue Mohammed el Korbi

Rue d'Angleterre

Rue Moussa

Blvd Chechaouni

Rue du Ravin

Route de l'Hôpital el Ghassani

Place Kennedy

Rue Mohammed el H

Rue Abou Hanifa

Av d'Espagne

Av d'Espagne

Rue de France

Rue de Beyrouth

Al Hoxamd

Place de Florence

Rue du Cot Metler

Ibn Moussaif

Rue el Fatouaki

Av des Forces Armées Royales (Av des Far)

Rue Mohammed Imam Malek

Rue Mohammed Amine

Blvd Ben Jerrah

Rue Tarik Ibn Ziad

Rue de Pologne

Banque du Maroc

Rue du Portugal

Blvd Mohammed

El Caher

Rue du Cot Metler

Grands Taxis to Sefrou

Ibn Didou

Rue de Russie

Synagogue

Rue de Belgique

Rue de Martiniere

Av Mohammed

Place Mohammed V

es Slaoui

Rue Mohammed

Rue Ibn Aïcha

Av Moulay Kameir

To 4

Rue Abdel Derad

Place Ahmed el Mansour

Rue Moh el Jai Cadi Ayad

Rue Abdelaziz Bouraleb

Av du Price Heritier

Av Allal Ben Abdalh

Prefecture

Rue Moulay Slimane

Av Youssef Ben Tachfine

Place Al Massina

Rue de l'Atlas

Ibn Sina

Coopartim Centre Artisanal

Place de l'Atlas

Place Bin Anzanane

Av Hussein de Jordanie

Place de l'Atlas

CTM

Av de Sefrou

To Airport & Ifrane

To Sefrou

➡ **Fès maps**
1 Fès: three cities, page 134
2 Fès el Bali, page 138
3 Fès el Jedid, page 148
4 Fès ville nouvelle, page 155

N

100 metres

100 yards

Where to stay 🛏
Amor **1**
Youth Hostel **2**

Restaurants 🍴
Café Les Ambassadeurs **1**
El Rincon de Espana **2**

Cremerie Skali **3**
L'Italien **4**
Restaurant MB **5**

panoramic views that extend over the medina to the north. Ultra-contemporary rooms are a tranquil haven with cool neutral stying blending stark Taza stone, lots of glass and slightly retro furniture design. All the bells and whistles are here, from the luxurious Givenchy Spa, a large outdoor pool, 2 restaurants and an exceedingly sleek rooftop bar. Wi-Fi and breakfast included.

€ Hotel Amor
31 Rue d'Arabie séoudite (coming from the train station, take a left as you come onto the Pl de Florence), T0535-622724.
A small hotel with 35 old but clean rooms (doubles 200dh, more for a/c) that are good value for the price being asked. Staff here are super-friendly and try hard to please. It also has a café-pâtisserie in the street below. Avoid street-facing rooms if traffic noise bothers you. Wi-Fi (in common areas only) and breakfast included.

€ Youth hostel
18 Rue Abdesslam Serghini, T0535-624085, www.fesyouth-hostel.com.
Widely considered to be Morocco's best youth hostel, this is a spotless and very professional outfit, worth considering even if you don't usually stay in youth hostels. There's a very pleasant courtyard and garden, with lilies, trees and birds, and they have single-sex dorms and smaller rooms for 2-7. You can do laundry on the roof, and good information is available. Reception is open 0800-2200 but the rooms are off-limits 1000-1200 and 1500-1800. No HI card necessary.

Camping

Camping du Diamant vert
Near Aïn Chkeff, right off the N6, is comparatively expensive by Moroccan

standards, but it does have some extra facilities like a shop and snack restaurant. There is plenty of shade, though the washing blocks are poorly maintained. To get there take bus No 19 from Fès from outside the **PTT**. If you do stay here, you can use the aqua-fun complex next door during the summer, but bear in mind this means the campsite gets packed and noisy during peak periods.

Camping international
On the Sefrou road, some 3 km from Fès.
This is possibly a better option. It is a well-maintained but expensive site with a pool, shops and even a bar serving alcohol. To get here take bus No 38 from Pl Atlas, T0535-731439.

Restaurants

Fès El Bali
The medina is changing fast; although the majority of places to eat are still traditional Moroccan restaurants or street food, there are an increasing number of hip, contemporary restaurants hidden down the narrow alleyways.

€€€ Dar Roumana
30 Derb el Amer, Zkak Roumane, T0535-741637, www.darroumana.com. Tue-Sun 1830-2230.
Classic French cooking techniques and Moroccan produce fresh from the market fuse effortlessly together at Dar Roumana, with chef Vincent Bonnin at the helm producing French-modern dishes that diners rave over (3-course menu, 350dh). The intimate atmosphere, with just a handful of tables within an opulently decorated salon replete with intricate tile and plasterwork, adds to the appeal. Booking is highly advised. The restaurant will send a staff member

to guide you to Dar Roumana. Alcohol served. Recommended.

€€€ Restaurant 7
7 Derb Zkak Rouah, T0694-277849, www.restaurantnumero7.com. Wed-Sun, dinner only.

Foodie-central, chefs on sabbatical from across the world head up the kitchen here for 1-4 month stints each, bringing an ever-changing menu which harnesses local produce and culinary traditions with the chefs' own cooking styles and techniques. It's a brilliantly creative concept resulting in some exceptionally interesting cooking. The 4- to 5-course menu (between 350-400dh) changes daily and highlights seasonal ingredients. Alcohol served.

€€ Fez Cafe
Le Jardin des Biehn, 13 Akbat Sbaa, Douh, T0664 647 679, www.jardindesbiehn.com. Daily for breakfast, lunch and dinner.

The garden restaurant of this riad – once a Pasha's summer palace – is a chilled-out oasis amid the medina; once the fairylights start twinkling in the evening, it has a rather magical ambience, full of colourful fun. The traditional Moroccan, or lighter French and Italian dishes, feature many home-grown products, and there are also pizzas baked in a wood-fired oven. Alcohol served.

€€ Mezzanine
17 Kasbat Chams, in front of the entrance to the Jnan Sbil Gardens, T011-078336. Daily 1200-0100.

Sleek and thoroughly contemporary, this bar-lounge overlooking the Jnan Sbil Gardens is a top-spot for a sundowner, particularly if you bag a comfy couch on the rooftop terrace. The tapas-style menu offers Mediterranean flavours from Morocco, France and Spain, such as grilled sardines and chorizo skewers, marinated aubergines and tapenade – great for grazers looking for light bites. There's a good alcohol selection here too, but it's pricey.

€€ The Ruined Garden
Derb Siaj, T0649-191410, www. ruinedgarden.com. Daily 1100-2130.

You could easily pop in for quick bite while out strolling in the medina and then find that you've lost an afternoon in this tranquil retreat amid the hustle. Shady tables are scattered amid columns, trees, flowers and shrubbery, offering relaxed, casual dining. The menu offers Moroccan dishes but with a few contemporary tweaks. The tapas plate here (85dh) is particularly delicious and imaginative if you're a fan of small-plate dining, while mains such as sardine and red olive tagine (110dh) and spiced onion tart (80dh) are tasty crowd-pleasers. Lots of options for vegetarians. Recommended.

€ Café Clock
7 Derb el Magana, Talaâ Kebira, T0535-637855, www.cafeclock.com. Daily 0900-2300.

In a beautiful old building just off Talaâ Kebira in the heart of the medina, Café Clock is so much more than just a café. It has become the epicentre of traveller and expat Fès since opening in 2006, and understandably so. Hip, young, and energetic, there always seems to be something going on, whether it's a photo exhibition by a local artist, Arabic conversation classes or a calligraphy lesson in one of the upstairs lounges. It's also a great place to eat, with a contemporary riff on Moroccan classics. People come from far and wide to get a taste of the eponymous camel burger (95dh), or to snack on roasted vegetable and cheese toasted sandwiches (55dh) and aubergine and goat's cheese quiche with ras el-honout potatoes (65dh) The roof has a stunning view of the minaret of the Medersa Bou Inania on the other side of Talaâ Kebira. Wi-Fi available, and if you want to find anything out about the city, you'll probably find someone here who will be happy to tell you. Recommended.

€ Café Medina
8 Derb Menissi. Daily 1000-2300.
Located just outside Bab Boujeloud
on the alleyway just to the right.
This is a peaceful spot to hang out on a roof terrace, and although its traditional Moroccan menu is a little bit more upmarket than its neighbours, it offers some seriously hearty cooking without all the restaurant-tout hustle and tustle just within the gate. The harissa soup, just like a Moroccan mamma would make it, is a highlight. The small menu troops through all the usual tagine and brochette subjects with set menus starting at 90dh, and mains from 60dh. Service is ultra-friendly.

€ Snak Restaurant Seffarine
Pl Seffarine. Daily 1000-2100.
A great spot to put your feet up and have lunch after trawling the souks, this lovely rooftop terrace looks out over Pl Seffarine with a soundtrack of metalworkers hammering below. It's a family-run affair with a simple menu of Moroccan staples, omelettes and snack-style food, and with friendly service to boot. You could easily waste an hour or two with a pot of mint tea while surveying the bustling square below.

€ Thami's
Rue Serrajine. Daily 1000-2300.
There is no shortage of cheap eats just inside Bab Boujeloud, where a row of

busy cafés with outdoor tables serve cheap and cheerful evening meals. Of these, local celebrity Thami's, tucked into a corner under the tree, is the most often recommended and the tastiest. His kefta and egg tagine is excellent, the lamb and prune tagine is melt in your mouth, and his steaming great cauldrons of *lobia* (white bean stew) and *maakouda* (potato pancakes with hot chilli sauce) are hearty and tasty. It's also arguably the best place in town for a spot of people-watching.

Cafés

Crèmerie de Place
On the northern point of Pl Seffarine.
A well-loved little spot for sitting out on the square and watching the copper-beaters at work. There's something almost musical about the chink, chink, chink of so many little hammers, and it's a good place to get to know locals who stop for a chat minus the endless haggle. Coffee, *panache* (mixed fruit juice) and cakes are all good here, and it's ideal for catching your breath after a couple of hours losing yourself in the souks.

Khamsa Café
Talaâ Kebira.
Right in the heart of the main street mayhem, head up through the scruffy entranceway to the roof terrace to chill out for a while with a fruit juice or pot of mint tea. It's a cheap and cheerful place with no frills, but there are good views over the rooftops and out to the tombs on the hill, and the staff are a friendly bunch who love to have a chat.

Fès ville nouvelle
The place to come if you feel like a change from more traditional Moroccan fare, the *ville nouvelle* has plenty of international options, though it's far from

having the same variety and choice as Marrakech. There are several good cheap places along Av Chefchaouni selling piping hot brochettes, lentils, Moroccan salads and other tasty street food.

€€€ Restaurant MB
12 Rue Ahmed Chaouki, T0535-622727, www.mbrestaurantlounge.com.
This ultra-cool customer is a top-ticket for fine dining in the city. It serves up a menu of classically French cooking, with just a smidgeon of Moroccan influences, in a suave, contemporary setting of sleek neutrals. It's a favourite among Fès's see-and-be-seen crowd, who come here to dine on the meat-heavy menu or to drink cocktails at the bar. Alcohol served.

€€ El Rincon de Espana
Av des FAR, T0535-942576. Daily 1100-2300.
Hankering after a taste of the sea? Spanish cuisine with an emphasis on seafood and paella is the name of the game here, with a couple of Moroccan tweaks thrown in for good measure. It's a casual and friendly place, with the seafood on a counter display; staff are happy to help you with choosing.

€€ L'Italien
Residence Longchamp, Av Omar Ibn Khattab, T0535-943384. Daily 1200-2300.
This Italian restaurant, with Scandinavian-styling of blonde wood, natty furniture and large communal tables, is about as far from Fès as you could be, but is a welcome respite from tagine overload. They serve top-notch home-made ravioli stuffed with spinach and ricotta, bread rubbed with rosemary and salt, and crisp-based wood-fired pizzas. Alcohol served.

Cafés

The wide boulevards of the *ville nouvelle* lend themselves to café society, and there are innumerable places to sit back with a *café noir* (black coffee) or a *nous nous* (half and half). The better ones include **L'Elysée** (4 Rue de Paris); **Café Les Ambassadeurs** (Pl de Florence), and **Crèmerie Skali** (Mohammed V), which has a huge juice and shakes menu, all freshly made on the spot.

Bars and clubs

For the classiest bar in the medina, go to the Sky Bar in **Riad Fès** (see Where to stay, above). Many of Fès's expats favour the bar in the **Hotel Batha** (Av de la Liberté, T0535-634860) for a beer, or for contemporary surroundings, try **Mezzanine** (see Restaurants, above).

Festivals

May Fès Festival of World Sacred Music (www.fesfestival.com). For 10 days Fès vibrates to the rhythmic drumming and soaring voices of the **Festival de Fès des musiques sacrées du monde**. From Sufi to gospel, the range is wide, and there is a scattering of dance too. Free open-air concerts take place in the square outside Bab Boujeloud, with other ticketed events at locations such as the Batha Museum and Bab Makina. Prices for individual concerts range from around 150dh to 600dh, or you can buy a pass for all the concerts for 2900dh. Tickets are available online.

Oct Fès Festival of Sufi Culture. Some of the finest Sufi musicians and singers from across the globe flock to the city for this 8-day festival which celebrates Sufi music and culture. A series of concerts is the highlight of the programme, but there are also a number of other events.

Shopping

Books and newspapers
Newspapers are available from the stalls in Av Mohammed V.
Librarie Konouz al Maarifa, *11 Talaâ Sghira, Fès el Bali*. A decent selection of English and, especially, French books, with Moroccan authors in translation as well as novels, travel literature and a few guidebooks.

Moroccan handicrafts
Fès has long been one of the great trading centres of Morocco. The souks, *kissaria* and boutiques offer a splendid selection for visitors. Many of the boutiques in the hotels, the *ville nouvelle* and near the important tourist attractions will try to charge inflated prices. As elsewhere, the large carpet shops have very experienced salesmen who work with guides to whom they pay a commission for sales completed. The best buy in Fès is probably the blue-and-white painted rustic pottery once typical of the city. For smaller gift items, slippers and traditional clothing explore the *kissaria* (clothes market) area between the Zaouïa of Moulay Idriss and the Qaraouiyine Mosque.
Coopartim Centre Artisanal, *Blvd Allal Ben Abdallah, T0535-625654. Daily 0900-1400 and 1600-1900*. A good selection of crafts in the *ville nouvelle*.

Supermarkets
Borj Fès, *Av de la Liberte, Ville Nouvelle*. The first shopping mall in the city has a big supermarket where you can stock up on travel needs. If you've got little ones in tow, this is where to come to purchase nappies and other baby products. Alcohol is also available.

What to do

Cookery
Clock Kitchen, *Café Clock, 7 Derb el Magana, Talaâ Kebira, T0535-637855, www.cafeclock.com*. Highly recommended cooking classes that take you through Moroccan culinary skills, from shopping for ingredients in the souk to cooking and finally eating your creations. The class runs 1000-1500 and costs 600dh per person.
The Ruined Garden Breadmaking Class, *The Ruined Garden, Derb Siaj, T0649-191410, www.ruinedgarden.com*. If you're interested in getting down to the specifics of baking Morocco's major staple, then this is the place to do it. You'll be guided through making 5 different local breads, including a trip to the community oven for baking, and learn how to handroll couscous. A 2-course lunch is included. 550dh per person.

Hammams
Hammam Mernissi, *Rue Serrajine, Fès el Bali. Daily women 0900-2000, men 2000-midnight*. This recently restored hammam (follow the sign down the narrow alleyway beside Thami's restaurant) is a good choice for a first public hammam experience. Staff here are used to tourists popping in, and the female attendants offer a tourist package complete with scrub 0900-2000.

Plenty of riads in the medina offer private hammam treatments, including:
Riad Laaroussa, *3 Derb Bechara, Fès el Bali, T0674-187639, www.riad-laaroussa. com. Daily 1100-2100*. A popular choice for a spa-style hammam treat, Riad Laaroussa's hammam offers a 45-min traditional hammam experiences for

350dh and a hammam and massage for 730dh. Booking is essential.

Riad Rcif Hammam and Spa, *Av Ben Mohammed el Alaoui, Rcif, Fès el Bali, T0535-740037, www.riadrcif.com*. This luxury spa-style hammam offers steam and scrub for 380dh or a full package of steam, scrub and full body clay mask, using traditional rasoul clay, for 420dh.

Language courses

Alif (Arabic Language in Fès), *2 Rue Ahmed Hiba (close to the Hotel Zalagh), T0535-624850*. Good reputation for organizing courses in Arabic, both literary and spoken Moroccan. They can cater for specific language needs, and at any one time have around 30 or more students from various backgrounds.

Tour operators

There are several good tour companies offering specialist trips aimed at independent travellers who want to experience a more authentic side of Morocco.

Culture Vultures Fez, *www. culturevulturesfez.org*. Arranges tours focused on the artisanal crafts of both Fès and Sefrou medinas. Half-day tours in Fès explore the wood, tanning, dying and metal workshops of the old city, while tours in Sefrou discover the traditional workshops of tailors, buttonmakers and ironmongers.

Tours Around Fez, *www.toursaround fez.com*. Hikes and sunset picnics on Mt Zalagh, or 4WD trips through the Middle Atlas, with a focus on responsible tourism.

Transport

Air

The small **Aéroport de Fès-Saiss** is 15 km to the south of the city, off the N8, T0535-624712. **Royal Air Maroc** (RAM; 54 Av Hassan II, *ville nouvelle*, T0535-625516/7, reservations T0535-620456/7) has a daily flight to/from Casablanca; for international connections, change there. To get to the airport, take bus No 16 from the train station, or catch a *grand taxi* (150dh).

Bus

Local Local buses cost 2dh. No 1 runs from Pl des Alaouites to Dar Batha, No 3 from Pl des Alaouites to Pl de la Résistance, No 9 from Pl de la Résistance to Dar Batha, No 10 from Bab Guissa to Pl des Alaouites, No 18 from Pl de la Résistance to Bab Ftouh and No 20 from Pl de Florence to Hôtel les Mérinides.

Long-distance Long-distance **CTM** buses depart from the station on Pl de l'Atlas (Av Mohammed V, T0535-622041) in the *ville nouvelle*. There are 9 departures daily to Casablanca (90dh, 6 hrs); 6 daily for **Marrakech** (160dh, 8-9 hrs); 9 to **Meknès** (25dh, 1 hr); 9 to **Taza** (50dh, 2 hrs); and a service to **Rissani** at 2130 (165dh, 10 hrs), among others.

　　Supratours buses depart from the train station and offer a daily bus to **Merzouga** via **Erfoud** and **Rissani** at 2030 (11 hrs). Most other private line buses leave from the new terminal off the Rte du Tour de Fès, below the Borj nord and not far from Bab Boujeloud, with regular services to Middle Atlas towns.

Car hire

Fès is a fairly easy city to navigate. There are several car parks dotted around the medina, usually fairly close to the one of the babs, where you can safely leave your vehicle for a day or two; a tip to the 'guardian' (security person) on leaving is expected. In case of breakdown, try **Mécanique Générale** (22 Av Cameroun), or for Fiat repairs, **Auto Maroc** (Av Mohammed V, T0535-623435). Car hire firms include: **Avis** (50 Blvd Chefchaouni, T0535-626746); **Budget** (adjacent Palais Jamaï Hotel, T0535-620919); **Europcar-Inter-Rent** (41 Av Hassan II, T0535-626545); **Hertz** (Kissariat de la Foire No 1, Blvd Lalla Meryem, T0535-622812; airport T0535-651823), and **Holiday Car** (41 Av Mohammed V, T0535-624550).

Taxi

Grands taxis to **Meknès** leave from just outside Bab Mahrouk; to **Sefrou** they depart from a stand on Blvd du Ravin in the *ville nouvelle*. Another taxi stand next to the **CTM** bus station serves other destinations. Red, cheap and a quick way to get around Fès, *petits taxis* generally have meters and most drivers are happy to use them.

Train

The railway station is at the end of Blvd Chenguit, in the *ville nouvelle*, T0535-622501. There are regular train services to **Rabat** (4 hrs), **Casablanca** (5 hrs) and **Marrakech** (8 hrs), all via **Meknès** (1½ hrs). Trains to **Taza** (2 hrs) depart at 1045, 1535, 1700 and 1845.

Around Fès

take time out from city life to explore scenic towns in the hills

Moulay Yacoub

Every bit a country spa town, Moulay Yacoub, 20 km northwest of Fès, is a short 45-minute journey through rolling countryside and some interesting capital-intensive irrigated farming. Taxis from Bab Boujeloud stop near the car park above the village from where steep flights of steps lead down into the centre. There are plenty of hammams, small shops, cafés and a number of cheap lodging houses, some with rudimentary self-catering facilities.

Moulay Yacoub is a destination for local tourists, and a visit to one of the **hammams** can be quite an experience. There are baths for both men and women. The buildings date from the 1930s and could do with some maintenance but, at the price, you can't complain. The men's hammam has a pool of extremely hot sulphurous water – a bucket of Moulay Yacoub water poured on your head is guaranteed to boil your brains. There are few foreigners; beware the masseur, who may well delight in making an exhibition of you with a poolside pummel and stretching designed for Olympic athletes. Merely bathing in the hot spring water will leave you exhausted – and hopefully rejuvenated. There is also a luxury spa down in the valley.

Sidi Harazem

In restaurants all over Morocco, Sidi Ali and Sidi Harazem are the most widely available mineral waters, along with sparkling Oulmès. The saintly Sidi Harazem is said to have died in Fès in 1164. He taught at the Qaraouiyin Mosque and, it is said,

BACKGROUND
Sefrou

Sefrou once lay astride the major caravan routes from Fès and northern Morocco, to the south and the Sahara beyond. Although it is now bypassed by new roads, it remains an important marketplace for the surrounding agricultural region. Sefrou was one of those small inland Moroccan towns that had a distinctive character because of its large Jewish population, which predated the Islamic conquest. Although many Berbers and Jews were converted to Islam by Moulay Idriss, Sefrou's Jewish element was reinforced with the migration of Jews from Tafilalet and Algeria in the 13th century. After the Second World War, large numbers of Jews emigrated to Morocco's large cities, Europe and Israel. The 1967 Arab-Israeli War was the final blow. Sefrou has fascinated American academics, with the likes of anthropologists Geertz, Rosen and Rabinow carrying out research here. Recently Sefrou was created capital of a new province, receiving new and badly needed investment. A town declining into shabby anonymity, it may yet rescue something of its heritage and find a place on the tourist map.

his classes and lectures were so interesting that even the *djinn*, the mischievous spirits of Moroccan folklore, attended. The village of Sidi Harazem, with its spring and spa centre, is only 4 km along the N6 from Fès, with buses leaving from the CTM bus station and Bab Boujeloud, and other buses and *grands taxis* from Bab Ftouh. The area around the thermal baths is still very popular for swimming and picnics. There is a 17th-century *koubba*, dating from the time of the village's establishment as a resort under Sultan Moulay Rachid.

★ Sefrou and around

Sefrou is 32 km south of Fès along the R503. It is not the sort of place you would visit if travelling south, as the N8/N13, via Ifrane and Azrou, is a better route from Fès to Er Rachidia and beyond. However, Sefrou is certainly worth visiting as a side trip from Fès for a morning or afternoon, or even for an overnight stay. Lying in a beautiful wooded valley, its historic medina is full of noodling back alleys of gently dilapidated houses with flaking whitewash. There's an air of tranquillity and a genuinely friendly atmosphere here that makes a nice break from the hustle and bustle of Fès. The town is known for olive and cherry production, and in June holds a three-day cherry festival (the **Fête des Cerises**) that sees the entire town come alive with music, a parade and a pageant to anoint that year's 'cherry queen'.

Sights Entering from the north, the road curves down to the Oued Aggaï, past the **Centre Artisanal** ① *Mon-Sat 0800-1200 and 1400-1900,* into the busy Place Moulay Hassan. From here, **Bab M'kam** is the main entrance to the medina, which lies north of the river, while **Bab Taksebt** is the main entrance into the *mellah*, over the bridge. Both are small, maze-like quarters, but it is difficult to get seriously lost. There is a clearly discernible difference in the design of the two areas, reflecting the strict regulations and conditions under which Jews in the *mellah* lived. Sefrou is quite remarkable, however, in that the *mellah* is as large as the medina.

As well as from Bab Taksebt, the **mellah** can also be entered from the covered marketplace through **Bab M'Rabja**. Beside a mosque built into the wall, turn right and down the main street, beside small restaurants, butchers' shops and craftsmen, and then left to reach one of several small bridges over the Oued Aggaï. Alternatively, take one of the small side turnings to discover the cramped design of the *mellah*, now mainly occupied by poor rural migrants, with houses often built over the narrow streets.

In the medina, the **Grand Mosque**, restored in the 19th century, lies beside the river and the souks just upstream. Past the souks is the **zaouïa of Sidi Lahcen ben Ahmed**. Avenue Moulay Hassan crosses the Oued Aggaï and continues as Avenue Mohammed V, the main street of the unexciting new town,

> **Tip...**
> The marketplace below and east of Avenue Mohammed V is a relaxed area in which to wander, best during the Thursday market.

with the post office and a few shops and simple café-restaurants. Turn into Rue Ziad by the post office, past **Hotel Sidi Lahcen Lyoussi**, and continue uphill on the black-top road. Camping is signed to the left but continue up to the **koubba of Sidi Bou Ali**, with its white walls and distinctive green-tiled roof. There is a café, a few stalls and a magnificent view. Another small excursion beginning south of the river leads west to a small **waterfall** (*les cascades*).

Bhalil Just 5 km before Sefrou, off the R503, is Bhalil. This small hill village may have had a Christian population before the coming of Islam. Behind the picturesque village are several **troglodyte dwellings**, with people still inhabiting the caves. The road takes you round the town, giving excellent views on all sides, and there are two good, clean cafés on the outskirts when approaching from the east.

Where to stay

Sidi Harazem

€€ Hotel Sidi Harazem
T0535-690135, www.sogatour.ma.
Pricey, for what it is, with 62 a/c rooms,
health facilities, restaurant and bar.

Sefrou

€ Riad La Maison des Lallas
304 Derb el Mittar, T0535-661116,
www.lamaisondeslallas.com.
Snuggled into the medina, this rather
charming guesthouse is a welcoming
place with plenty of home-from-home
appeal. Filled with traditional character,
rooms (€32-40) have stark walls offset
by original tiled floors, wrought-iron
features and colourful bedspreads. It's a
lovely place to stay if you want to escape
Fès and get a taste of the quieter side of
Morocco. Breakfast and Wi-Fi included.

Camping

Camping de Sefrou
2 km from the town, follow Rue Ziad,
by the post office on Av Mohammed V,
T0535-673340.
This large 4-ha site has a bar and café,
a grocery shop and good bathrooms.

Transport

Sefrou

Grands taxis from Fès leave from Blvd
du Ravin in the *ville nouvelle* and drop
passengers off right in front of Bab
M'Kam, on Pl Moulay Hassan.

East of
Fès

discover a medina far from the madding crowds

There was a time when Taza was quite a happening place, given its strategic location controlling the easiest route from the Moroccan heartland of Fès and Meknès to the eastern plains. The town, rather quiet today, is divided into three quite separate parts: the area around the railway and bus station; the *ville nouvelle*, dating from the early 20th century, around Place de l'Indépendence (for hotels, restaurants, banks and other services), and the older attractive medina on the hill with its narrow streets. After the hurly-burly of Fès, low-key Taza makes a good base from which to explore up into the hills of the Jbel Tazzeka National Park.

Essential Taza

Finding your feet

Taza is easily accessible by public transport from Fès, 120 km to the west. Coming from eastern Morocco, you will pass through Taourirt and Guercif, a major meeting of the roads some 40 km from Taza. Trains, buses and *grands taxis* from all directions arrive to the north of town, about 1 km from Place de l'Indépendence, which is at the centre of the *ville nouvelle*. The medina is another 2 km further south. There is only one hotel in the medina, so you will probably stay in the *ville nouvelle*. (There are three hotels on Place de l'Indépendence.)

Getting around

There is a regular bus service from Place de l'Indépendence to Place Moulay Hassan in the medina, or a light blue *petit taxi* will cost you around 3dh from the station to Place de l'Indépendence, and 6dh from the station to the medina.

> **Tip...**
> From the bottom of the hill there is an interesting short cut to the kasbah via a flight of steps which provide remarkable views. Beyond this point, further along the main road on the right, are the Kifane el Ghomari caves, inhabited in Neolithic times.

BACKGROUND

Taza

The site was first settled in Neolithic times. Later it was developed by Meknassa Amazigh groups, eventually becoming an important, but ultimately unsuccessful fortification against the advance of the Fatimids from the east. The Almohads under Sultan Abd el Moumen captured the city in 1141-1142, making it their second capital and using it to attack the Almoravids. The Almohads built a mosque and expanded the fortifications.

Taza was the first city taken by the Merinids, who extended the Almohad city considerably. Its important defensive role continued under the Merinids and the Saâdians, and was again pivotal in the rise to power of the Alaouites, who further extended and fortified the city, later using it as a strong point in their defence against the threat from French-occupied Algeria to the east.

The eccentric pretender, Bou Hamra, 'the man on the she-donkey', proclaimed himself sultan here in 1902 and controlled much of eastern Morocco until 1912, when he was caught and killed. He was known as a wandering miracle-maker, travelling Morocco on his faithful beast. Taza was occupied by the French in 1914 and became an important military centre, located on the route linking Algeria with the Atlantic plains of *le Maroc utile*, between the remote mountains and plateaux of eastern Morocco and the great cities to the west.

Today, with the decline in cross-border trade with Algeria, Taza, like its distant neighbour Oujda, sees far less passing traffic than it did and has a distinctly sleepy feel to it. A couple of the hotels have been upgraded, however, and you could well stay here for a couple of nights if exploring or birdwatching up in the Jbel Tazzeka National Park.

Medina
Note that the main historic buildings in the medina are closed to non-Muslims.

The transport hub of the old town is **Place Moulay Hassan**, just outside the main entrance to the **souk**. The focus of the old quarter is the main street, commonly called the Mechouar from end to end, which runs behind Place Moulay Hassan along the entire length of the medina, from the Andalucían Mosque to the Grand Mosque at the opposite end of town by the Bab er Rih gate. Between the two mosques are the various souks. Hassle is practically non-existent, as there are few articles thought to interest the tourist. The fact that there is no motor traffic in the medina makes it all the more pleasant. The best thing to do is just wander – the old neighbourhoods are quite small and sooner or later you will come out on the outside road ringing the town.

Turning left just past the main gate to the souk, by the **Cinema Friouato**, is the jewellery section of the souk. From here you can turn left along a very straight and narrow section of road towards the Andalucían Mosque, or right towards the Grand Mosque. Following the latter route, the food and spice souk is off to the left, behind the broader section of the Mechouar. Further along, you may get a glimpse of the **Zaouïa of Sidi Azouz** (note its beautiful wall-basin by the door). It is difficult to gain a good view of the **Grand Mosque**, built by the Almohads in the second half of the 12th century, with further elaboration by the Merinids in the late 13th century, and the Alaouites in the 17th. In its

Tip...
For snacks to munch while you're exploring the medina, head to Pistacherie Rayane, 5 Avenue Moulay Hassan, by the entrance to the old town. It sells a big variety of factory-fresh nuts, much cheaper than elsewhere.

classic proportions of 1:5, the minaret resembles that of the Koutoubia Mosque in Marrakech. Only Muslims can view the beautiful chandelier bearing 514 oil lamps, which lights the mosque.

To the right of the Grand Mosque, down a steep flight of steps, you reach a section of the **ramparts** (which have been well restored in recent years), with good views over the surrounding countryside, lower Taza, and the mountains beyond. Going left after the steps to start a rampart tour, the first section, with some steep drops, is referred to as **Bab er Rih**, 'the Gate of the Wind'. From here you have perhaps the best view of the Almohad minaret. Eventually, keeping to the outside of the town, you could look out for the circular **Sarasine Tower**, also dating back to the Almohad times – and showing clear European influence.

Taza medina

200 metres
200 yards

Restaurants 🍴
Café Andalous 1
Café en Ghissani 2

At the far end of the Mechouar from Bab er Rih is the **Andalucían Mosque**, with its 12th-century minaret. Just before, on the right, stands the 14th-century **Medersa of Abu el Hassan**, named after a Merinid sultan. This is closed, but the exterior shows a carved lintel in cedar wood and a porch roof overhanging the road. In a lane to the right of the mosque, Zankat Dar el Makhzen, there is the former house of Bou Hamra the pretender. The weekly **market** takes place outside the walls at this end of town, outside **Bab Titi**.

Listings Taza *map p168*

Where to stay

€ Grand Hotel du Dauphiné
Av de la Gare and Pl de l'Indépendence,
T0535-673567.
The rooms (190dh) are nothing spectacular but this old timer is handily located in the centre, close to cafes with plenty of breads and pastries for snacks. All the rooms were renovated a few years ago and, although all its period details have gone, there are some modern touches that make it more comfortable.

€ Hotel de la Gare
At the main crossroads near the station,
T0535-672448.
This cheap and cheerful hotel near the train station – great for early travel starts – has spic-and-span rooms (200dh) and very friendly owners. There's a decent café next door. It's a 2-km stroll to the medina from here.

Restaurants

€€ Grand Hotel du Dauphiné
See above.
The huge 1950s dining hall here dishes up good-value meals, as long as you don't mind a limited menu (sometimes only steak and chips). On the plus side, they do serve a nice cold bottle of beer.

For more basic eats try **Café Restaurant Majestic** (**€**), Av Mohammed V, which does solid Moroccan food, while the **Snack Bar Youm Youm** (**€**) (behind **Hotel de la Poste** on Blvd Moulay Youssef), serves tasty brochettes.

Cafés

Taza is a great place for people-watching and has a thriving café scene.

Café Andalous
In the old town.
With a terrace overlooking the animated Pl Moulay Hassan, this is probably the top spot to sit and observe the local scene.

Café des Jardins
Av Ibn Khatib.
Located in the municipal gardens en route to the old town. Chill out on the shady terrace with views, after a morning in the medina.

Café el Ghissani
Opposite Café Andalous by the main entrance to the souk.
This is a good place to catch your breath and is hugely popular with locals.

Pâtisserie des Festivités
1 Blvd Mohammed V, just off Pl de l'Indépendence.
Provides a cosy nook and is good for breakfast and cakes.

Transport

Bus CTM buses leave from their office on Pl de l'Indépendence. There are several departures daily for **Casablanca** (155dh, 6½ hrs); **Fès** (45dh, 1½ hrs); and **Meknès** (70dh, 3¼ hrs); plus 2 services at 1515 and 1715 to **Oujda** (80dh, 3 hrs). Other companies operate from near the railway station; turn right at the north end of Av de la Gare. There are plenty of services to **Oujda/Guercif/Taourirt** (4 hrs); buses to **Fès** hourly; and regular departures for **Nador** (4 hrs), **Al Hoceïma** (4 hrs) and **Aknoul** (1 hr). Make sure you take a new-looking bus by a reliable company for Al Hoceïma and Nador.

Taxi *Grands taxis* leave from the transport cafés by the bus station to **Oujda**, **Fès**, **Al Hoceïma** and **Nador**, amongst other places.

Train At Taza the ONCF locomotives switch from electric to diesel, hence speed heading eastwards is slow. There are at least 3 daily departures for **Oujda** (4 hrs), stopping at **Guercif** and **Taourirt**. **Casablanca** is 7 hrs away; **Tangier**, a good 8 hrs away, if you are lucky with the connection at **Sidi Kacem**. **Fès** is 2 hrs by train; **Meknès,** 3 hrs.

Jbel Tazzeka National Park

one of North Africa's greatest caving experiences

An area of fine mountain scenery, the Jbel Tazzeka National Park, south of Taza and the N6, can also be visited with your own transport on a long but rewarding day trip from Fès. The region's cork-oak forest and its undergrowth have plenty to keep ornithologists happy – look out for the rare black-shouldered kite. Scenery and kites apart, however, the main reason for doing this trip is to go intrepidly down into the Gouffre de Friouato, an immense series of hobbity caverns with scrambles, stalactites and mud aplenty.

Along the S311
The map shows distances between major points and the quality of the roads.

From the plateau of old Taza, the S311 winds its way south and west, eventually linking up with the the the N6 some 31 km further west. If you have parked up close to the walls of Taza, head back as though you were returning to new Taza, leaving the Préfecture on your left, and go straight ahead at the next roundabout. (Without a car you might bargain for a *grand taxi* to take you part of the way, from the rank by the railway station.) With no stops, a careful driver will take 1¾ hours to reach the N6. (Take water in case the engine overheats.)

After a rainy winter, the **Cascades de Ras el Oued**, a few kilometres out of Taza and a popular picnic spot, might be worth a look. Next stop, some 14 km along the route, is the **Vallée des oiseaux**, which starts with a thick stand of cork oak. Nearby lies the **Dayat Chiker**, a seasonal lake. Next you will reach a fork in the road signed Maghraoua (left) and Bab Boudir (right). Go right, and 3 km further on, about 35 minutes from Taza, you will reach the turn-off right heading uphill to the Gouffre de Friouato (see below).

After the caves, the next major stopping point, 30 km from Taza, is an unlikely *station estivale*, with red-roofed houses and various seasonal eateries, including the **Café Bouhadli**. Continue on to the Bab Taza pass, from which a rough and challenging track goes north up to the **Jbel Tazzeka**, where there are incredible views of the surrounding mountains. After, or avoiding, the Jbel Tazzeka, the road continues through cork forest, past another signed picnic area, the **Vallée des Cerfs**, and then down and through the narrow gorge by the Oued Zireg and back to the N6.

★ Gouffre de Friouato
5dh, guide 200dh (recommended). Torches, overalls and shoes can be rented on site.

A descent into this magnificent cave system is not for the weak-kneed. Near the car park is a stone-built *guichet* building, where smiling, bright-eyed Mustapha Lachhab presides over piles of biscuits, sweets, torches and batteries – everything an amateur caver could need. The officially authorized organizer of guides, he also has photocopied sheets with a cross-section of the caverns.

The site admission fee gives you access to the first flights of steps; if you've hired a guide you can continue down 520 steps (a further 230 m), push through a narrow squeeze (easier on the way back) and then scramble into the **Salle de Lixus**, as the first main cave is rather grandly known, after the Roman site near modern Larache. Here there are stalactites, including a sort of crystal platform that looks for all the world like a Renaissance pulpit; other shapes include a be-turbaned individual (use your imagination) and a *hallouf* (pig). From here the caves run on at

Jbel Tazzeka National Park

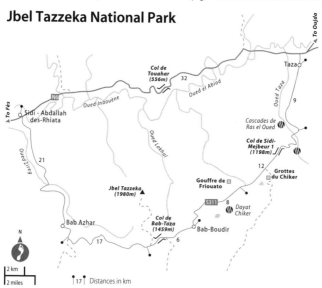

least a further 2 km, an exploration best left to the enthusiastic and well equipped. Getting down and back from the Salle de Lixus will take you about an hour.

If you're a real speleologist, it would definitely be worth spending time in the region as there are further caverns elsewhere. Note that, having done the descent so many times, the local guides really do know how to pace a group. They now also have quite a lot of ropes and other material left behind by cavers.

Listings Jbel Tazzaka National Park

Where to stay

€€€-€€ Auberge Aïn-Sahla
59 Oued Amlil, T0661-893587, T0670-196094, www.ainsahla.com.
Located in the heart of the Tazzeka National Park, this place is a gem for those who like to get out into the wilds in style. It has 17 rooms and 3 suites, some with private gardens or terraces,
all beautifully decorated with lots of outdoor spaces for chilling out (singles/doubles from 550/700dh). The pool is fed by the Aïn-Sahla spring, and the home-cooked food is excellent. It's a great base for keen walkers, and the friendly owners are an excellent source of information on the hidden corners of the park. Wi-Fi and breakfast included. Half-board and full-board options also offered.

Middle Atlas east of Taza

the rural heartland of the Middle Atlas

Oujda Msoun
Some 20 km to the east of Taza along the N6 is the fortified farming village of Msoun. Built around 1700 in Moulay Ismaïl's reign to guard the approaches to the strategic Taza Gap, it is still inhabited by members of the semi-nomadic Houara tribe. The village has a shop, post office and even a teahouse. The compact, walled settlement stands isolated on a hillside, clearly visible from the main road where there is the convenient **Motel-Restaurant Casbah** and a petrol station. It is possible to walk to the village from here, just 2 km.

Guercif
Guercif is an unremarkable modern agricultural town noted for its olives and shoe industry. In the 14th century, it became a stronghold of the Beni Ouattas Tribe, who later overran Taza and replaced Merinids to form the Ouattasid Dynasty. The main part of

Tip...
From Guercif, the N15 heads south along the Oued Moulouya to Missour (see page 203) and Midelt (page 201).

town, which lies to the south of the main road, is centred round Boulevard Mohammed V, its solid 19th-century mosque and two adjacent squares. The railway station is reached via a driveway from the opposite side of the main road. Market day is Sunday. There's a **pharmacie centrale** on the market square.

Taourirt and around

Halfway between Taza and Oujda, Taourirt is an important commercial centre with a large **market** on Sunday. In the past the town functioned as the junction between two major trade routes: the east–west trans-Maghreb route and the route from Melilla to the Tafilalet. The centre of town is located around the junction of the N6 and the Debdou road (the ancient caravan route to the south), which is packed with shops, garages, cafés and small workshops. The **Pharmacie Echifa** is opposite the new mosque. The only tangible historic attraction is the remains of the **kasbah** on the hill 1 km to the northwest, unfortunately spoiled by electricity pylons but with excellent views.

There are several excursions around Taourirt that make it worthwhile stopping for a day or two, if you have time. Providing there is enough water in the *oued* (unlikely between August and December), the **Zaâ waterfalls** make an enjoyable picnic and bathing destination, and camping is possible. To get there, turn right at the signpost 6 km along the Taza road. It is a further 9 km north to the waterfalls. The track continues to Melga el Ouidane and the large lake known as **Barrage Mohammed V**. There are a number of picnic spots along the route. Southeast of Taourirt, the **Zaâ gorges** are deep, very impressive and well worth the journey. As you leave Taourirt on the Oujda road, there is a turning off to the right. You cannot drive through the narrow defile, so leave the car where the road ends and walk from there.

Debdou

Nestling in a verdant bowl formed by the surrounding massif, Debdou, 50 km southwest of Taourirt, is an island of rural tranquillity. The fact that it's on a road to nowhere has helped to preserve its identity. The surrounding area is very scenic and provides good opportunities for walking and exploration. There is an interesting kasbah halfway up the mountainside above the main village. There are no tourist facilities, and transport links are poor.

Until the 1960s over half the population of Debdou were Jewish, and most were the descendants of Jews from Taza who fled the persecution and chaos of Bou Hamra's rule (1902-1908). The 'main street' branches off the main road at the entrance to the village and zig-zags for about 1 km, past store houses, to a square at the top end of the village known as **Aïn Sbilia**. Overlooking the square is a balcony shaded by plane trees. A small sluice gate allows water to flow into a channel bisecting the square below, which has a café. It is all very restful, the locals playing cards or backgammon and drinking mint tea.

High above the village is the still-inhabited **kasbah of Caïd Ghomriche**, built by the Merinids in the 13th century and subsequently handed over to the Beni Ouattas, a related tribe, around 1350 when the Merinids ruled Morocco. Follow the signposted track (2 km) starting from the bottom end of the village. Note the colourful hammam, which is still heated by a wood stove. Along the way there are pretty views of the town on the right and the waterfalls high above on the left. Just before the kasbah there is a grassy ledge with good views over the valley, and the entrance to a **cave**. The settlement is a mixture of ancient ruins, small vegetable gardens and mud houses.

At the back of the village, past the walls and a dry moat, is a field where jagged stones stick out of the ground – the sunken headstones of tombs. By crossing the field and turning left for 30-40 m and then sharp right, there is a path (1 km) linking up with the main road and the source of the Oued Debdou. The same location can be reached by the main road, which swings to the left just before Debdou and runs along the mountain crest, or **Gaada de Debdou**, for 5 or 6 km. There are fantastic views from here and good walking opportunities. Beyond this, the road descends from the plateau down into the arid Rekkam plain where it becomes a rough track, eventually leading to Outad Ouled el Hadj. **Market** day is Wednesday.

El Aïoun

Halfway between Taourirt and Oujda, and within easy reach of the **Beni Snassen Mountains**, El Aioun was founded by Moulay Ismaïl in 1679. It has a small kasbah, restored in 1876 by Sultan Moulay Hassan in response to the threat of French expansion from Algeria. To the south of the town is a **cemetery**, where those who died fighting colonialism are buried. During the first half of the 20th century, El Aïoun became a centre of the Sufi Brotherhood of Sheikh Bou Amama, whose *zaouïa* is located here. The weekly **souk** is held on Tuesday and frequented by members of the local Ouled Sidi Sheikh tribe.

Listings East of Taza

Where to stay

Taourirt

€ Hotel Mansour
On the Debdou road just off main crossroads, T0536-694003.
The large rooms here are adequately clean and there's a good café below. Hot water available.

Transport

Guercif
CTM has departures to **Oujda**, **Fès**, **Midelt** and **Er Rachidia**. CTM offices are between the central square and Pl Zerkatouni. Private buses serve **Taourirt–Oujda** and **Taza–Fès**. Buses for **Er Rachidia** depart from le complexe on the main road. ONCF train services run to **Taourirt/Oujda** and **Taza/Fès/Casablanca**.

Taourirt
Buses for **Oujda** (every ½ hr) and **Nador** (around 5 a day) depart from the Agip petrol station past the main crossroads. **Guercif/Taza/Fès** (virtually every 30 mins during the day and hourly at night) depart from near the Shell petrol station on the same road, as do the *grands taxis* that ply the N6. *Grands taxis* for **Debdou** leave from the rank on the Debdou road. There are trains to **Oujda**

0530, 0800, 1800, 1930 (approximate times); **Taza/Fès/Casablanca** 0830, 1045, 2030, 2230 (approximate times). Once the new Nador line opens, Taourirt's transport options will increase. **Petrol** is available at the south end of the main boulevard before the bridge.

Debdou

There's an early morning and an early afternoon bus departure to **Taourirt,** as well as taxis (most frequent in the morning and early evening – if you don't want to get stuck here, try to leave before 1800).

Meknès
& around

Meknès never set out to be an 'imperial city'. But, as chance would have it, the inhabitants of Fès and Marrakech showed little enthusiasm for 17th-century ruler and builder Moulay Ismaïl, and so he turned his attentions towards Meknès. Strategically situated at the heart of Morocco, Meknès became his capital, and he embarked on a massive building programme. Meknès is known as a city of minarets – gentle green or grey in colour, the tall, angular, linear towers dominate the old town, which, with its cream colour-washed houses and terraces sits above the narrow valley of the Oued Boufekrane. There are pleasant souks, a *medersa* – but, above all, an easy pace that is almost relaxing after the tension and press of Fès. The most famous monument is the great Bab Mansour el Aleuj. Although there's little left except for vast *pisé* walls, once upon a time this great gate to a palace complex was worthy of the *Thousand and One Nights*. Meknès also offers some rewarding side trips – to the Roman site of Volubilis, and to the pilgrimage centre of Moulay Idriss.

Essential Meknès and around

Finding your feet

It's just over an hour by train from Fès to Meknès. By road, take the N6 west; *grands taxis* depart from Bab Mahyrouk in Fès regularly throughout the day. If you're driving up from Marrakech, there are some beautiful views on the Azrou to Meknès route (the N13) via the Belvédère d'Ito, or you can turn onto the R212, which will take you from Mrirt through fine landscapes to join the N13 north of El Hajeb.

Meknès has two train stations. If you are going to stay in the *ville nouvelle*, get off at the **Meknès Amir Abdelkader** station, the first of the two as you come from Casa/Rabat. This station is just below Avenue Mohammed V and within easy walking distance of the hotels. The main train station is further east, 1 km from the centre (a 10dh taxi ride to the central *ville nouvelle*/about 15dh to the medina). The **CTM** bus station is close by, while the bus station for other private long-distance buses is at Bab el Khemis, on the far side of the medina from the *ville nouvelle*. Private local buses arrive at the terminal below Bab Mansour. See Transport, page 189, for further details.

Getting around

Meknès is a fairly spread-out place. It takes around 30 minutes to walk between the *ville nouvelle* and the medina, or you can jump in one of the pastel-blue *petits taxis*. Nearly all Meknès taxi drivers use their meter without asking. A ride between Av Mohammed V in the *ville nouvelle* and Bab Mansour in the medina costs around 8dh. Meknès is one of the easiest imperial cities to explore independently, but there is no shortage of faux guides offering their services in Place el Hedim and nearby. If you need assistance, obtain an official guide from the tourist office or one of the larger hotels. About 150dh is a realistic fee.

Time required

Allow two days for Meknès, plus a day trip to Volubilis and Moulay Idriss.

Tip...

Lovers of Moroccan red wines will find place names in the region south of Meknès familiar. The country's best vineyards are located near Aït Souala, Aït Yazm and Agouraï. Quality is improving, with foreign investors putting money into improved vinification methods and makers from Bordeaux and other renowned wine regions bringing their knowledge to the industry.

Meknès is a striking town, a fact accentuated by the distant backdrop views of the Jbel Zerhoun, which rises to over 1000 m to the north. The wooded foothills and orchards of olives, apples and pears below provide a green setting to the city for much of the year. Meknès is now more memorable for its impressive sense of scale and feeling of space rather than for any existing historic architecture.

1 Meknès

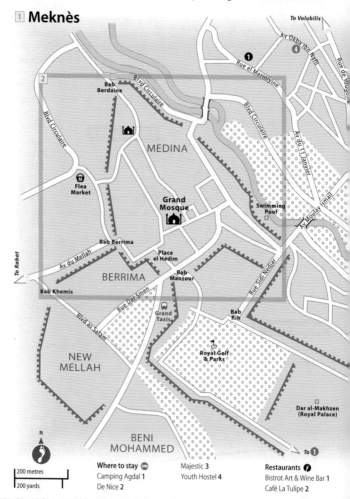

Where to stay
Camping Agdal 1
De Nice 2
Majestic 3
Youth Hostel 4

Restaurants
Bistrot Art & Wine Bar 1
Café La Tulipe 2

The medina includes the intricately decorated Medersa Bou Inania, vibrant souks, the Dar Jamaï palace museum and numerous mosques. The cream-washed walls and daily life of the residential areas just behind Rue Dar Smen still carry an antiquated 'Morocco that was' feel about them. To the east of the medina, on the opposite bank of the Oued Boufekrane, there stands the early 20th-century *ville nouvelle*. Carefully laid out by planner Henri Prost, the new town commands impressive views over both medina and the imperial city. It has a relaxed atmosphere and is a calm place to drink a coffee or tea and watch the evening promenade.

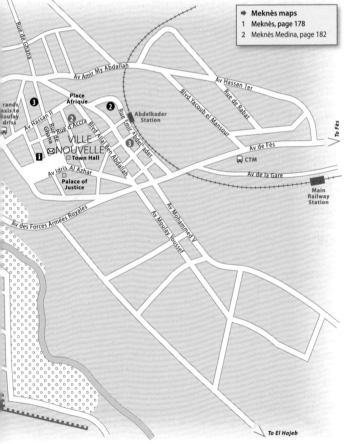

➡ **Meknès maps**
1 Meknès, page 178
2 Meknès Medina, page 182

Gambrinus **3**

BACKGROUND

Meknès

Meknès was originally a kasbah from the eighth century, used by the Kharajite Berbers against the Arabs. The town itself was founded by the Zenata Amazigh tribe called Meknassa in the 10th century and then destroyed by the Almoravids in 1069. A later kasbah was destroyed by the Almohad Sultan Abd el Moumen in order to build a new grid-patterned medina, some features of which still remain. This city was ruined during the conflict between the Almohads and the Merinids but was partially rebuilt and repopulated in 1276 under Sultan Moulay Youssef. A fine *medersa* was built under the Merinids, as they sought to expand Sunni orthodoxy to reduce the influence of Soufi leaders.

The reign of Moulay Ismaïl

The reign of the Alaouite sultan, Moulay Ismaïl (1672-1727), saw Meknès raised to the status of imperial capital. Even before his succession to the imperial throne, Moulay Ismaïl developed the city. Situated in a belt of fertile countryside, Meknès was chosen as his capital rather than the rebellious and self-important rivals of Fès and Marrakech. Moulay Ismaïl is renowned for his ruthless violence, but many of the stories recounted by the guides may be apocryphal. What is certain is that he made an impression on European visitors to the court. Meknès was described as a Moroccan Versailles. Indeed, some suggest that the sultan was trying to rival Louis XIV, then involved in building his palace complex outside Paris. Having conquered Morocco, Moulay Ismaïl left his mark all over the country. Kasbahs were built by his troops as they pacified the tribes, while cities acquired mosques and public buildings.

Moulay Ismaïl's vision of Meknès was vast and, although much of the *pisé* and rubble walls are in ruins, those still standing are testimony to its original

Place el Hedim

Place el Hedim (the Square of Destruction), opposite Bab Mansour, is the centre of Meknès' old city and the best starting point for exploration. The biggest open square in the city, it was once as busy as the Jemaâ el Fna in Marrakech (see page 43), filled with acrobats, storytellers and snake charmers plying their trade, but these days there's just a few vendors touting for business and a line of cheap cafés along its southwest wall. In the evening, though, this is prime strolling territory. To the left of the square is a crowded covered **food market**, with bright displays of fresh vegetables and pickles, that's definitely worth a look. On the right-hand corner of the square down a few steps is **Dar Jamaï Museum** ① *T0535-530863, Wed-Mon 0900-1700, 10dh,* a 19th-century palace, owned by officials at the court of Sultan Moulay Hassan. Built in 1882, it was the residence of the Jamaï family, two members of which were ministers to Moulay Hassan. It was used as a military hospital after 1912 and in 1920 became a museum. Exploring the house gives an insight into the lifestyle of the 19th-century Muslim élite. On display is scale. The city was built by a massive army of slaves, both Muslim and Christian, and the sultan was notorious for his barbaric treatment of these people, supposedly having them buried alive in the walls among other horrors. He built several palaces to accommodate his wives, concubines, children and court, as well as quarters for his army, the Abid Bukhari, an élite praetorian guard of black slaves, the chief instrument of his power. The city contained within it all that was necessary for such a large military machine, with store houses, stables, armouries, gardens and reservoirs.

After Moulay Ismaïl

After Moulay Ismaïl's death, Meknès gradually declined. His huge court and army could not be held together without his immense ego, and his successors, Moulay Abdallah and Sidi Mohammed, returned the emphasis to Fès and Marrakech. Furthermore, the earthquake of 1755 destroyed many of Moulay Ismaïl's creations. The French revitalized Meknès, appreciating its strategic position in the corridor linking eastern Morocco and Algeria with the coastal belt around Rabat and Casablanca. They built their *ville nouvelle* on the east bank of the Oued Boufekrane, apart from the medina and the imperial city, as part of their policy of separate development of Moroccan and European quarters. During the Protectorate, Meknès became the most important garrison town in Morocco and continued as an important military town after independence.

Meknès today

Although Meknès is perhaps overshadowed by its near-neighbour Fès, it is today the fifth largest city in Morocco. After a period of relative stagnation, Meknès is re-emerging as an important town for tourism, industry and agricultural. National planners made the city the capital of the Meknès-Tafilalelt region, which extends southeast to Er Rachidia, Erfoud and Rissani, down one of the country's most strategic lines of communication.

a selection of Moroccan arts, including wrought iron, carved wood, weaving, leather and metalwork, and various antique household items. Look out for richly painted wooden chests and panels. Upstairs is a furnished reception room. The garden planted with cypress and fruit trees is a pleasant halt in the heat of the day.

Souks

The medina of Meknès has seven traditional **souks**, which, while not quite of the order of those in Marrakech or Fès, are nevertheless well worth exploring. Immediately to the left of the Dar Jamaï a small entrance leads to the souks. The alley bends around to the right behind Dar Jamaï past some undistinguished clothes shops. Just before a carpet shop, turn left. The passage, now covered, widens slightly and continues past a range of shops selling modern goods, a bank and various minor side turnings. At the junction, on the left is **Souk Nejjarine**, which includes textile-sellers and carpenters, another entrance to the carpet souk and a fondouk hardly changed since it was built. This route passes the Almoravid

Nejjarine Mosque. At the end, one can turn left towards the *mellah* or Place el Hedim or right into the dusty and noisy **Souk Sraira**, just inside the city walls, used by carpenters and metalworkers. At the very end, on the left, is the 12th-century Almohad **Bab Jedid**, around which are some interesting stalls selling musical instruments. **Souk Cherchira**, initially occupied by tent-makers, runs parallel to Souk Sraira but outside the city walls. **Souk Sebbat** is the right-hand turning opposite Souk Nejjarine and includes sellers of *babouches*, modern clothes and caftans, several tourist and handicraft shops, a *fondouk* on the right and another on the left, before the Bou Inania Medersa. A turning on the right opposite the *medersa* leads directly onto Rue Dar Smen, a good alternative route to remember.

Medersa Bou Inania
Daily 0900-1800. 10dh/child 3dh.

Best approached from Souk Sebbat, the **Bou Inania Medersa** was founded circa 1345 by Merinid Sultan Abou el Hassan as a college of religious and legal

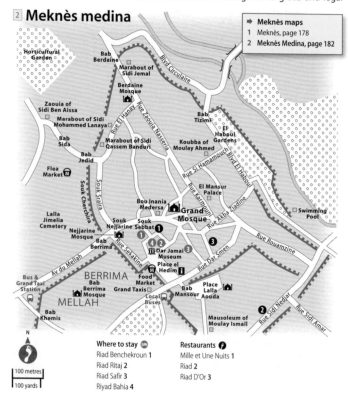

2 Meknès medina

➡ **Meknès maps**
1 Meknès, page 178
2 Meknès Medina, page 182

Horticultural Garden
Bab Berdaine
Marabout of Sidi Jemal
Berdaine Mosque
Blvd Circulaire
Zaouia of Sidi Ben Aissa
Marabout of Sidi Mohammed Lanaya
Rue El Hanay
Rue Zaouia Nasseria
Bab Tizimi
El Haboul Gardens
Bab Sida
Marabout of Sidi Qassem Banduri
Koubba of Moulay Ahmed
Bab Jedid
Rue Si Hamamouch
Blvd El Haboul
Flea Market
Souk Sraira
Souk Cherchira
El Mansur Palace
Rue Karmouni
Bou Inania Medersa
Grand Mosque
Rue Akba Zaâline
Swimming Pool
Lalla Jimelia Cemetery
Nejjarine Mosque
Souk Nejjarine
Souk Sebbat
Bab Berrima
Rue Sekakine
Dar Jamai Museum
Place el Hedim
Rue Dar Smen
Rue Rouamzine
Av du Mellah
BERRIMA
Bab Berrima Mosque
Food Market
Grand Taxis
Bab Mansour
Place Lalla Aouda
Rue Sidi Nejjar
Rue Sidi Amar
Bus & Grand Taxi Station
MELLAH
Local Buses
Mausoleum of Moulay Ismaïl
Bab Khemis

N
100 metres
100 yards

Where to stay 🛏
Riad Benchekroun 1
Riad Ritaj 2
Riad Safir 3
Riyad Bahia 4

Restaurants 🍴
Mille et Une Nuits 1
Riad 2
Riad D'Or 3

instruction. The door to the *medersa*, part of a cedar screen, is just under a dome (notable for its ribbed design) at an intersection in the souk. Altogether, the college had 40 cells for its students on two floors, around an oblong courtyard including a pool, with arcades surrounded by a screened passageway. As with many of the *medersas*, there is

Tip...
Climb up onto the roof for a view of the medina, including the lovely green-tiled roof of the Great Mosque, the minaret of the Nejjarine and other mosques.

eye-catching *zellige* tiling and carved wood lintels. Take a look at the green-and-yellow tiled prayer hall. The doorway is ornamented with *zellige* tiling as well as the customary and, perhaps, a little over-the-top stalactite-style plasterwork.

Nearby, the **Grand Mosque**, situated in the heart of the medina, is a 12th-century Almoravid foundation with 14th-century alterations. It is one of the oldest in Meknès and also the largest. Non-Muslims are not permitted to enter the mosque.

Mellah

To the west of Place el Hedim, through a street popular with hawkers of household goods, turn left into Avenue de Mellah. On the left is the *mellah*, built by Moulay Ismaïl in 1682 for the large Jewish community and walled off from the Muslim medina. The **Bab Berrima Mosque** dates from the 18th century, a time when the *mellah* was becoming increasingly Muslim. Few members of Meknès's once important Jewish community remain today.

Bab el Khemis to Bab Berdaine

Heading southwest towards Rabat, the city wall is broken by Bab el Khemis, built by Moulay Ismaïl, with a range of different arches, decoration and calligraphy. This is the only remaining piece of the garden quarter attributed to Moulay Ismaïl. The rest was destroyed by Moulay Abdallah, son of the great Moulay Ismaïl, who was not pleased by the reception he received from the inhabitants when he returned from an unsuccessful campaign. After this, the Boulevard Circulaire leads past a cemetery containing the 18th-century tomb of Sidi Mohammed Ben Aissa, founder of the important religious brotherhood of the Aissoua. It's closed to non-Muslims but worth a look from a respectable distance. The Ben Aissa religious ceremonies are still held on the Mouloud (Prophet Mohammed's birthday). The Boulevard Circulaire continues round to Bab Berdaine, the entrance to the north medina.

Northern medina

Less frequented by tourists, the northern medina is reached by either weaving through the streets from the *medersa* or the souks or, more easily, coming round on the Boulevard Circulaire. **Bab Berdaine** dates from the 17th century, a building decorated by Jamaâ el Rouah and flanked by two immense towers. Inside, on Place el Berdaine, is the **Berdaine Mosque**. Travelling south, the streets continue through an area of the traditional medina, only occasionally spoilt by insensitive new building. Here you are in traditional neighbourhoods where private and public space are clearly differentiated, each quarter having its own mosque, hammam and public oven.

Back on the Boulevard Circulaire, the next major gate around towards Oued Boufekrane is **Bab Tizmi**, near to Restaurant Zitouna. Opposite Bab Tizmi is the quiet **Parc el Haboul**, part of an area of gardens and recreational facilities in the valley, dividing the medina and the *ville nouvelle*.

Bab Mansour

Claimed by some to be the finest gateway in North Africa, Meknès is dominated by this monumental gate at the top of the hill in the medina, opposite Place el Hedim. It dates from the reign of Sultan Moulay Ismaïl and was completed by his son Moulay Mohammed Ben Abdallah in 1732. It is named after one of the sultan's Christian slaves, Mansour the Infidel. The gate marks the entrance to the huge grounds of the imperial city; its huge size serves more as a testimony to the might of the sultan than as an effective defensive structure and is clearly more about imperial splendour than anything else. The decorated flanking towers do not even have firing posts. The outrepassé arch is surrounded by a blind arch, including the usual lozenge network motif and *zellige* tiling. Between the arch and framing band is a black-tiled area with floral patterns. The overall effect of the main gate is exuberant and powerful. The gate has come to be a symbol of Meknès, even of Morocco as a whole.

Imperial city

Immediately through Bab Mansour from Place el Hedim is **Place Lalla Aouda**, once the public meeting point during the period of Moulay Ismaïl and now a relaxing and pleasant area to rest. In the far corner is the **Lalla Aouda Mosque**, which was supposedly built by Princess Aouda as penance for eating a peach during the Ramadan fast.

Directly opposite Bab Mansour, in the right-hand corner of the square, a space in the walls leads through to a second square, the **Mechouar**. To the right note the domed **Koubat al Khayyatine** ⓘ *10dh*, a plain building with pleasing simple décor, is situated in a small park behind a fence. In the 18th century this was used to receive ambassadors and, later, to make uniforms. Koubat el Khayyatine translates as 'the tailors' dome'. Inside is a display of photos of old Meknès. Outside, right of the entrance, a flight of stairs leads down to dank and vaulted underground chambers, said by guides to be the prison of the Christian slaves, although why one should want to keep a workforce down here is anyone's guess.

In the wall opposite the small park the right-hand gate leads to a golf course. This was originally to have been a lake but was converted to its present use by the king. Behind the golf course is a later palace of Moulay Ismaïl, the **Royal Palace** or **Dar al Makhzen** ⓘ *closed to visitors*, still in use and now heavily restored.

South of Place Lalla Aouda, the **Mausoleum of Moulay Ismaïl** ⓘ *access via the monumental entrance in the cream wall opposite an arcade of craft shops*, contains the tombs of Moulay Ismaïl, his wife and Moulay Ahmed. Unusually for religious buildings in Morocco, the mausoleum is open to non-Muslims. Although the room containing the actual tomb cannot be entered, visitors can enter the ornate annex to the mausoleum salon and admire from there the plaster stucco, *zellige* tiling and distinctive and exuberant colouring. The guardian normally allows visitors to take photos of the interior of the mausoleum from the annex.

Just past the mausoleum is an entrance to **Dar el Kebira** ('the big house'), Moulay Ismaïl's late 17th-century palace. The palace is in ruins, but the nature of the original structure of the building can be discerned. Since the 18th century, houses have been built into the walls of the palace.

Back out on the road, pass under the passage of the **Bab ar Rih** ('Gate of the Winds'), a long, arched structure. Follow the walled road, running between the Dar el Kebira and the Dar al Makhzen and turn right at the end. Carry on straight ahead through another arch and, after around 200 m, you reach another chunky *pisé* wall, the Heri es Souani building.

Heri es-Souani
Daily 0830-1200, 1430-1830.

Close to the city campsite and a hefty 35-minute walk from the medina, Heri es Souani, also called Dar el Ma ('the Water Palace'), is a large, impressive structure, also dating from the reign of Moulay Ismaïl and used variously as granary, warehouse and water point to provide for the court, army and followers in either the normal run of events or in case of emergencies, such as conflict or drought. It is a good indication of the scale of Moulay Ismaïl's imperial ambitions. From the roof there would be a good view, if one were allowed up. The nearby Agdal basin is now used for storing water for irrigation purposes; once it was presumably a vital reserve in case of siege. Popular with strollers at weekends and on summer evenings, the location is a little stark on a hot summer afternoon, so have a post-visit drink at the café in the nearby campsite.

Listings Meknès *maps p178 and p182*

Tourist information

Office du Tourisme (ONMT)
27 Pl Batha-l'Istiqlal, T0535-521286.
Helpful, although not overly endowed with information.

Where to stay

Meknès medina
At peak times, especially spring holidays, book in advance or arrive early.

€€€-€€ Riad Safir
1 Derb Lalla Alamia, Bab Aissi, T0535-534785, www.riadsafir.com.
This riad combines 2 quite different, though equally stylish, spaces. The first house is cosy and bohemian, filled with warm red and orange textiles and lots of carved wood detailing. The second offers a more contemporary interpretation of Moroccan architecture, with cooling greys and greens. All 7 rooms (€70-130) have bags of character and plenty of

space. There are lounges for relaxing, a massage room and spacious roof terrace. The food is good too, but needs to be booked 3 hrs in advance (better still in the morning).

€€ Riad Ritaj
13 Derb Sidi Amar Bouaouada, T0535-534808, www.riadritaj.com.
Rooms may lack the antique, cosy charm of smaller riads but make up for it with space and amenities. The groundfloor courtyard still has plenty of old riad pizazz with a flurry of tiles but upstairs the 14 large rooms are more modern and decorated in the smart if rather staid style of a mid-range hotel; all are equipped with satellite TV, a/c and good-sized bathrooms. Wi-Fi and breakfast included.

€€-€ Riad Benchekroun
8 Derb Tiberbarine, T0535-535406, www.riadbenchekroun.com.
The snug rooms here (doubles from €50) are full of traditional woodwork features and trimmed with stained-glass details. Opening out onto the courtyard, they can be a tad dark so bag one of the rooms on the upper floor if possible. The rooftop has daybeds for chilling out and admiring the rooftop views and a beautifully restored green tiled fountain. Wi-Fi and breakfast included.

€ Riyad Bahia
13 Derb Tiberbarine, T0535-554541, www.ryad-bahia.com.
This guesthouse has a comfortable, laid-back vibe and is one of the best run small hotels in Morocco, thanks to genial owners Abdellatif and Bouchra who are well travelled themselves and so understand the needs of other like-minded souls. Rooms (single/double/family 400/500/900dh) are decorated

with antique wooden hand-painted doors, low tables and cushions, and all have big beds with soft linens and roomy walk-in showers, a/c and heating. Some have windows onto the street as well as the lushly planted courtyard. There are plentiful alcoves scattered with cushions where you can sprawl out after exploring and a multi-levelled terrace, brimming with pot-plants and with good views over the city. Evening meals are cooked by Bouchra and are highly recommended. Wi-Fi and breakfast included. Recommended.

Meknès ville nouvelle
There are some very reasonably priced central hotels here. Some of the older ones near the top end of Av Mohammed V and the Av des FAR, however, tend to be noisy, due to the number of bars in the vicinity.

€€ Hotel de Nice
10 Rue d'Accra, T0535-520318.
This is a reasonable mid-range option, centrally located, squeaky clean and comfortable, with some welcome modern touches. Although it's not exactly brimming with personality, all rooms are en suite with pretty, planted balconies. It also has a restaurant (breakfasts are generous and varied), a licensed bar and safe parking.

€ Hotel Majestic
19 Av Mohammed V, T0535-522033.
Most visitors only stay at the Majestic for 1 night to make the most of its location very near to the train station, but this quirky, and in some ways quite fabulous, old 1930s-style place has plenty to offer. It's good value, friendly and provides a taste of old Morocco for lovers of kitsch and fans of the creaky, old-school traveller boltholes that are

disappearing fast these days. There are 47 clean and good-sized rooms, with original floor tiles and dark wood and red velvet furniture. Rooms on the street side can be noisy, so it's worth opting for a quieter inner room. Breakfast is an extra 60dh. Wi-Fi only works in the groundfloor salon.

€ Youth hostel
Av Okba Ibn Nafii, near the municipal stadium and Hotel Transatlantique, T0535-524698, www.hihostels.com. Open 1000-1200 and 1600-1700.
This is the HI's headquarters in Morocco and is one of the best and most friendly hostels in Morocco, with dorms arranged around a garden. Clean, comfortable and well maintained, it has a total of 60 beds costing 25-35dh per night, a communal kitchen and meals available on request. It's 25 m from the bus stop, and just over 1 km from the main train station.

Camping

Camping Agdal
2 km out of Meknès centre, opposite the Heri es Souani, T0535-551828.
To get here take buses Nos 2 or 3, or better, a *petit taxi* from Meknès town centre. The 4-ha site has a shop, café, laundry, electricity for caravans, hot showers, plenty of shaded areas for pitching a tent and is clean and well organized. It now offers some rooms, which are a cheap alternative to a hotel. The site serves alcohol and it can get a bit noisy near the café area, especially once the piped music gets going, but it's a great little site for one so close to the city.

Camping Belle-Vue
On the road to Moulay Idriss some 15 km north, T0668-490899.

This is a smaller site of around 3 ha set in beautiful countryside. It costs 60dh for 2 people with car and tent, and has a small shop, showers, laundry, electricity for caravans and petrol just 100 m away. But the toilet blocks could do with some maintenance.

Meknès medina
Pl el Hédim's cafes serve up similar menus of paninis, pizza and brochettes. There's not much to choose between them, so take a wander and see what takes your fancy. There are plenty of cheap restaurants along Rue Dar Smen and Rue Rouamzine where you can get a meal for less than 50dh.

€€ Restaurant Riad
79 Ksar Chaacha, T0535-530542.
This rather good medina restaurant offers a range of traditional Moroccan menus concentrating on the classics, such as beef and prune tagine, pigeon *pastilla* and couscous on Fri. It has no alcohol licence and can fill up with tour groups, but one of its great advantages is being able to eat outside in a garden filled with flowers and cacti beside a small, slightly unkempt pool.

€€ Riad Bahia
13 Tiberbarine, T0535-554541, www.ryad-bahia.com (see also Where to stay, above).
One of the best places in the medina, offering an excellent and varied range of tagines, including lamb and aubergine or apricots, chicken and preserved lemon, and beef with prunes. It's all very calm and orderly, yet authentically Moroccan, with leather pouffes, abundant carved wood and a well-planted courtyard. Advance booking essential. Recommended.

€ Mille et Une Nuits

An intimate family-run place where all the ingredients are bought fresh from the market that day and the small menu of tagines are rustled up from scratch when you order. This means waiting times can be long so it's a great idea to pop your head in the door earlier in the day and order for dinner.

Meknès ville nouvelle

There are plentiful cheap and cheerful roast chicken shacks dotted around the centre of the *ville nouvelle* where you can get a filling meal for less than 30dh.

€€ Bistot Art & Le Wine Bar
Hotel Transatlantique, Rue el Marinyen, T0535-525051.

The restaurant has an extensive international menu, a great wine list and wonderful views over Meknès medina from its hilltop location, which is the main reason to come here. If you're suffering from tagine-overload or simply fancy a relaxing drink while taking in the cityscape, this place is just the ticket.

€ Café Restaurant Gambrinus
Rue de Ghana, opposite the market, off Av Hassan II, T0535-520258.

This friendly little place serves French, Spanish and Moroccan cuisine, and it's a reliable lunch stop for refuelling. Interesting wall murals give it the edge over similar spots.

Cafés

Meknès produces the best mint in Morocco, so don't pass up a chance to get your fix of mint tea here.

Café la Tulipe
Pl Maarakat Lahri, Ville Nouvelle, T0535-511094.

This big bustling place, with tables spread under an awning between the trees, is a charming place to enjoy a pot of mint tea while watching the world go by. It also serves excellent cakes and pastries and good ice cream in the summer. Wi-Fi.

Bars and clubs

Meknès has a surprisingly lively drinking scene, though it's very male-orientated and the bars (mostly strung along Blvd Allal ben Abdallah in the *ville nouvelle*) aren't welcoming to women. For a more relaxing drink head to Bistrot Art & Le Wine Bar in the Hotel Transatlantique (see Restaurants, above), where you can have a quiet drink with great views over the medina.

What to do

Cultural centres
Institut Français, *zankat Farhat Hachad, Av Hassan II, T0535-524071.* Organizes lectures and films, hosts occasional concerts and plays. Closed mid-Jul to early Sep. A bright note in Meknès' rather sleepy cultural life.

Hammams
Hammam des Jardins, *aka Hammam Maha, very handy for the ville nouvelle.* Heading towards the medina on Av Hassan II, take a right between **BCM** and **Agora** salon de thé. After 25 m, drop left down some steps, then go right. The hammam, with separate entrances for men and women, overlooks a semi-abandoned small park.
Hammam Sidi Omar Bou Aouada, *turn right as you face Dar Jamaï museum on Pl Hedim, baths on your right about 25 m further on, unmarked.*

Transport

Air
The closest airport is at Fès (see page 132). **Royal Air Maroc** has an office in Meknès at 7 Av Mohammed V, T0535-520963/523606.

Bus
Local buses No 5, 7 and 9 run between the *ville nouvelle* and the medina. The long-distance bus station is just off Av de la Gare. **CTM** has regular services to Casablanca (85dh, 5 hrs) and **Fès** (25dh, 1 hr), plus departures for **Ifrane** (25dh, 1¾ hrs) and Azrou (35dh, 2 hrs) at 1145 and 1515. Private line buses go from the terminal below Bab Khemis.

Car hire
Cars are available from **Stop Car** (3 Rue Essaouira, T0535-525061) and **Zeit** (4 Rue Antsirebe, T0535-525918).

Taxi
Grands taxis are a particularly good option for getting to **Fès** and **Azrou**. They leave from the car park below Bab Khemis, opposite the private line buses; ask the drivers hanging around for the destination. For **Moulay Idriss** (10dh) *grands taxis* leave from near the Shell station on your right as Av Hassan II descends.

Train
The main station is east of the central *ville nouvelle*, T0535-520017/520689. Abdelkader Station, right in the centre on Rue Emire Abdelkader, is the easier station to use. There are regular departures for **Rabat**, **Casablanca** and **Marrakech**, and eastwards for **Fès**, **Taza** and **Oujda**.

Moulay Idriss and Volubilis
a sleepy pastel-washed village and a grandiose Roman ruin

The shrine town of Moulay Idriss and the Roman ruins at Volubilis make an easy and thoroughly rewarding day trip from Meknès. The rambling ruins of Volubilis, covering over 40 ha, are home to once-grand mansions that still preserve intricate floor mosaics, a noble forum, triumphal arch dedicated to Emperor Caracalla and a long decumanus. The vanished splendour of Volubilis is echoed by legendary evocations of early Islam at Moulay Idriss nearby. This most venerable pilgrimage centre, set between steep hillsides, was founded in the eighth century by one Idriss Ben Abdallah, great-grandson of Ali and Fatima, the Prophet Mohammed's daughter. Today he is referred to as Idriss el Akbar, 'the Great'. His son, Idriss II, is buried and venerated in Fès. Moulay Idriss is a sleepy kind of place for most of the year (except during the annual moussem in August) and its winding lanes, with walls washed in pink, blue and green hues, are a charming place to explore.

Essential Moulay Idriss and Volubilis

Finding your feet

Moulay Idriss is 30 km north of Meknès. To get there, take a *grand taxi* from the corner of Rue Benghazi and Avenue Hassan II, just past the petrol station in Meknès's *ville nouvelle* (a 10dh ride). There are also regular buses from below Bab Mansour. The last bus back is at 1900. Volubilis is clearly signposted 5 km from Moulay Idriss, a pleasant walk (about 40 minutes) on a nice day, or a short taxi ride. Alternatively, for Volubilis bargain in Meknès for a *grand taxi* to take you all the way. If travelling by car, leave Meknès by Rue de Yougoslavie in the *ville nouvelle*, and follow the R410 as far as Aïn el Kerma, and from there take the N13 to Moulay Idriss.

When to go

This area can be oppressive in midsummer. Volubilis, set in open fields, is a delight in spring, with wild flowers abounding. When visiting, start early to avoid the heat and the tour buses which usually begin arriving by 1030.

> **Tip...**
> Make sure you have plenty of water; the ruins cover a large area, and once you're within the site there's nowhere to buy refreshments. Some areas of the site are clearly roped off; it is advisable to respect this to avoid the whistle and wrath of the otherwise very friendly guardian.

★ Moulay Idriss

Coming round the last bend from Meknès, Moulay Idriss is a dramatic sight with its houses spilling down two rocky outcrops, with the *zaouïa* (sanctuary) in between. The centre of the Jbel Zerhoun region, Moulay Idriss is a major pilgrimage centre and Morocco's holiest town because it is home to the tomb of its namesake, Idriss Ben Abdallah Ben Hassan Ben Ali, the great-great-grandson of the Prophet Mohammed.

Moulay Idriss came to Morocco from Arabia after defeat at the Battle of Fakh in 786. In 788 he was accepted as imam by the Amazigh Aurora tribe at Volubilis. He spent the rest of his life in Morocco winning over the loyalty of the tribes to the Idrissid dynasty and spreading the faith of Islam before he was poisoned in 791. This town and Fès were two of his major legacies. The town is an alternative to Mecca in Morocco for those unable to do the ultimate pilgrimage.

The town of Moulay Idriss was mainly developed in the 18th century by Sultan Moulay Ismaïl, in part using materials lifted from nearby Volubilis, which the sultan plundered without restraint. Moulay Idriss was closed to non-Muslims until 1912 and, even today, is primarily a Muslim sanctuary and a place of deep reverence for Moroccans. During the religious festival, or *moussem*, held here in August the town is transformed by an influx of pilgrims and a sea of tents.

Buses and taxis stop just below the main square where there are some good local restaurants serving tagines and brochettes and cafés. The green-roofed mausoleum and mosque complex is at the end of the square, surrounded by shops selling pilgrimage items and a delicious array of nougats, candies and nuts. Non-Muslims cannot enter the mausoleum complex.

Looking up from the square, the medina clings to the two hills, on the left is Khiba, while Tasga is on the right. From the square, walk through the white arch to explore the steep pastel-washed alleys that snake up through the residential areas. At the top of town, there are two terraces with rewarding views over the tumble of houses down to the mausoleum.

★ Volubilis

5 km from Moulay Idriss along the N13, signed from the road. Daily 0800 to sunset. 10dh, children 3dh. Local guides hang out by the entrance and charge around 100dh for a 1-hr tour.

Volubilis is by far the most impressive Roman site in Morocco and sits in a spectacular spot, with the hills and Moulay Idriss behind and vast views over the plain below. While much has been removed, either to adorn other cities over the centuries or to be displayed in museums, the structure of the town is largely intact and the design of the buildings is clearly discernible from the ruins. Many floor mosaics remain, remarkably unaffected by the passing centuries.

Entrance and olive press complex From the ticket office the entrance to the city is by the southeastern gate. A path, with sculptures and tombstones alongside it, leads down to a bridge across the Oued Fetassa. On the other side of the river is an area of small houses and industrial units, among which are the remains of an **olive press complex**. The mill stones for crushing the olives and the tanks for collecting and separating the oil can be seen. Olive presses can be found through much of the city, as olive oil production was as essential to the Volubilis economy as it is in the area today. Many of the same techniques are still used.

House of Orpheus Right of the olive press is the House of Orpheus, a large mansion. The first entrance gives access to a room with an intricate dolphin mosaic, to a kitchen with a niche for religious figures, and to a paved bathroom and boiler room. Note the complex heating system. The second entrance leads to an open court with a mosaic of the goddess Amphitrite, with living rooms around it, including a dining room with an Orpheus mosaic, showing the hero playing his harp.

Basilica, forum and capitol Roman imperial settlements, even the most provincial, had an impressive array of public buildings to cement their Roman identity. Volubilis was no exception. Heading further down into the site and then to the right, you'll reach the **Baths of Gallienus**, public baths that are the distant ancestor of the Moroccan hammam. Beyond this, the large public square in front of the Basilica is the **Forum**, which has a number of monuments to leading Roman figures. The **Basilica** is one of the most impressive ruins, with a number of columns still intact. This third-century building was the court house for the city. Beside the

Basilica is the **Capitol**, also with columns. In the court in front there is an altar and steps leading up to the **temple** dedicated to Juno, Minerva and Jupiter Optimus Maximus. This building had great state importance, being the place where the council would assemble on great occasions. Adjacent to the Forum is the **House of the Athlete**, named after the mosaic of an athlete winning a cup.

Volubilis

BACKGROUND

Volubilis

Archaeological evidence points to the possibility of a Neolithic settlement at Volubilis, while recovered tablets show that it was a Phoenician settlement during the third century BC. In AD 24 it was the western capital of the Roman kingdom of Mauretania, and from AD 45 to 285 the capital of the Roman province of Mauretania Tingitana. Under the Romans the immediate region prospered from producing olive oil. As Volubilis was at the southeastern extremity of the province, only connected to Rome through the Atlantic ports, its weak position had to be bolstered by extensive city walls.

Under the Emperor Diocletian, Rome withdrew to the coastal areas, leaving Volubilis at the mercy of neighbouring tribes. The city survived, but its Christian and Jewish population diminished in importance, becoming the Christian enclave of Oualila during the eighth century. Though he was proclaimed sultan in Volubilis, Moulay Idriss preferred Fès, and by the 11th century, Volubilis was totally deserted. It suffered again when Moulay Ismaïl ransacked the ruins to build Meknès and, further, in the earthquake of 1755. French excavations and reconstruction began in 1915; the metal tracks on the site date from this period.

Triumphal arch The Triumphal Arch dominates the skyline. It was built in AD 217 to honour Emperor Caracalla and his mother, Julia Domna. Originally finished with fountains and medallions, the arch was heavily reconstructed by French archaeologists. Although not of the same finesse as the honorary arches surviving in the Roman cities of Tunisia and Libya, it is nevertheless impressive.

Decumanus Maximus From the arch, the Decumanus Maximus (main street) leads to the Tangier Gate. It had a colonnade with small shops in front of a series of large houses, some containing interesting mosaics. Starting on the left, from just beside the Triumphal Arch, the **House of the Ephèbe** was built around a courtyard with a pool. The house is named after the bronze statue of a beautiful boy or *ephebos* found in the ruins. Adjacent is the **House of Columns** and then the **Knight's House**, which has an interesting mosaic of Bacchus, good-time god of wine. In a more serious taste, the **House of the Labours of Hercules** has a mosaic with individual pictures of Hercules' life, and another of Jupiter. Further up, the **House of the Nymphs Bathing** has a mosaic showing nymphs undressing. The largest house on this side, the **Gordian Palace**, is fronted by columns, but the remains are quite plain. This may have been the governor's residence from the time of Gordian III, with both domestic quarters and offices.

House of Venus On the right-hand side of Decumanus Maximus from the Triumphal Arch there is a large **public bath and fountains**, fed by an aqueduct. Three houses up is the **House of Nereids** with a pool mosaic. Behind this and one up is the House of Venus, which has one of the best arrays of mosaics. The central courtyard pool has a mosaic of chariots. There are also mosaics of Bacchus, on the left, and Hylos and two nymphs, on the right. Nearby is a mosaic of Diana and the horned Actaeon. From the House of Venus cross back over the Oued Fetassa to the remains of the **Temple of Saturn**, a Phoenician temple before the Romans took it over. From here, follow the path back to the entrance, perhaps for refreshments in the café.

Listings Moulay Idriss and Volubilis *map p192*

Where to stay

There is a handful of small guesthouses in Moulay Idriss and also a hotel at Volubilis (T0535-544405), which is useful if you want to get a really early start on the ruins to beat the oppressive heat during summer.

€€ Dar Zerhoune
Moulay Idriss, T0642-247793, www.darzerhoune.com.
Far and away the best place in town. A boutique-style guesthouse with just 4 rooms (single/double 410/620dh), all simply but very comfortably decorated, with large bathrooms, quality bed linens and some great details, such as the sea serpent table legs and flea market finds. The New Zealand owner, Rose Button, makes the experience a special one, and you'll find lots of great homely touches here, from highly sociable breakfasts and dinners on the roof to arranging henna sessions, carpet-buying trips and cooking classes with local women. Wi-Fi and breakfast included. Recommended.

Camping
Zerhoune Belle Vue (T0663-569856) is a site between Meknès and Moulay Idriss. The proprietor of the café at Volubilis allows people to camp opposite the turning to the site.

South of
Fès

From Fès or Meknès there are a number of interesting towns to visit in the Middle Atlas, possibly as stopovers to break a journey south to Marrakech, or as places to escape the summer heat and do some walking in the hills and cedar forests. In a week you could comfortably combine Fès and Meknès (plus Volubilis and Moulay Idriss) with a circuit southwards, which might include overnights in Azrou, Ifrane, Sefrou or Immouzer du Kandar. A loop southwest of Azrou would take you down to Khénifra and back up via the Aguelmane Azigza and Oum er Rbia, Morocco's largest river, which flows into the Atlantic at Azzemour.

Essential South of Fès

Getting around

There are buses to the main towns in the Middle Atlas – Azrou, Ifrane, Midelt – but the only way to fully explore the countryside is to hire a car with or without driver.

Time required

For a decent taster of the Middle Atlas, a few days in the countryside around Ifrane and Midelt could be followed by a road trip up to Taza (see page 166) before travelling back to Fès.

Azrou, 70 km south of Meknès, is a small Amazigh market town and hill resort at the heart of the Middle Atlas. The name means 'rock' in Tamazight and refers to the rock in the middle of the town next to the large new mosque. The ruined kasbah was built by Moulay Ismaïl. The town has a relaxed air, and there's good hiking in the wooded vicinity. If you have a car, there are some very scenic routes south of Azrou where the landscapes are truly spectacular. One loop would take you up to Aïn Leuh, past Lac Ouiouane and across the Plateau des cèdres to the source of the Oum er Rbia (Morocco's major river) and onto the Aguelmane Azigza and Khénifra (a possible overnight stop), or back up from Khénifra on the main N8 to Azrou via Mrirt (large Thursday souk).

Sights

Azrou's traditional character, once created by the green-tiled roofs of the arcades round the market square, has taken a beating. Although there are a few good hotels and it is ideally located as a base for exploring the cedar forests, it has yet to find its place in the tourist market. It seems to function as a sort of suburb to its more upmarket neighbour, Ifrane. The heart of Azrou, **Place Mohammed V**, is to the right on leaving the bus stop. There is a covered **market** near Place Mohammed V, while the **Ensemble Artisanal** ⓘ *daily 0830-1200, 1430-1800*, is situated off Avenue Mohammed V, with a fixed-price shop and a number of craftsmen working on the premises – look out for the Middle Atlas carpets. A large **Amazigh souk** is held just above the town on Tuesday, with vegetables, textiles and some interesting Middle Atlas carpets, as well as traditional entertainment from musicians and others.

Around Azrou

If you have time, seek out the region's largest and most famous cedar, the **Cèdre de Gouraud**, named after some half-forgotten French military commander. This is signposted to the right off the Azrou to Ifrane road, down a narrow, winding road. Barbary apes will be eagerly waiting among the trees to share the contents of your picnic.

Of more specialized interest is the abandoned **Benedictine monastery** at **Tioumliline** ⓘ *head out of Azrou on the Midelt road and turn right a few hundred metres up the hill after the Ifriquia petrol station*. The monastery, founded in 1920, was finally relinquished in 1963, becoming a vocational training centre, abandoned along with the dispensary in the 1980s. Low stone buildings, a cloister planted with cypress, lilac and a Judas tree survive on this beautiful site, as does the church building and the graves of five fathers. The monastery was important as a meeting place for Moroccan intellectuals in the heady days after Independence, providing a refuge to abstract painter Gharbaoui, amongst others. The location is lovely, and birdwatchers may find things of interest in the mixed deciduous/cedar woodlands here.

One of Azrou's claims to fame is that under the French Protectorate, it was chosen to be home to the Collège berbère, a training school for Moroccan Berbers, which was founded on the premise that Arabs and Imazighen were fundamentally different and should be educated and ruled as such. The divide-and-rule policy backfired – it was in the interests of neither Arabs nor Imazighen for a colonial regime to continue to control Morocco; in any case, loyalty to Islam and the Alaouite throne proved to be stronger than ethnic ties, a fact which somehow escaped French colonial ethnographers. After Independence, the Collège berbère became the Lycée Tarik Ibn Zayid, symbolically named after the Arab conqueror of Andalucía.

Azrou to Khénifra

At 19 km south of Azrou, a turning off the N8 leads to **Aïn Leuh**, an Amazigh village with a Wednesday souk important to the semi-nomadic Beni M'Guild tribe, a ruined kasbah from the reign of Moulay Ismaïl, and nearby waterfalls. You then follow a narrow road through cedar forest and across a plateau, past **Lac Ouiouane** and its 1930s chalets to the source of the River Oum er Rbia, 20 km away. In places, the cedar forest has been cut back to form a thick green crown on the tops of the hills. The villages here are desperately poor; there is little traffic, and children will come racing out at the first sign of a passing vehicle. Many of the houses are little more than stone shelters with crude plank roofs, now partly rendered more watertight with plastic. Drive slowly as the road is narrow.

Eventually, you drop down to the **Source de l'Oum er Rbia** (a series of waterfalls and springs) clearly visible with its water works from above. There is a car park (lots of men wanting to guard your car) and steps leading to a series of concrete platforms built on the rocks where the river waters come boiling out from between the boulders. (Some of the springs are said to be sweet, others salty.) After the platforms, you can clamber up to see where the water comes crashing into a small but not actually very deep pool (no diving).

After the source, you can head west on a narrow and in places much deteriorated metalled road through beautiful landscape to join the main N8 south of Mrirt. The other option is to continue on south to **Aguelmane Azigza**, a crater lake surrounded by forest and ideal for swimming. The tree-lined spot has its devoted followers among Moroccan campers and is a fine location for some birdwatching. There also may be accommodation on offer in a local café. The road continues to rejoin the N8 at Khénifra.

Khénifra

Khénifra, capital of the Zaïane region, is 81 km southwest of Azrou and 96 km southwest of Ifrane. It is a relaxed (if rather dull) Middle Atlas town with a population of around 100,000. The town's men are famed for their horsemanship.

It has large Wednesday and Sunday **souks** – the place perhaps to pick up an Amazigh rug. The town, with its strategic location at the heart of the Middle Atlas, was developed by Moulay Ismaïl in the late 17th century. In the late 19th century, Sultan Hassan I named local strongman Moha ou Hammou ez Zaïani as caïd. The French had considerable difficulty in bringing Khénifra under their control and suffered a major setback there in 1914 at the hands of Moha ou Hammou. The town only came under the Protectorate's control in 1921, when he was killed in a battle with French forces. A few kilometres south of the town on the N8 is a **monument** to this resistance hero.

Khénifra still has a somewhat military feel to it. There is a main avenue with the usual buildings on stilt-legged arcades. At the north end of town near the horse-monument roundabout are a large number of steep-roofed French buildings, often topped with storks' nests, while, over the river, is the **kasbah** area with an old bridge and one or two historic buildings drowned in a mass of new construction. A possible place for a coffee stop might be the **Café des Cascades**, on a low rise between the town centre and the horse roundabout. There is a **tourist office** at Immeuble Lefraoui, Hay Hamou-Hassan.

Listings Azroud and around

Where to stay

Azrou

€€€ Le Palais des Cerisiers
Rt du Cedre Gourad, T0535-563830, www.lepalaisdescerisiers.
Looking like it's fallen off the lid of a Swiss chocolate box, this smart alpine-style hotel on the road to Ifrane (4 km from Azrou centre) is the most comfortable choice for miles around. Rooms (single/double from 950/1300dh) are decorated in a classic European hotel style, with plentiful soft colours and neutrals, pretty art on the walls, satellite TVs and comfy sofas. There are also bags of facilities: restaurant, spa, pool and lots of hiking and horse riding excursions available. Wi-Fi and breakfast included.

€ Hotel Panorama
T0535-562010, panorama@extra.net.ma.
As the name suggests, the chalet-style hotel has the best views in town. All of

the 38 rooms are showing a bit of wear and tear but have a balcony or terrace and a TV, should you have a penchant for late-night Arabic talk shows. It's a pleasant-enough place, with some good quality contemporary photographs decorating the walls and a decent restaurant and bar for a sundowner. It's a short walk out of the centre of town. Breakfast included.

€ Riad Azrou
Pl Moulay Hachem ben Salah, T0661-064242, www.riadazrou.com.
The best place in the centre to spend the night, Riad Azrou is a well-kept riad-style guesthouse bang in the centre of town. Rooms (from €38) are rather simple but have tiled floors and a/c, and management are switched on about hiking and other activities in the local area and are happy to help. Wi-Fi and breakfast included.

Restaurants

Azrou

€€ Hotel Panorama
T0535-562010 (see also
Where to stay, above).
With its crackling wood fire and 100dh menu, including mountain delicacies such as Middle Atlas trout and *lapin à la moutarde*, this is a solid choice, especially after a hard day's hiking.

€€ Hotel Restaurant des Cèdres
Pl Mohammed V, T0535-562326.
Behind the net curtains there are 2 fixed menus, one 'gastronomique', one 'touristique', though you may find that you can order the same things à la carte for cheaper. Service is attentive and the fish is good.

€ Boulangerie Pâtisserie L'Escalade
5 Pl Hassan II, T0535-563419.
Excellent little baker with very good cakes and biscuits.

Transport

Azrou is situated at a crossroads of routes leading up from **Marrakech** (via Beni Mellal and Khénifra) and **Er Rachidia** (via Midelt). There are plenty of private-line buses north to **Meknès** and **Fès**. CTM buses depart from near Pl Mohammed V, with services to **Casablanca** at 0815 and 1215 (130dh) via **Meknès** (30dh); **Fès** at 0615 and 1415 (30dh); **Marrakech** at 0800 and 2125 (150dh); **Midelt** at 1400 and 2230 (50dh); and **Meknès**. There are also daily services to **Rissani** and **Er Rachidia**. Numerous *grands taxis* head to **Khénifra**, **Ifrane**, **Immouzer du Kandar**, **Meknès** and **Fès**, departing from the centre of town. Azrou is a one-horse sort of place, so there are no difficulties getting around town.

Ifrane and the lakes

Morocco's lake district

Ifrane

Ifrane, 17 km north of Azrou and 63 km south of Fès, is a mountain resort founded by the French in 1929 which today has numerous large villas and chalets, as well as a royal palace and hunting lodge. It still manages to have something of a colonial hill-station feel to it, despite the arrival of a large new campus university, housed in chalet-type buildings, and vast new social housing developments on the Azrou side of town. When the palace is occupied by the king, the town becomes busy with staff and politicians. From the town there are good walks in the cedar forests and a drivable excursion round the *dayats* (crater lakes). There is some skiing to be had at the nearby resort of **Mischliffen**, and a small airport is maintained for private and royal flights.

Dayat lakes

North of Ifrane, leave the N8 to the east for a tour of the dayats, seasonal limestone lakes that are a haven for wildlife, especially birds. There are four lying between the N8 and the R503: Aaoua and Ifrah are the largest, but you can also visit Afourgah and Iffer. **Dayat Aaoua**, 12 km from Ifrane, is a scenic place to picnic if the lake is full, which is not the case in drought years and can make the area disappointing for birdwatchers. In good circumstances, however, the dayats are home to coots, herons and egrets; look out for the black-winged stilt and numerous reed warblers. The surrounding woodland, made up mainly of holm-oak and cedar, is alive with birds: tits, chaffinches, short-toed treecreeper, jays, greater spotted woodpeckers and raptors, including black and red kite, Egyptian vulture and booted eagle. In the woodland Barbary apes can be seen and, where the woodland gives way to more open plateau, look out for the jackals.

Immouzer du Kandar

A small hill resort, 80 km south of Fès and beautiful in spring with the apple blossom, Immouzer is a popular excursion from Fès, easily accessed with regular buses and *grands taxis*. It is also a lively place during the Fête des Pommes in July. Market day takes place on Mondays in the ruined kasbah. Just north of Immouzer du Kandar are the popular picnic/camping springs, **Aïn Seban** and **Aïn Chifa**, clearly signposted to the west of the road. In drought conditions they are less attractive.

Listings Ifrane and the lakes

Where to stay

Ifrane

€€€€ Michlifen Ifrane Suites and Spa
Av Hassan II 18, T0535-864000,
www.michlifenifrane.com.
This swanky spa hotel brings a touch of glamour to the alpine-esque town of Ifrane. Expect 5-star service with bells on. There's a luxury spa and hamman, beautiful bedrooms (doubles from 2050dh), several excellent restaurants and stunning views of snow-capped mountains. Design-wise, think American lodge luxury and sleek, Nordic minimalism, with plenty of wow factor. There's even a log fire by the indoor pool. Wi-Fi and breakfast included.

€€-€ Hotel Le Chamonix
T0535 566028.
A good, mid-range option, with 64 bright clean rooms (doubles from 550dh), with fairly chintzy communal areas and simple, comfortable decor in the rooms.

It could do with a bit of TLC these days, but friendly service and a willing attitude make up for it. The restaurant serves alcohol, and you can hire skis from the bar. Wi-Fi and breakfast included.

€ Gîte Dayet Aoua
Rte d'Immouzer a Ifrane, Km7,
T0535-604880, T0661-351257,
www.gite-dayetaoua.com.
Located about 7 km outside Ifrane, this basic gîte is set in stunning countryside. Peacocks and chickens roam the gardens, decor is a cut above most gîtes of this level, each room (doubles from 250dh) individually and carefully decorated with local textiles and crafts. Don't expect modern luxuries, but if you want to get away from the mob, sample home-cooked Moroccan food served in a Berber tent, or go on long walks from your back door, it's a winner. They can also arrange bivouacs for camping in the hills, canoe trips and guides.

Camping

Camping International
Signposted from the town centre,
T0535-566156.
Very busy in the summer but open year round for those brave enough to face the winter chill. The 6-ha site is fairly basic with no shop or restaurant, though it does have laundry facilities and showers. Petrol is only 2 km away.

Restaurants

Ifrane
Ifrane is not exactly a gastronomic destination but there are some reasonable options, lots of mid-range places and a handful of cafés, including **Le Croustillant Boulangerie Pâtisserie**, which does reasonable coffee and has a good selection of pastries in a setting reminiscent of a European cafeteria.

€ **Café de Pax**
Av de la Mare Verte.
For your pizza, pasta or calzone craving, this little place hits the spot, plus the coffee is decent and there's a small menu of tagine options.

What to do

Ifrane
Skiing
Near Ifrane, Mischliffen is a small area with cafés and ski lifts but little else. The season is Jan-Mar, and the resort has good but short slopes, sometimes with patchy snow cover. Hire equipment from the **Hotel Le Chamonix** in Ifrane and take a taxi to the resort. During summer the area is popular with walkers.

Transport

Ifrane
There are regular buses from Ifrane to both **Azrou** and **Fès**.

Midelt and around

prosaic but well-placed base for off-the-beaten-path excursions

For many, the rough-and-ready town of Midelt is a handy overnight stop about halfway between the imperial cities and the Tafilalet. Midelt works well as base for excursions to the abandoned mines of Ahouli in a defile of the Oued Moulouya, or for an off-road trip to the Cirque de Jaffar, a natural amphitheatre in the side of Jbel Ayyachi, paramount peak of the region. In the heart of the eastern High Atlas, Imilchil (see page 125) is now also feasible as a long day trip on the metalled road via Rich.

Midelt
Despite high unemployment, the town has a calm, friendly atmosphere and a souk on Sunday. Those in need of a little retail therapy should think carpets in Midelt. Located north of the town centre, the Kasbah Meriem is the local name for the monastery of **Notre Dame de l'Atl**

> **Tip...**
> As elsewhere in this plateau region, the winters are very cold and the summers very hot, so the best time to visit is late spring. May or even early June are recommended for walking.

as, which still has a tiny community of Trappist monks who relocated here from Algeria. It is home to the weaving school, **Atelier de Tissage** ⓘ *Sat-Thu 0900-1200 and 1400-1800*, which employs local Berber women and helps develop their weaving skills. Visitors to the atelier are also welcome to take a look around the monastery grounds. To get there, head north out of Midelt town centre, take a left turn onto the track after the bridge, follow the track towards the kasbah village, where you then take a sharp right and go almost immediately left up the hill. After about 1 km, the Kasbah Meriem is signed on the left, down a dip and up again, its presence indicated by trees. The atelier is left of the large metal gate. Inside, there is a simple church with a small icon of the seven sleepers of Ephesus, symbol of a myth present both in Christianity and Islam.

Jbel Ayachi

Midelt is the jumping-off point for treks up to Jbel Ayachi, which at 3747 m is eastern Morocco's highest mountain, an impressive 45 km stretch of solid mountain, unbroken by any peaks. First conquered in July 1901 by the Marquis de Segonzac, the heights can remain

> **Tip...**
> Make sure you have plenty of water. Even in summer, it can be very cold at the summit.

snow-covered well into late June. In the right conditions, on a long summer's day, the climb can be done up and back in 12 hours, but it's probably better to take two days and bivouac out on the mountain. To tackle Jbel Ayachi, head first for **Tattiouine**, 12 km from Midelt (*grand taxi* transport available). Here it should be possible to find mules and a guide.

Impressive and seemingly impenetrable with its snow-capped heights, the Jbel Ayachi functions as a water tower for southeastern Morocco, its meltwater feeding both the Moulouya to the north and the Oued Ziz to the south. Jbel Ayachi derives its name from the local Aït Ayyach tribe. Within living memory, caves in the cliffs were occupied by freedom fighters resisting the Makhzen and the incoming French. The last of such mountain strongholds were only finally taken by the central authorities in 1932.

Cirque du Jaffar

One of Morocco's best known 4WD excursions takes intrepid off-roaders up to the Cirque de Jaffar (map NI-30-II-3), one of the natural arenas hollowed out on the north side of the Jbel Ayachi. In fact, in a good off-road vehicle, it is just about possible to travel over from Midelt, via the Oued Jaffar, to **Imilchil**, a distance of 160 km. The initial part through the Oued Jaffar gorges is the most scenic. The route is not to be attempted in winter, however, and certainly not risked in spring if there are April snows. Consult the **Gendarmerie royale** in Midelt or the people at **Ksar Timnay** on the Zeïda road (see page 204).

Mines of Ahouli

For those with a hire car, this excursion north from Midelt goes along the S317 to **Mibladene** (10 km) and over the head of the Oued Moulouya to the abandoned mining settlement of Ahouli. The road is signed right a few metres north from the central bus station junction in Midelt. The first long straight section is badly potholed as far as Mibladene, a former mining community to the right of the road, but it then improves slightly

Tip...
Men will try to flag the car down en route to Mibladene. Most will be selling fossils or stones of some kind. With all three mines in the region (Mibladene, Ahouli and Zaïda) now closed, there is a lot of poverty and selling stones may be their only source of income.

as it winds into spectacular gorges. The road deteriorates again after an Indiana Jones-style bridge, parts of it washed away by floods.

Ahouli must once have been a hive of activity. Copper and lead were the main products. The gorge is beautiful, with poplar, oleander and even the odd weeping willow. Mine infrastructure and housing clings to the cliffs. The community even had its own rather splendid cinema (now sanded up) and swimming pool. The lower floors of the houses had heavy metal doors to keep out eventual floodwater. There is a caretaker here, and he or his son may show you round.

After Ahouli, you can drive up out of the gorges on a well-made track, turning left to more abandoned dwellings on the plateau. Turning left, a couple of kilometres brings you to the small village and semi-abandoned ksar of **Ouled Taïr** next to the *oued*, reached by a wobbly footbridge.

Oued Moulouya

Ten kilometres east of Midelt, the N15 branches off the N13 and heads northeast to cross the high plain of Aftis before joining the valley of the Oued Moulouya. Two fortified kasbahs built by Moulay Ismaïl around 1690 to guard the imperial route from Fès to Sijilmassa are still inhabited: **Ksabi** and **Saida**. The inhabitants, originally forming an agglomeration of 10 *ksars*, are mostly descendants of Alaouite guardsmen from the Tafilalet. At over 1000 m, the freshness of the air and quality of light in this remote region are exhilarating. Past Saida, the road runs along an attractive stretch of the Oued Moulouya, with *pisé* villages and richly cultivated riverbanks. Beyond Tamdafelt the road continues for about 30 km through a bare but dramatic landscape that would make a good Western film set to Missour.

Missour

A tranquil town with many donkeys and unpaved roads, Missour comes alive for the weekly market. There is a fair medium-priced hotel here, and, although they're unaccustomed to foreigners, the locals are helpful. If you are lucky enough to be here on a Wednesday, there is a large local **souk** situated on the hill by the water tower, past the new mosque. The lower part of the market is disappointing, but the top end of the main enclosure has the fruit and vegetable market, and a separate area beyond encloses the livestock market. Both enclosures have tea tents. There is a view of the town and the mountains from the adjacent hill.

Listings Midelt and around

Where to stay

Midelt

€ Hotel Bougafer
7 Av Mohammed V, T0535-583099.
Up the hill round behind the bus station, this place has good, clean en suite rooms (300dh), simple 3-bed rooms on the top floor, a restaurant and friendly management. It's one of the best budget hotels in town. Breakfast included.

€ Ksar Timnay
Aït Ayach, halfway between Midelt and Zeïda on the N13, 20 km from Midelt, T0535-360188, www.ksar-timnay.com.
This is an efficient set-up, with a range of accommodation, including a choice of bright, simple rooms (and some swankier room options in a separate building onsite – Riad Mimouna), camping, nomad tents and sites for campervans. There is a restaurant, shop, pool and sprawling gardens; also 4WD rental, with a guide for exploring the region, and good day trips can be arranged to Canyon de Tatrout. Wi-Fi included.

Restaurants

Midelt
There are some cheap roadside places just up from the station offering mainly tagines – try **Restaurant Lespoir** or **du Centre**.

€ Restaurant de Fès
2 Av Mohammed, T0662-057754.
Couscous is the order of the day here, along with some excellent options for vegetarians. Choose from 7 different *salades Marocaine* and an excellent 10-vegetable tagine. Small, welcoming and enthusiastic, it gets filled up with groups, so it's worth trying to bag your table early. 3-course menu for 80dh.

What to do

Midelt
For hiking opportunities and other possible excursions in the area, ask at **Ksar Timnay** (see Where to stay, above).

Deserts
& gorges

With their arid mountains and gentle oases, a volcanic massif and some splendid canyons, the great valleys south of the High Atlas have some of the finest scenery in Morocco.

Whether heading south from Fès, via the crumbling *ksar* at Rissani, or east from Marrakech, many people's aim is Erg Chebbi, the cinematic sand dunes near Merzouga. Here you can sleep in nomad tents and ride out on camels into the sunset. To the west, the spectacular, winding valleys of Dadès and Todra become narrow gorges before they rise into the High Atlas, their red rocks glowing in the southern sun. To the south there are alternative tastes of desert life to be had as you follow the Drâa Valley through miles of lush oases and sleepy villages until the ribbon of tarmac finally stutters to a halt at M'Hamid el Ghizlane and the Sahara beckons. Here, the dunes of Erg Chiggaga are the star attraction, some 50 km away across turbulent desert *pistes* and stony *hammada*.

Almost all travellers will pass through Ouarzazate, where the Tizi-n-Tichka route over the mountains from Marrakech meets the main east–west axis from Er Rachidia to Agadir, running parallel to the south side of the High Atlas. Ouarzazate may be no beauty itself but it's a fine base for planning further desert exploits and excursions to the stunning kasbah of Aït Ben Haddou.

Best for
Camel riding ▪ Hiking ▪ Off-roading ▪ Star gazing

Er Rachidia to Erg Chebbi.... 210
Er Rachidia to Ouarzazate ... 222
Ouarzazate & around....... 232
Drâa Valley................. 244

Footprint
picks

★ **Erg Chebbi**, page 219

Camel trek to this vast dune field on the western edge of the Sahara.

★ **Dadès Gorge**, page 227

Hike through lush gardens and tiny villages to crumbling kasbahs and orange-tinged cliffs.

★ **Aït Ben Haddou**, page 241

Explore the twisty alleyways through one of Morocco's prettiest kasbahs.

★ **Drâa Valley**, page 244

Take a road-trip along the old caravan route from Ouarzazate to Zagora, via crumbling fortified villages lined with palm groves and hemmed in by barren hills.

★ **Erg Chiggaga**, page 253

Sleep under the vast desert sky amid the rippling dunes of Erg Chiggaga.

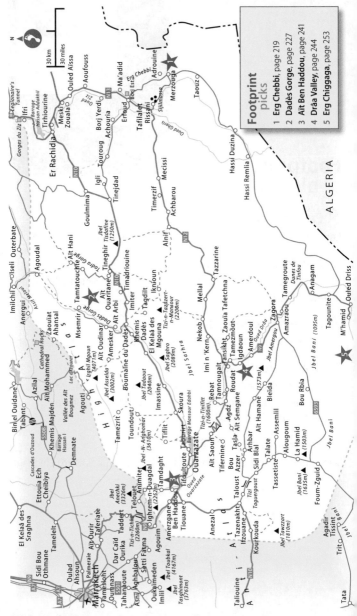

Footprint picks

1 Erg Chebbi, page 219
2 Dadès Gorge, page 227
3 Aït Ben Haddou, page 241
4 Drâa Valley, page 244
5 Erg Chigaga, page 253

Essential Deserts and gorges

Finding your feet

Ouarzazate, Boulmane du Dades, Tineghir and Er Rachidia can be used as overnight stops on an Atlas tour from Fès to Marrakech or vice versa, with other possible overnights at Midelt, Beni Mellal or Azilal. Boumalne and Tineghir can be used as bases to explore the Dadès and Todra gorges, although keen hikers might opt to stay in the auberges and small hotels in the gorges themselves, near to the best trekking.

Getting around

Although all of the highlights of the region are easily accessible by public transport, it's definitely worthwhile hiring a *grand taxi* privately on some routes (such as down into the Drâa Valley), so that you can stop off along the way to visit the kasbahs and ksour. To fully explore, you'll need a 4WD vehicle. Those driving should take care: the main roads are narrow and wind up and over high passes. They can also get busy with vehicles driven fast by experienced local drivers.

When to go

Overall, April and May are the best times to visit with pleasant temperatures

out in the desert and almond and fruit blossom in the valleys and gorges. From December to February, be aware that the Tizi-n-Tichka Pass (the main access route to Ouarzazate from Marrakech) can be closed due to snow. It can also be exceedingly cold at night in the desert during these months. Bring adequate warm clothing if you're travelling in winter. Due to extreme heat, July and August are not the months to be venturing out on sand dune trips from M'Hamid or Merzouga; much of the tourist infrastructure in these towns, shuts down in the height of summer.

Time required

Allow at least a week to get a full taste of the desert, valleys and gorges, or longer if you're planning on a more extensive desert adventure. Keen hikers may also want to spend more time exploring the Todra and Dadès gorges.

> ### Tip...
> To avoid confusion, remember that a *ksar* (plural *ksour*) is a fortified village, whereas a kasbah is a fortified dwelling, usually occupied by the ruler or chieftain.

Weather Ouarzazate

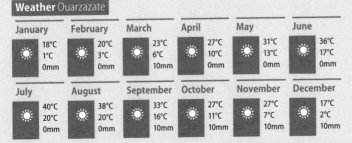

January	February	March	April	May	June
18°C	20°C	23°C	27°C	31°C	36°C
1°C	3°C	6°C	10°C	13°C	17°C
0mm	0mm	0mm	10mm	0mm	0mm

July	August	September	October	November	December
40°C	38°C	33°C	27°C	27°C	17°C
20°C	20°C	16°C	11°C	7°C	2°C
0mm	0mm	10mm	10mm	10mm	10mm

Er Rachidia
to Erg Chebbi

The variety and scale of the landscapes is the attraction of east-central Morocco. North of Er Rachidia the Oued Ziz carves it way through a spectacular narrow gorge, while to the south it waters the palm-filled canyons of the Tafilalet, one of the biggest oases in the world and famous for its dates. Further south, there are crumbling kasbahs and *ksour* (fortified villages) at Rissani and high dunes at Merzouga, site of many a Saharan fantasy, where travellers and filmmakers flock to ride camels out into a photogenic desert landscape.

Er Rachidia

Er Rachidia was previously known as Ksar es Souk or 'the village of markets', due to its importance as a trading crossroads for the trans-Saharan caravans. It was renamed after Independence after the first Alaouite leader, 17th-century sultan Moulay Rachid. The present town was established by the French, initially by the Foreign Legion as a military centre, a role it retains today, due to its position near the Algerian border. The town, with its mix of new concrete and older mud-walled buildings, has little in the way of sights beyond the 19th-century Ksar Targa, 5 km from the centre, but it is a convenient stopping point at the meeting of routes to Ouarzazate, Erfoud (south), Midelt and Meknès (north), and distant Figuig (east), and so has reasonable facilities and a relaxed atmosphere. Er Rachidia is generally used by visitors as an overnight stop on a circuit of the High Atlas, before they head down to the kasbahs of Rissani and the dunes of Merzouga. The grid-iron street pattern, so typical of French garrison towns in the Sahara, makes orientation simple, and the central town area is small enough that everything can be reached on foot. The main road, Avenue Moulay Ali Cherif, leads down to the new bridge over the Oued Ziz and has ATMs, banks, cafés and restaurants along its length. Evenings in the town are pleasant, with lots of people out strolling in the streets after the heat of the day; the main market days are Sunday, Tuesday and Thursday.

Gorges du Ziz

The N13 north of Er Rachidia is a superb route which follows the Oued Ziz for the first 20 km. Caves can be seen cut into the cliff, no doubt used to store crops. On your right is the western shore of the **Barrage de Hassan Addakhil**, completed in 1971. The dam supplies water to Er Rachidia and the region's oases. It also limits the potentially destructive flash flooding of the Oued Ziz. Migrating birds stop over on the lake, too. If you travel along this route in the evening, the sun accentuates the landforms, highlighting bands of hard rock with screes between. Then you come to the **Gorges du Ziz**, a spectacular ride in a narrow defile 2 km in length. The small settlement of **Ifri** is around 29 km from Er Rachidia, where a bridge crosses the river; picnicking and camping are possible here.

If you have lots of time, then continue on the N13, through the Legionaire's Tunnel, to the hot springs of **Moulay Ali Cherif**, 42 km north of Er Rachidia with the N10 a few kilometres east of Er Rachidia, near the airport.

> **Tip...**
> If you are travelling north on the N13 from Er Rachidia to complete a High Atlas circular tour, Midelt (see page 201) is the next major town with decent accommodation, 156 km from Er Rachidia.

Tourist information

Er Rachidia

There is a **tourist office** in Er Rachidia at 44 Rue My Abdellah (near bus station), T0535-570944, Mon-Fri 0830-1630.

Where to stay

There is not a huge choice of hotels in Er Rachidia.

€€ Hotel Le Riad
Zone touristique d'Errachidia,
Rte de Goulmima, T0535-791006,
www.hotelleriad.com.
A smart hotel outside the city, centred round a good-sized pool. The 24 big a/c rooms (from 800dh) are elegantly decorated in a European style and come with satellite TV, minibar and bathrooms with tubs. Wi-Fi and breakfast included.

€ Auberge Tinit
Rtd de Goulmima, T0535-791759,
www.auberge-tinit.info.
This auberge has a modern, block-colour approach in its rooms (single/double 300/500dh), which are good-sized, bright and airy, and have just a touch of Moroccan-inspired style with Berber motifs adorning the walls. It's just out of town, along the main road. Wi-Fi and breakfast included.

€ Hotel Errachidia
31 Rue Ibnou Batouta, T0535-570453.
This is a reliable, clean and modern cheapie, just behind the bus station. Rooms (100dh) are nothing special but have TVs, desk and comfy beds. It's far from beautiful, but it does the job.

Restaurants

There are plenty of cheap places along Av Mohammed V.

€ Hotel-Café La Renaissance
19 Rue Moulay Youssef, T0535-572633.
Reliable restaurant with excellent couscous.

€ Restaurant Imilchil
Av Moulay Ali Cherif, T0535-572123.
Moroccan standards served on a terrace overlooking the main drag.

Transport

Bus

The *gare routière* is in the town centre on Rue M'Daghra. **Supratours** and **CTM** are located here too (T0535-572024). Heading west, CTM buses leave for **Casablanca** (200dh, 10 hrs), via **Meknès** (125dh, 8 hrs) at 0830 and 2145; **Marrakech** (165dh, 10½ hrs) at 0630 daily; and **Fès** (130dh, 9 hrs), via **Meknès** at 2130. **Supratours** have a 1030 departure for **Marrakech**; and a 2130 service to **Fès**. Going east, 1 CTM bus heads to **Erfoud** (30dh) and **Rissani** (40dh, 2 hrs) at 0530; **Supratours** buses depart at 0500 and 1830 on the same route, but continue to **Merzouga** (2¼ hrs). There are also other private-line buses to **Casablanca**, **Marrakech**, **Meknès** and **Fès**, and several buses a day for **Erfoud**, **Rissani**, **Midelt** and **Tineghir**.

Car

If you're driving yourself, vehicle parts and tyre repairs are available at a place opposite the **Hotel Meski**.

Grand taxi
Grands taxis can be found 200 m north of the *gare routière* in a parking-lot 2 blocks off the main road. There are frequent *grands taxis* to **Erfoud** and **Meski**, **Goulmima** and **Tinejdad**.

Tafilalet

head south through the fertile Ziz valley

The southern stretch of the Ziz valley, known as the Tafilalet, is particularly fertile. Historically, the region was of considerable importance, due in part to its location on the trans-Saharan trade routes. In the eighth and ninth centuries the region was a separate kingdom and became known as a centre of religious unorthodoxy – of the Kharijite Berber heresy and later of Shi'ism. The ruling Alaouite Dynasty originated in Rissani. From 1916 to 1931 French control of the region was challenged and effectively thwarted by local forces. Many of the settlements of the valley were destroyed in a flood in 1965. Today the region produces figs, olives and dates, but is noted especially for its tamarisk trees.

Meski

Heading towards the Tafilalet from Er Rachidia, it's a 94 km journey to Rissani. Meski, lying to the west of the Erfoud road about 18 km east of Er Rachidia, is the first halt, famed for its natural springs, known as the **Source Bleu**. Developed by the Foreign Legion,

Fact...
Dried tamarisk fruit is used in the leather industry for its tannin, essential to the curing process.

the springwater pool is surrounded by palms and has a popular campsite next door, the **Camping de la Source Bleu**. Overlooking the springs are the 500-year-old ruins of ksar Meski, which form an attractive backdrop.

Along the Ziz canyon

Continuing south on the N13 towards Erfoud, you could easily miss one of the most spectacular views in Morocco over the huge oasis-canyon of the Oued Ziz to the right (west). Keep an eye out for a track, marked by a small cairn, which runs to the edge of the gorge. The view is magnificent – there will be others admiring the scenery too.

Tip...
If you have time, take a 4WD and a guide along the small roads by the river rather than speeding along the N13. Here you will see a great contrast between the green fertile ribbon of palms and oasis gardens and the surrounding scorched landscape.

After the viewpoint, the road soon drops down into the valley, some 20 km long. In each loop of the river stands a *ksar* (fortressed village) made of mud brick, guarding the valley and providing protection for the village as well as supervision for the trade in slaves and precious metals that once used this route.

At 28 km from Er Rachidia, the main road descends the cliff to the valley floor. **Zouala** is the first settlement and good place to explore the oasis, with bare crags soaring above the palms.

Further on, the large settlement strung out along the main road is **Aoufouss**, about 45 km from Rachidia. There is an **Afriquia** petrol station and a CTM stop here. Red-washed concrete houses line the road, but the old *pisé* dwellings are clearly visible further back. For a break, try the café attached to the petrol station where food is usually good and the bathrooms are clean.

The road then rises out of the canyon floor onto an arid plain. At **Borj Yerdi**, 14 km north of Erfoud, the first small dunes come into view; if you're driving, watch out for sand on the road, despite the tiny fences of palm fronds put up to control the shifting dunes. North of Erfoud, on the eastern side of the road, is the *ksar* of **Ma'adid**. Here it is said the streets are so narrow and the arrangement so complicated that only locals can find their way in and, more importantly, out. Take a guide if you visit.

Erfoud

Erfoud is a southern Moroccan garrison town, founded by the French in the 1930s to administer their desert territories. It is now the modern centre of the Tafilalet region. Although many travellers bypass it in favour of Merzouga, which is nearer to the dunes, Erfoud makes an excellent base for exploring the valley and nearby

> **Tip…**
> There is a **BMCE** ATM next to the Total garage on the east side of the main drag, just before the Hotel Tafilalet, as you go north.

desert areas: 4WD trips out to the Erg Chebbi dunes are easily arranged with hotels and local desert tour agencies, and Rissani, with its *ksar* and the historic Sijilmassa site, can be reached by *grand taxi*.

On the other side of the river from the town of Erfoud is the **Borj Est**, a military fort overlooking the village and palms, the Tafilalet oasis and the desert. There's no admittance, but it's worth getting a taxi up to the top for the view. There is a **market** on Sunday in the centre.

> **Tip…**
> Lovers of dates should try to time their visit to coincide with the annual date festival held in October, though it is a movable feast and hard to pin down.

The Erfoud area is known for its trilobite fossils. The main digging areas are out of town on the road to Merzouga. To learn more about the geology of the area, head to Tahiri's **Museum of Fossils and Minerals**, on the main road to Rissani, which displays important fossils found here.

Where to stay

Along the Ziz canyon

€€ Kasbah Xaluca Maadid
205 Rte Errachidia, Ma'adid,
T0535-578450, www.xaluca.com.
Part of a Spanish chain, this large neo-kasbah is 7 km north of Erfoud in the village of Ma'adid. It has spacious rooms (single/double 830/1080dh) and large suites with all mod-cons, decorated in local traditional style with palm beams and marble bathrooms. The host of facilities include huge outdoor pool, indoor pool, spa, restaurant and bar. Wi-Fi and breakfast included.

Camping

Camping Tissirt
30 km south of Er Rachidia towards
Erfoud, T0662-141378, www.
campingtissirtziz.free.fr.
On the edge of the Ziz canyon, the site has great views, a shaded garden and a big Berber tent dormitory (50dh per person). It's 65dh for a caravan, 2 people and electricity and 15dh to pitch a tent, plus 20dh per person. Good-value meals are available here.

Erfoud

Erfoud has a clutch of luxury hotels on the Rissani (southern) side of town, facing towards the distant Merzouga dunes. Many are slightly garish modern takes on the traditional kasbah. Coming from Er Rachidia, cheaper hotels and eateries in the town centre are reached by going left onto Av Mohammed V, at the crossroads with the post office.

€€-€ Hotel Kasbah Tizimi
2 km out of town on the Tinghir road,
T0535-576179, www.kasbahtizimi.com.
Very popular with tour groups, Kasbah Tizimi has 65 rooms (€50) with wrought-iron furniture and *beldi* tiled floors, centred round a patio with pleasant pool. Take a look at a few rooms before deciding, as some of the bathrooms could do with a revamp. There are also 8 suites (€90) and a couple of bigger apartment-style studios. The restaurant here serves good-value meals. Wi-Fi and breakfast included.

€ Hotel Farah Zouar
Av Moulay Ismail, on right as you leave
Erfoud for Rissani, T0535-576230.
This solid budget place has small but spick-and-span a/c rooms and a restaurant serving European and Moroccan food, with good views from roof terrace.

€ Hotel Merzouga
114 Av Mohammed V, T0535-576532.
One of the better cheapies in the centre of town, this basic place has friendly management and en suite rooms (100dh) that are nothing to write home about. Those watching their dirham can sleep on the roof terrace for 25dh.

Camping

Tifina Camping
8 km from Erfoud towards Rissani, T0610-
231415, www.tifina-morocco.com.
Constructed from local materials in vernacular style, this modern camping complex has all the bells and whistles and is extremely well-run. Facilities include a pool and restaurant, and it also has disabled access.

Restaurants

The Kasbah Xaluca lunch-buffet is delicious for 210dh (see Where to stay, above).

Erfoud

You can eat in (relative) luxury at any of the hotels in Erfoud. For those on a budget, there are places on Av Moulay Ismail and Av Mohammed V.

€€ Dadani
103 Av Mohammed V, T0535-577958.
An excellent little café-restaurant with traditional (and comfortable) Moroccan seating upstairs and a Western-style café downstairs. Very good *kalia*, though don't expect it to come in a hurry. There's even an apartment for rent, should you like it so much you want to stay.

€ Café-Restaurant des Dunes
Av Moulay Ismail, near the Ziz petrol station.
This well-known place serves up surprisingly authentic pizzas.

Transport

Meski
It is best to have your own transport to explore the Tafilalet, although you can get to Meski from Er Rachidia by *grand taxi*, paying the same price as for Erfoud (the Source and campsite are a few hundred metres from the road). Moving on from Meski, you might be able to get a bus, or (easier) hitch a lift with other tourists.

Erfoud
Erfoud is easily accessible from Ouarzazate and the Dadès Valley to the west via Tineghir and Tinejdad (change buses here). **Er Rachidia** to Erfoud is 1½ hrs. There is also a daily bus from **Fès** (11 hrs). The **CTM** office is on Av Mohammed V. The daily **CTM** service from Rissani to **Er Rachidia**, **Meknès** and **Fès** picks up passengers in Erfoud at 2000; in the other direction, the morning bus to **Rissani** pulls into town at about 0700. Other private-line buses and **Supratours** operate out of Pl des FAR. **Supratours** has 1 daily departure to **Fès** at 2130; and 1 to **Marrakech** at 0930. Their services to **Merzouga** pull into town at 0615 and 1930. Regular minivans and *grands taxis* (from Pl des FAR) ply the road to Rissani and are the quickest and easiest way of getting there.

Rissani and around

discover the atmospheric remains of this once-prosperous oasis

Rissani, 22 km south of Erfoud is a sprawling modern village close to the site of the ruined town of Sijilmassa. It has a 17th-century *ksar*, which houses most of the population, and the main street has a bank and a few cafés. If you are feeling energetic and have your own transport, you may want to explore other local *ksour* on a heritage trail known as the *circuit touristique*. Accommodation options aren't great in Rissani, but it makes a good day trip from either Merzouga or Erfoud.

Sights

The ruins of **Sijilmassa**, little of which remain, are located between the town and the river. Sijilmassa was founded in 757 by the Arab leader Moussa ben Nasser. For many centuries it was the Berber capital of the Tafilalet region and a major trading centre, thanks to its location on the major Sahel to Europe trade route from Niger to Tangier. The town enjoyed considerable importance and prosperity from trading in gold, and, as its fame grew, so did its size. The current Alaouite Dynasty settled in the surrounding region in the 13th century before gaining the Moroccan sultanate in the 17th century. A major new kasbah was built by Moulay Ismaïl, but the Aït Atta tribe destroyed the town in 1818. The ruins are really of historical interest only and the guides are often not very well informed, although they can be entertaining: tales of earthquake destruction, for example, are on the fanciful side.

To find out more about Rissani's past, you might call in at the **Centre d'Études et Recherches Alaouites (CERA)** ① *T0535-770305, Mon-Fri 0830-1630*, located in the large austere *ksar* on the main square, just along from the **Hotel Sijilmassa**. There is a library and a small museum, consisting of just a few small cases displaying pots from recent excavations and large panels with information in French about the region's history. There is also a detailed 1:100,000 scale map of the region. Some of the staff may speak English.

Around Rissani

The Rissani oasis has a rather Mesopotamian feel, with mud monuments crumbling away to fine dust. The former prosperity of the region is obvious from the palace buildings that are dotted around; these were designed by architects, unlike the more makeshift *ksar* villages. The isolation of Rissani, separated from Erfoud by salt flats, means that the lost palaces of the Tafilalet, now much eroded by the action of the wind, sun and occasional floods, must have been truly impressive for wandering nomads and caravans coming up from far-distant Mali.

To the southeast of Rissani is the **Zaouïa of Moulay Ali Cherif**, the founder of the Alaouite dynasty, who was buried here in 1640. This is a new building as the previous one was destroyed by flash flood. Non-Muslims may not enter and are prevented therefore from viewing the beautiful glazed tilework and the central courtyard with fountain, surrounded by palms.

Near here is **Ksar Akbar**, a ruined Alaouite palace from the 19th century, which once held vast treasures – not to mention members of important families who had fallen out of favour. It is also said to be the palace of Moulay Abd el Rahmane, brother of reforming 19th-century sultan Hassan I.

About 2 km to the south is the **Ksar Ouled Abd el Helim**, nicknamed the 'Alhambra of the Tafilalet'. It was built in 1900 by Moulay Rachid, elder brother of Moulay Hassan, as a governor's residence. Its decorated towers, monumental gateway and cloistered courtyards provide a little grandeur in the oasis.

Ksar Tinrheras is the most southerly *ksar* at 770 m above sea level. There is a splendid view from the walls, looking out to the *hammada* (rocky desert) to the south and the oasis to the north.

Off the road to Erfoud, in the vicinity of the **Hotel Kasbah Asmaa**, are some more minor sights, including **Ksar Jebril**, a large, still-populated village to the west, and **Al Mansouria**, another village to the east, about 300 m into the palm groves. Here there are yet more crumbling remains of vanished palaces, including a rather spectacular gate.

Listings Rissani and around

Restaurants

There are not that many eating options in Rissani, but Restaurant Café Merzouga on Av Moulay Ali Cherif, near the main market, is a solid choice and La Baraka, next to the market, does a fine line in Berber pizza.

Shopping

Rissani has a lively market on Sun, Tue and Thu, and there are several handicraft shops. People with large vehicles may like to pick up a hefty chalky-white *khabiya* (water jar) or two, which are still used in the region.

Transport

Although there is a new *gare routière* before the ceremonial arch as you come into town from the north, lots of buses still come into the main square. **CTM** buses have their own office in the centre (T0535-770238). CTM's daily service to **Erfoud**, **Er Rachidia**, **Meknès** and **Fès** leaves at 1930. **Supratours** service to **Marrakech** leaves at 0830; and to **Fès** to 1930. There are regular *grands taxis* to **Merzouga** or **Erfoud**.

Merzouga and the dunes of Erg Chebbi

rippling Saharan dunes are the star attraction

Some 61 km southwest of Erfoud, Merzouga has one attraction: the 150-m-high dunes of Erg Chebbi, a vast pile of sand stretching into the Sahara. There is little else here, beside the other tourists and a small village with a Saturday souk, but the calm and the wilderness are a big part of the appeal.

There is occasionally good birdwatching in the adjacent **Dayat Merzouga**, when it has water. Another (summer) option is to have a sand bath, said to be good for rheumatism. Beyond Merzouga, the *piste* continues south to **Taouz**, where the 4WD brigade can now travel west along the once 'forbidden track' (shown as the *piste interdite* on the maps) to Remlia and the confluence of the dry river valleys of the Gheris and Ziz.

★ Erg Chebbi

The dunes of Erg Chebbi are an offshoot of a much bigger area of dunes across the border in Algeria and, because of their relative accessibility, have often been used as a film set by Hollywood directors. It's not hard to see why: as the sun shifts across the sky during the day, the dunes change colour, from the palest cream to deep oranges and reds, and their beautiful shapes and patterns are constantly sculpted by the wind. Despite the popularity of the dunes, it's easy to escape any sign of human habitation, especially if you get up early for a walk.

> **Tip...**
> Although the dunes might at first appear to be no more than a lifeless expanse of sand, they are, in fact, a fragile ecosystem. Bear this in mind before signing up for an environmentally harmful quad bike tour.

All of the hotels along the edge of Erg Chebbi organize **camel treks** into the dunes – usually out to semi-permanent tent encampments where you stay a night before coming back to the hotel. The cheaper trips tend to go a short distance to a communal camp, where you may find that the romance of a night under the bright Saharan stars is spoiled by the crowds. Pay a bit more, and you should get a small camp, with varying degrees of comfort. Camps on the northern or southern slopes of the dunes tend to be quieter.

Listings Merzouga and the dunes of Erg Chebbi

Where to stay

Spread out along the edge of the dunes, most of Merzouga's hotels are north of the village itself. In fact, those further away from town tend to be preferable, as they generally have more space and easy access to the less-visited areas of the dunes. Most have obligatory half-board and do their own excursions. Many close in the summer, when it becomes too hot

> **Tip...**
> Note that there are numerous faux guides in the area who will do their best to convince you that certain auberges are closed and lead you elsewhere. If you have GPS, contact the auberge for their precise location.

to go out on the dunes. Signs off to the east of the new sealed road from Rissani lead across the sand on bumpy pistes, to ubiquitous kasbah-style accommodation, with high *pies* walls around a large central courtyard. Most hotels will offer to meet you out on the main road, which is highly advisable.

€€ Auberge du Sud
T0661-216166 (mob),
www.aubergedusud.com.
20 differently themed rooms (doubles €70-100); the better ones have their own private terrace overlooking the dunes, and each has a/c, heating and solar panels providing hot water and electricity. There's a nice pool area, and they run good sunset camel trips (€40 per person) involving 2 or 3 hrs' trekking and an overnight camp with dinner

and breakfast. The hotel provides free collection from Rissani if you tell them in advance. Wi-Fi and breakfast included.

€€ Auberge Kasbah Derkaoua
T0535-577140, www.auberge derkaoua.com.
At the northern end of the dunes, Derkaoua is best reached heading southeast out of Erfoud, rather than from the Rissani–Merzouga road. Popular, and a cut above many of the other options, it has a licensed restaurant, a pool, hammam and a tennis court. Rooms (doubles 700dh) are decorated with Moroccan fabrics, and the food is magnificent. Book in advance. Wi-Fi and breakfast included.

€€ Kasbah Mohayut
T0666-039185 (mob), www.hotelmohayut.com.
The colourful rooms and suites at this popular mid-range option are big and bright and come with a/c and minibar. The best ones have private terraces overlooking the dunes. There's a restaurant and bar, and a very nice pool setup with a camel fountain. Breakfast and Wi-Fi included.

€€-€ Auberge Ksar Sania
by the Grand Dune and the seasonal lake, T0535-577414, www. ksarsaniahotelmerzouga.com.
For something a little bit different, Ksar Sania is an unusual mudbrick, hexagonal eco-lodge ran by Gérard and Françoise Tommaso. Attractive rooms (single/double €40/60) are shaped from traditional materials, palms and *tadelakt* and have plenty of rustic desert charm. There's also budget adobe huts (single/ double €30/40) in the garden that

surrounds the pool, or you can pitch your tent for 25dh per person. Wi-Fi and breakfast included.

€ Auberge Camping Sahara
Hassi Labied, T0535-577039, www.aubergesahara.com.
Simple and homely family-run auberge with cosy guest rooms (200-300dh) and a shaded camping site to pitch your tent in (25dh per person). Service is super-friendly; the restaurant does decent meals, and they can set up all sorts of dune excursions.

€ Chez Julia
right in the centre of Merzouga, T0535-573182, www.chez-julia.com.
This place offers a very different experience to all the kasbah-style hotels. Small and personal, it's run by the eponymous Austrian owner. The 5 rooms (180-250dh), decorated in soft pastel tones, have good big beds; the room at the top has good views over Merzouga to the dunes. Facilities are shared, but everything is spotlessly clean. Breakfast (40dh) is taken on the roof terrace, and there are lots of Moroccan choices for dinner – especially good for vegetarians – and Austrian desserts too.

Restaurants

Most people eat where they're staying, so there are not many standalone eateries.

€ Café Nora
T0667-612191, in Khamlia, 7 km south of Merzouga on the Taouz road.
Well worth a visit for a tasty organic lunch or mint tea prepared by Hassan and Souad. Combine it with a visit to the Dar Gnawa next door.

What to do

Most people book their dune trips directly through their hotels. Overnight camel treks start from 400dh per person, sunset camel treks are about 200dh. 4WD trips and excursions are 400-500dh.

Dar Gnawa Khamlia, *7 km south of Merzouga on road to Taouz, T0668-247150, www.khamlia.com*. Next to **Café Nora** is this open house of local Gnaoua musicians. Gnaoua music was brought to this region by slaves from sub-Saharan Africa. Hamad Mahjoubi will teach you to play, or organize a ceremony for you. Ideal for sandstorm days.

Transport

A *grand taxi* from Rissani to Merzouga will cost around 50dh. **Supratours** have 1 service daily to **Marrakech** at 0800; and to **Fès** at 1900.

Er Rachidia
to Ouarzazate

The 'Road of the Thousand Kasbahs', as it is marketed, runs between Er Rachidia and Ouarzazate, through arid plains and oases with a backdrop of harsh mountain landscapes, where semi-nomadic Berbers pasture their flocks. Piercing the mountains are dramatic gorges that entice trekkers and birdwatchers. The modern world has arrived here, however: tourist buses and 4WDs bring visitors to the growing villages at the start of the gorges, and new buildings replace crumbling kasbahs with concrete breeze-blocks rather than *pisé*. Nevertheless, there is plenty to see in the steep valleys, as well as myriad walking opportunities. Those with 4WDs can try the bumpy mountain tracks leading into the Massif du Mgoun, or the rugged gorge-to-gorge route from Tineghir to Boumalne.

Goulmima

Goulmima is one of a series of expanding small towns, mainly Amazigh in population, on the eastern side of the High Atlas. Much of the town is located north of the road in the main oasis. The centre is pretty prosaic, with ATMs, and cafés for refuelling after a long drive. For visitors, the main attraction is the *ksar* out in the palm groves. Market day is Monday.

There is a road north from Goulmima leading to the villages of the High Atlas (only suitable for 4WD). It is surfaced for the 55 km to **Amellago**, from where it is possible to circle back to the Todra and/or the Dadès gorges.

Tinejdad

At the junction of the Er Rachidia, Tineghir and Erfoud roads, Tinejdad is an Amazigh and Haratine town in a large oasis, with some significant kasbah and *ksour* architecture, notably the Ksar Asrir. The central square has a post office, the town gardens, town hall, telephones, taxis and a petrol station. Just under 1 km from

> **Tip...**
> There are a lot of bicycles in Tinejdad, so be particularly careful if driving through.

the centre, the **Oasis Museum** ⓘ *inside Auberge Ksar el Khorbat, T0535-880355, www.elkhorbat.com, daily 0900-2100, 20dh, children free*, does a fine job of showcasing the history and culture of southern Morocco with photographs, displays on agriculture, trade, tribal systems and ceremonial use, and plentiful information boards in English and French. It's a very worthwhile stop for anyone interested in furthering their understanding of Amazigh culture.

Tineghir

Once a tiny oasis settlement of the Aït Atta tribe, Tineghir is now a modern administrative centre, its population swelled by technicians and staff working for the local mining company. Because of its position, the town is an ideal stay on the road to or from the Tafilalet, although the central hub, ribboning east and west along the N10, is a bustling and dusty place.

The older kasbah settlement is a few kilometres north of the modern town, overlooking the irrigated plain as you climb out of the town towards the Gorges du Todra. The contrast of magnificent barren mountains and verdant oases is stark. For the rushed, there are views from the gorge road, otherwise you might explore on foot with a guide for 40dh, or rent a bike from **Hotel l'Avenir** (see page 224. You will find olive and fruit trees inter-cropped with cereals and vegetables, herds of sheep and goats out to pasture in the foothills. As elsewhere in the region, there is much new building along the roads, and the old *ksar* is partly abandoned to the side. Try to visit the **Kasbah el Glaoui** on the hill above the town. Although officially closed, it is normally possible to get in.

South from Tineghir

The village of **Aït Mohammed** is southeast of Tineghir and clearly visible from the main road. It stands on the minor road that goes along the *oued* to **El Hart-n'Igouramène**. A track due south leads towards the village of **Iknioun**, which nestles under the central heights of the **Jbel Saghro**; it eventually connects with the desert road from Erfoud to Zagora.

Listings West from Er Rachidia

Where to stay

Goulmima

€€-€ Chez Pauline
Tadighoust, 15 km from Goulmima, T0535-885425, www.gitechezpauline.com.
This French-run guesthouse is a rural hideaway surrounded by peach, fig and olive trees, with the odd chicken scuttling across the farm. 4 rustic whitewashed rooms with a/c and walls hung with African artefacts (440-660dh) in the main house sleep 2-5 people, while 2 garden annexes (for 4-/8-people, 770/1000dh), brimming with old-fashioned charm and with shaded private patios, are a great choice for families or groups of friends. Camping and campervan space is also available. Breakfast is 50dh.

Tinejdad

€ Ksar el Khorbat
T0535-880355, www.elkhorbat.com, just under 1 km from Tinejdad centre.
Built within an 18th-century *ksar*, the 10 huge, characterful rooms (single/double 475/550dh) here are scattered with richly hued Moroccan rugs, local art, colourful textiles and cushion-strewn seating areas to chill out on after a long day's drive. There's a pool, restaurant amid the palm-shaded gardens, library, communal terraces, and even a museum. Staff can help organize excursions and

if you're using public transport, staff will pick you up from the bus station upon arrival if you book in advance. Breakfast and Wi-Fi included. Recommended.

Tineghir

€€ Hotel Tomboctou
126 Av Bir Anzane (take 1st major left coming into Tineghir from west), T0524-835291, www.hoteltomboctou.com.
The airy rooms (single/double €45/53) in this restored mid-20th century kasbah have a nicely modern feel despite the mudbrick walls and traditional textiles. This is a great choice for travellers with kids in tow, with spacious good-value family rooms available (from €63). A wide range of excursions and activities – from pottery workshops to climbing in the Todra Gorge – can be easily arranged, or you could simply pluck a book from the vast library and take the day off poolside. The hotel has serious sustainable travel values, helping to support local heritage conservation efforts. Breakfast and Wi-Fi included. Recommended.

€ Hotel l'Avenir
On the 2nd square, T0524-834599.
On the 1st floor above a pharmacy, this solid budget option has 12 small but clean rooms (160dh) and a roof terrace where you can crash on a mattress (40dh). Note that the square below is

very noisy, so it won't suit light sleepers. Bike hire is available here.

Camping

Camping Ourti
South of the road at western end of town, opposite Hotel Kenzi Bougafer, T0524-833205.
Very secure site with electricity for campervans, a restaurant, bungalows and pool, but quite a walk from town.

Tinejdad
By far the best place to have a meal is the restaurant in **Ksar el Khorbat** (see Where to stay, above). **Café el Fath**, **Café Assagm** and **Café Ferkla** are possibilities for refreshment. **Café Oued Ed-Dahab**, stands north of Tinejdad at the junction with the road to Erfoud.

Tineghir
The main roads of Av Hassan II and Av Mohammed V have plenty of cheap and cheerful options. **Hotel Oasis** (Pl Principale, Av Mohammed V) has a decent restaurant, and **La Kasbah** (Av Mohammed V) is a friendly place with good food.

Tineghir
There is a souk on Tue, behind the **Hotel Todra**, and there are small shops on the main square (Pl Principale). **Chez Michelle Supermarket** (T0524-834668) sells alcohol, snacks and trekking supplies.

Tineghir
All buses leave from Pl Principale. The **CTM** service via **Ouarzazate** (55dh, 3 hrs) to **Marrakech** (130dh, 8 hrs) leaves at 0845; another service terminating in Ouarzazate leaves at 2000. Heading east, **CTM** have 2 buses heading to **Er Rachidia** (40dh, 2¼ hrs) at 1045 and 1540. **Supratours** have 2 daily services to **Ouarzazate** and **Marrakech** at 0530 and 1300. There are also private-line buses running these routes as well as services to **Erfoud** (3 hrs). All services heading to Ouarzazate can drop passengers off at **Boumalne du Dadès**, **El Kalaâ** and **Skoura**. *Grands taxis* at Pl Principale go to **Boumalne du Dadès**, **Ouarzazate**, and **Er Rachidia**, and *grands taxis* and minivans here also run up through the Todra Gorge.

Gorges du Todra

head here for hiking and climbing adventures

The Todra Gorge is narrower and more winding than the Dadès Gorge and is particularly spectacular in the evening, when the rocks are coloured in bands of bright sunlight and dark shadow. There are campsites and places to stay near the narrowest part of the gorge and these are highly recommended for a break from the activity of the major towns.

Tineghir to Tamtatouchte

The 14-km route up the gorge is very narrow: you will have to slow down for kids playing near the road and watch out for the tyre-splitting road edge when you make way for a bus thundering towards you. (Tourist buses and 4WDs head up to the gorge for lunch.)

Just north of Tineghir, as the road climbs up, is the village of **Aït Ouaritane**, which has good views and some stopping places on the road. The safest place to stop is generally picketed with camels; the most spectacular has fossil and scarf sellers. Neat strips of crops in the oasis gardens and crumbling kasbah villages are spread out below.

Some 9 km from Tineghir are campsites in an idyllic location in a palm grove. About 6 km further on is the most visited section of the gorge, where the high cliffs leave just enough space for the road and river. As you might imagine, rocks, palm groves and river make this a good environment for birds. There are some hotels (eg **La Vallée**) before the ford (which should present no problems for ordinary cars), and you can then carry on up to the next two hotels, **Les Roches** and **Yasmina**, which squat in bogus kasbah style under a spectacular overhanging bit of gorge.

Tamtatouchte and beyond
The more adventurous will want to continue beyond the narrow confines of the Gorges du Todra to the village of Tamtatouchte, a steady uphill drive of about four hours. The **Auberge Baddou**, the **Auberge Bougafer** and various other rudimentary establishments provide food and accommodation here. A few trucks use this route and may provide you with a lift, if necessary. With a 4WD, many of the smaller villages to the north can be reached, or, with a good driver, connections can be made west to the Dadès Gorge (see below) or north towards Imilchil (see page 125).

Gorge to gorge
Though rough, the 42-km route west from Tamtatouchte to **Msemrir** and the Dadès Gorge is popular with the 4WD brigade and can be done in five hours. The road rises to 2800 m and is best tackled in a good 4WD vehicle with reliable local driver. Ensure that tyre pressure is higher than normal, as tracks are very stony, and that you have a full petrol tank. This route is best undertaken between May and September, but even then you should find out about the condition of the piste before departure. At other times of year, potential flash floods make it dangerous. At Msemrir, a popular base village for treks, there are a couple of simple places to stay, including the **Auberge el Ouarda** and the **Auberge Agdal**.

> **Tip...**
> It is probably best to start this route from the Todra Gorge so that you do the most difficult pass, just beyond Tamtatouche (2800 m), first.

Where to stay

In winter it gets pretty chilly at night and, in late summer, the river can swell suddenly after thunderstorms in the mountains, so choose your camping place with care.

€€ Dar Ayour
Km 13, just before the narrowest point of the gorge, T0524-895271, www.darayour.com.
This stylish guesthouse, with *tadelakt* walls, Berber rugs and a warm welcome, is built right on the edge of the river, overlooking the gardens. Rooms (single/ double €35/60-80 with half-board) are cosy and colourful; try to bag one of the rooms with a private terrace. A comfortable home-from-home place. Wi-Fi included. Recommended.

€ Hotel Kasbah Amazir
Km 10, just after Camping Les Poissons Sacrés, T0524-895109.
The 15 a/c rooms (6 triple, 9 double from €40) in this stone-clad building are simple and spick-and-span with sturdy pine furniture. The garden terrace is shaded by towering date palms, and there's a pool for cooling off after a day out hiking. Staff are helpful and friendly. Breakfast and Wi-Fi included.

€ Hotel-Camping du Soleil
Aka Chez Bernard, T0524-895111, www.hotelcamping.
A bit lacking in shade, otherwise an excellent site. Has a small pool, washing machines and they can put you in contact with a local for mule rides in the region.

Transport

Grands taxis and minivans from Tineghir run up through the Todra Gorge.

★ Gorges du Dadès
scenic hikes, sleepy villages and striking rock formations

The R704 leaves the N10 at Boumalne and follows the Oued Dadès through limestone cliffs, which form the striking Dadès Gorge. The principal destination is the section of the gorge following Aït Oudinar, but the track continues up into the High Atlas, with public transport as far as Msemrir. Off the main route, there are very basic pistes into the mountains and across to the Todra Gorge (see page 225). The gorges and crags offer a good environment for golden and Bonelli's eagles and lammergeiers, and the scree slopes are inhabited by blue rock thrushes.

Boumalne du Dadès
Boumalne is a small town, with a reasonable selection of hotels, though most people prefer to stay in the Dadès valley to the north. The town grew from a very basic settlement to its current size mainly in the second half of the 20th century. In the Muslim cemetery there is the domed shrine of one Sidi Daoud. He is commemorated in an annual festival, when bread is baked from flour left at the grave and fed to husbands to ensure their fertility. Wednesday is market day.

Approaching from the west, there is usually a Gendarmerie royale checkpoint at the intersection before the bridge, so slow down.

From a high point above the town, a barracks and some hotels look out over the harsh and rocky landscape. If you are a birdwatcher, you may well want to head off south to the **Vallée des Oiseaux** (on the road from Boumalne to Iknioun). The track southeast, which leaves the N10 road just east of Boumalne, gives easy access into the desert. It rises steadily to Tagdilt and provides possibilities for spotting desert birds and, less likely, desert fauna.

Through the gorge

Just beyond Boumalne is **Aït Arbi**, where there are a series of striking red-earth kasbahs above the road. The road snakes past an area of unusual rock formations known locally as the 'monkey fingers', with excellent day-hiking in the vicinity, then continues through Tamnalt and **Aït Oudinar**. At Km 27 a small off-shoot from the main valley has hiking trails that lead up into the hills to visit nomad caves and over the mountain for views of the valley from above. The valley narrows after Aït Oudinar, with the road and oued squeezed between red cliffs. The road continues alongside the *oued* as far as **Msemrir**, after which it branches right onto a difficult track that runs east across the pass (2800 m) to link with the R703 through the Todra Gorge, or up into the High Atlas.

Listings Gorge du Dadès

Where to stay

Boumalne du Dadès

€€ Xaluca Dades
Heading east out of town on the Er Rachidia road, signposted off to the left, T0524-830060, www.xaluca.com.
This former 1970s state-owned hotel as 114 rooms (double 1080dh), with stone walls, satellite TV and a pan-African theme. There's a myriad of facilities here to keep you busy, including pool, spa and hammam, restaurant, bar, gym and tennis courts. Wi-Fi and breakfast included.

€ Auberge de Soleil Bleu
Up a slightly rough track past Hotel Xaluca, T0524-830163.
Popular with hikers and birdwatchers, this place can organize treks into the High Atlas and Jbel Saghro. The 12 good-sized rooms (from €49) have fine views across the countryside, and campers can pitch their tent in the garden.

€ Horwl Al Manader
Av Mohammed V, uphill from Banque Populaire on the Er Rachidia road, T0524-830172.
The rooms (300dh) themselves may be rather bland, but they're big (with generously sized bathrooms), clean and come with a/c and tiny balconies overlooking a swath of orange-hued hills with the snow-capped tips of the High Atlas beyond. Staff are super-friendly and willing to help with any query, and they make a mean café nuss-nuss for breakfast in the morning. It's within easy walking distance of the bus and *grands taxis* stands. Wi-Fi (on ground-floor common areas only) and breakfast included.

Gorge du Dadès

All accommodation in the gorge can provide lunch and dinner and many have half-board options. They can all also organize hiking guides for excursions.

€ Auberge des Gorges Dadès
Km 23, Aït Oudinar, T0524-831719, www.aubergeaitoudinar.com.
Good camping (20dh per person) shaded by trees alongside the river and 32 decent-sized rooms (250dh) with Berber motifs decorating the walls, a/c and slightly sagging beds. Go for one of the rooms with a balcony if you can. A solid budget choice in a great location at the start of Aït Oudinar village. Breakfast and Wi-Fi included.

€ Auberge Tissadrine
Km 27, Aït Oudinar, T0524-831745, www.auberge-tissadrine.com.
This charming guesthouse has 10 generously sized rooms (300dh) with wood-fire heaters for colder months and rustic charm provided by dinky seating areas and colourful old rugs. The best have little balconies where you can contemplate gorge life, while staring up at the towering red cliffs. It faces a side canyon with good walking opportunities out to nomadic encampments and caves. Set menus for dinner are 100dh. Multilingual staff go out of their way to make you feel comfortable. Wi-Fi (in communal areas) and breakfast included.

€ Jardin de la Source
Km 11, Aït Ibirne, T0600-685129 (mob).
A relaxing place to stay with an exceptionally warm welcome and helpful management, near to the Dadès Gorge's famous 'monkey fingers' rock formation. Simple, spacious rooms (from €27) with traditional *tataoui* ceilings look out onto a garden where shady seating areas are scattered amid the flowers and trees (heaters are provided in winter). A fabulous choice for a few days' hiking and chilling out. Plus the meals here are delicious. Recommended. Wi-Fi and breakfast included.

€ Kasbah de Victor
KM 31, T0622-290268.
An intimate and friendly choice with 4 bright rooms (with heating in winter) in a French-run guesthouse perched out on the rocks. There's a pool with a Berber tent alongside for slothing in, and a restaurant serving up exceptional Moroccan food, including interesting variations on Berber standards, such as lamb tagine with apple, or camel tagine with harissa. Wi-Fi and breakfast included.

Restaurants

Boumalne du Dadès

There are decent, basic cafe options in the central square.

Café Atlas
In the centre.
Good for food or just a tea or coffee.

Restaurant Chems
Just outside Boumalne, on the Er Rachidia road.
Perhaps the best option with its pleasant terrace.

Snak Adrar
In the centre.
Rustles up good juice, sandwiches and coffee, and has a shaded terrace and friendly service.

What to do

Trekking

Most travellers to the Dadès Gorge book day hikes through their accommodation once they've arrived. Nearly all the guesthouses and auberges in both Boumalne du Dadès and in the gorge itself can hook you up with a guide to explore on foot. You can also try the **Bureau des Guides** (bottom of Av Mohammed V, main street, Boumalne, T0667-593292).

Transport

All bus services between **Tineghir** and **Ouarzazate** can drop passengers off at **Boumalne du Dadès** (see Tineghir transport, above). *Grands taxis* and minivans run the length of the gorge all the way from the central square in Boumalne to **Msemrir** (10dh). There's usually only a short wait before leaving, as the minivans and *grands taxis* pick-up and drop-off passengers along the way. Coming back to Boumalne, you simply hail a *grand taxi* or minivan on the road.

El Kalaâ des Mgouna and the Vallée des Roses

Morocco's rose capital

El Kalaâ des Mgouna, 1¼ hours' drive from Ouarzazate, is the capital of the Moroccan rose-essence industry and centre of the Mgouna tribe. (The name means 'Citadel of the Mgouna' and is also spelt Qalat Mgouna.) The former French administrative centre has become a sprawling town, with two banks right on the main intersection, a pharmacy on Boulevard Mohammed V, police, small shops for provisions, petrol and a Wednesday market. The blooms in the Vallée des Roses flower in late spring. The rose festival is held in early May, with dances and processions under a shower of rose petals to celebrate the harvest.

One of the rose essence factories (in a kasbah-like building) can be visited. Children at the roadside will try to sell bunches of roses and garlands of rose petals, and there are plenty of shops selling rose water, *crème à la rose*, rose-scented soap and dried roses. There is also a dagger-making workshop and showroom, **Co-operative Artisan du Poignards Azlag**, on the eastern outskirts of the town. This craft tradition was developed by the now-departed Jewish communities in the region; most of the present-day artisans are concentrated in Azlague, south of the Coopérative.

Massif Mgoun
While based in El Kalaâ, energetic visitors could head northwards for 15 km up the Mgoun Valley to the **Ksar de Bou Thrarar** at the entrance to the **Mgoun Gorge**. In late spring and summer more ambitious walkers may want to try to climb **Irhil Mgoun** itself, which at 4068 m is one of the highest peaks in the central High Atlas. A good seven-day circuit would take you up to Amesker and back via Aït Youl. For other trekking options in the Massif Mgoun, see page 230.

BACKGROUND
El Kalaâ des Mgouna and the Vallée des Roses

A picturesque local legend tells that pilgrims travelling back from Mecca brought with them 'the Mother of All Flowers', the Damascus rose, thus initiating the Moroccon rose industry. It may be more likely, however, that sometime in the 20th century, French perfumers realized that conditions in this out-of-the-way part of southern Morocco would be ideal for the large-scale cultivation of the bushy *Rosa centifolia*. Today, there are hundreds of kilometres of rosebush hedges, co-existing with other crops, and two factories distilling rose essence. To produce a litre of good quality rose oil requires around five tonnes of petals. The locals feel, however, that the price paid by the factories is too low, and so they prefer to sell dried rose petals at the local markets. Pounded up, the petals can be mixed with henna or other preparations.

Listings El Kelaâ des Mgouna and the Vallée des Roses

Where to stay

El Kalaâ

€€ **Kasbah Itran**
3 km from El Kelaâ des Mgouna heading to Bou Tharar, T0524-837103, www.kasbahitran.com.
This welcoming auberge, run by a Spanish-Moroccan partnership, is perched up on a cliff on the road up to Bou Tharar and the Massif du Mgoun. Rooms with balcony (single/double from €34/41) and simpler rooms with shared bathroom (single/double €20/26) have a rustic, traditional ambience, with bright layered carpets on the floor and *tataoui* ceilings, while the views down onto the valley are spectacular. A wide range of activities and excursions, as well as local trekking, can be organized easily here. Wi-Fi and breakfast included.

€ **Kasbah Assafar**
5 km from El Kelaâ des Mgouna on the road to Bou Tharar, T0524-836577, www.kasbahassafar.com.
Fantastic views of the Rose Valley from this authentic converted kasbah that brims with local character. The small rooms (single/double 250/400dh) are basic but colourful and share clean bathrooms. Staff here can dish out oodles of local knowledge, and official mountain guides are on hand for trekkers. Breakfast included.

Restaurants

El Kalaâ

Café-Restaurant Rendez-Vous des Amis
Av Mohammed V, T0661-871443.
Popular and reliable for tasty tagines and snacks.

What to do

El Kalaâ
Trekking
El Kelaâ is a good base for trekking. Kasbah Assafar (see page 230) has plenty of contacts with guides and organizes trekking trips. The **Bureau des Guides de Montagne** is 1 km before the town centre, on south side of road, T0524-836577, T0661-796101 (mob).

Ouarzazate
& around

The name 'Ouarzazate' (pronounced *wah-za-zatt*) may be highly evocative of a dusty desert fort but the reality is, unfortunately, a little more prosaic. As a result of the lucrative film industry, this once-isolated French military outpost, sitting amid the rolling landscape of the rock-pitted *hammada*, now has an international airport, a core of luxury hotels alongside its kasbah and a Cinematography School. Though the garrison remains, the needs of the regional administration and migrant worker remittances have resulted in the creation of a large, low-rise concrete town.

Nevertheless, although it may not be a picture-perfect lonely outpost, Ouarzazate is a major transit point for journeys into the mountains and the desert and is a useful base for exploring valleys and oases south of the High Atlas. The region is at its best in early spring, when blossom is on the almond trees and snow still covers the summits of the Atlas.

Finding your feet

Taourirt airport is 2 km northeast of Ouarzazate but although there are regular **RAM** services from Casablanca and charter flights from France, most visitors come in by road. Tour companies often sell Ouarzazate as a long day trip from Marrakech but this is only really worthwhile if the journey includes Telouet (see page 117). A much better idea is to hire a car and make an overnight stop in Ouarzazate after a leisurely drive over the Tizi-n-Tichka pass, taking in the kasbahs at Telouet and Aït Ben Haddou. The following day, you could explore sights east from Ouarzazate (Skoura, El Kelaâ des Mgouna and the Rose Valley), making a loop via Bou Thrarar and the Dadès Gorge if you have a 4WD vehicle, before the long drive back.

If you're using public transport, **Supratours** buses drop passengers off outside their office on Avenue Moulay Abdallah, at the western end of town. The *gare routière*, for private-line buses, and the main *grands taxis* stand are both nearby. It's a hefty walk from either to the centre of town, so it's best to take a *petit taxi*. **CTM** have their bus terminal slap in the centre of town on Avenue Mohammed V, next to the post office. See Transport, page 239, for further details.

Getting around

Petits taxis whizz down Avenue Mohammed V and can be flagged down anywhere along the road. Short taxi rides within town cost around 7dh. Getting to the spectacular kasbah at Aït Ben Haddou is awkward without your own car. The easiest way to do the trip is to hire a *grand taxi* privately (the going rate for a return trip with one hour waiting time is 200dh). A few kilometres out of Ouarzazate, just off the Marrakech road, Tifoultoute Kasbah and the Atlas Film Studios are easily reached by *grand taxi*. Skoura, east along the Boumalne du Dadès N10 road, is easily accessible by local bus or *grand taxi*. Both Aït Ben Haddou and Skoura have good accommodation options.

Orientation

A lot of streets in Ouarzazate have yet to get name plaques, which can make navigation tricky. Heading east from the bus station on Avenue Mohammed V, the large Place du 3 Mars is on your left. Here there are a few tour agencies, cafés and the Palais des Congrès. Further along the main street are banks with ATMs, hotels, restaurants, cafés, shops, car rental agencies, tour companies and petrol stations. The old market area is closed to traffic and offers some interesting clothing, jewellery, spice and ceramics stalls before opening out onto to the Place Al Mouahidine, which in turn offers pavement snack-restaurants, an excellent patisserie and several desert tour agencies. The famous Kasbah Taourirt is located at the eastern edge of town and is an easy walk from the town centre.

Ouarzazate

Strategically placed at the confluence of three rivers, Ouarzazate has had a military presence since the Almohad period. In the late 19th century, it came under control of the Glaoui family, who used it as a power base to develop their control of the south. In 1926, the first airfield was built and, in 1928, a regular French military garrison was installed. Ouarzazate was henceforth the main administrative town for the region and the nerve centre for the Lyautey method of expanding French influence into tribal areas. A few buildings from this period straggle along the main street, but most of the town's blocky architecture was built in the 1980s. Since the filming of *Lawrence of Arabia* at Aït Ben Haddou in 1961-1962, the Ouarzazate region has become increasingly popular as a film location, favoured by directors for its access to mountains and desert. In the 1990s and 2000s, as the film industry blossomed, infrastructure in the town was radically improved to cater for visiting stars, crews and local workers.

Sights

The historic highlight of Ouarzazate is **Kasbah Taourirt** ① *east of the town centre along Av Mohammed V, daily 0800-1830, 20dh.* Constructed largely in the 19th century by the Glaoui family, the building had its heyday in the 1930s and

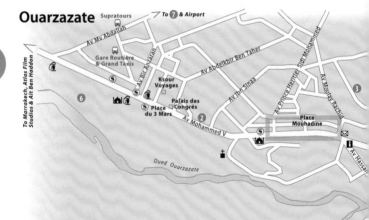

Ouarzazate

N

Not to scale

Where to stay ⊜		Restaurants ⑦
Amlal **1**	Camping Municipal **4**	Chez Dmitri **1**
Azoul **2**	Dar Daif **5**	Douyria **2**
Berbere Palace **3**	Dar Rita **6**	Habouss **3**
	Le Petit Riad **7**	

would have housed the Glaoui chief's extended family, servants and followers, as well as a community of tradesmen, artisans and cultivators. Today it's one of Ouarzazate's poorest areas, although the part adjacent to the road, which probably served as quarters for the Glaoui family, has been maintained and can be visited.

West of town, 5 km along the road to Marrakech, mock Egyptian statues signal the entrance to **Atlas Studios** ① *T0524-882212, www.studiosatlas.com, Mar-Oct daily 0815-1815, Oct-Feb daily 0815-1715, 50dh, children 35dh.* These are the major studios where numerous famous movies were made, including *Lawrence of Arabia*, *Kingdom of Heaven*, *Kundun* and *Gladiator*. You can see various bits of set and props on a 30-minute guided tour.

Listings Ouarzazate *map below*

Tourist information

Délégation du Tourisme
Corner Av Mohammed V and Av Hassan II, T0524-882485.
Mon-Fri 0900-1200, 1430-1600.

Has a few brochures and friendly enough staff but is not particularly useful for advice or information.

Where to stay

Hotels are scattered throughout town with most of the budget options in the

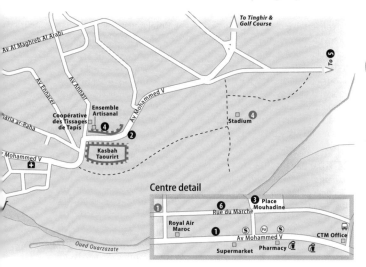

Le Kasbah Café **4**
Le Kasbah de Sables **5**
Massanisa **6**

centre around Av Mohammed V and more luxurious options further east in the Av Moulay Rachid area.

€€€€ Hotel Berbère Palace
T0524-883105, www.hotel-berberepalace.com.

The hotel has 249 contemporary rooms decked out in soft neutrals and large suites that feature garden patios. There's pretty much every facility at your fingertips here, with a pool, piano bar, tennis courts, a plethora of restaurants dishing up Moroccan, Italian and pan-European cuisine and a hammam. Past guests include film producers and even the odd star. Ouarzazate's snazziest place to sleep by far. Wi-Fi included.

€€ Le Petit Riad
Av Moulay Abdallah 1581, T0524-885950, www.lepetitriad.com.

Northeast of the centre, in the Hay Al Wahda neighbourhood, Le Petit Riad is a comfortable, colourful choice, with rooms (from €69 in high season) decked out in blues, soft greens and lemons and decorated with local art. The big plus-point here, though, is the courtyard pool with sunbeds and shaded tables set temptingly around it – just the place to sit back and relax with a book after a few days of dusty desert exploits. Breakfast and Wi-Fi included.

€€-€ Dar Daïf
Talmasla, next to the Kasbah des Cigognes on the Tabount side of town, T0524-854232, www.dardaif.ma.

About 5 km out of town, this traditional restored kasbah has good-sized rooms (single/double €38-60 €45-80 in high season, good discounts in low season) and roomy suites (from €140 for 4 people), some with private terraces, all decorated with lovely glazed tile details

and vibrant carpets. It's well looked after by its French-Moroccan owners who can also organize a wide range of activities. The restaurant here provides hearty meals. Breakfast and Wi-Fi included.

€ Dar Rita
39 Rue de la Mosque, T0613-797347, www.darrita.com.

If you don't mind being out of the centre, Dar Rita is a charming place to stay. This homely and intimate 7-room guesthouse is hidden in the mostly residential Tassoumant neighbourhood, west of the centre, where Ouarzazate's traditional mudbrick architecture still survives. Rooms (single/double €35-45/40-50) are large, cheerful and bright, with tiling, stained-glass, metal lamps, wrought-iron window decor and textiles adding lots of traditional touches. Showers are solar-powered, and the hotel is making worthy efforts to limit its waste.

€ Hotel Amlal
24-25 Rue du Marché, T0524-884030, www.hotelamlal.com.

As long as you're not expecting any frills, the Amlal is a solid budget find in a central location, near Ouarzazate's main mosque – the call-to-prayer guarantees you won't need an alarm clock here. The 28 rooms (single/double 200/250dh), some with slim balconies are clean and decently sized, with a/c and bathrooms that pump out hot water. The family who run this place are extremely sweet and helpful. Wi-Fi available. Breakfast is an extra 50dh.

€ Hotel Azoul
Av Mohammed V (near Place 3 Mars), T0524-883015, www.hotelazoul.com.

Location, location, location. The Azoul is a solid choice slap in the centre of town. Sure, their contemporary take on kasbah architecture is a bit questionable, but all the rooms (single/double 330/440dh) are pleasant, clean and come with a/c and satellite TV. Staff are keen to help. Grab a room with a titchy balcony if you can. There's also a mini-cinema where you can chill out and watch a movie that was shot in town. Wi-Fi and breakfast included.

Camping

Camping Ouarzazate
Next to the Stade Municipale, off the N10 heading out of town on the Skoura road, T0524-888322, www.camping-ouarzazate.jimdo.com/.
Running water, café, restaurant, pool at complex next door, hot showers, electricity for caravans, grocery shop and petrol 800 m away. Caravan parking 50dh per night with electricity, camping 15dh per person plus 15dh for the tent.

Restaurants

There are a growing number of eateries doing more than just multiple tagines and couscous. The cheapest places are around the Rue du Marché and on the Pl al Mouahidine. Near the kasbah there are a few newer restaurants worth checking out.

€€ Chez Dmitri
22 Av Mohammed V, T0524-887346. Daily for lunch and dinner.
Once the focus of Ouarzazate, as the bar of the Foreign Legion, this restaurant serves decent pasta and even a Greek moussaka, along with brochette dishes. The interior, with old photos displayed on the walls, gives the place a rather lovely historic ambience, and the service is smooth and rather refined. A great choice if you're looking for something

other than tagines and if you'd like a wine or beer with your meal.

€€ Le Kasbah des Sables
195 Ait Kdif, 4 km east of the centre, T0524-885428, www.lakasbahdessables.com.
Definitely worth the taxi ride out here, Le Kasbah des Sables is an oriental fantasy of a place which radiates a subtly sumptuous ambience. Dining is in 6 arched and pillared salons, all decorated with hanging lamps, antiques and gorgeous objets d'art. The menu merges Moroccan and European cooking styles with rarely seen flair, offering dishes such as gently spiced rabbit confit glazed with honey and peach nectar reduction, and chicken tagliatelle with Atlas mushrooms. Alcohol served. Recommended.

€ Douyria
Av Mohammed V, next to Kasbah Taourirt, T0524-885288, www.restaurant-ouarzazate.net. Daily 1000-2300.
Contemporary Moroccan cuisine in a converted old house, with a roof terrace and stylishly simple salons. All the usual Moroccan pastilla, tagine, couscous and brochette options are served (mains 60-130dh) with some imaginative flavour flourishes, and there are goat and camel dishes for more adventurous diners. Good, solid cooking topped off by great presentation. Alcohol served. Recommended.

€ Habouss
Pl Al Mouahidine, T0524-882699. Daily 0700-2200.
It is no surprise that this large place, right on the main square, is always bustling with locals. Not only is it famed for its scrumptious cakes, ice cream and Moroccan pastries, but it also churns out cheap and cheerful dishes for lunch

and dinner. Sandwiches, pizzas, tagines and brochettes feature heavily on the menu and are served in good-value portions. The brochettes, in particular, are excellent, coming with vegetables, chips and mashed potato (just in case you need more carbohydrates in your life). Habouss is also the No 1 spot in town to pull up a pew and sip mint tea or freshly squeezed fruit juice while people-watching. Recommended.

€ Massanisa Restaurant
Rue du Marché. Daily 1000-2300.
On a cold night, eat in the cosy dining room with candles flickering on the tables, or on a balmy summer evening head upstairs to the terrace. Massanisa is a fine choice in town for both Moroccan tagines and Italian pasta staples, such as lasagne (mains 60-90dh). Friendly service makes it a great choice for solo female travellers.

Cafés

Le Kasbah Café
Opposite Kasbah Taourirt.
Climb the steps leading up from the **Ensemble Artisanal** to reach this rather tranquil café with multiple terraces overlooking the Kasbah Taourirt opposite. With plenty of shady seating, it's a good place to sit back with a coffee or mint tea in the late afternoon.

Bars

Hotel La Perle du Sud
40 Av Mohammed V (near Pl 3 Mars).
The only hotel in town that has a bar open to locals and tourists alike. It can get a bit smoky and rather lively later in the evening.

Ibis Ouarzazate
Av Moulay Rachid.
The rather bland, contemporary lounge bar is open to non-guests and has an open fireplace and a good range of wine, beer and cocktails.

Festivals

Events tend to be a bit ad hoc, so always try to check in advance to confirm dates. **Mar-Apr Marathon des Sables**, www. marathondessables.co.uk. Billed as the toughest footrace on earth, this 6-day ultra-marathon has its start in Ouarzazate though the actual course of the 250-km race changes annually.
Aug-Sep Moussem of Sidi Daoud. Held in town annually.

Shopping

Sun cream, batteries, a good selection of snack food and pretty much all your other essentials can all be obtained on Av Mohammed V at the supermarket opposite **Chez Dimitri**. It even sells alcohol – the last place to do so before the deserts south beyond M'Hamid, or Tineghrir to the east. Along this strip there are also a number of shops selling the ubiquitous *cadeaux berbères*: carpets, *babouches*, knick-knacks, jewellery and traditional desert robes or *gandoura*. The covered market and the shops around the edge of Pl al Mouahidine have some cheap Western clothing and household goods as well as a few spice sellers. There is a reliable pharmacy next to the Shell petrol station, opposite Pl al Mouahidine. The Sun evening market on the block of Rue du Marché that leads on to Pl al Mouahidine is full of popcorn vendors, plastic-fantastic household goods and cheap clothing. It's good for a stroll.

Ensemble Artisanal, *Av Mohammed V, opposite Kasbah Taourirt*. Multiple traders sell a good range of local handicrafts. **Shop No 4** stocks a fine range of well-priced Tuareg and Berber artefacts, while **Coopérative des Tissages de Tapis**, at the rear, is a fixed-price shop selling carpets handmade by local women of the Ouzgita tribe (closed Sat and Sun).

What to do

Cycling and motorbiking
Bikers Home, *www.bikershome.net*. Dutch-based operator offering motorbiking tours of the Atlas Mountains and off-road tours into the desert starting from Ouarzazate. **Said Mountain Bike**, *T0524-422111, www. saidmountainbike.com*. Mountain biking expeditions are the speciality and good-quality mountain bikes can be rented.

Trekking and tour operators
Amzrou Transport Touristique, *41 Av Mohammed V, T0524-882323*. Rental of 4WD vehicles with driver, plus treks and circuits for small groups. **Désert et Montagne Maroc**, *contact via Dar Daïf guesthouse, see Where to stay, above, or on T0524-854947*. Sets up mule and camel treks in the surrounding countryside visiting Berber villages as well as longer 4WD and trekking trips into the desert and gorges. **Desert Majesty**, *T0524-890765, www. desertmajesty.com*. Ouarzazate-based tour agency which can set up private 4WD tours into the desert with multi-lingual guides. Also operates day trips to outlying attractions, including Aït Ben Haddou, the Drâa Valley and the Dadès Gorge. **Ksour Voyages**, *11 Pl du 3 Mars, T0524-882840, www.ksour-voyages.com*.

Arranges fully customized tours, 4WD excursions and desert trips with multi-lingual guides as well as running a wide range of day trips. To get to the office turn left before the Palais des Congrès as you come from Marrakech.

Transport

Air Taourirt airport, T0524-882348, just to the northeast of the centre, has regular services to **Casablanca**. From the airport, get a *petit taxi* to your hotel for around 30dh. The **RAM** office is on Av Mohammed V (T0890-000800).

Bus CTM buses (T0524-882427, www. ctm.ma) leave from their terminal on Av Mohammed V next to the post office. There are 6 services daily to **Marrakech** (85dh, 5 hrs); 4 departures to **Casablanca** (150dh, 9 hrs) at 0830, 1100, 2215 and 2330; 3 buses at 0530, 1615 and 1630 to **Zagora** (55dh, 2¾ hrs), with the 1615 service continuing on to **M'Hamid** (80dh); and 1 departure at 1200 to **Er Rachidia** (95dh, 5½ hrs) via **Boumalne du Dadès** (40dh, 2½ hrs).
    Supratours (www.oncf.ma) have their office west of the centre on Av Moulay Abdallah. They have buses to **Marrakech** at 0830, 0845 and 1600 (80dh); 1 daily service down the Drâa Valley to **Zagora** (50dh, 2½ hrs) at 2030; and buses to **Tineghir** (55dh, 3 hrs) via **Boumalne du Dadès** (40dh, 2 hrs) at 1300 and 2000.
    All other private-line buses leave from the from the *gare routière*, just off Av Moulay Abdallah (near to the Supratours office). There are several services a day to **Zagora**, east to **Boumalne**, **Tineghir**, **Er Rachidia**, and west to **Taroudant** (5 hrs) and **Agadir** (7½ hrs). For long-distance destinations, get your ticket the day before.

Car hire Vehicles are available from **Budget** (4 Av Mohammed V, near **RAM** office, T0524-884202); **Hertz** (33 Av Mohammed V, T0524-882084); **Europcar** (Pl du 3 Mars, T0524 882035). Other local agencies have offices around Pl du 3 Mars. For petrol, there is a **Shell** station in the centre and service stations at the main exits from town.

Taxi *Grands taxis* have their stand next door to the *gare routière*. Destinations include **Agdz** (35dh), **Boumalne** (35dh), **Marrakech** (100dh), **Skoura** (20dh) and **Zagora** (70dh). For **M'Hamid**, get a *grand taxi* to Zagora and change there. Prepare to wait around for a while as cars can take a long time to fill up. If you're heading to Aït Benhaddou, you'll have to hire the entire taxi; drivers at the *grands taxis* stand charge 200dh for the return trip, including 1-hr waiting time.

Around Ouarzazate

dramatic kasbahs amid the big-sky scenery of the *hammada*

Mansour Eddahbi Dam

To the east of Ouarzazate, the Mansour Eddhabi Dam on the Oued Drâa has created a lake over 20 km long. Birdwatchers come here to see the wintering and migrating wildfowl, including spoonbills and flamingos, when there is sufficient water in the dam. In recent years, water levels have fallen spectacularly (the lakeside golf course is a ghost of its former self) and the villas built as pricey lakeside retreats are now a good distance from the water. About 13 km from Ouarzazate, tracks from the N10 lead down towards the northern shore; one is signed into a gated reserve. (You should be able to enter if you show your binoculars and say you are a birder.) Another access point is via the Royal Golf club. The southern shore is more difficult to reach and access to the dam itself is prohibited. The best time to visit the lake is in spring or autumn.

Skoura oasis

The large oasis fed by the Oued Dadès has irrigated land growing palms, olives and cereals. The river crosses the road on the western side of Skoura. To the left of the road (if coming from Ouarzazate), and before the actual village, is **Kasbah Amerhidl**, the largest of Skoura's kasbahs. The main road now bypasses the town itself, but it's worth stopping to see the white square mosque with cupola and two further kasbahs formerly occupied by the El Glaoui family, **Dar Toundout** and **Dar Lahsoune**. The palm groves can also be explored on foot, bicycle or even on horseback.

Tip...

For those with 4WDs or hardy cars, the oasis of Fint is a possible destination, out in the desert west of Ouarzazate, across the Tabount causeway. This is a good place to sample a slice of rural Moroccan life amid the oasis's tiny agricultural villages, although there's not much to actually do here.

Kasbah of Tifoultoute
T0524-882813, 10dh.

Take the N9 from Ouarzazate north towards Marrakech. After 6 km, turn left on the road marked for Zagora and Agdz. After 1 km turn left again and after about 7 km you will come to the village of Tifoultoute with its splendid kasbah built for the Glaoui family in the early 20th century. It stands alongside the Oued Igissi. Still owned by the family, it has adequate food, guesthouse accommodation and magnificent views. You can climb up to the roof terrace for views over the countryside and a close-up look at the stork's nest on one of the turrets. A visit to the kasbah of Aït Ben Haddou (see below) can easily be combined with a visit here.

★ Aït Ben Haddou

Up on a dramatic hillside, the Kasbah of Aït Ben Haddou, 30 km from Ouarzazate, is one of the largest complexes of traditional packed-earth buildings in Morocco, hence its place on the UNESCO-sponsored World Heritage List. The place's fame has spread far and wide, helped in part by being used as a film and TV location for (among others) *Lawrence of Arabia*, *Jewel of the Nile*, *Gladiator*, *Jesus of Nazareth*, for which part of the settlement was actually rebuilt, and *Game of Thrones*. In high season, coachload after coachload of visitors drives up, pauses for a few photographs to be taken and then leaves.

The turn-off for Aït Ben Haddou is clearly signed from the N9, 22 km from Ouarzazate. A large *marabout* with ridged cupola and crenellated edges on the tower is a prominent landmark to make sure you don't miss your way. The route follows the valley, with the *oued* on the right. The first village is **Tissergate**. After a further 10 km the much-filmed kasbah comes into view on the right, set up above the bright green of the irrigated fields. The kasbah towers offer views across the area, and the old village also includes a large *agadir*, or store house. The **Kasbah Tebi** hotel (see Where stay, below) at the bottom of the kasbah allows visitors to explore some of its interior rooms and climb up the stairs to its towers for good views for 10dh.

Aït Ben Haddou grew because of its strategic location on the south side of the Atlas, near the convergence of the Drâa and Dadès Valley routes. Today despite its popularity with the tour bus crowds, the place is an awesome sight and largely unspoilt.

Tamdaght

The road continues north from Aït Ben Haddou into the mountains and to the ford at Tamdaght. A bridge has been constructed and the road has been resurfaced recently, allowing most vehicles to carry on for the remaining 40 km or so up to Tourhat, along the Asif Ounila and then west to Telouet (see page 117).

Where to stay

Skoura oasis

€€€-€€ Jardins de Skoura
www.lesjardinsdeskoura.com.
Hammocks by the pool, breakfast in the gardens and open fires for cold winter evenings. Surrounded by the date palms of the palmeraie, Jardins de Skoura is the chicest place in Skoura. Beautiful *pisé* rooms (€75-125 in high season) and family suites (€155-170) merge modern comfort and Moroccan artistry with ease and come with big *tadelakt* bathrooms. It's all so comfortable and well-run that you may find it difficult to move on.

€€ Kasbah Aït Ben Moro
3 km west of Skoura, T0524-852116,
www.kasbahaitbenmoro.com.
A beautifully refurbished building a few metres off the main bypass. Rooms (from €65) are dark and cool and have held onto plenty of original features, and from the roof terrace and garden there are views over the palm groves to the Kasbah d'Amerdihil. 3 tower rooms have shared bathrooms.

€ Dar Lorkam
T0524-85 2240, www.dar-lorkam.com.
Over the river, snuggled amid Skoura's *palmeraie*, you'll find this attractive and peaceful adobe guesthouse with just 6 rooms (from 400dh with half-board) and 1 spacious family suite, decorated with plenty of colourful textiles and an eye for rustic minimalism. It's very relaxing and tranquil, surrounded by date palms and lush green shrubs, and there's a very attractive pool to splash about in.

Aït Ben Haddou

Staying in Aït Ben Haddou is a quieter alternative to Ouarzazate and gives visitors the opportunity to experience the village in the evening and early morning when it is free of tour buses. Most of the accommodation is in the modern village, offering good views of the kasbah across the river, and there are some interesting choices in the outlying countryside as well. For those who want to sample a taste of life within the ancient kasbah walls, there are a couple of special options, but note that Aït Ben Haddou kasbah doesn't have electricity, so if Wi-Fi and other mod cons are important to you, it's best to stay on the other side of the river. At peak times of year, try to reserve accommodation in advance.

€€€-€€ Kasbah Ellouze
Tamdaght, T0524-890459,
www.kasbahellouze.com.
4 km north of Aït Ben Haddou, next to Tamdaght Kasbah, Ellouze is a new building constructed in traditional fashion and overlooking almond orchards. Cosy and warmly lit a/c rooms (single/double/suite €68/86/124 with half-board) come with plentiful arches and tiles. It is a quiet place to relax and soak up the scenery or to base yourself for day excursions. There's a pool with shaded terrace, and staff can organize kasbah tours and camel rides well away from the tourist buses.

€ Auberge Etoile Filante d'Or
T0524-890322, www.etoilefilantedor.com.
Along the main road into town, this is a great base for a few days if you're exploring the region on foot or by

bike (which can be rented here). The 19 spacious rooms (single/double €25/35) come with a/c, solid pine furniture and traditional bamboo ceilings. There's a remarkably elegant TV lounge and restaurant, and a roof terrace for star-gazing. Half-board and full-board options are available too. Wi-Fi and breakfast included.

€ Auberge Kasbah du Jardin
T0524-888019,
www.kasbahdujardin.com.
Well located at the far end of town and near the footbridge across to the kasbah, this friendly auberge has 15 simple, spick-and-span rooms (single/double 380/500dh) and a dormitory in a traditional Berber-style tent (150dh per person). Although the rooms are nothing fancy, the auberge has a pool, a well-priced restaurant and a terrace with fantastic panoramic views. Rooms by the pool are the best. Breakfast included.

€ Kasbah Tebi
Inside Kasbah Aït Ben Haddou, 0661-941153, www.kasbahtebi.com.
Sleep in one of the kasbah's restored towers. One of the Kasbah Aït Ben Haddou's original families has created a guesthouse within the walls that brims with local charm and character. Cosy, curvy mudbrick rooms (from 400dh

per person), reached by wonky narrow stairs, are rustically stylish and full of colourful kilims and fabrics. Climb to the top of the tower to take breakfast on the rooftop, from where there are great views down to the river and palmeraie below. There's no electricity (but there is heating and hot water), so expect romantic candlelight after the sun sets. Breakfast included.

€ Said Aitmalak's Homestay
Inside Kasbah Aït Ben Haddou, T0671-734799, saidcouscous@hotmail.com.
Multi-lingual Said and his mother provide a taste of local life inside their family home within the kasbah. Basic rooms with homespun appeal (half board 180-200dh) open out onto a terrace with a sweeping view over the river. Said can provide plenty of advice on walks and activities in the area and can also act as a guide. No electricity.

What to do

Skoura oasis
Horse riding
Skoura Equestrian Centre, *2 km from Skoura on Toundout road, T0661-432163 (mob).* Lessons and treks through the Skoura oasis. For beginners and experienced riders.

Drâa
Valley

★ The Drâa River was once one of the longest rivers in northwest Africa, and the lush green valley fed by its waters made this area a vital section of the caravan routes between sub-Saharan Africa and the north. Today, bountiful reminders of the Drâa's trade-post history remain in the crumbling fortified villages that line the road. Many travellers heading along this route are making a beeline for M'Hamid, where the road runs out and desert begins, in order to take in the dunes of Erg Lehoudi and Chiggaga, but it's well worth spending a day meandering down the road at a relaxed pace. Ksar Tamnougalt is a real highlight, but if you have the time, then Kasbah Ouled Othman, Ksar Tinzouline, and Ksar Tissergate are all good options for exploring.

Essential Drâa Valley

Getting around

The N9 is in excellent condition. Buses and *grands taxis* connect Ouarzazate, Agdz, Zagora and M'Hamid. **CTM** buses run between Ouarzazate and M'Hamid, while the **Supratours** service only runs as far as Zagora. A car allows you to make photo stops at will and to visit the smaller, less spoilt oases and villages. If you're self-driving, the most difficult section of this route is between Ouarzazate and Agdz, with a winding climb up to the Tizi-n-Tinifitt. With a 4WD, there are opportunities for some off-road driving along the *circuit touristique* that runs parallel to the main road from Tamnougalt.

BACKGROUND
Drâa Valley

The Drâa Valley was not always so arid, as is attested by the rock carvings of the wild animals that once thrived here, which have been discovered in the lower Drâa. The river was known to the ancient writers: for Pliny, it was the *flumen Darat*; for Ptolemy, the *Darados*, and Polybius mentions it as a river full of crocodiles. Today, the river only very rarely runs its full course from the sandy Debaïa plain near M'Hamid to the Atlantic coast near Tan Tan, some 750 km away (the last time was in 1989). In years of sufficient rainfall, however, there is good grazing for the nomads in the Debaïa, and even some cultivation.

Southeast of Ouarzazate

enjoy the varied scenery of this stunning oasis valley

Agdz
The road southeast from Ouarzazate to Zagora winds its way in a spectacular switchback over the **Tizi-n-Tinifitt** and across the craggy moonscape of the Jebel Anaouar before threading down to the Drâa. After the Tizi-n-Tinifitt, the modest town of Agdz comes into view, with the sprawling *palmeraie* beyond, backed by the Jebel Kissane. The Glaoui kasbah here will whet your appetite for the Drâa's glut of desert fortification architecture. It's not always open but if you hang around at the entrance for a while, one of the neighbours will probably fetch the key for you. The building has a dark modern history as it was used as a prison for dissidents during King Hassan II's reign.

Tamnougalt
South of Agdz, you are entering one of the most beautiful oasis valleys in Morocco: a slash of vivid green snakes across the land, speckled with plenty of dusky earth-walled kasbahs and ksour and hemmed in by barren hills.

Six kilometres east along the N9 from Agdz, veer off the highway and take the road through the *palmeraie* to reach the photogenic, half-toppled remains of **Ksar Tamnougalt** ⓘ *free, but the guide at the entrance will expect 50dh tip*. One of the oldest *ksour* in the area, Tamnougalt dates from the 16th century and probably began life as a garrison during the Saadian era, later gaining importance as a vital stop along the caravan routes. The external walls of the fortified village are still imposing, though within the labyrinth alleys some of the buildings have crumbled and lie in ruins. Thread your way to the *mellah* (the guide has a key), which still retains much of its original decoration motifs, and then visit **Kasbah Tamnougalt** ⓘ *10dh*, which has been fully restored and contains a small museum.

Where to stay

Agdz

€€€-€€ Kasbah Azul
T0524-843931, www.kasbahazul.com.
This beautiful kasbah-style guesthouse
in the palm groves surrounding Agdz is
run by a French artist and a Moroccan
musician. There is style in abundance
within the 7 rooms (€80-130) and curvy
tadelakt bathrooms. Outside, poolside
lounging is the name of the game, with
the expansive gardens and shady date
palms providing plenty of reasons to
sit back and do nothing. The best place
around by miles. Breakfast and Wi-Fi
included. Dinners cost €20.

€ Casbah Caïd Ali
*2 km from Agdz, T0524-843640,
www.casbah-caidali.net.*
Run by a local family, the simple rooms
(€20) here are in a renovated kasbah
amid extensive palm grove gardens.
There's also excellent camping in the
grounds, with electricity and clean
bathrooms. There's a pool to cool off
in, free Wi-Fi, and the owners can help
organize local excursions and treks.
Breakfast is €2, other meals upon request.

Tamnougalt

€ Chez Yacob
*Tamnougalt, 6 km south of Agdz
on road to Zagora, T0524-843394,
www.lavalleedudraa.com.*
In a restored house right next to the Ksar
Tamnougalte, Chez Yacob is best known
for its restaurant (popular with passing
tour groups) but staying here is a great
get-away-from-it budget choice. Built
in the traditional *pisé* style, the rooms
(from 300dh) are simple but good-sized,
and there are lovely views over the
surrounding Drâa oases from the terrace
and the restaurant. Breakfast included.

What to do

Agdz

Agdez Aventures, *on the main square,
T0671-732622 (mob), www.agdez.com.*
Rents out mountain bikes and
arranges hiking and biking tours
as well as 4WD excursions.

Zagora is the main town at the southern end of the Drâa Valley and the favoured spot to overnight before heading off into the desert. In the 1990s the town woke up to tourism: the arrival of 4WD vehicles and improvements to the N9 road brought an influx of desert-tripping travellers to its door. In the space of a decade, the desert settlement founded by an Arab tribe in the 13th century was transformed out of all recognition. Once famed for its '52 Days to Timbuktu' road sign (which has been sadly taken down by the authorities), today this low-level town of salmon-pink concrete block buildings wouldn't win any beauty awards, but there's still a real desert outpost atmosphere that harks back to Zagora's trading heyday. The town is still a vital trading centre for surrounding communities, and the twice-weekly souk on Wednesdays and Sundays is an important hub for the exchange of livestock and produce for the surrounding region. South of town is an expansive *palmeraie*, a green escape from all that pink concrete.

Essential Zagora

Finding your feet

All public transport stations are along the main road, Av Mohammed V. The *grands taxis* stand is behind the main mosque in the centre of town. **Supratours** and **CTM** buses are both a little further along the road. The *gare routière* (for other private-line buses) is north of the central town.

Getting around

Petits taxis whizz all the way down Av Mohammed V to Amazrou. They cost 5dh per trip. As long as it's not too hot, it's a pleasant 2 km walk between central Zagora and the start of the date palm oasis.

Tip...

Given the poverty levels here, many locals compete fiercely for the tourist trade. To avoid potential hassle, try to make travel arrangements into the desert in advance, either through your hotel or through recommended agencies. If you arrive in town without any prior desert plans, don't pay too much attention to hotels and travel agencies badmouthing each other's businesses while you're scouting for tours; a lot of it is hot air. Pick a company you feel comfortable with and ensure that you thoroughly understand the itinerary they're offering. An alternative to making desert arrangements in Zagora is to continue on to M'Hamid, which is closer to the dunes.

Making tracks

Always check that you have a good spare tyre before setting out into rough country.

From the N12 to the N10

With a solid 4WD, there are a couple of routes from the N12 across wild country to the N10 Er Rachidia–Ouarzazate road. Heading east out of Nekob, you will find a sign showing right for Tazzarine and left for Iknioun, a settlement some 65 km to the north in the Jbel Saghro. It is best to travel this route with a local as the tracks are confusing and some of the better ones lead up to mines. After crossing the Tizi-n-Tazazert-n-Mansour (2200 m), you will have the option of going north on a rather better piste to Boumalne at the head of the Dadès Gorge (about 42 km), or right to Iknioun and Tineghir, via the Tizi-n-Tikkit, a rougher but more beautiful route.

The easiest route up from the N12 to the N10 heads north from Alnif (65 km northeast of Tazzarine). Although it is best tackled in a 4WD, it can just about be done in a hire car with high clearance. After the Tizi-n-Boujou, the track reaches the N10 some 20 km east of Tineghir, or 35 km west of Tinejdad.

West from Zagora to Foum Zguid

This route was off-limits for years due to the risk of Polisario rebel incursions from neighbouring Algeria. It is a difficult journey best attempted in a 4WD with accompanying vehicles. Much of the road (the 6953) is a very poor surface and 124 km in these conditions are not to be undertaken lightly. However, the thrill of the open spaces, the wide horizons and the faint prospect of sandstorms make this a memorable journey. Basically, the road runs east–west, following the line of the Jbel Bani to the south. From Foum Zguid, further rough tracks take you southwest and west towards Tata in the Anti-Atlas.

Around Zagora

Although there are few architectural traces of Zagora's life before tourism, the paths through the date palm groves to the various *ksour* can help you imagine a time when the world was slower. One of the more pleasant walks, despite the potential pestering, is around the date palm oasis of **Ksar Amazrou** across the river. There is also some accommodation here and a kasbah once famed for its silverwork. Another *ksar* that's worth visiting is imposing Ksar Tissergate, 8 km north of Zagora. It's a maze of a place with plenty of dark and narrow, high-walled alleys to lose your bearings in. Also here is the very worthwhile **Musée des Arts et Traditions de la Vallée du Drâa** ① *T0661-348388 (mob), 20dh,* which has plenty of information on the Drâa Valley's history and an interesting, and eclectic collection of local antiquities. Displays have both English and French explanations.

Glowering over the town is the craggy peak of **Jebel Zagora**. There are excellent views over the valley and towards the desert on the two-hour (return) hike towards the summit. You can begin the ascent by taking the narrow track up the hill directly opposite the **Riad Sofian** hotel: cross the river 2 km south of town, then take the left-hand fork at the small roundabout. Alternatively, walk another 3 km along this road until the wide dirt road that threads up the mountain begins. If you choose the latter option, there are sparse ruins of an 11th-century **Almoravid fortress** along the way. Note that the military base on the summit of Jebel Zagora means that you can't walk to the very top.

Routes north and east of Zagora

From Zagora there are two routes north and east to Rissani in the Tafilalet (see page 216). The first is the rough track that runs northeast from Zagora to Tazzarine, a settlement on the main metalled N12; it is for 4WD only and needs careful planning. In a hire car, a better route is to backtrack 60 km up the Ouarzazate road as far as **Tansikht**, then head east on the N12 through some wonderful arid scenery all the way to Rissani. Although this route can easily be driven in half a day, there are a number of auberges and converted kasbahs offering an overnight halt at **Nekob** (42 km from Tansikht). There is also a helpful **Bureau des Guides** in Nekob, T0667-487509 (mobile), that can organize trekking excursions in the Jbel Sarhro area from October to May. For onward 4WD routes from here, see Making tracks, opposite. After Nekob, Mellal is the next settlement before **Tazzarine** (conveniently located 75 km from the junction). Tazzarine is a small settlement, with petrol station and basic shops, where the direct north–south track from Zagora joins the road. It is a good base for searching out the *gravures rupestres* (prehistoric rock carvings) at **Tiouririne** or **Aït Ouazik**.

Listings Zagora and around

Tourist information

Maison du Pays d'Accueil Touristique de Zagora
Southern end of Av Mohammed V, near the provincial administration building.
Relatively new tourist office in central Zagora. Unfortunately though, it never seems to be open.

Where to stay

Zagora

€ Auberge Chez Ali
Av Atlas-Zaouite, Zagora, T0524-846258, www.chez-ali.com.

Simple, colourful, comfortable rooms in Saharoui style are offered here, all surrounding a large garden abloom with pink bougainvillea where a peacock roams freely. Rooms with en suite and a/c come with titchy balconies (250-350dh), and there are also dinky cottages with shared bathrooms. After a dusty overnight desert excursion, the pool beckons for a lazy afternoon. There's decent food on offer too. Wi-Fi and breakfast included. It's popular so book ahead. Note that hot water can be erratic.

€ Hotel La Palmeraie
Av Mohammed V, near the road junction south of town, T0524-847008, www.hotellapalmeraie.com.
It's fallen out of favour lately and certainly needs some updating, but the oldest hotel in town is still a real budget find with exceptionally good-value rooms (single/double from 100/200dh), most with a/c and all painted in zany, hilarious colour combinations. Service is friendly and there's a pool, too.

Camping

Camping Les Jardins de Zagora
Av Hassan II, next to Hotel Ksar Tinzouline, T0524-846971.
This campsite is in town rather than out in the palm groves. Camping in Berber tents is available from 40dh per person, or there's space to pitch your own or park your caravan. Meals on request for 80dh.

Prends Ton Temps
Hay El Mansour Dahbi, just to the north of central Zagora, T0524-846543, www.prendstontemps.com.
Pitch up or park up in this exceedingly well-run site with gardens, Wi-Fi, restaurant, clean bathrooms with hot water, and friendly staff. There's a range of simple guest rooms with en suite in the auberge here, too.

Around Zagora

€€ Kasbah Ziwana
Ksar Tissergate (8 km north of Zagora), T0524-892280, www.kasbah-ziwana-zagora.com.
Snuggled inside Tissergate's large ksar (next door to the Musée des Arts et Traditions de la Vallée du Drâa), this intimate guesthouse is chock-a-block full of rustic, homely charm. Adobe rooms

(€60 including half-board), arranged around a central courtyard, are home to plentiful local textiles, while the rooftop gives good views across the ksar. A great option if you have your own transport and are looking for a tranquil alternative to dusty Zagora.

€€ Riad Dar Sofian
Rte de Nekhla, Amazrou, T0524-847319.
The elaborate façade is built in grand riad style and the doorway is graced with intricate *tadelakt* design and adobe decoration, but, once inside, there's a feeling of light-filled contemporary comfort. Good-sized rooms (single/double 660/880dh) use lots of white and lilac and have colourful tiled bathrooms. Two rooms on the rooftop come with private terraces. There's a glorious traditionally tiled courtyard with a bar that leads onto a large, welcoming pool area, where an afternoon lounging on a sunbed after a dusty desert trip would be time well spent. Breakfast and Wi-Fi included.

€€ Riad Lamane
Amazrou (off the road to M'Hamid just after the bridge, turn right at the mini-roundabout), T0524-848388, www.riadlamane.com.
A rather special escape amid a garden bursting with colourful flowers. Individually designed bungalows and rooms brim with distinctive Berber and African touches including coloured *tadelakt* walls and huge beds. There's also some very luxurious 'tent' rooms that – with a/c and bathroom – are definitely 5-star glamping. A pool, convivial bar and a restaurant under a rather magnificent tent top off the experience. It's all very romantic and incredibly peaceful. Desert excursions and camel trips can be arranged. Breakfast and Wi-Fi included.

€€ Villa Zagora
Rte de Nekhla, Amazrou, T0524-846093,
www.mavillaausahara.com.
An oasis within an oasis, this tiny
guesthouse has 6 elegant rooms all
named after plants (single/double
€40-50/€70-90) and a roomy 6-bed
Berber tent with private terrace for
budget travellers (€18 per person). Eat
locally grown, freshly cooked food in the
garden or on the terrace, then spend a
lazy afternoon poolside. Rooms have
a fresh, contemporary feel with lots of
light yellow and white, and local kilims
adding vibrant splashes of colour. Most
have views over the rambling garden and
some have fireplaces. Excellent half-day
trips exploring the palm groves and
Amazrou village as well as longer desert
excursions can be arranged. Breakfast
and Wi-Fi included.

Camping

Camping Auberge Oasis Palmier
Route de Nekhla, next to Riad Dar Sofian,
T0524-846724, pixameharee@hotmail.fr.
Highly popular with over-landers, this
large campground in the palm groves
offers campervan space (50dh), tent
pitches and basic beds in Berber tents
(100dh per person). There's a restaurant,
Wi-Fi, electricity, and the bathrooms
have hot water. It's well run, friendly and,
best of all, campers get to use the pool
of neighbouring **Riad Dar Sofian**.

Routes north and east of Zagora

€ Kasbah Ennakhile
Nekob, T0524-839719,
www.kasbah-nkob.com.
Friendly service and a choice of
6 colourful traditional rooms with shared
bathrooms (single/double €22/36 with
half-board), or 9 standard rooms (single/

double €34/58 with half-board) with
traditional *tataoui* ceilings, stone floors
and attached bathrooms with inventive
use of Berber water pitchers. There are
great views over the oasis from the
terrace salon and from some rooms,
and there's a pool. Local trekking
organized. Wi-Fi included.

€ Ksar Jenna
2 km west of Nekob, T0524-839790,
www.ksarjenna.com.
A relaxed and elegant retreat, with
7 gorgeous rooms (from €40) complete
with traditional flourishes and mosaic-
tiled bathrooms. There's a restaurant
with a magnificent painted ceiling, a
fountain and bar plus gardens blooming
with jasmine. A great place to overnight
on the road north or south. Breakfast
and Wi-Fi included.

Camping

Camping Amasttou
Tazzarine, T0524-838078,
www.amasttou.com.
Signposted as you arrive from Nekob
into Tazzarine. Excellent well-organized
campsite with a pool, restaurant and
plenty of space within the mature garden
to pitch your tent (15dh per person plus
12dh per tent) or park up the campervan
(36dh including electricity). Also has a
large Berber tent dormitory (60dh per
person) and simple adobe rooms (single/
double 80/130dh). Good-value meals
available and a range of excursions and
activities on offer.

Restaurants

As in many southern towns, cheap
eateries need to be treated with
caution. If worried, stick to food cooked
in front of you, such as brochettes and

grilled meats, or tagines that have been simmering for hours. Almost all of the good places to eat or drink in Zagora are attached to hotels.

€€ Villa Zagora
Rte de Nekhla, Amazrou, T0524-846093.
Set menus at €15 offer locally sourced ingredients and home-style cooking appeal. They're a great chance to get stuck into traditional Moroccan flavours. Seasonal specialities such as lamb tagine with quince are also offered. Dining is inside during winter evenings and outside amid the guesthouse's lovely gardens or on the terrace when warm. Bookings are essential.

€ Café Litteraire
Av Mohammed V. Daily 1100-1400 and 1600-2100.
Step through the bland arcade arches outside and you'll discover a hidden garden of creeping vines, flowers and comfy, shaded seating nooks. At the far end of the garden a little room showcases interesting black and white photographs of Zagora in the 1940s and '50s and a small exhibition of local artwork. The short menu concentrates on tagines and brochettes with a few omelettes and sandwiches chucked in for good measure (mains 20-40dh). It's also a lovely place to just relax with a coffee or tea. Wi-Fi.

€ Café Magana
Av Mohammed V, opposite the main mosque, 1000-2100.
One of the most popular places in town to kick back with a pot of mint tea or panache (mixed juice), with a large street terrace that's perfect for people-watching. The Magana's menu serves up the standard range of tagines, but they're all well executed and tasty, plus there are

> **Tip...**
> For a drink you could try the bars at Riad Lamane (see Where to stay) and Hotel La Fibule du Drâa (Rte de M'Hamid, Amazrou).

a few alternative options: pizza, pasta, delicious merguez sandwiches, and omelettes. Service here is super friendly. Mains start from 40dh, while sandwiches are 20-25dh.

Festivals

Zagora
During the *moulid* there is a major religious festival held in Zagora, the **Moussem of Moulay Abdelkader Jilala**.

What to do

Zagora
Caravane du Sud, *Amazrou, T0524-847569, www.caravanesud.com.* Camel-trekking, mountain-biking and 4WD trips in the desert around Zagora.
Discovering South Morocco, *T0524-846115, www.zagora-desert.info.* 1- to 10-day trekking (€35 per person per day) or camel-treks (€45 per person per day) into the desert.

Transport

Zagora
The **Supratours** bus to **Ouarzazate** (50dh, 2 hrs) and **Marrakech** (130dh, 7½ hrs) leaves at 0600. The **CTM** bus from M'Hamid, heading to Marrakech and **Casablanca**, pulls into town at 0745 (see below for details). *Grands taxis* leave from the car park beside the main mosque for **Ouarzazate** (70dh) and **M'Hamid** (25dh), but you'll have to wait for the cars to fill up. There are also *grands taxis* and

minibuses shuttling between **M'Hamid**, **Tagounite** and Zagora. If you're driving, the **Total** station on the Ouarzazate road can do minor vehicle repairs, and there is a larger garage opposite the police station, on your left as you come from the Ouarzazate direction.

South of Zagora

Tamegroute and around

Tamegroute lies on the left bank of the Oued Drâa, 20 km southeast from Zagora, and is visited mainly because of the *zaouïa* founded in the 17th century. It is the headquarters of the influential Naciri Islamic brotherhood, which had great importance in the Drâa region until recently, and is visited by scholars from the Islamic world. The outer sanctuary and library are open to public view (closed 1200-1500), the latter containing a number of impressively old Korans and 12th-century antelope hide manuscripts. The village is also interesting to explore, with its inhabited underground kasbah, and there's a community pottery that for centuries has been producing the green-glazed and brown ceramics typical of the region. Some 8 km south of Tamegroute, the **Tinfou dunes** are a small and popular but nevertheless memorable area of Saharan sand.

Tagounite

Driving south from Tinfou, the road takes you up over the Jbel Bani and down into oasis country again around the village of Tagounite. There are basic shops here and the last petrol station before the desert. Tracks connect to **Merzouga** to the east (see page 218) or **Foum Zguid** to the west, only advisable with a guide and 4WD (see Making tracks, page 248).

★ M'Hamid and Erg Chiggaga

An alternative to Merzouga in the east, M'Hamid is popular as a base for camel trips into the dunes. The village of M'Hamid itself marks the end of the tarmac road and has a few basic shops, souvenir sellers, desert tour agents and a Monday souk. Across the river in 'old' M'Hamid is an interesting kasbah to explore and outlying villages. The most common destinations are the sands of the **Erg Lehoudi**, some 8 km north of M'hamid, and the magnificent unspoiled dunes of **Erg Chiggaga**, 55 km out towards the Algerian frontier, a two-hour drive by 4WD, or a three-day camel trek. There are plenty of outfits (and hustlers) here who will set you up with a trip of any length, from a short camel ride and a single night in a camp under the stars to a week-long camel trek west to Foum Zguid. Shop around and make sure you know what you're getting.

The days of the great camel caravans led by indigo-swathed warriors are a mirage from the past, but you may catch a glimpse of some 'blue men of the desert' at the Monday souk (more for the benefit of tourists than tradition), and there's a celebration of their cultural heritage at the annual **International Nomads Festival** in March (see Festivals, below).

Tamegroute and around

€€ Kasbah Sahara Sky
Tinfou, T0667-351943 (mob),
www.hotel-sahara.com. Closed Jul.
A well-appointed observatory on the
roof, very dark skies and cold beer attract
astronomers to this comfortable and
friendly modern hotel, built in kasbah-
style, next to the dunes. Spacious rooms
come with a/c and satellite TV as well as
great views over the desert, and ground-
floor rooms have disabled access.

M'Hamid
There is a sprinkling of boutique
guesthouses and hotels in the palm
groves of Ouled Driss just before the
village, and more simple hotels in the
village itself.

€€€€-€ Dar Azawad
T0524-848730, www.darazawad.com.
Closed Jul.
This luxury boutique hotel in the oasis
5 km before M'Hamid is what desert
dreams are made of. The 9 charming
kasbah-style rooms (single/double
€40-70/50-90) and 6 luxurious suites,
with bells and whistles such as Nespresso
machines and iPod speakers (€120-250),
merge contemporary comfort with
rustic-chic decor. There's a heated pool,
extensive gardens, plus a hammam and
spa offering massages, so you can scrub
that desert dust off and emerge shiny,
relaxed and new. They also have a deluxe
tented bivouac at the Chiggaga dunes
for exclusive hire. Wi-Fi and breakfast
included. Dinners available.

€€ Dar Sidi Bounou
In the oasis 4 km before M'Hamid, T0524-
846330, www.darsidibounou.com.
Tranquil and relaxing, this arty retreat
is a place to savour the desert on the
doorstep and also to dig a bit deeper into
local culture. The rooms (€40 per person
half-board) in a converted traditional
house are authentically decorated, plus
there are adobe huts (€39 per person
half-board) and a Berber tent (€30 per
person half-board) in the garden. Camel
treks and desert trips can be arranged.

€€ Kasbah Azalay
T5024-848096, www.azalay.com.
This Spanish-owned kasbah-style
hotel has 43 good-sized a/c rooms, a
restaurant and a bar where you can raise
a toast to your desert exploits. There's
a rather over-the-top, opulent indoor
pool and a huge marble hammam. They
can arrange transfers from Ouarzazate
or Marrakech airport and offer their own
excursions into the desert.

€ Auberge Hamada du Drâa
T0524-848086, www.hamada-
sahara.com.
This auberge is a friendly budget choice
with 10 simple a/c rooms (single/double
€23/36) cheerfully kitted out with bright
African motifs on the walls. There's a
restaurant, nice pool and a small, lush
garden to relax in. There is also space to
park up your campervan or pitch your
tent. The usual desert excursions can be
arranged plus camping overnight at their
tented bivouac at the Chiggaga dunes.

Festivals

M'Hamid

Mar Nomads Festival (www. nomadsfestival.org). A showcase and celebration of nomadic cultures with 3 days of concerts, cultural activities and workshops.

What to do

M'Hamid

Sahara Services, *T0661-776766, www. saharaservices.info*. A good reputation for dune excursions. The 'sunset tour' is €45 per person, including food and a night's accommodation, or you can do a whole day's trek, getting you deeper into the desert, for €56.

Zbar Travel, *T0668-517280, www. zbartravel.com*. Reliable local operator with sunset tour including overnight in the desert plus sandboarding for €35, and longer treks by camel and multi-day safaris in 4WD. Another office in Ouarzazate.

Transport

M'Hamid

Daily **CTM** bus departs at 0600 from M'Hamid to **Casablanca** (255dh, 14 hrs) via Zagora (35dh, 2 hrs), **Ouarzazate** (80dh 5 hrs) and **Marrakech** (160dh, 10 hrs). There is also a slower private bus departing M'Hamid at 0700 along the same route as far as Marrakech. *Grands taxis* head to **Zagora** when full.

Background

History 257
Modern Morocco 268

History

Morocco's location has always been a central factor in shaping the country's history. The westernmost country in the Muslim world, for centuries it was *El Maghreb el Aqsa*, 'the Land of the Farthest West', to the Arabs. Despite being the closest Arab land to Europe, Morocco was the last to come under European domination.

Moroccans are highly aware of the particularities of their location, and are convinced that their history has given them a civilization combining the virtues of the Arabs, Berbers, Andalucíans, Jews and Christians who converted to Islam.

Conventionally, Moroccan history is divided into two major periods: the distant pre-Islamic past, marked by the Phoenicians and Romans, and the better-documented times of the Islamic dynasties, at their most brilliant during a period roughly equivalent to the European Middle Ages. From the 16th century onwards the rulers of Morocco were constantly fighting back the expansionist Iberian states and, later, France, under whose rule the majority of the Cherifian Empire (as it was called by the colonizers) came from 1912 to 1956. The last areas under colonial rule, the former Spanish Sahara, were retaken in the 1970s. The later 20th century saw the formation of the modern Moroccan State.

Pre-Islamic times

Human settlement in Morocco goes back millennia. Rock carvings in the High Atlas and Sahara, and objects in stone, copper and bronze have survived from early times. Nomadic pastoralism is thought to have existed in North Africa from around 4000 BC, among a population today referred to by historians as Libyco-Berber, probably part of the wider Hamito-Semitic group that eventually sub-divided into the Egyptians in eastern North Africa and the Berbers to the west.

The enterprising Phoenicians traded along North Africa's coast. Utica in Tunisia is thought to have been their first port in North Africa. Carthage (also in modern Tunisia) was founded in 814 BC and was to develop an extensive network of trading posts along the Mediterranean and African coasts. Archaeological excavations at Russadir (Melilla) on the Mediterranean and at Larache and Essaouira on the Atlantic coast have shown that these towns started life as Phoenician settlements. Daring Carthaginian seafarers also undertook journeys far to the south, along the West African coast.

Lost in the mists of ancient times is the history of the Imazighen, the Berber peoples of inland Morocco, referred to by the Romans as the Maures – hence the Latin name 'Mauretania' for the kingdom that seems to have taken shape in the fourth century BC over part of what is now Morocco. This early state may have had its capital at Volubilis, near modern Meknès and no doubt traded with the maritime Carthaginian empire.

After the defeat and destruction of Carthage in 146 BC, and the establishment of the Roman province of Africa, it was only natural that the empire of the Caesars develop an interest in the lands of the Maures – always a potential source of

BACKGROUND

Chronology: ancient Morocco

6000-3000 BC Neolithic era. Tumulus (burial mounds) of Mzoura, near Larache, dates from this time.

3000 BC onwards Proto-historic period. Bronze tools manufactured in Morocco, to judge from evidence of rock-carvings.

7th century BC First confirmed Phoenician presence in the form of trading posts in Morocco, notably near the sites of modern Essaouira and Larache.

5th century BC Carthage establishes trading posts on the coast.

4th-3rd centuries BC Kingdom of the Maures established.

146 BC Fall of Carthage to Rome. Northwest Africa (or Mauretania, as it is referred to by the Latin authors) comes under Roman influence.

33 BC King Bocchus II leaves the Kingdom of the Maures to Rome.

24 BC Juba II comes to the Mauretanian throne. Augustus rules in Rome.

AD 40 Ptolomy, son of Juba II and Cleopatra Selene, is assassinated on the orders of Emperor Caligula.

AD 42 Northwestern Morocco becomes a Roman province as Mauretania Tingitana, with its capital at Tingis, modern Tangier.

3rd century Christianity appears in Morocco. Rome abandons the province south of the Oued Loukkos.

4th century The elephant becomes extinct in northwestern Africa.

AD 429 The Vandals invade north Africa, but fail to establish a lasting presence in Mauretania Tingitana.

AD 533 During the reign of Justinian, the Byzantine Empire re-establishes control of the coastal cities of Ceuta and Tangier.

trouble. Roman forces had had considerable problems in putting down the revolts of the Berber kingdoms, the most difficult campaigns being in the eastern Maghreb against Jugurtha, 109-105 BC. To establish stable rule in northwestern Africa, Augustus entrusted Mauritania to Juba II, son of Juba I, an enemy of Julius Caesar, who had committed suicide after Pompey's defeat in the civil war between Caesar and Pompey.

A cultured monarch, Juba II married Cleopatra Selene, daughter of Cleopatra and Mark Anthony. From 25 BC, he reigned over much of what is now Morocco. Fluent in Amazigh, Greek, Latin and Punic, he was interested in the arts, sciences and medicine. His portrait in the form of a fine bronze bust was discovered during the excavation of the ancient city of Volubilis near Meknès.

An independent-minded Mauretanian monarchy was too much for Rome. The last king, Ptolomy, grandson of Anthony and Cleopatra, was put to death by the Roman emperor Caligula, and the client kingdom was transformed into a Roman colony. Roman northwestern Africa was reorganized as two provinces, with capitals at Iol-Caesarea (Cherchell in Algeria) and Tingis, today's Tangier.

Roman administration and Latin culture were grafted onto Punic and Berber peoples. The army was an important influence: until 19 BC there was fighting in North Africa, and the army continued to extend its influence. A major Berber revolt, led by one Tacfarinas, took seven years to suppress. Such tensions were probably aggravated by Roman centurions settling to farm wheat and olives on lands once grazed by the nomads' flocks. The towns had all the trappings of Romanized urban life and flourished until the third century AD.

The third to eighth centuries AD are a hazy time in northwest Africa's history. The Amazigh rebelled frequently, while Romanized populations protested against the low prices of wheat, wine and olive oil supplied to the metropolis. Although Christianity became Rome's official religion in AD 313, it proved insufficient glue to hold the Empire together against the Germanic invasions. The Vandals swept down from Spain and across into the eastern Maghreb in the fifth century. Although the Byzantine Empire was to take back certain territories in the sixth century, its unity was undermined by struggles within the Church. Mauretania Tingitana was never effectively ruled again by a Roman administration.

Arrival of Islam

The key event in shaping Morocco's history was the conquest by the Muslim Arabs in the eighth century AD. Islam, the religion of the Prophet Mohammed, was born in the oases of Arabia in the seventh century AD. It gave the warring Arab tribes and oasis communities – formerly pagan, Jewish and maybe Christian – the necessary cohesion to push back the Byzantine and Sassanian Empires, exhausted by years of warfare.

In eighth-century North Africa, Islam was welcomed by the slaves – who freed themselves by becoming Muslims – and by Christian heretics, who saw the new religion as simpler and more tolerant than Byzantine Christianity. In 711, therefore, it was an Islamized Amazigh army that crossed the Straits of Gibraltar under Tariq Ibn Ziyad, conquering the larger part of the Iberian peninsula. Along with North Africa, the southern regions of the peninsula, referred to as Al Andalus (whence Andalucía), formed a unified socio-cultural area until the 15th century.

Islam, which vaunts a spirit of brotherhood within a vast community of believers and condemns petty clan interests and local loyalties, was to prove an effective base for new states based on dynastic rule, with central governments drawing their legitimacy from their respect for the precepts of the Koran and the Hadith, the codified practice of the Prophet Mohammed.

From the moment that Islam arrived, Morocco's history became that of the rise and fall of dynasties, often ruling areas far wider than that of the contemporary nation state. Simplifying heavily, these dynasties were the Idrissids (ninth century), the Almoravids (11th century), the Almohads (12th-13th centuries), the Merinids (13th-15th centuries), the Wattasids (15th-16th centuries), the Saâdians (16th century) and, finally, the Alaouites, rulers of Morocco from the 17th century to the present. Almost all these dynasties arose from politico-religious movements.

To return to the early centuries of Islamic rule in North Africa, the new religion took hold fairly slowly, as struggles between rival dynasties in the Middle East – the

BACKGROUND

Chronology: medieval and early modern Morocco

622 Prophet Mohammed is forced to leave Mecca for Medina. His *hijra* ('emigration') on account of his beliefs is the start of the Muslim era.

703 Moussa Ibn Nusayr conquers Morocco and begins the conversion of Berbers to Islam.

704 Tangier falls to the Muslim armies with the help of Count Julian.

711 Tariq Ibn Ziyad crosses the straits which today bear his name (Jabal Tariq) to begin the conquest of Iberia, which lasts until 732.

740 Berber revolt against central authorities in Damascus. Their heretic, Kharijite brand of Islam leads to a political break with the Arab Near East.

786 Idriss I, descendant of caliph Ali and the Prophet's daughter Fatima, reaches Morocco, fleeing the Abbasids of Baghdad.

788 Idriss becomes religious leader of the Berber tribes of the Middle Atlas.

789 Foundation of Fès.

791 Idriss I poisoned at orders of Haroun Errachid.

803 Idriss II on the throne.

809 Fès re-founded by Idriss II.

817-818 Hundreds of Jewish and Muslim families move to Fès from Córdoba and Kairouan.

1048 Abdallah Ibn Yassin, a religious reformer from Sijilmassa, creates a fortified settlement or ribat, home to warriors (*murabitoun*) – hence the name of the dynasty he founded, the Almoravids.

1062 Youssouf Ibn Tachfine founds Marrakech.

1086 The minor kings of southern Spain appeal for help to the Almoravids, who go on to beat Alfonso VI at the Battle of Sagrajas.

1125 Ibn Toumert declares himself mahdi, 'the rightly guided one', at Tin Mal in the High Atlas. The purist Almohad movement is launched.

1126 The Almohad Abd el Mu'min Ibn Ali (ruled 1130-63) takes the title of caliph. Goes on to conquer North Africa and Iberia up to the Guadalquivir.

1143-1147 Collapse of the Almoravid Empire.

1148-1197 Construction of major mosques, including the Koutoubia in Marrakech, the Tour Hassan in Rabat and the Giralda, Seville.

1244-1269 Almohad Empire falls apart, having lasted barely 100 years.

1248 Fès falls to the Merinids. They begin the construction of Fès el Jedid.

1269 Fall of Marrakech marks the beginning of the Merinid era.

1300s Merinid rule is at its height.

1400s Internal anarchy in Morocco. Merinid collapse in 1465.

1492 Fall of Granada to the Catholic monarchs, Ferdinand and Isabella.

1509 Spain takes Oran.

1525-1659 Saâdian rule.

1578 Battle of the Three Kings ends Portuguese threat to sultanate.

1578-1607 Reign of Ahmed el Mansour ed Dahabi.

1664 Alaouite rule established at Fès under Moulay Rachid.

1672-1727 Moulay Ismaïl rules with an iron hand.

1757-1790 Sidi Mohammed Ben Abdallah rules a stable country.

1817 Corsairing is banned.

Ummayads and the Abbasids – divided the Islamic heartlands. The Islamic ideal was certainly not the only interest of the Arab governors sent out by the caliphs. Power was often exercised despotically, with repression leading to a major revolt against the Arab rulers (740-780) in the name of Islam. The revolt was of Kharijite inspiration – the Kharijites considering that they practised the most pure and egalitarian form of Islam. They rejected the split between Sunni and Shi'a Muslims and refused to submit to the authority of the caliphs of Damascus and Baghdad. Even at the end of the struggle between Umayyads and Abbasids, in 750, and the victory of the latter, central Islamic power was slow to reassert itself in the northwestern extremities of Africa, which remained, along with the northern Sahara, independent as the Berber Kharijite Kingdom of Tahert. Then, in the mid-eighth century, an Ummayad descendant of the Prophet, fleeing the Middle East, founded the first great Muslim dynasty in 788. Idriss I founded Fès in 789. A further refugee Umayyad prince was to build a kingdom in Al Andalus, centred on Córdoba.

The ninth and 10th centuries saw the development of the trans-Saharan caravan trade, notably in gold. There were routes leading up into what is now Tunisia and Libya, and other, longer routes across the western regions of the Sahara. The shorter, western route finished in the Drâa Valley and the southern slopes of the Atlas. Sijilmassa, close to today's eastern Moroccan town of Rissani, was to be the capital of this trade, the mustering place from which the caravans headed onwards to the Middle East and the Mediterranean ports. Sijilmassa was to be taken by a Shi'ite group who, thanks to their control of the gold trade, were able to found the Fatimid dynasty – named after Fatima, daughter of the Prophet and wife of Ali, considered by the Shi'ites as the legitimate caliph or successor of the Prophet Mohammed.

Tribal dynasties and religious causes: Almoravids and Almohads

The Saharan gold trade in the 11th century was to be dominated by a nomad Berber group based in fortified religious settlements (*ribats*), hence their name, *el murabitoun*, which transposes as Almoravid. Based in the northern Sahara, they founded a capital at Marrakech in 1062. Their empire expanded to include much of Spain and present-day Algeria.

In the 12th century, the Almoravids were overthrown by the Almohads, *el muwahhidoun* or 'unitarians', whose power base lay in the Berber tribal groupings of the High Atlas. United by their common religious cause, the Almohads took Sijilmassa, the 'gold port', and their empire expanded to include the whole of present day Morocco, Algeria and Tunisia, along with Andalucía. This political unity lasted from about 1160 to 1260. Towns expanded, distinctive mosques were built (along the lines of the Koutoubia at Marrakech), trade grew with southern European merchant cities and Arabic took root as the language of the urban areas.

The Almohad dynasty disintegrated towards the end of the 13th century. The ruling tribal elite lost its sense of cohesion and the feudal Christian rulers of Spain reacted quickly: Seville fell to the Christians in 1248 and Granada became a Protectorate. The Almohad Empire split into three separate kingdoms, roughly corresponding to the independent states of today. Ifrikiya (Tunisia) was ruled by the Hafsids, who initially ruled in the name of the Almohads; the Abdelwadids ruled from Tlemcen in modern Algeria; in Morocco, the Merinids established their capital in Fès.

Merinids: from tribal to urban dynastic rule

The Beni Merini, rulers of Morocco from the mid-13th to mid-15th centuries, were not champions of any particular religious doctrine. Nomads from the Figuig region, they appear in Moroccan history in the late 12th century and grow in influence during the early 13th century.

In the 1250s, the Merinid forces took the main cities under Abou Yahya el Merini, and Abou Youssef Yacoub (1258-1286) consolidated their rule. The 14th and 15th centuries saw the Merinids build a state centred on Fès – but they were more or less constantly involved in struggles with mountain tribes and neighbouring dynasties: the Tlemcen-based Zayyanids, the Hafsids further to the east, and the Nasrids to the north in Granada.

Home to the Merinid court and administration, Fès grew as a centre of religious learning, too. Having conquered power in a land where political authority depended closely on religious credentials the Merinids tried to build legitimacy by sponsoring theological education. *Medersas*, operating rather like the colleges of some early European universities, were founded at Fès and in other cities, providing teaching reflecting the urban elite's piety. Students, however, came from both town and country. In attempting to build an educated group with formal theological and legal training, the Merinids sought to counter the influence of Sufi leaders in rural areas.

Merinid power, unlike that of previous dynasties, was not based on a single tribe – probably because large settled communities of merchants and artisans were emerging. Subsequent dynasties, although they had to use tribal support initially, never maintained a single tribal affiliation. The European threat which emerged in the 15th century (Ceuta was occupied by the Portuguese in 1415) led to a resistance based on religious ideals, with leaders referred to as *cherifs*, descendants of the Prophet Mohammed. When the Merinids proved ineffective in fighting back the Europeans, alternative local leaderships appeared, suitable symbols around which unity could be built due to cherifian descent. The Saâdians exemplify this trend.

Morocco and marauding Europe

The routes of the gold caravans linking sub-Saharan Africa to North Africa meant that any Moroccan dynasty had importance. However, as of the 14th century, new routes opened up, reducing the significance of northwest Africa. The Mamlouks in Egypt fought back the Christian kingdoms of Nubia; Spain and Portugal began the quest for sea routes to the 'gold coasts' and the epoch of the great discoveries began, as the Portuguese explored the Atlantic coast of Africa. In 1492, Granada, the last Muslim stronghold in Andalucía, fell to Ferdinand and Isabella, and Columbus sailed for America. The era of European imperialism had begun, and the Maghreb was first in the firing line as the Catholic monarchs continued the Reconquista into Africa. The two Iberian powers occupied strong-points along the Atlantic and Mediterranean coasts (the Spanish garrison towns of Ceuta and Melilla date from this time). However, under Iberian powers, resources were soon taken up with the commercially more important development of far-flung empires in the Indies and Americas. And the people of North Africa put up solid resistance.

In 1453, the last bastion of eastern Christianity, Constantinople, fell to the Ottoman Empire. Muslim resistance to the Christian powers in the western Mediterranean was led by corsairs, who called on the Ottoman sultan in Istanbul for support. By the end of the 16th century, the eastern part of the Maghreb had been divided into three Ottoman *ilayet* or regencies: Algiers, Tunis and Tripoli. Morocco, however, remained independent, ruled by dynasties of cherifian origin. The Saâdians (late 15th-16th century) sprang from the Souss region (Taroudant) and, under Ahmed el Mansour (1578-1603), destroyed an invading Portuguese army, re-established (for a short while) the gold trade, developed sugar cane plantations in the Souss and re-founded Marrakech.

Alaouites and the foundations of the Cherifian state

After the decay of Saâdian power, a second cherifian dynasty, the Alaouites, originally from the oases of the Tafilalet (southeastern Morocco), came to power. The first sovereigns, Moulay Rachid (1666-1672) and Moulay Ismaïl (1672-1727), a tireless builder, restored order. As Fès and Marrakech had risen against him, he created a vast new capital at Meknès; with a large palace and four mosques, he transformed a provincial town into a regal city.

There seems to have been major political and strategic motives behind the decision to centre Alaouite authority on Meknès. It enabled the sultan to avoid identifying himself too closely with the interests of either Fès or Marrakech. Meknès was also very central, and better situated for campaigning against the Middle Atlas Berbers and it was more distant than Fès from Turkish-dominated lands further east.

Moulay Ismaïl's authority depended on a special corps of black slave troops, the Abid Bukhari. By the end of his long reign, Moulay Ismaïl had a loyal force of some 150,000 men, ever ready to deal with Ottoman encroachments or Sanhaja Berber rebellion. By 1686, the sultan's authority was complete, with only remote mountain areas outside his control. Such a security force required considerable resources, which meant resorting to rather un-Islamic forms of taxation. Repressive taxation produced resentment in the already defiant cities, notably Fès.

After a period of chaos in the 1730s, the work of Moulay Ismaïl continued under Mohammed Ben Abdallah (1757-1790). Stability was restored and the influence of Moulay Ismaïl's Abid army was ended. Many of the *presidios* were re-taken, including Mazagan (today's El Jadida), while Essaouira was fortified. In 1760, the port of Anfa (today's Casablanca) was fortified, and Christian merchants were exempted from customs duties as an incentive to settle. Morocco came to be respected by the European powers.

Mohammed Ben Abdallah was the first Alaouite sultan who was keen to gain the real support of the urban religious elite, the *ulema*. While previous sultans – and especially Moulay Ismaïl – had relied on their cherifian lineage as an ideological prop for their rule, Mohammed Ben Abdallah sought *ulema* support for his policies. He won them over because of his piety and scholarly interests. Thus the Moroccan State, although dependent on tribal soldiery, began to become identified with the interests of Morocco's city dwellers. This trend continued under Mohammed Ben Abdallah's successor, Moulay Suleyman (1792-1827).

The 19th century: colonialism held at bay

In 1798, Napoleon Bonaparte led an expedition to Egypt. The lands of Islam became aware of the newly acquired technological power of European armies. Modernization was essential, despite the high financial costs, if colonial rule was to be avioded. The European peace of 1815 established conditions favourable to colonialism, and France, anxious to re-establish lost prestige, looked towards North Africa. Algiers was taken in 1830, and French colonial expansion continued throughout the 19th century, with a settler population of largely Mediterranean origin putting down roots. European farming grew, thanks to the redistribution of land confiscated after revolts and modern land registration. New European-style cities were constructed. Although Algiers fell with little resistance, the central Maghreb was occupied at a terrible price to the local population.

Because of the development of French Algeria, Morocco increasingly found itself isolated from the rest of the Islamic world and subject to severe pressure from the European powers who were steadily growing in confidence. France attacked Morocco for providing shelter to the Algerian leader, the Emir Abdelkader, defeating the Moroccan army at the Battle of Isly in 1844. Great Britain forced Morocco to sign a preferential trade treaty in 1856, while, in 1860, a Spanish expeditionary force took the key northern city of Tetouan. Sultan Aberrahman was forced to accept unfavourable peace terms, with customs coming under foreign control by way of an indemnity; an ill-defined Saharan territory, was ceded to Spain. The departure of Spanish troops in 1862 left Morocco considerably weakened.

A reform policy had been launched, however, under a series of bright, dynamic sultans: Abderrahman (1822-1859), Mohammed IV (1859-1873) and Hassan I (1873-1894). Despite the latter's efforts to expand his power base with the support of the High Atlas tribes, further treaties were imposed by Great Britain, Spain and France. The country ran into increasing debt problems with foreign banks. The situation continued to worsen under the weak rulers who succeeded Hassan I.

In 1906, the Conference of Algeciras brought 12 nations together to discuss the Moroccan debt. France and Spain emerged as key contenders for occupation. In 1907, following the killing of some Europeans during unrest, France occupied Casablanca. A new sultan, Moulay Hafidh (great-uncle of the present king), was

Chronology: modern Morocco

1844 Battle of Isly. Moroccan sultan's forces defeated by the French near Oujda.

1880 Conference of Madrid, while recognizing Morocco as an independent kingdom, confirms the major European powers' trade interests.

1905 Kaiser William II visits Tangier and makes a speech proclaiming himself 'defender of Islam'.

1907 France uses major riots in Casablanca as a pretext for sending in troops.

1912 30 March. Proclamation of a French Protectorate over central Morocco.

1942 Allied landings at Casablanca (8 November).

1943 Allied conference at Anfa, Casablanca.

1947 Sultan Mohammed V calls for independence.

1953 Mohammed V deposed and sent into exile, replaced by puppet ruler Mohammed Ben Arafa.

1956 Moroccan independence.

proclaimed the same year. In 1911, with Fès surrounded by insurgent tribes, he called in Algerian-based French forces to end the state of siege.

The last act came in 1912, when the Treaty of Fès, signed by France and Moulay Hafidh for Morocco, established the French Protectorate over the Cherifian Empire. A subsequent Franco-Spanish treaty split the country into a northern zone, under Spanish control, a vast central area under French rule, and a southern zone, also assigned to Spain.

The Protectorate: separate development and exploitation

The full occupation of Morocco was an arduous affair, with tribes putting up resistance and an area of the Rif (northern Morocco), establishing itself as an independent republic for a short period in the 1920s, threatening the Protectorate system's stability.

The Protectorate bore the firm imprint of the first French resident-general, Maréchal Lyautey – and the work accomplished during his 12-year rule was to leave a long-lasting mark on the country. Lyautey, a Roman Catholic aristocrat who had seen service in Algeria, Indochina and Madagascar – and witnessed at first hand what he considered to be the errors of the colonial system – was fascinated by Morocco; as something of a monarchist, he had respect for the sultanate, and was not disposed to intervene in the new Protectorate's traditional life.

Thus, the first period of French rule saw local institutions consolidated, alongside the gradual occupation of the main cities and the coastal plains. The sultan remained ruler, although executive and legislative powers were shared with the French resident-general. To govern the vast southern regions, the French relied on local Berber chiefs – Marrakech and its region was ruled by co-opting a local potentate, T'hami el Glaoui, for example. This meant that large-scale forces did not

Monarchs, battles and freedom fighters

Moroccan city streets tend to draw on the same selection of names. The biggest avenue in any town will be named after **Mohammed V** (1909-1961). Third son of Sultan Moulay Youssef, the young Mohammed was chosen by the French to be sultan because he was thought to be more malleable. In the event, he ruled Morocco from 1927 to 1961, seeing the country to Independence in 1956. His son, **Hassan II**, who ruled 1961-1999, also has many streets named after him, as does **Prince Moulay Abdallah**, the late king's younger brother. There are also streets named for dynasties (avenue des **Almoravides**, des **Almohades**, des **Saâdiens**, des **Alaouites**) and for major monarchs (ninth-century founder of Fès, **Idriss II**, 16th-century **Mansour Eddahbi**, 'the victorious and golden').

In any self-respecting town, central streets also bear the names of freedom fighters and the battles of the resistance. **Oued el Makhzen** was the battle in 1578 near modern Larache, where Mansour Eddahbi wiped out the invading Portuguese. The **Amir Abdelkader** fought the French in Algeria in the 19th century, while **Abdelkarim el Khattabi** was the leader of the Rif rebellion that set up an independent republic in northern Morocco in the 1920s. At the Battle of **Anoual** in 1921, he won a famous victory over Spanish forces. In the 1950s, **Mohammed Zerktouni** lobbed a bomb into a market much frequented by French shoppers in Marrakech, thus ensuring his commemoration on numerous major boulevards. Imprisoned, he took his own life to avoid torture.

have to be committed at a time when they were needed elsewhere. Exploitation of Morocco's natural wealth turned out to be a capitalist venture, rather than a settler one. French private banks financed public and private building works and exploited mineral concessions through the Compagnie Générale Marocaine and the Omnium Nord Africain. Infrastructure development was impressive: 1600 km of railway lines were created, a major new port was constructed at Casablanca. Rabat was chosen as the capital, and other new towns were planned using the most up-to-date techniques. Working closely with the planner Léon-Henri Prost, Lyautey ensured that Morocco's traditional cities were preserved and carefully separated from the elegant new European quarters.

It was quickly realized, too, that the lands controlled by the sultan's government, the *bilad el makhzen* (the coastal plains, along with the Fès, Meknès and Oujda regions), were the most fertile – hence the term *le Maroc utile*, 'useful Morocco'. An increasingly dynamic European community undertook to develop the country's resources to its own advantage, helped by tax concessions. By 1951, the European population had reached 325,000.

But for Lyautey, Morocco was not to be a settler colony, like neighbouring Algeria, where the French had shattered local society. Efforts were made to understand Moroccan society – the rural areas were administered by the specially trained *officiers des affaires indigènes*, and special government departments were created to catalogue and restore Morocco's heritage of historic buildings and crafts.

Lyautey may have been too 'pro-Moroccan' to satisfy a growing settler lobby. The fatal moment came in 1925. The Rif uprising, led by the enterprising Abdelkrim el Khattabi, imperilled the two Protectorates. In July 1921, the Rif armies had captured or killed around 15,000 Spanish soldiers at the Battle of Anoual. Lyautey was recalled to France, replaced by Maréchal Pétain at the head of a large army which finally defeated the Rifans in 1926 in co-operation with Spain. Fighting to defeat tribes resisting colonial incursions elsewhere in Morocco continued into the early 1930s.

Hardly had Morocco been 'pacified' than a nationalist movement arose. A focal point for nationalist resentment was the so-called Berber *dahir* (decree) of 1933, an attempt to replace Muslim law with Berber customary law in the main Berber-speaking regions. French colonial ethnography, which had provided the reasoning behind this project, had made a fundamental miscalculation: Morocco could not be divided into Berbers versus Arabs. The educated urban bourgeoisie demanded a reform programme in 1934 and, with the Second World War, the international situation clearly shifted to favour independence. The urban elite formed the Istiqlal (Independence) Party in 1944, with the goodwill of Sultan Mohammed V. Although closely watched by the French, the Alaouite sultan came to be seen as an instrument of French policy.

Tension grew in the early 1950s; under the Pacha of Marrakech, contingents of tribal horsemen converged on Rabat to demand the deposition of the sultan. In 1953 the resident-general, in violation of the Protectorate treaty, deposed Mohammed V and replaced him with a relative. The royal family found themselves in exile in Madagascar, which gave the nationalist movement another point of leverage. The sultan's return from exile was a key nationalist demand.

The situation elsewhere in the French Empire was to ensure a fast settlement of the Moroccan question. France had been defeated in Indochina in 1954, and there was a major uprising in Algeria, considered an integral part of France by Paris. The La Celle-St Cloud agreements of November 1955 ensured a triumphal return from exile for the royal family, and independence was achieved in March 1956, with Spain renouncing its Protectorate over northern Morocco at the same time. The issue of the southern desert provinces under Spanish rule, like Río de Oro, was left to one side.

Thus, Morocco's independence was achieved under the leadership of the country's traditional ruler. The Istiqlal Party had fostered political consciousness in the Moroccan middle classes, and a confrontation between a colonial regime and the people had developed into a conflict between colonial rulers and the Muslim ruler. The sultanate under foreign protection became an independent kingdom, with a unique position in the Arab and Mediterranean worlds.

Modern
Morocco

Morocco today is a complex and rapidly changing country. In political terms, the country is one of the most interesting Arab states, with a degree of media freedom and debate (within certain limits) rare in Northern Africa and the Middle East.

Recent political history

After independence, the national pact was increasingly criticized by the urban elite, who thought to push the monarchy aside – rather as had happened in Egypt, Tunisia and Iraq – and rule the country under a one-party system supported by the educated middle classes. The Istiqlal and socialist parties jockeyed for leadership; a revolt in the Rif was put down. The monarchy proved to be durable, however. After the death of his father, Mohammed V, in 1961, the new king, Hassan II turned out to be an able political player. An alliance with conservative rural leaders ensured the success of the constitutional referendum of December 1962. After the Casablanca riots of 1965, the army was called in to guarantee order. The Left lost its leader, Mehdi Ben Barka, assassinated in Paris in November 1965. As of July 1965, Hassan II was to rule without parliament.

The 1970s and 1980s

Such a centralized system was fraught with risk, as was realized following two attempts on the King's life: the Skhirat Palace attempted coup in 1971 and the attempt to shoot down the royal plane in 1972. So the King sought to rebuild a political system which would end the monarchy's relative isolation on the political scene and leave considerable room for manoeuvre. The 'Moroccanization' of the remaining firms still (mainly) in French hands, launched in 1973, was part of the strategy, winning the support of the middle classes. Spanish Río de Oro and Saquiet el Hamza were regained in the mid-1970s; the army was to be kept busy in these new Saharan provinces, fighting the Polisario, often at bonus pay rates. A number of key players emerged to second the King on the political scene. Foremost among them from the early 1980s was Driss Basri, Minister of the Interior. The dialogue between the King and Abderrahim Bouabid, head of the left wing UNFP in the mid-1970s, was to give the opposition a chance to express itself and represented a return to the methods used by Mohammed V after independence. In the 1990s, Parliament came to be dominated by the ruling conservative Wifak grouping and the opposition bloc, the Koutla. The early 1990s saw the King actively working to bring the opposition into government. Finally, in November 1997, elections produced a parliament with an opposition majority, led by the USFP (Union socialiste des forces populaires).

The 1990s: l'alternance or bringing the opposition to power

It is clear that Hassan II was trying to leave Morocco in good running order for his son, Crown Prince Sidi Mohammed. By the late 1980s, the Palace was aware that the political elite born of the independence struggle was running out of steam and that the opposition criticism of the inequalities in living standards (*la fracture sociale*, in Moroccan political parlance) had good grounds. World Bank 'remedies', strenuously applied in the 1980s and early 1990s, only helped to impoverish a large section of the population. Drought and poor harvests accelerated the rural exodus, rendering the split between poor and wealthy all the more visible in the cities. The first opposition government of 1998 thus had a very clear remit to 'do something' – and quickly – for the poorest in Moroccan society.

Underlying the opposition's coming to power was a fear that a large part of the *bidonville* (shanty town) population might be tempted by radical Islam. The middle classes have everything to lose should the country head towards an Algerian-type scenario, where thousands died in the 1990s.

July 1999: a new reign

The equation changed on the death of Hassan II on 23 July 1999. His eldest son, crown prince Sidi Mohammed, came to the throne as Mohammed VI. The battle against social inequality soon figured at the top of the royal agenda. And, for the first time in decades, areas of the country never visited by the reigning monarch received a royal visit. In long-ignored Tangier and the north, crowds turned out in the rain to welcome the king. In the palace, a new cohort of reform-minded counsellors joined the royal cabinet.

The new king moved quickly to improve the human rights situation. Former political prisoners and the families of those who 'disappeared' during the repression of the 1970s and 1980s received compensation payments; the house arrest of a leader of Islamist movement El Adl wal Ihsane, the ageing Cheikh Yassine, was ended. In early 2001, the International Federation of Human Rights held its annual conference in Casablanca.

The 2000s: slow, gradual reform

The Youssoufi government was much criticized for its inability to deal with deeply entrenched networks of economic cronyism. There were no spectacular reforms. Gentle but constant improvement was felt to be the best way – and, given the shortage of competent personnel, probably the only one. Most Moroccans realized that the habits of decades could not be changed overnight. Reform continued in the civil service, the security forces and justice; dynamic young ministers were appointed to the key portfolios of communications, housing and regional development, tourism and transport.

2003 and 2011: Islamist urban bomb attacks

In early May 2003, Morocco celebrated the birth of Crown Prince Hassan. Shortly after, on 16 May, tragedy struck. The country was dumbstruck by suicide bomb attacks in the centre of Casablanca. Targets included a Jewish social club and a downtown hotel. Over 40 people were killed, all Moroccans, and many were injured. The bombers were members of the Salafiya-Jihadiya purist Islamist movement. Several hundred arrests in Islamist circles swiftly followed.

Morocco's tourist capital was the target for another terrorist attack, on 28 April 2011, when a bomb exploded in a café overlooking the Jemaâ el-Fna square in Marrakech, killing 17, most of whom were foreign tourists. Though initially blamed for the attack, Al Qaeda denied responsibility. In October, Adel al-Olthmani was sentenced to death for his role in the attack and seven others received prison sentences for their part. For the Moroccans, the bombings were shocking: undermining an assumption that unprovoked urban slaughter of this kind could only happen elsewhere – notably in neighbouring Algeria.

2011 and beyond

Morocco did not escape the effects of the Arab Spring, which began in neighbouring Tunisia in December 2010. On 20 February 2011, tens of thousands took part in demonstrations calling for political reforms, including further devolved powers from the king to parliament and a more independent judicial system. A group called the **20 February Movement** was formed, which, like other protest movements around the Arab world, was led by young people and created through social networking. On 11 March, the king promised 'comprehensive constitutional reform' but, despite these guarantees, the demonstrations continued, led by the 20 February Movement. This prompted the televised announcement by the king of a series of reforms to be put to a national referendum on 1 July. Again, the protest movement rallied against the proposed reforms, arguing that they did not go far enough.

The referendum went ahead and, following a resounding vote in favour of the reforms (98% voted 'yes' with an estimated turnout of 73%), the new constitution enshrined the following changes: the new prime minister is selected from the party that receives most votes in an election rather than chosen by the king; the prime minister is able to appoint government officials and is also able to dissolve parliament. The king does retain significant powers however, he is the key power-broker in matters of security, religion and the military, and continues to chair the Council of Ministers and the Supreme Security Council.

Pro-democracy protests continued, with the 20 February Movement taking to the streets on 3 July to reject the new constitution. Following these demonstrations, early elections for the National Assembly of Representatives were held on 25 November 2011. The moderate **Islamist Justive and Development Party (PJD)** became the largest party, more than doubling their number of seats from 46 in 2007 to 107, though this was still short of an overall majority. Abdelilah Benkirane, leader of the PJD, was appointed prime minister and formed a coalition goverment with the centre Independence Party (who won 60 seats out of total of 395) and the Popular Movement (who won 32 seats).

Challenges for the 21st century

Things have moved forward considerably since the 1970s and, on the whole, the situation in the early 21st century looks positive. While Morocco, with (for the moment) no oil resources of its own, suffers from fluctuating oil prices, the country's proximity to Europe and an expanding internal market has made it an ideal base for relocating manufacturing industry. Due to the referendum called after the 2011 protests, Morocco has managed to sidestep the destabilization and strife that have affected its North African neighbours. The question, however, remains how to reduce poverty and social inequality and, at the same time, increase media freedom and civil liberties.

Practicalities

Getting there 273
Getting around 279
Essentials A-Z 286
Index. 299
Credits 304

Getting there

Air

The main international airports in Morocco are **Aéroport Marrakech Menara**, page 38; and **Aéroport Casablanca Mohammed V**, page 274. Other airports, including those at Fès and Essaouira, receive mainly domestic flights and just a handful of international services. Trains connect Casablanca's Mohammed V with the central city and pass through Casa Voyageurs train station, where you can pick up onward trains northeast to Fès and southeast to Marrakech. Marrakech Menara has a regular bus service from the airport into the central city. Both airports have *petits taxis* and *grands taxis*.

Major European airlines run frequent scheduled flights to Casablanca-Mohammed V and Marrakech Menara with most flights operating from France and Spain. National carrier **Royal Air Maroc (RAM)** ⓘ *www.royalairmaroc.com*, is reliable. Prices are similar to **Air France** and **British Airways**. The cheapest flights are usually with budget airlines **EasyJet** and **Ryanair**. Charter flights, run by package holiday companies, also fly into Marrakech Menara and are another possible cheap option.

From the UK

EasyJet ⓘ *www.easyjet.com*, flies daily from London Gatwick to Marrakech and twice weekly from Birmingham, Bristol and Glasgow airports. They also have two departures per week from London Luton to Essaouira. **Ryanair** ⓘ *www.ryanair. com*, flies to Marrakech twice a week from London Luton and London Stansted.

Budget airlines aside, the best direct flight option from the UK to Morocco is with **Royal Air Maroc** ⓘ *www.royalairmaroc.com*, which flies daily from Heathrow to Casablanca. Most other carriers include a stop in Europe.

TRAVEL TIP

Packing for Morocco

In summer light cotton clothing is best, with a fleece or woollen jumper for evenings. During the day you will need a hat, sunglasses and high-factor sunscreen. For winter packing clothes you can easily layer is a great idea. Thermal underwear is handy for chilly nights.

Trekkers should bring a sleeping bag and comfortable walking boots that have been worn in, water-purification tools (iodine drops, tablets etc), and a medical kit.

Female travellers should note that tampons are difficult to find outside of the big supermarkets in major cities.

ON THE ROAD

Casablanca

If you're arriving in or departing from Casablanca's **Mohammed V Airport**, Morocco's biggest city is worth an overnight stay before you continue your journey.

Essential Casablanca

Mohammed V Airport is 30 km south of the city. Trains between the airport and Casa Voyageurs train station leave hourly from 0600 to 2200. *Grands taxis* also wait for passengers outside the Arrivals hall (300dh to downtown). From Casa Voyageurs train station it is just five stops west on the city's fast and efficient tramway (every 15 minutes, single 7dh) to Place Nations Unies in the centre of town. If arriving by bus, the CTM terminal is on Rue Léon l'Africain in the downtown area, an easy walk to most hotels. *Petits taxis* are plentiful, but be aware that taxi drivers here are renowned for overcharging.

Sights

Hassan II Mosque (Boulevard Sidi Mohammed Ben Abdallah, T0522-482886) is the world's fifth biggest mosque and was inaugurated in 1993 after five years of intensive labour by over 30,000 workers and craftsmen. Although in many ways impeccably modern, its lavish traditional decorative detailing of carved plasterwork, *zellige* tiling and painted wood is often heralded as a symbol of the renaissance of Moroccan craftwork. The mosque has space for 80,000 worshippers and the minaret – inspired by the minaret of the Koutoubia Mosque in Marrakech – is 200 m high. The mosque is open to non-Muslims by 45-minute guided tour only from the western side of the mosque, from Saturday to Thursday at 0900, 1000, 1100 and 1400, and on Friday at 0900, 1000 and 1400, 120dh. The tour takes visitors into the prayer hall (which has a retractable roof), the ablutions room and down to the mosque's own hammam.

Elsewhere, the central city is home to fine examples of decaying French colonial architecture. Stroll from Marché Centrale tram-stop, down **Blvd Mohammed V** and up **Av Hassan II** to Pl Mohammed V to spot ornate neo-Moorish facades that blend art deco with a dash of traditional Moroccan design. From Pl Mohammed V, head up Blvd Rachidi to the dilapidated **Cathédrale du Sacré Coeur**. Its tall white towers, pinpricked by stained glass, have nods to Moroccan as well as European architecture.

Casablanca's *medina* is a ramshackle quarter, dating primarily from the 19th century. Still densely populated, it can be explored in a couple of hours. Originally there were three main sections: a bourgeois area with consuls, merchants and Europeans; a *mellah*, or Jewish neighbourhood; and the *tnaker* housing rural migrants (the term refers to a compound with a cactus hedge). The medina's **Grand Mosque** was built by Sultan Sidi Mohammed Ibn Abdallah at the end of the 18th century to celebrate the recapture of Anfa from the Portuguese.

For further insight into Morocco's Jewish community, it's worth making the easy 20-minute stroll from Beauséjour tram-stop to the **Jewish Museum**

(81 Rue Chasseur Jules Gros, Quarter Oasis, T0522-994940, www.casajewish museum.com, Mon-Fri 1000-1700, Sun 1100-1500, 50dh). This villa, once a home for Jewish orphans, now holds a collection of photographs, religious items, jewellery, costumes and artisanal objects.

Quartier des Habous is a suburb planned by the French to resemble the architecture of a traditional Moroccan medina and to provide housing for migrants flooding into Casablanca. If you've got souvenir shopping to do, the souk here sells all the typical Moroccan crafts, including carpets, slippers and leatherware. It's 4 km southeast of the central city. The easiest way to get here is by *petit taxi*.

Where to stay

€€€ Hotel Les Saisons
19 Rue el Oraibi Jilali, T0522-481898,
www.hotellessaisonsmaroc.ma.
The contemporary rooms here are a comfortable choice and come with all the mod-cons. Staff are helpful, there's a decent restaurant on site and the central location, very near the medina, is a bonus. Breakfast and Wi-Fi included.

€€ Hotel Transatlantique
79 Rue Chaouia, T0522-294551,
www.transatcasa.com.
In business since 1922, the Transatlantique claims to be Casablanca's oldest hotel. Public areas are replete with bundles of carved wood and art deco detailing, although the rooms themselves are rather plain. Downstairs there's a piano bar and nightclub, so go for a room on a higher floor to avoid the noise. Breakfast and Wi-Fi included.

€ Hotel Guynemer
2 Rue Mohammed Belloul, T0522-275764, www.guynemerhotel.net.
Exceptionally friendly and helpful, the Guynemer is one of Casablanca's top budget choices. The small rooms (from 350dh) with a/c and satellite TV are suffering from some wear and tear, but it's quiet, clean and very central. Breakfast and Wi-Fi included.

Restaurants

€€€ Rick's Cafe
248 Rue Sour Jdid, T0522-274207.
Something of an institution among visitors to the city, this restaurant plays on Casablanca's Hollywood connection with a piano player and *Casablanca* on a continuous loop downstairs. The menu has something for everyone from classic French to Moroccan, and there's ambience in spades. Alcohol served.

€€ Sqala
Av des Almohades, T0522-260960.
Tue-Sun.
Popular for good reason. The Moroccan and French dishes served up here are some of the best in the city, and the location, set in the 18th century fortified bastion at the edge of the medina, can't be beaten. Come here for lunch in the garden, scattered with fountains and cannons.

€ Ifrane
Rue Tata.
Seriously good value. Ifrane serves up a big selection of brochettes, French mains and sandwiches. Service is swift and on-the-ball, and portions are generous. Bag a table streetside to watch the world go by.

From the rest of Europe

Budget airlines **EasyJet** and **Ryanair** fly direct to Marrakech from multiple European cities including Barcelona, Berlin, Frankfurt, Madrid, Nice, Paris and Rome. RAM flies direct out of main western European airports to Casablanca. Air France ⓘ *www.airfrance.com*, flies out of Paris to Casablanca as well.

From North America

RAM flies to Casablanca from Montreal and New York. (Flight time New York to Casablanca, six hours 40 minutes.) Flights with most other carriers operating out of North America include a change of planes.

From Africa and the Middle East

RAM runs regular services between Casablanca and many African cities including Cairo, Dakar, Tunis and the Canary Islands (Las Palmas). Middle Eastern RAM destinations from Casablanca include Beirut and Istanbul. A number of other regional carriers fly direct from their hub cities to Casablanca; these include Egypt Air ⓘ *www.egyptair.com* (from Cairo); **Emirates** ⓘ *www.emirates.com* (from Dubai); and **Turkish Airlines** ⓘ *www.turkishairlines.com* (from Istanbul).

Sea

If your trip is focusing on central Morocco then you are most likely to fly in to Marrakech. However, **ferries** are also a viable option from southern Europe. The shortest ferry crossings from Europe to Morocco are from Tarifa, Algeciras or Gibraltar to Tangier or Ceuta. Longer crossings run from Almería and Sète, France, to Melilla and Nador. Ceuta and Melilla are Spanish enclaves so you cross a land border in Africa. Algeciras to Ceuta is fast but the advantage is lost at the Fnideq land border crossing into Morocco. This means that in most cases Algeciras to Tangier is the most convenient crossing; Tangier is the northernmost point on the Moroccan rail network and (almost) the starting point of the autoroute down to Casablanca.

When you leave Spain for Morocco, your passport is checked by the Spanish authorities before boarding. Moroccan border formalities are undertaken on board: you fill in a disembarkation form and have your passport stamped at a *guichet*, generally as you get on board. Leaving Morocco, you fill in an embarkation form and departure card, which are stamped by the port police before getting on the boat. (Various people will offer to sell you the police *fiches* but they can be found free when you check in.) When you travel from Spain to Spanish enclaves Ceuta and Melilla, this does not apply.

A good website providing details of all main services (boats and hydrofoils) between Europe and Morocco is www.directferries.com.

Services to Tangier

The main ferry route between Spain and Morocco is the Algeciras–Tangier passenger and car service (note that it is booked solid for cars in summer and around Muslim feast days). **Baleària** ① www.balearia.com, **FRS** ① www.frs.es, and **Trasmediterranea** ① www.trasmediterranea.es, are the three main companies operating on this route. The ferry terminal in Algeciras is near the town centre. It has a ticket office and money-changing facilities. There are similar facilities in the Tangier terminal. The journey takes 1½ hours, with between six and 10 services a day in each direction, with some seasonal variation. One-way passenger fares start from passenger only/including car €29/133, children from four to 12 years old are half price and under four-year-olds are free.

FRS run a weekly high-speed **hydrofoil** service from Gibraltar to Tangier (usually on Fridays). The crossing time is 1½ hours and fares start from passenger only/including car €52/185. **FRS** and **InterShipping** ① www.intershipping.es, are the main ferries running from Tarifa to Tangier. Between them, there are 10 departures daily from Tarifa with a one-hour journey time to Tangier. Fares cost from €39.50 passenger only or €125 including car.

Ferry travel tips…

- Book early if you want to travel in the summer months with a car; ferries are booked solid months in advance, as Moroccans working in Europe return home to visit family.
- Be early for your ferry, allowing at least an hour to clear the police and customs, particularly when departing from Tangier.
- Be cautious about scheduling onward journeys on the same day, in view of the delays.
- It is usually cheaper to buy a return, rather than two singles.
- Tickets can be bought at either the ferry terminals or at numerous ticket agents in port towns.
- The ferries have adequate facilities, including bars, restaurants, lounges, as well as a bureau de change.
- On board food and drink are on the expensive side and can be paid for in both dirhams and euro.

Grandi Navi Veloct runs car and passenger ferry services from Sète in the South of France, two-to-three times weekly to Tangier. Book via www.southernferries.co.uk. Single fares passenger only/including car from Sète to Tangier start at 71/300. These are relatively luxurious services, with a journey of 36 hours.

Arrival in Tangier Arriving by ferry in Tangier can be a pain in the neck. Getting off the boat and going through customs can take ages, and various hustlers will be on hand to misinform innocents abroad as they emerge from the ferry terminal. For inexperienced travellers, arrival by ferry in Tangier can be intimidating.

Passport formalities are accomplished on board. Once off the boat, there are various exchange facilities but ATMs are only available at banks in the city centre.

Onward transport options from Tangier are train (**ONCF**) or bus. Trains run from the Tangier-Moughougha station (also spelt Morora), out beyond the old bull ring and the city limits, 10 km away. Take a sky-blue *petit taxi*, or a Mercedes share taxi. Generally, there are four train departures a day from Tangier-Moughougha to Casa-Voyageurs in Casablanca. The night departure, around 2130, goes through to Marrakech, arrival 0800, and has couchettes.

Inter-city **CTM** buses for main northern Moroccan towns run from outside the port gates. If there is no departure to suit you, take a *petit taxi* (15dh) to the main bus station (*gare routière*), which is 2 km away. There are six-passenger Mercedes taxis here for Tetouan (20dh) and other destinations.

Services to Ceuta
Algeciras to Ceuta connections are operated by the same ferry companies that run to Tangier, and from the same terminal in Algeciras. The crossing takes one hour with FRS and 1½ hours with other companies, with each company running four-to-five departures daily. Fares one way passenger only/including car are from €35/120. It is possible to buy tickets at either terminal or from numerous agents. It's important to note that should you need to overnight, accommodation in Ceuta is more expensive than in Morocco.

Arrival in Ceuta Ceuta is a popular port. Once off the ferry, you take a bus to the border from Plaza de la Constitución in the town centre. Spanish customs is generally quick; the Moroccan customs can be slow for those with their own car. From Fnideq on the Moroccan side of the frontier, Mercedes taxis to Tetouan cost 20dh a head. Moroccan banks have exchange facilities near the frontier.

Services to Melilla and Nador
Almería to Melilla is an eight-hour crossing, run by **Trasmediterranea**. The service is much used by migrant workers originating from the eastern Rif. One-way passenger fares start at passenger only/including car €37/131. The Almería to Nador service has daily sailings in winter, and up to 18 sailings a week in summer. Fares cost from passenger only/including car €50/185. The company also operate a further service between Málaga and Melilla, daily at 1430 (excluding Mondays). The crossing takes 7½ hours and fares cost the same as from Almeria to Melilla. **Grandi Navi Veloct** runs car and passenger ferry services from Sète in the South of France, two-to-three times weekly to Nador. Book via www.southernferries.co.uk. Single fares from Sète to Nador passenger only/including car €62/259. These are relatively luxurious services, with a journey time of 36 hours.

Arrival in Nador Buses and Mercedes taxis leave from a terminal at the end of the Avenue des FAR, close to the waterfront (buses for Melilla from here). There is another bus terminal (CTM and others) in the town centre, close to the Municipality.

Arrival in Melilla The Spanish-Moroccan border is best reached by bus from the central Plaza de España, 10 minutes' walk from the ferry terminus. The border can be crossed in five minutes on a good day. At peak times of year (Easter Week, end of August), the process can be much slower. You need to fill out a Moroccan entry card before getting to the passport window. Various people will try to sell you these, otherwise ask for one at the window and return to your place in the queue at the window. Once over on the Moroccan side at Beni Enzar, there are Mercedes taxis and a bus to Nador.

Getting around

When planning a trip in Morocco, remember that the distances are great and that long trips on buses can be tiring. Bus journeys are often excruciatingly slow, even over relatively short distances. To make maximum use of your time, especially if you don't mind dozing on a bus, take night buses to cover the longer distances. If you have sufficient funds, then there is always the option of internal flights – although these may not always fit in with your schedule. Public transport is reasonably priced, and the train network is good and receives plenty of investment, although it doesn't cover the whole country. Car hire can be expensive; although you may be able to get a small car for 1800-2500dh a week, you still have petrol or diesel costs on top of this. In many places, however, a car enables you to reach places which are otherwise inaccessible.

Air

Royal Air Maroc ① www.royalairmaroc.com, operates domestic flights, most routed via Casablanca and requiring waits in the airport. Cities served include Essaouira, Fès, Marrakech, and Ouarzazate. There are also limited direct flights between Marrakech and Fès. For **RAM** enquiries, call T089-000 0800. All major towns have RAM agencies, generally on the main boulevard.

Road

Bicycles and motorcycles

Mountain bikes, mopeds and sometimes small motorcycles can be hired in tourist towns. There is no shortage of mechanics to fix bikes and mopeds. Trains, buses and even *grands taxis* will take bikes for a small fee. Some European companies now run cycling holidays, with bikes being carried on vans on the longer stretches. Off-road biking is popular in the Gorges du Dadès.

If you go touring with a bike or motorcycle, beware of the sun. Wear gloves and cover those bits of exposed skin between helmet and T-shirt. For motorcyclists, helmets are compulsory, and *gendarmes* will be happy to remind you of the fact.

Riding a motorbike in Morocco is even more testing than driving a car. Watch out for stray pedestrians and note that vehicle drivers will not show you much respect. Where flocks of animals are straying across the road, try not to drive between a single animal and the rest of the flock, as it may well try to charge back to join the rest. Use your horn. If you are going to go off-road, wear boots and make sure your tyres are in tiptop condition.

Theft from bicycle paniers is a problem. Anything loosely attached to your bike can disappear when you are being besieged by a horde of children in an isolated village.

Bus

Domestic bus services are plentiful. Price variations are small, but the quality of service varies enormously. Broadly speaking, don't bother with the small bus companies if a suitable alternative is available to your destination (train, **Supratours** bus, CTM bus or *grand taxi*). For early morning services it's worth getting your ticket in advance; this rule also applies at peak times, such as the end of Ramadan and around Aïd el Kebir (two months after the end of Ramadan), when many Moroccans are travelling. You usually have to pay for baggage to be stored under the bus (5dh). On smaller buses, where there's no luggage compartment, you will find that there is a man who helps stow luggage on the roof; it's common practice to tip him a couple of dirhams.

The safest and most comfortable service is with **Supratours** ⓘ *www.oncf. ma*, which is run by the national railway company and covers the destinations not reached by the rail network. Next best is CTM (**Compagnie de transport marocain**) ⓘ *www.ctm.ma*. Often (but not always) CTM services have their own separate terminal away from the main *gare routière* (inter-city bus station). Both **Supratours** and CTM buses usually run on time, and their buses are comfortable, modern and come with air conditioning.

Local bus companies Other private bus companies are generally much slower, apart from a few *rapide* services – try **Trans-Ghazala**. There are regional companies, like **SATAS** (which serves much of the south), and all sorts of minor companies with names like **Pullman du Sud**. While such buses get to parts that CTM and **Supratours** cannot reach, they are often slow. Bus terminals have a range of ticket windows (*guichets*), displaying destinations and times of departure. Several companies may serve the same destination and, as you head into the bus station, you may be approached by touts who will urge you to prefer one company over another. In rural areas, there are also minivan services between villages not serviced by the bigger bus companies. These generally don't operate to a schedule and leave when the driver has enough passengers. Vehicles used by many private bus companies do not conform to high safety standards. Drivers are severely underpaid and, to make up for their low wages, may leave half-full, aiming to pick up extra passengers (whom they won't have to declare to their employers) en route. This makes for a slow, stop/go service. On routes worked by several companies, drivers race each other to be first to pick up passengers in the next settlement. Given the poor condition of the vehicles and the often narrow roads, accidents are inevitable.

City buses Most towns have city buses although these can be exceedingly crowded, and, as they rarely have air-conditioning, they are extremely hot in the height of summer. It's usually more preferable to take a *petit taxi*.

Car hire See also box, opposite.
As distances are great, having a car makes a huge difference to the amount of ground you can cover. All the main hire car companies are represented, and there are numerous small companies, which vary hugely in reliability. A good deal would give you a Fiat Uno for 500dh a day, unlimited mileage, although some Marrakech agencies can be cheaper. The Peugeot 205 is felt to be a more reliable small car, with slightly higher clearance and better road holding. If you're planning to drive on unsealed routes, hire a suitable off-road vehicle (see Off-road driving, below). In general, you will need dirhams to pay, as only the larger agencies take credit cards. They will take an imprint of your credit card as a guarantee.

There is huge demand for hire cars during the Christmas and Easter breaks. Before hiring, check for scratches and especially tyre condition (this includes spare tyre), presence of jack and warning triangle (not compulsory but very useful), working lights and safety belts. Always try to have the mobile phone number of an agency representative in case of emergency.

Car insurance The best agencies will provide all-risk insurance. A good agency will also have agreements with garages across Morocco for repairs. The garage will talk to the agency about the nature of the repairs, and the matter will be handled. If the damage is your fault (eg because you have taken the car onto rough tracks in breach of contract), you will be responsible for covering the cost of repairs. In the case of an accident, report to the nearest gendarmerie or police post to obtain a written report, known as a *constat de police*, stating who is at fault; otherwise the insurance will be invalid. Depending on the type of insurance, the client pays a percentage of the cost of repairs: a *sans franchise* contract means that you will have nothing to pay; a 50% franchise means that you pay 50% more than rental cost, so that in a case of an accident, you pay only 50% cost of repairs.

Taking your car to Morocco

Foreigners are allowed temporary import of a private vehicle for up to six months in total (be it one or several visits) per calendar year. Documents required are car registration documents and a Green Card from your insurance company, valid in Morocco, which will be inspected at the border along with your International Driving Licence (or national licence). The car will be entered in the driver's passport and checked on leaving the country to ensure that it has not been sold without full taxes being paid. It should be noted that some car hire companies do not allow customers to take cars into Morocco from Europe. The minimum age of driving is 21. Car entry is not possible from Mauritania.

On arrival, complete customs form D 16 bis, called 'Declaration d'importation temporaire', and specify the intended duration of stay. Visitors arriving at the border without valid recognized insurance cover may take out a short-term policy available at any frontier post. A customs carnet is required for a trailer caravan but not for motor caravans. If using a vehicle or caravan of which you are not the owner, carry with you a letter of authorization signed by the owner. Customs officials may require a detailed inventory in duplicate of all valuable items but routine items such as camping equipment need not be listed.

Fuel and other costs Hire cars in Morocco generally run on petrol (*super*) rather than diesel. You may have to pay for the petrol already in the tank of your hire car, but, usually, the car will be almost empty, and you fill up yourself. In April 2016, diesel in Morocco was around 7.5dh per litre, petrol 12.5dh. A fill-up (*le plein*) for a Fiat Uno or a Clio costs around 400dh. In such a car, 250dh does the four-hour trip on winding mountain roads from Marrakech to Ouarzazate. A fill-up with diesel for a Pajero 4WD costs around 600dh, and on this the vehicle will do the 800-km trip from Marrakech to Zagora and back.

Many cars do not as yet use unleaded petrol (*sans plomb*) – if you have one that does, you may find it difficult to refill your tank, especially in the south. In any case, you should remember to fill up whenever possible in remote areas, preferably at one of the larger petrol stations (**Shell**, **Mobil**, **CMH** in most cities; **Ziz** in the south). There have been cases of petrol being watered down, with unfortunate results, in certain places; new-looking service stations in towns are best.

Should you need tyre repairs, prices vary. Expect to pay upwards of 50dh as a foreigner in a hurry in a small town, rather less if you have time to wait in some rural outpost.

Road safety Always drive more slowly than you would in Europe. There are a number of dangerous stretches of road which you may have to negotiate in your hire car. The new N11 Casablanca to Marrakech motorway has much improved road transport between the two cities, but care must be taken on the Rabat to Fès N1, especially as there are few crash barriers. Other roads, such as Ouarzazate to Skoura and Agdz to Nekob, seem to be in excellent condition but can also be hazardous, tempting you to drive too fast and then surprising you with sudden dips and turns. Much concentration is needed on the four-hour drive along the winding, mountainous N9 from Marrakech to Ouarzazate, via the Tizi-n-Tichka, where fog and icy surfaces are possible in winter.

Tip...
Road accidents cost the Moroccan state about US$1.2 billion a year, according to official figures. In 2013 6870 people were killed on the roads in Morocco.

In the Middle and High Atlas barriers are put across the road on routes to Azrou, Ifrane, Midelt and over the Tizi-n-Tichka and Tizi-n-Test when snow blocks roads.

Highway code The Moroccan highway code follows the international model. Speeds are limited to 120 kph on the autoroute, 100 kph on main roads, 60 kph on approaches to urban areas and 40 kph in urban areas. Speed restriction signs do not always follow a logical sequence. The wearing of seat belts is compulsory outside the cities and is strictly enforced by the police. There are two types of police on the roads: the blue-uniformed urban police and the grey-uniformed gendarmes in rural areas. The latter are generally stationed outside large villages, at busy junctions or under shady eucalyptus trees near bends with no-overtaking marks. It is traditional to slow down for the gendarmes, although as a foreigner driving a hire car you will generally be waved through. Note that the police are empowered to levy on-the-spot fines for contravention of traffic regulations. Fines are now quite severe in response to the high number of fatal accidents due to careless driving.

Off-road driving Off-roading is increasingly popular for exploring the remote corners of Morocco. In addition to well over 10,000 km of surfaced road, Morocco has several thousand kilometres of unsurfaced tracks, generally referred to as pistes. Some of these can be negotiated with care by an ordinary car with high clearance. Most, however, require a 4WD vehicle. Remember that you are responsible for damage if you take a standard car into areas suitable only for 4WD vehicles. Those available in Morocco include the Suzuki Gemini (two people) and the Vitara (four people), at around 800dh per day; long-base Mitsubishi Pajeros (six people) are hired at 900-1000dh per day. Toyotas are said to be the best desert option. Landrovers are very uncomfortable for long cross-country runs on road, especially in summer without air conditioning. When hiring an all-terrain vehicle, try to ascertain that the agency you are hiring from has a reliable, well-maintained fleet. Make sure that the vehicle will go into four-wheel drive easily.

Fans of 4WDs should plan their trips carefully, noting that bad weather can impede travel. Snow blocks mountain tracks in winter, while rain and melt-water can make them impassable. Ask locals about conditions. In many areas, pistes are no longer well maintained as they have been made superfluous by the presence of a new tarmac road. What's more, not all road improvement works are of very high quality: a hard winter can destroy mountain tarmac or wash large quantities of rubble and clay on to the road surface.

If you are driving into remote areas, always travel with two vehicles so that there is always a spare vehicle to get you out if something goes wrong in the hostile desert environment. If you are unused to off-road vehicles, you can employ the services of a driver (around 300dh a day). He will know the routes well and be able to chat to locals and other drivers about the state of the tracks. When out in wild country, never take an unknown piste if a storm is on its way or as night is falling. Check the names of villages on your route before you leave, and remember that some tracks lead to abandoned mining operations rather than helpful hamlets. Do not go full tilt into a ford without checking the depth of the water first by wading in. You do not want to be stranded in an *oued* in full flood. Remember that progress will be slow, and that, after wet weather, you may have to dig/pull vehicles out. Distances tend to be measured in hours rather than in kilometres.

Car parking Parking is fairly easy in towns, although parking meters rarely function. Usually, a watchman, identified by blue overalls and a metal badge, will guard your car from theft and damage; give him some spare change, say 10dh, when you return to your vehicle. At night, it is essential to leave your vehicle in a place where there is a night watchman (*le gardien de nuit*); all good hotels and streets with restaurants will have such a figure who will keep an eye out. Note that red and white curb markings mean no parking.

Hitchhiking

It is possible to hitchhike in Morocco. There are trucks which go to and from Europe, and drivers can sometimes be persuaded to take a passenger. In remote areas, vans and trucks may pick up passengers for a bargained price. However, don't count on hitching, as vehicles out in the sticks are generally packed with locals. Landrover taxis (jeeps) and Mercedes Transit vans are not run for hitchhikers – they are *grands taxis* and charge a price for a ride. It's not advisable to hitch anywhere as a solo traveller, particularly as a solo female traveller.

Taxi

Grand taxi Long distance *grands taxis*, generally Mercedes 200 saloon cars, run over fixed routes between cities or between the city centre and outlying suburbs. There is a fixed price for each route and passengers pay for a place. There are six spaces in a Mercedes, nine in a Peugeot 504 estate car. In a Peugeot estate, the best places are undoubtedly at the front, or, if you are quite small, right at the back. The middle place in the middle row is probably the worst. Taxis wait until they are full before departing.

> **Tip...**
> You may wish to pay for two places in a *grand taxi*, in order to be comfortable at the front (and be able to wear a safety belt) or to start your journey more promptly.

Between towns, *grands taxis* are quicker than trains or buses and, normally, only a little more expensive. Each town has a rank for *grands taxis*, which is generally next to the main bus station. The drivers cry out the name of their destination and, as you near the taxi station, you may be approached by touts eager to help you find a taxi.

In mountain areas, the same system applies, although the vehicles are Mercedes transit vans (where there is tarmac) or Landrovers; these have spaces for two people next to the driver and 10 in the back.

Petit taxi *Petits taxis* are used within towns and are generally Fiat Unos and Palios. They are colour-coded by town. Officially they are metered, with an initial minimum fare, followed by increments of time and distance. There is a 50% surcharge after 2100. A *petit taxi* may take up to three passengers. In Marrakech drivers are renowned for not using their meters and trying to charge whatever they like. In Fès and Mèknes, nearly all drivers will switch on the meters without being asked. In some cities (notably Casablanca but also in Marrakech) drivers allow themselves to pick up other passengers (up to three in total) en route if they are going the same way, thus earning a double fee for part of the route. Taxi drivers welcome a tip; many of them are not driving their own vehicles and make little more than 100dh a day. In terms of price, a short run between old and new town in Marrakech will set you back 10-15dh.

Rail

The ONCF (**Office National des Chemins de Fer**) ⓘ *www.oncf.ma*, runs an efficient though generally slowish service between major cities. There is 1900 km of railway line, the central node being at the railway town of Sidi Kacem, some 46 km north of Meknès. Coming into Casablanca airport, you can take the blue Bidhaoui shuttle train to Casa-Voyageurs station on the main north–south line. This line runs from Tangier to Marrakech, with significant stations being Kénitra, Sidi Kacem, Salé, Rabat, Casa-Voyageurs, Settat, and Benguerir. The ONCF's main west–east route does Casa-Voyageurs to Oujda, the main stations on this route being Rabat, Sidi Kacem, Meknès and Fès. A fast double-decker service connects Casablanca with Fès in three hours 20 minutes. There are also frequent trains from Marrakech to Fès. ONCF timetables are available at all main stations and can be accessed through their website. The **Supratours** timetable connects with arriving and departing trains from Marrakech and Fès train stations, and you can book your connecting bus journey when you purchase your train ticket.

Fares and journey times
Prices are reasonable. A first-class single ticket, Marrakech to Fès (around eight hours), is 311dh in first class, 206dh in second class. Services between Casablanca and Marrakech (3½ hours) are 148dh in first class and 95dh in second class. Fès to Mèknes (45 minutes) is 32dh. First-class compartments are spacious and generally quieter than second class. Second-class rail fares are slightly more expensive than CTM bus fares, but the train is also faster, safer and more reliable. Trains normally have a snack trolley.

Essentials A-Z

Accident and emergency

Police: T19 (T190 in Marrakech).
Fire brigade: T15 (T150 in Marrakech).
Larger towns will have an **SOS Médecins** (private doctor on-call service) and almost all towns of any size have a pharmacy on duty at night, the *pharmacie de garde*. Any large hotel should be able to give you the telephone/address of these. For most ailments, a *médecin généraliste* (GP) will be sufficient. In Marrakech there is a **private ambulance service** at 10 Rue Fatima Zohra, T0524-443724.

Children

Moroccans love children, which means that travelling with children in Morocco can be a particularly rewarding experience.

If you hire a car via an international agency, specify the sort of child seats you require and do not be surprised if your requirements get lost somewhere along the way. Most local car hire agencies will be unlikely to have children's seats. Overall your best bet is to bring one from home. If you will be doing a lot of driving, make sure you have things in the car to entertain kids. When walking around busy streets and squares, keep a tight hold of children, as the traffic and throngs of people are often hectic.

On the health front, make sure your kids are up to date with all their vaccinations. Be particularly aware of the hazards for children of too much sun and heat: they should use a very high-factor sunscreen, wear a hat and keep well hydrated. Tap water in major cities is safe to drink, but some children may still react to drinking different water. The best idea is to stick to bottled water rather than risk it. In rural areas, always give children bottled drinks or mineral water. Try and stay in hotels with pools to keep children happy and cool. For other health advice, see page 288.

Customs and duty free

Foreign currency may be imported freely. Visitors may take in, free of duty, 400 g of tobacco, 200 cigarettes or 50 cigars and personal items. You may also take your pet to Morocco. It will need a health certificate no more than 10 days old and an anti-rabies certificate less than 6 months old.

Prohibited items

There are severe penalties for possession of or trade in narcotic **drugs**: 3 months to 5 years' imprisonment plus fines (see also Drugs, below). Be aware that **wild animal pelts** and some other items openly on sale in Morocco cannot be legally imported into the EU. This includes products made of animal pelts. Live wild animals may not be exported from Morocco and their import into EU is in most cases illegal.

Disabled travellers

Morocco really cannot be said to be well adapted to the needs of the disabled traveller. However, don't let this deter you. Some travel companies are beginning to specialize in exciting holidays, tailor-made for individuals depending on their level of disability. *Nothing Ventured* edited by Alison Walsh (Harper Collins) gives personal accounts of worldwide journeys by disabled travellers, plus advice and listings.

Dress

In coastal resorts, you can wear shorts and expose arms and shoulders. However, when wandering round medinas and heading out into the countryside, both men and women should cover shoulders and wear at least knee-length shorts and skirts. Expect lots of remarks and attention if you do go wandering round the souks in your running shorts. In the High Atlas wear trousers rather than shorts and T-shirts rather than vests, even if you're trekking in mid-summer, to show respect for the local culture. A lot of importance is given to looking smart and respectable in Morocco and the unkempt, deliberately scruffy European traveller is really a bit of an alien to them. Dressing tidily will go a long way in helping you interact with locals.

Tip...
Inland, winter is cold. Night temperatures in the desert and at altitude are low all the year, so a fleece is handy, even as a pillow.

Drugs

Kif or marijuana represents a good source of income for small farmers in the Rif. However, the European Union has put pressure on Morocco to stop production. There is no serious attempt to stop Moroccans from having a gentle smoke, and kif is also consumed in the form of *maâjoun* cakes, a local variant of hash brownies, which have been known to lead to much merriment at otherwise staid occasions. However, as a tourist, under no circumstances do you want to be caught by the police in the possession of drugs of any kind. Anyone caught exporting illegal drugs can expect a harsh penalty.

Electricity

Morocco has a fairly reliable electricity supply of 220V, using continental European round 2-pin plugs. In some more remote areas, however, there is no mains electricity.

Embassies and consulates

For all Moroccan embassies and consulates abroad and for all foreign embassies and consulates in Morocco, see http://embassy.goabroad.com.

Gay and lesbian travellers

Same-sex sexual activity is illegal in Morocco and can be punished with up to 3 years' imprisonment and fines. Although this law is only sporadically enforced (and very unlikely to be enforced at all on foreigners) gay travellers should be discreet about their sexual orientation while in public, particularly if they have a Moroccan partner. Despite this, Morocco and, in particular, Marrakech, attracts a large number of gay travellers. Same-sex couples should find they have no problems booking double bedrooms, as long as they steer clear of the cheapest budget options. Gay male travellers should note that body language is very different in Morocco. Physical closeness between men in the street does not necessarily indicate a gay relationship.

Health

Before you go

No vaccinations are required unless you're travelling from a country where yellow fever and/or cholera frequently occurs. You should be up to date with **polio**, **tetanus**, and **typhoid** protection. If you are going to be travelling in rural areas where hygiene is often a bit rough and ready, then having a **hepatitis B** shot is a good thing. You could also have a **cholera** shot, although there is no agreement among medics on how effective this is.

Health risks

Acute mountain sickness This can strike from about 3000 m upwards and, in general, is more likely to affect those who ascend rapidly (for example by plane) and those who over-exert themselves. Acute mountain sickness takes a few hours or days to come on and presents with headache, lassitude, dizziness, loss of appetite, nausea and vomiting. When trekking to high altitude, some time spent walking at medium altitude, getting fit and acclimatizing is beneficial.

Stomach upsets Some form of **diarrhoea** or intestinal upset is almost inevitable; the standard advice is to be careful with drinking water and ice; if you have any doubts about the water then boil, filter and treat it. In a restaurant, buy bottled water or ask where the water has come from. Food can also pose a problem: be wary of salads if you don't know whether they have been washed or not. In major cities, tap water should be fine to drink, though many visitors stick to bottled water to make sure. Out in the sticks you should definitely only drink the bottled variety.

Malaria There is a very minimal risk of malaria in Morocco. Usually prophylaxis is not advised, but check before you go; if you are going to be travelling in remote parts of the Saharan provinces, then a course of malaria tablets may be recommended.

Rabies A rabies vaccination before travel can be considered but, if bitten, always seek urgent medical attention – whether or not you have been previously vaccinated – after first cleaning the wound and treating with an iodine-base disinfectant or alcohol.

Medical services

Fès There is an all-night chemist at the **Municipalité de Fès**, Blvd Moulay Youssef, T0535-623380 (2000-0800). During the day try **Bahja**, Av Mohammed V, T0535-622441, or **Bab Ftouh** at Bab Ftouh, T0535-649135. **Hôpital Ghassani** is at Quartier Dhar Mehraz, T0535-622776.

Marrakech Pharmacie Centrale, 166 Av Mohammed V, T0524-430151. **Pharmacie de Paris**, 120 Av Mohammed V, T0524-447663. There is also an all-night chemist, **Pharmacie de Nuit**, at Rue Khalid Ben Oualid, Guéliz, T0524-430415 (doctor sometimes available). Private hospitals are **Polyclinique du Sud**, 2 Rue de Yougoslavie, T0524-447999, and **Polyclinique Les Narcisses**, Camp el Ghoul, 112 Route de Targa, T0524-447575.

Meknès **Pharmacie d'Urgence**, Pl Administrative, T0535-523375, daily 0830-2030. **Hôpital Mohammed V**, T0535-521134. **Hôpital Moulay Ismaïl**, Av des FAR, T0535-522805. Probably the best of the bunch is **Polyclinique Cornette-de-St-Cyr**, 22 Esplanade du Docteur Giguet, T0535-520262.

Further information
Fit for Travel (UK), www.fitfortravel. nhs.uk. A-Z of vaccine and travel health advice requirements for each country. **Foreign and Commonwealth Office (FCO) (UK)**, www.fco.gov.uk. **National Travel Health Network and Centre (NaTHNaC)**, www.nathnac.org. **World Health Organisation**, www.who.int.

Insurance

Before departure, it is vital to take out full travel insurance. There is a wide variety of policies to choose from, so shop around. At the very least, the policy should cover personal effects and medical expenses, including the possibility of medical evacuation by air ambulance to your own country. Make sure that it also covers all activities that you might do while away: trekking or surfing, for example. There is no substitute for suitable precautions against petty crime, but if you do have something stolen while in Morocco, report the incident to the nearest police station and ensure you get a police report and case number. You will need these to make any claim from your insurance company.

Internet

Internet cafés can be found in city centres and even quite out-of-the-way places. Areas of cheap hotels attracting budget travellers will have several cybercafés. In the main tourist centres, most accommodation options and many cafés and restaurants have Wi-Fi.

Language

Darija (Moroccan Arabic) and Tamazight (Berber) are the official language of Morocco, but nearly all Moroccans with a secondary education have some French and a smattering of English. In many situations French is more or less understood. However, you will come across plenty of people who have had little opportunity to go to school and whose French may be limited to a very small number of phrases. Moroccan Arabic in the cities and the various Tamazight dialects in the mountains remain the languages of everyday life. Attempts to use a few words and phrases, no matter how stumblingly, will be appreciated. Those who have learnt some Arabic elsewhere often find Moroccan Arabic difficult. It is characterized by a clipped quality (the vowels just seem to disappear), and the words taken from classical Arabic are often very different from those used in the Middle East. In addition, there is the influence of the Berber languages and the use of a mixture of French and Spanish terms, often heavily 'Moroccanized'.

If you wish to learn Moroccan Arabic, **ALIF** (Arabic Language Institute in Fès, T0535-624850, www.alif-fes.com), an offshoot of the American Language Centre, has a very good reputation. They organize a range of long and short courses in both classical and Moroccan Arabic. Courses in Amazigh languages can be set up, too.

Media

Press

Moroccan newspapers are produced in Arabic, French and Spanish. The main political parties all have their newspapers. From the mid-1990s, the general tone of the press became increasingly critical, dealing with issues once taboo. Of the daily newspapers, *Le Matin* (www.lematin.ma) gives the official line. The party press includes *L'Opinion* (www.lopinion.ma), *Libération* (www.libe.ma) and *Al Bayane*. These newspapers are cheap and give an insight into Morocco and its politics. Coverage of overseas news is limited, but sheds interesting light on attitudes to major international issues.

More interesting, and generally better written, are the weekly newspapers, which include *Maroc-Hebdo* and *La Vie économique*. The best discussion of contemporary issues is provided by *Le Journal*, which also provides major economic and business coverage. Morocco's best news magazine is *Tel Quel*, (www.telquel-online.com). *Téléplus* has some cultural events coverage.

For Moroccan news in English, check out the website www.moroccoworld news.com. The main foreign newspapers are available in town centre news kiosks, generally on the evening of publication. As these are expensive for most Moroccans, some kiosks run a 'rent-a-magazine' service for loyal customers. Occasionally, an issue of a foreign news publication with a very critical article on Morocco will fail to be distributed.

Television and radio

Radio Télévision Marocaine (RTM) is the state service, predominantly in Arabic and French. The news is given in Arabic, French and Spanish, with early afternoon summaries in the 3 main Berber languages. All agree that the **RTM** provides humdrum fare – hence the huge popularity of satellite television and alternative local channels **2M** and **Médi 1 TV**. 2M broadcasts North American and European feature films and some local current affairs programmes, while **Médi 1 TV** has mostly entertainment with some current affairs.

The most popular radio stations are **RTM-Inter** and commercial radio station **Médi 1** (www.medi1.com), which gives news and music in Arabic and French.

Money

Currency

US$1 = 9.63dh, UK £1 = 13.89dh, €1 = 10.96dh (May 2016).

The major unit of currency in Morocco is the dirham (dh). In 1 dirham there are 100 centimes. There are coins for 1 centime (very rare), 5, 10, 20 and 50 centimes, and for 1, 2, 5 and 10 dirhams, as well as notes for 20, 50, 100 and 200 dirhams. The coins can be a little confusing. There are 2 sorts of 5 dirham coin: the older and larger cupro-nickel ('silver coloured' version), being phased out, and the new bi-metal version, brass colour on the inside. There is a brownish 20 dirham note, easily confused with the 100 dirham note. The 50 dirham note is green, the 100 dirham is brown and sand colour, and the 200 dirham note is in shades of blue and turquoise. Currency is labelled in Arabic and French.

Note that dirhams may not be taken out of Morocco. If you have excess dirhams, you can exchange them back into euros at a bank on production of exchange receipts, or more easily at an exchange office. There is a fixed rate for changing notes and no commission ought to be charged for this.

Moroccans among themselves sometimes count in older currency units. To the confusion of travellers, many Moroccans refer to francs, which equal 1 centime, and reals, though both these units only exist in speech. Even more confusingly, the value of a real varies from region to region. Unless you are good at mental arithmetic, it's easiest to stick to dirhams.

ATMs

By far the easiest way to manage your money in Morocco is by using your debit or credit card. ATMs (*guichets automatiques*) are plentiful in the centres of towns, though in cities such as Marrkech, Fès and Mèknes, ATMs are few and far between within the medina areas and you may need to go to the *ville nouvelle* to draw out cash. Most ATMs will only allow you to withdraw 2000dh at a time, which unfortunately means that bank withdrawal fees can add up. At weekends and during big public holidays, airport and city-centre ATMs can be temperamental. The most reliable ATMs are those of the **Wafa Bank** (green and yellow livery) and the **BMCI**; **Crédit du Maroc** and **Banque Populaire** are also reliable. In southern towns, **Banque Populaire** is often the only choice. Note that in very rural areas, ATMs are non-existent, so plan ahead and stock up on cash beforehand.

Cash

Most high-end hotels and riads will accept euros as currency, particularly in Marrakech and Essaouira. You can also quite often use euros to pay for tours and excursions at travel agencies and in some large souvenir emporiums. Changing money at a bank is generally a slow, tortuous process. It's a much better idea to use a foreign exchange office.

Credit cards

Credit cards are widely accepted at banks, top hotels, restaurants and big tourist shops. For restaurants, check first before splashing out. Remember to keep all credit card receipts – and, before you sign, check where the decimal marker (a comma in Morocco rather than a dot) has been placed, and that there isn't a zero too many. You don't want to be paying thousands rather than hundreds of dirhams. To reduce problems with card fraud, it makes sense to use a credit card for payments of large items like carpets and hotel bills. If a payment is not legitimate, it is a lot less painful if the transaction is on the credit card rather than drawn from your current account.

Cost of travelling

As a budget traveller, it is possible to get by in Morocco for 350-400dh per day. Your costs can be reduced by having yoghurt and bread and cheese for lunch and staying in rooms with shared bathroom facilities (100dh a night or less). In small towns you can

> **Tip...**
> Buy a Moroccan SIM card for your mobile. If you make more than a couple of Moroccan calls, it will save you money.

TRAVEL TIP

Cost of living for Moroccans

Although prices for many basics can seem very low indeed to those used to prices in European capitals, the cost of living is high for most Moroccans. At one end of the scale, in the mountainous rural areas, Morocco remains a poor country, still on the margins of the cash economy. In these regions, families produce much of their own food and are badly hit in drought years when there is nothing to sell in the souk to generate cash to buy oil, extra flour and sugar. This precariousness means much 'hidden' malnutrition.

Conditions are improving for the city shanty-town dwellers. Here, families will be getting by on 2000dh a month, sometimes much less. The urban middle classes, those with salaried jobs in the public and private sectors, are doing fairly well. A primary school teacher may be on 3000dh a month; a private company employee at the start of their career will make around 3000dh a month, too. This category has access to loans and is seeing a general improvement in living standards. Morocco's top-flight IT technicians, doctors and business people have a plush lifestyle, with villas and servants, available to few Europeans. And, finally, a very small group of plutocrats has long been doing very, very well, thank you.

To put the contrasts in perspective, there are parents for whom the best option is to place their pre-adolescent girls as maids with city families in exchange for 300dh a month. The Amazigh-speaking boy who serves you in the corner shop may be given 50dh a week, plus food and lodging (of a sort). His horizons will be limited to the shop; there will be a trip back to the home village once a year; he may never learn to read. At the other, distant end of the scale, there are couples who can easily spend 40,000dh a semester to purchase an English-language higher education for one of their offspring at the private Al Akhawayn University in Ifrane.

often find accommodation for less than 80dh and during summer there are often options to sleep on the roof (usually around 30dh).

Tip…

Unless you're in a fixed-price emporium, haggling is the name of the game for all the crafts and souvenirs you can buy in Morocco. If you're shopping for fruit in the market, however, note that prices for food are fixed.

Accommodation, food and transport are all relatively cheap compared to Europe and America, and there is a lot to see and do for free. However, this budget does not allow much room for treats, unexpected costs like the frequent small tips expected for minor services, and stocking up on necessities – notably cosmetics and toiletries. Allowing 450dh per day is more realistic.

In top-quality hotels, restaurants, nightclubs and bars, prices are similar to Europe. Marrakech tends to be more expensive for accommodation and dining, though there are still plenty of budget options. Around the 200dh mark, you can get a much better meal in a restaurant than you can in Western Europe.

Opening hours

The working week for businesses is Mon to Fri, with half-day working Sat. On Fri, the lunch break tends to be longer, as the main weekly prayers with sermon are on that day. Official business takes considerably longer during Ramadan.
Banks Open 0830-1130 and 1430-1600 in winter; afternoons 1500-1700 in summer; 0930-1400 during Ramadan.
Museums Many close on a Tue. Hours generally 0900-1200 and 1500-1700, although this can vary considerably.
Post offices Open 0830-1230 and 1430-1830, shorter hours during Ramadan.
Shops Generally 0900-1200 and 1500-1900, although this varies in the big towns.

Post

Posting letters is relatively easy, with the **PTT Centrale** of each town selling the appropriate stamps. Postage costs to Europe are 6dh for a letter and 6.5dh for a postcard. It is best to post the letter in the box inside or just outside this building as these are emptied most frequently. Each **PTT Centrale** will have a post restante section, where letters are kept for a number of weeks. There is a small charge on collection. **American Express** post restante is handled by Voyages Schwartz. Letters to or from Europe can take up to a week.

Public holidays

1 Jan New Year's Day.
1 May Fête du Travail (Labour Day).
9 Jul Fête de la Jeunesse.
30 Jul Fête du Trône. Commemorates the present king Mohammed VI's accession.
20 Aug Anniversaire de la Révolution.
6 Nov Marche Verte/El Massira el Khadhra. Commemorates a march by Moroccan civilians to retake the Spanish-held Saharan territories of Río de Oro and Saguiet El Hamra.
18 Nov Independence Day. Commemorates independence and Mohammed V's return from exile.

Religious holidays

Religious holidays are scheduled according to the Hijna calendar, a lunar-based calendar. The lunar year is shorter than the solar year, so the Muslim year moves forward by 11 days every Christian year.
1 Muharram First day of the Muslim year.
Mouloud Celebration of the Prophet Mohammed's birthday.
Ramadan A month of fasting and sexual abstinence during daylight hours. During Ramadan, the whole country switches to a different rhythm. Public offices open part time, and the general pace slows down during the daytime. No Moroccan would be caught eating in public during the day, and the vast majority of cafés and restaurants, except those frequented by resident Europeans and tourists, are closed. At night, the change in ambience is almost palpable. There is a sense of collective effort, shared with millions of other Muslims worldwide. People who never go out during the rest of the year visit friends and stroll the streets during Ramadan.

Shops stay open late, especially during the second half of the month. Ramadan is an interesting and frustrating time to visit Morocco as a tourist, but probably to be avoided if possible if you need to do business.

Eid el Fitr (the Lesser Aïd) A 2-day holiday ending the month of Ramadan.
Eid el Kebir (the Great Aïd) A 1-day holiday that comes 70 days after Aïd el Fitr. Commemorates how God rewarded Ibrahim's faith by sending down a lamb for him to sacrifice instead of his son. When possible, every family sacrifices a sheep on this occasion.

Safety

Morocco is basically a very safe country, although there is occasional violent street crime in Casablanca and (very rarely) Marrakech. Travelling on public transport, you need to watch your pockets. Do not carry all your money, cards and other valuables in the same place. A money belt is a good idea. Never have more money than you can afford to lose in the pockets of your jeans. Thieves operate best in crowds, getting on and off trains and at bus and taxi stations where they can quickly disappear into an anonymous mass of people.

Be aware of the various skilled con-artists in operation in certain places. Hasslers of various kinds are active in tourist destinations with all sorts of ruses used to try and extract a little money from tourists (though the worst of the hassle has dissipated in recent years). You need to be polite and confident, distant and sceptical and even a little bored by the whole thing. Learn the values of the banknotes quickly (the yellow-brown 100dh and the blue 200dh are the big ones, a red 10dh is no great loss). Keep your wits about you. Remember, you are especially vulnerable stumbling bleary-eyed off that overnight bus.

Should you be robbed, reporting it to the police will take time – but may alert them to the fact that there are thieves operating in a given place. For safety matters with regard to women travelling alone, see page 296.

Security and terrorism

On the night of 14 May 2003, Casablanca was shaken by co-ordinated suicide bomb attacks targeting a Jewish social club and a major hotel. Over 40 Moroccans were murdered. Salafiya-Jihadiya fundamentalist groups organized these murders and the national security forces reacted with a wave of arrests. After 2003, Morocco saw little urban terrorism and violence until the Marrakech bombing of 2011, see page 269. The Moroccan government claims to have broken up 55 terrorist cells since 2003, and there are around 1000 Islamists in the country's jails on terrorist charges. There is tight monitoring of all fundamentalist activity and zero tolerance of anything which might lead to violence. As anything Jewish is an obvious target, there are police outside most synagogues.

Student travellers

Morocco is a good place for the student traveller, as food and accommodation costs are reasonable. Public transport is also very cheap considering the distances covered, but often slow for getting to out-of-the-way places. The youth hostels have been upgraded and most are now well run. However, there are few student discounts of the sort available in Europe.

Telephone

Lots of Moroccans have mobile phones but there are also phone shops or *téléboutiques*, clearly marked in distinctive blue and white livery. They stay open late in summer, are always supervised, have change available and (generally) have telephone directories (*annuaires téléphoniques*). The machines are sometimes old French coin phones, and international calls are no problem. For internal calls, put in several 1dh coins and dial the region code (even if you are in the region), followed by the number (a total of 10 digits beginning 0). For overseas calls, put in at least 3 coins of 5dh, dial 00 and wait for a musical sequence before proceeding. Calls can also be made from the *cabines téléphoniques* at the **PTT Centrale**. Give the number to the telephonist who dials it and then calls out a cabin number where the call is waiting. Note, it is significantly more expensive to phone from a hotel. When calling Morocco from abroad the code is 212 and you then drop the first zero.

Mobile phones

Mobile phone coverage in Morocco is reasonably good, though international roaming prices are expensive. If you're going to be in the country for a decent stint of time and have an unlocked phone, it's well worth buying a local Moroccan SIM card on arrival. SIM cards cost around 20dh and there are various pay-as-you-go packages available that include data usage for smartphones. The main mobile phone companies are **Maroc Telecom** (www.iam.ma) and **Meditel** (www.meditelecom.ma). You will need to bring your passport along when you are purchasing a SIM card.

Time

Morocco follows the UK all year round, with GMT in winter and GMT+1 in summer. Ceuta and Melilla work on Spanish time.

Tipping

This can be a bit of a hidden cost during your stay in Morocco. Tipping is expected in restaurants and cafés, by guides, porters and car park attendants and others who render small services. Make sure you have small change at the ready. Tipping taxi drivers is optional. Do not tip for journeys when the meter has not been used, because the negotiated price will be generous anyway. For porters in hotels, tip around 3dh, on buses 3dh-5dh, and 5dh on trains and in airports.

Tour operators

There are a number of companies that specialize in Morocco. Some of the trekking companies have many years of experience.

UK and Ireland

The Best of Morocco, Delta Pl, 27 Bath Rd, Cheltenham, Gloucestershire, GL53 7TH, T0800-171-2151 (UK only), T01242-77-6500, www.morocco-travel.com. Luxury travel operator offering unlimited flexibility using quality hotels.
Exodus Travels, T0845-805-0348, www.exodus.co.uk. Well-established worldwide operator.
Explore Worldwide, 1 Frederick St, Aldershot, Hants GU11 1LQ, T0845-013-1537, www.exploreworldwide.com. Offers small-group tours throughout the country.

Imaginative Traveller, Camp Green, Debenham, Suffolk, IP14 6LA, T0845-287 2962, www.imaginative-traveller.com. Small-group tours of 8-15 days, with some specialist cycling and trekking tours.
Naturally Morocco, T01239-710814, www.naturallymorocco.com. Recommended, environmentally responsible Morocco-specialist company with lots of Moroccan experience and expertise.

North America
Heritage Tours, 121 West 27th St, Suite 1201, New York 10001, T1-800-378 4555, www.htprivatetravel.com. Custom-designed in-depth itineraries. Specialize in cultural and historic tours, sahara encampments, crafts and architecture.
Sahara Trek, T1-727-421 0218, www.saharatrek.com. Offers weekly inclusive adventure and sightseeing tours. Package to custom-designed. Desert trekking, imperial cities, golf, whitewater rafting, beach resorts, skiing.

Tourist information

For **Moroccan National Tourist Board (ONMT)** locations worldwide, see www.visitmorocco.com.

Morocco on the web
www.emarrakech.info News of the Red City, regularly updated but in French only.
www.north-africa.com Weekly analysis on economics, politics and business. Subscriber service.
www.riadzany.blogspot.com Titled 'The View From Fez', this blog is actually a great round-up of what's going on in Morocco as a whole.

Visas

No visas are required for full passport holders of the UK, USA, Canada, Australia, New Zealand, Canada, Ireland and most EU countries. Passports must be valid for at least 6 months, from the date of entry. On entry travellers will be required to fill in a form with standard personal and passport details, an exercise to be repeated in almost all hotels and guesthouses throughout the country. From the point of entry, travellers can stay in Morocco for 3 months.

Visa extensions
To extent your stay in Morocco requires a visit to the Immigration or Bureau des Etrangers department at the police station of a larger town, as well as considerable patience. An easier option is to leave Morocco for a few days – preferably to Spain, the Canary Islands, or to one of the two Spanish enclaves: Ceuta or Melilla – then return for a further 3 months. People coming into Morocco from either of these Spanish enclaves for a second or third time have on occasion run into problems with the Moroccan customs. With numerous foreigners resident in Marrakech, it may be easiest to arrange visa extensions there. Approval of the extension has to come from Rabat and may take a few days.

Weights and measures

Morocco uses the metric system.

Women travellers

Despite a rather fearsome reputation, Morocco really isn't that difficult to travel in as a solo female traveller. Much of the low-level harassment solo female travellers experience stems from a belief that foreign women have a looser set of morals than Moroccan women – an attitude not helped by the huge number of female tourists having holiday flings with Moroccan men. Yes, you will attract attention and more hassle than male travelling counterparts and, yes, you may have to swat off declarations of love on a semi-regular basis which can all become wearisome, but a street-savvy attitude can limit a lot of potential problems.

Dressing slightly conservatively helps a lot: wear T-shirts instead of strappy singlets, and trousers instead of shorts. Young hustlers are less likely to try on their charms with someone who looks like they know and understand Moroccan traditional culture. Dark sunglasses are a great idea, particularly if you have blue eyes. In more rural areas, some female travellers choose to don a headscarf; although this is unnecessary it can help to ward off would-be harassers.

Stay away from the cheapest of the budget hotels; some moonlight as brothels. It's a much better idea to pay a little extra for your accommodation in order to feel comfortable and safe. Trust your instincts when you walk in: if a place feels a little bit dodgy, it probably is.

Try to sit next to local women on public transport, particularly in buses and *grands taxis*. Most *grand taxi* drivers will go out of their way to arrange the seating allocation so that you, as a solo female traveller will get a good seat. If you're the only female in the taxi, some will offer you the entire front passenger seat.

Away from the cities, where there are thoroughly modern contemporary bars, Moroccan bars are a male domain. Walking into a local bar by yourself is guaranteed to bring a lot of unwanted attention, and you won't feel

Tip...
If you do encounter any serious harassment, don't hesitate to complain to the Brigade touristique. These plain clothes officers are in action at a number of main tourist centres, stamping down on hassle.

particularly welcome either. It's best to avoid them completely.

Most importantly, don't let a few bad eggs taint the whole basket. Not all men who approach you are trying to harass you, woo you or trying to marry you in order to bag a visa to your country. Many are just being friendly and want the opportunity to chat with a foreign woman – as opportunities for young, single Moroccan men to interact with the opposite sex are few and far between in traditional households. You'll find that chivalry is alive and well in Morocco and many men will go out of their way to help you (which can be annoying on a completely different scale). A bus driver in a remote town may drop you off right outside your hotel door rather than the bus stop, because he doesn't want you walking by yourself down the street, or you'll be offered the only seat at the *grands taxis* car park and brought mint tea and cake by the driver while you're waiting for the car to fill up.

Working in the country

Morocco has a major unemployment problem. University-educated young adults find it hard to get work, especially those with degrees in subjects like Islamic studies and literature. At the same time, industry and business are desperately short of qualified technicians and IT-literate staff. Low salary levels mean that the qualified are tempted to emigrate – and many do, fuelling a brain-drain that has reached worrying levels. In cities, adults with a low level of skills find it hard to get work, basically as many simple jobs in small companies are done by badly paid, exploited adolescents. For the foreigner, this means that there are few opportunities for work, although international companies setting up in Morocco do employ foreign managerial staff, generally recruited abroad. Basically, the only opening if you want to spend time in Morocco is through teaching English, which is badly paid even with organizations like the British Council or the American Language Centres. It is your employer who will help you deal with the formalities of getting a *carte de séjour* (residence permit). For you to be able to work, your employer has to be able to satisfy the relevant authorities in Rabat that you are doing a job in an area in which Morocco has a skills shortage.

Europeans can obtain residence relatively easily, providing they can prove that they have a regular source of income and that regular transfers of funds are being made into their Moroccan bank account. Towns where the police are used to processing the official paperwork for foreign residents include Essaouira, Marrakech and Fès.

Index

Entries in bold refer to maps

A

Abid Bukhari 181, 263
accident and emergency 286
accommodation 23
  price codes 23
Adwa al Andalus (Fès) 146
Agdal Gardens (Marrakech) 60
Agdz 245
Ahouli 203
air travel 273, 279
Aït Ben Haddou 241
Aït Mohammed 224
Alaouites 259, 263
Al Mansouria 218
Almohads 259, 261
Almoravids 259, 261
Amazigh culture 196, 223
Amizmiz 103
Anergui 126
Animiter 117
Arabic 289
Arab Spring 270
Asni 104
Atlas Studios 235
ATMs 291
Azilal 120
Azrou 196
  history 197

B

Bab Agnaou (Marrakech) 54
Bab Berdaine (Meknès) 183
Bab Boujeloud (Fès) 135
Bab el Khemis (Marrakech) 54
Bab el Khemis (Meknès) 183
Bab Mansour (Meknès) 184
Bab Sba' (Fès) 150
Bab Semmarine (Fès) 150
Bahia Palace (Marrakech) 58
ballooning 17, 77
begging 103
Beni Mellal 123
Bhalil 164
bicycles 279
birdwatching 17
bomb attacks 69, 269, 294
Bou Hamra 167
Boujaâd 124
Boumalne du Dadès 227
bus travel 279

C

camel trekking 17, 219, 253
camping 26
car hire 281
Casablanca 274
Casa Voyageurs station (Casablanca) 273, 274, 277
Cascades d'Ouzoud 120
cash 291
Ceuta 263, 276, 278, 296
children 103, 140, 286
Chouara tanneries (Fès) 146
Chraïbi, Driss 135
Cirque du Jaffar 202
climate 14
  see also weather
coffee 32
Collège berbère 197
colonialism 264
cost of living 292
cost of travelling 291
credit cards 291
cuisine 27
currency 290
customs 286

D

Dadès Gorge 227
Dar Bellarj 52
Darija 289
Dar Si Said (Marrakech) 58
dates 214
dayat lakes 199
Dayat Merzouga 218
Debdou 173
Demnate 120
Deserts and gorges 206-255
dirham 290
disabled travellers 287
Drâa Valley 244-255
  history 245
dress 287, 297
drink 31
driving 280
driving 282-284
  see also car hire
drugs 286, 287
dunes 219, 253
duty free 286

E

Eastern High Atlas 119-127
El Aïoun 174
El Badi Palace (Marrakech)
  55
electricity 287
El Kalaâ des Mgouna 230
embassies and consulates
  287
Erfoud 214
Erg Chebbi 219
Erg Chiggaga 253
Er Rachidia 210, 211
Essaouira 34, 82-97, **85**, **86**
  essential 83
  harbour 84
  history 87
  listings 88
  medina 84
  sights 84

F

Fassi pottery 141
ferries 276
Fès 128, 131-162, **134**, **155**
  essential 132
  hammams 145
  history 136
  listings 151
  mellah 148
  palaces 149
  souk 142
  weather 132
Fès el Bali 134, **138**
Fès el Jedid 148, **148**
**Fès, Meknès and Middle
  Atlas 128-205**
festivals 15
Fête des Cerises 15, 163
film industry 232, 234

Fint 240
food 27-30, 33
fossils 214
Foum Zguid 248, 253
four-wheel drive
  see off-road driving

G

gay and lesbian travellers
  287
Glaoui family 149, 234, 241
Gnaoua music 15, 95, 221
Gorges du Dadès 227
Gorges du Todra 225
Gorges du Ziz 211
Gouffre de Friouato 171
Goulmima 223
Grande traversée de l'Atlas
  marocain 125
grand taxi 284
Guercif 172

H

haggling 22, 140, 292
hammams 18, 78, 95, 145,
  160, 162, 188
Hassan I 264
Hassan II 268
Hassan II Mosque
  (Casablanca) 274
health 288
Heri es-Souani 185
Heritage Museum
  (Marrakech) 53
High Atlas 98-127
history 257-267
hitchhiking 284
horse riding 18, 79, 96, 243
hotels 23
  price codes 23

I

Ibn Toumert 105
Idriss I 'el Akbar' 16, 136,
  189, 190, 193, 260, 266
Idriss II 136, 144, 189,
  260, 266
Idriss Ben Abdallah
  see Idriss I
Idrissids 190, 259
Ifrane 199
Île de Mogador 88
Îles Purpuraires 84, 88
Imilchil 125
Imi-n-Ifri 120
Imlil 108
Immouzer du Kandar 200
imperial city (Meknès) 184
independence 267
insurance 289
internet 289
Islam 259

J

Jardin Majorelle
  (Marrakech) 59
Jbel Ayachi 202
Jbel Tazzeka National Park
  170, **171**
Jbel Toubkal 109, **110**
Jemaâ el Fna (Marrakech)
  43, **44**
Jewish community
  59, 84, 148-150, 163,
  173, 183, 274
Juba II 258

K

kasbah 209
Kasbah Mosque
  (Marrakech) 54

Kasbah quarter
(Marrakech) 54
Kasbah Tadla 124
Kasbah Taourirt 234
Khénifra 197
Koubba el Baroudiyine
(Marrakech) 51
Koubba el Khamsiniya
(Marrakech) 55
Koutoubia Mosque 46
ksar 209, 217
Ksar Akbar 217
Ksar Amazrou 248
Ksar Jebril 218
Ksar Ouled Abd el Helim
217
Ksar Tinrheras 217

L

Lac Tislit 126
Lalla Takerkoust 102
language 289
Lawrence of Arabia 234
Lazama Synagogue 59
Lyautey, Maréchal 265

M

Maison de la Photographie
(Marrakech) 52
Maison Tiskiwin
(Marrakech) 58
Mansour Eddahbi Dam 240
marijuana 287
markets 106
Marrakech 34, 37-81,
40, 44
accommodation 61
bars and clubs 72
entertainment 74
essential 38
festivals 74
hammams 78

history 48
mellah 59
modern Marrakech 49
ramparts 42
restaurants 67
shopping 75
sights 42
tourist information 61
transport 79
weather 39
**Marrakech and Essaouira
34-97**
Marrakech Museum for
Photography and Visual
Arts (MMPVA) 56
Massif du Mgoun 121, 230
Mauretania 257
Medersa Ben Youssef
(Marrakech) 51
Medersa Bou Inania (Fès)
135, 137
Medersa Bou Inania
(Meknès) 182
Medersa el Attarine (Fès)
144
media 290
medical services 288
Meknès 128, 176-194,
178, 182
essential 177
history 180
listings 185
mellah 183
sights 178
souks 181
Melilla 278
mellah 59, 84, 148-150,
164, 183
Menara airport 38, 79, 273
Menara Gardens
(Marrakech) 60
menu reader 33
Merinids 136, 148, 167,
259, 260, 262

Merinid Tombs (Fès) 147
Merzouga 218
Meski 213
M'Hamid 253
Middle Atlas 128, 172, 195
Midelt 201
mineral waters 162
Mischliffen 199, 201
Missour 203
mobile phones 295
modern Morocco 268-271
Mohammed Ben Abdallah
263
Mohammed V Airport 274
Mohammed VI 269
money 290
mosques 47
motorcycles 279
Moulay Ali Cherif 217
Moulay Brahim 103
Moulay Hafidh 264
Moulay Idriss 189, 190
see also Idriss I
Moulay Ismaïl 176, 180,
184, 263
Moulay Yacoub 162
mountain accommodation
25
mountain biking 19
Moussem des fiançailles
16, 126
Moussem of Moulay Idriss
16, 143, 190
Moussem of Setti Fatma 16
Msemrir 226, 228
Musée Berbère
(Marrakech) 59
Musée Boucharouite
(Marrakech) 53
Musée Dar Batha (Fès) 141
Musée de Marrakech 51
Musée de Mouassine
(Marrakech) 52

N

Naciri Islamic brotherhood 253
Nador 278
Nejjarine Museum of Wooden Arts (Fès) 143
Nekob 249
newspapers 290
Nomads Festival 15, 253, 255

O

Oasis Festival 16
off-road driving 283
  routes 114, 126, 127, 202, 213, 214, 218, 223, 226, 240, 244, 248, 249, 253
opening hours 293
Ouarzazate 232-240, **234**
  weather 209
Oued Ksob 87
Oued Melah 148
Oued Moulouya 203
Oued Ziz 210, 211, 213
Ouirgane 104
Oujda Msoun 172
Oukaïmeden 19, 114

P

packing 273
Palmeraie (Marrakech) 60
parking 284
petit taxi 285
pistes
  see off-road driving
post 293
pottery 141
prices 292
Prophet Mohammed 259
Protectorate 265
public holidays 293

Q

Qaraouiyine Library (Fès) 142, 145
Qaraouiyine Mosque (Fès) 136, 144

R

radio 290
rail travel 285
Ramadan 15, 29, 293
religious holidays 293
residence permit 298
restaurants 27
  price codes 23
riads 24, 63
Riad Zitoun el Jedid (Marrakech) 58
Rif uprising 267
Rissani 216
Road of the Thousand Kasbahs 222
road safety 282
road travel 279
Romans 191, 193, 257
rose essence 230, 231
Rose Festival 15, 231
route planner 9

S

Saâdians 48, 55, 137, 259, 263
Saâdian Tombs (Marrakech) 54
safety 294
Sefrou 163
Setti Fatma 113
shopping 22, 76
Shrine of Moulay Idriss II (Fès) 144
Sidi Harazem 162
Sijilmassa 216, 217, 261

skiing 19, 114
Skoura oasis 240
souks 22, 50, 76, 134, 143, 167, 181, 275
student travellers 294
Sultan Abou Inane 142
surfing 19, 96

T

Tafilalet 210, 213
Tagounite 253
Talaâ Kebira (Fès) 142
tamarisk 213
Tamazight 289
Tamdaght 241
Tamegroute 253
Tamnougalt 245
Tamtatouchte 226
Tangier 276
tanneries 56, 146
Taourirt 173
Taouz 218
taxis 284
Taza 166-170, **168**
tea 31
telephone 295
television 290
Telouet 117
terrorism 294
Tifoultoute 241
time 295
Tineghir 223
Tinejdad 223
Tin Mal 104
  history 105
tipping 295
Tizi-n-Test 106
Tizi-n-Tichka 116, 209
Todra Gorge 225
Toubkal Circuit 111
Toubkal National Park 108-113
tourist information 296

FOOTPRINT

Features

A child's survival guide to Fès 140
A day by the pool 80
Bathtime stories 145
Café culture 69
Chronology: ancient Morocco 258
Chronology: medieval and early modern Morocco 260
Chronology: modern Morocco 265
Cost of living for Moroccans 292
Country markets 106
Dishes for Ramadan 29
Eating in people's homes 31
Hammams 18
Inside the mosque 47
Jemaâ el Juice 45
Making tracks 248
Marrakech for kids 43

Monarchs, battles and freedom fighters 266
Moussem des fiançailles 126
No rules of the road 280
Packing for Morocco 273
Pottery and belief 141
Saintly Sultan Abou Inane 142
Taking your car to Morocco 282
Tanning secrets 56
The desert and the mountains 42
The Fès effect 135
The palaces of Fès 149
The riad experience 63
Trekking 20
Un stylo, un bonbon, un dirham 103
Where to buy what in the souks 76

tour operators 295
train travel 285
transport 273-285
travel photography 12
Treaty of Fès 265
trekking 20, 108-111, 121, 126, 202, 229, 230

V

vaccinations 288
Vallée des Aït Bougmez 121

Vallée des Roses 230
  history 231
vegetarian food 31
visas 296
Volubilis 189, 191-194, **192**

W

weather 14, 39, 132, 209
weights and measures 296
Western High Atlas 101-118
windsurfing 19, 96

wines 32, 177
women travellers 296
working 297

Y

youth hostels 25

Z

Zagora 247
Zaouïat Ahansal 127
Ziz canyon 213

Credits

Footprint credits

Editor: Sophie Blacksell Jones
Production and layout: Emma Bryers
Maps: Kevin Feeney
Colour section: Patrick Dawson

Publisher: Felicity Laughton
          Patrick Dawson
Marketing: Kirsty Holmes
Sales: Diane McEntee
Advertising and content partnerships:
Debbie Wylde

Photography credits
Front cover: Stock Up/Shutterstock.com
Back cover top: Maurizio De Mattei/
Shutterstock.com
Back cover bottom: Marcel
Baumgartner/Shutterstock.com
Inside front cover: John Copland/
Shutterstock.com, © Steve Davey/
stevedavey.com 2009, Jose Ignacio Soto/
Shutterstock.com.

Colour section
Page 1: © Steve Davey/stevedavey.com 2008.
Page 2: © Steve Davey/stevedavey.com 2008.
Page 4: Matej Kastelic/Shutterstock.com,
John Copland/Shutterstock.com.
Page 5: KajzrPhotography.com/Shutterstock.
com, klempa/Shutterstock.com.
Page 6: OPIS Zagreb/Shutterstock.com.
Page 7: Inu/Shutterstock.com,
Rudolf Tepfenhart/Shuttestock.com,
© Steve Davey/stevedavey.com 2008.
Page 8: © Steve Davey/stevedavey.com 2009.

Duotones
Page 34: John Copland/Shutterstock.com.
Page 98: Pack-Shot/Shutterstock.com.
Page 128: takepicsforfun/Shutterstock.com.
Page 206: Alberto Loyo/Shutterstock.com.

Printed in Spain by GraphyCems

Publishing information
Footprint Morocco
1st edition
© Footprint Handbooks Ltd
July 2016

ISBN: 978 1 910120 85 9
CIP DATA: A catalogue record for this
book is available from the British Library

® Footprint Handbooks and the
Footprint mark are a registered
trademark of Footprint Handbooks Ltd

Published by Footprint
6 Riverside Court
Lower Bristol Road
Bath BA2 3DZ, UK
T +44 (0)1225 469141
F +44 (0)1225 469461
footprinttravelguides.com

Distributed in the USA by
National Book Network, Inc.

Every effort has been made to ensure
that the facts in this guidebook are
accurate. However, travellers should still
obtain advice from consulates, airlines,
etc about travel and visa requirements
before travelling. The authors and
publishers cannot accept responsibility
for any loss, injury or inconvenience
however caused.